INTERNATIONAL GARDEN PHOTOGRAPHER OF THE YEAR

COLLECTION FIVE

CONTENTS

Design and production: Nick Otway
Copy editing and proof reading: Hannah Powell Smith
Image retouching and colour repro: Michael Moody

A catalogue record for this book is available from the British Library.

ISBN: 978-0-9563-9731-7

Printed and bound in the UK by Butler Tanner & Dennis Ltd

www.igpoty.com
www.alphaforme.co.uk

GREAT BRITISH BOOKS
PUBLISHED & PRINTED IN THE UK

SPONSORS AND SUPPORTERS

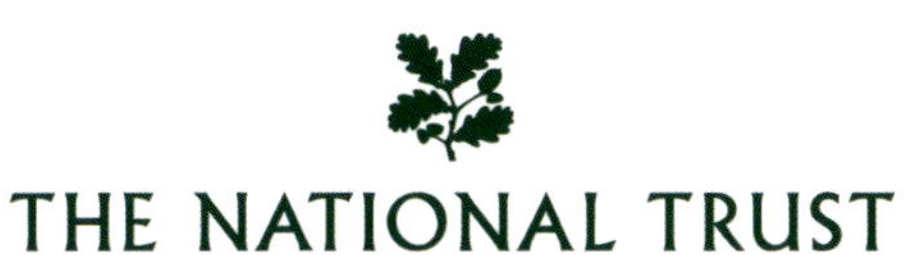

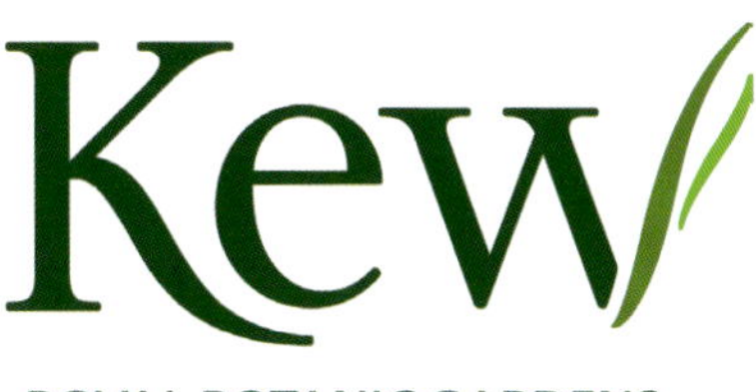

ROYAL BOTANIC GARDENS

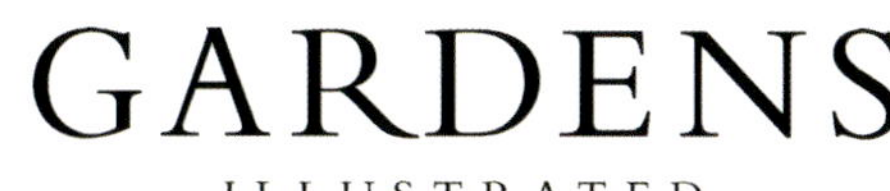

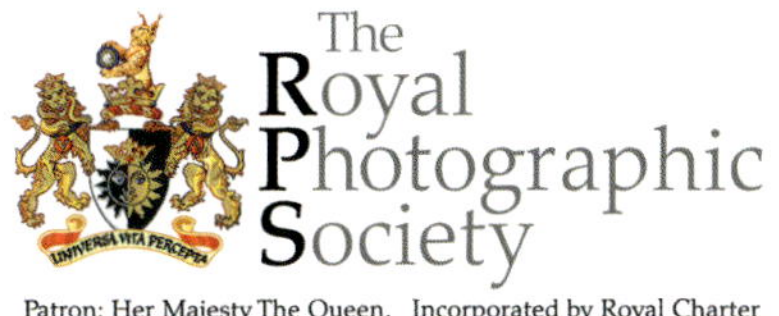

Patron: Her Majesty The Queen. Incorporated by Royal Charter

THE NEW YORK BOTANICAL GARDEN

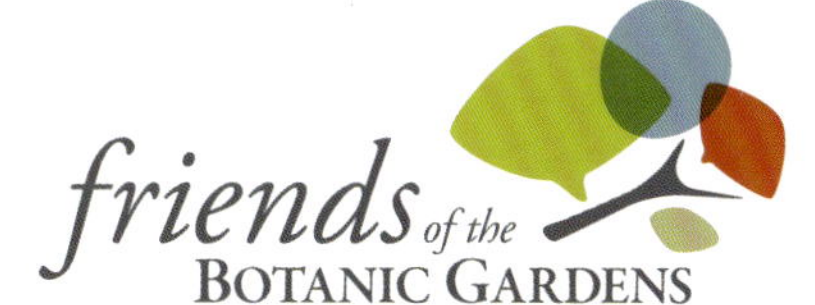

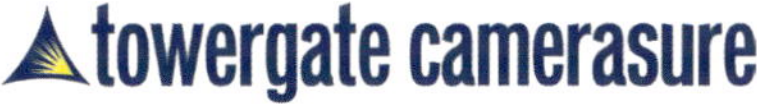

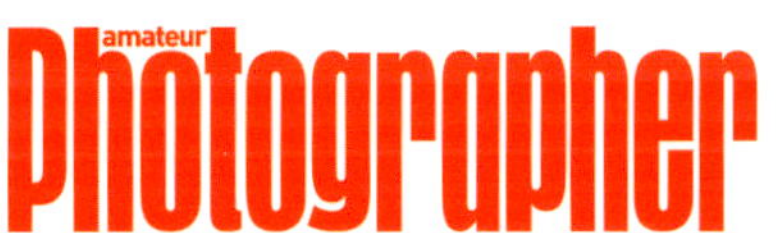

bobbooks.co.uk

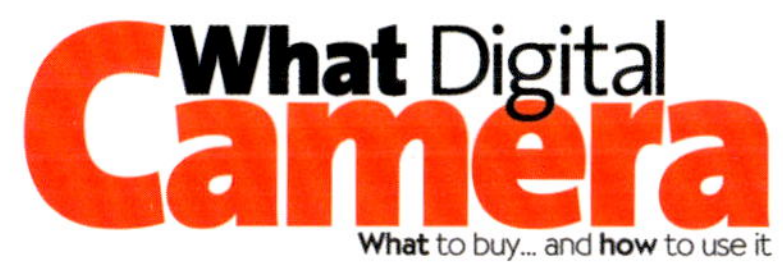

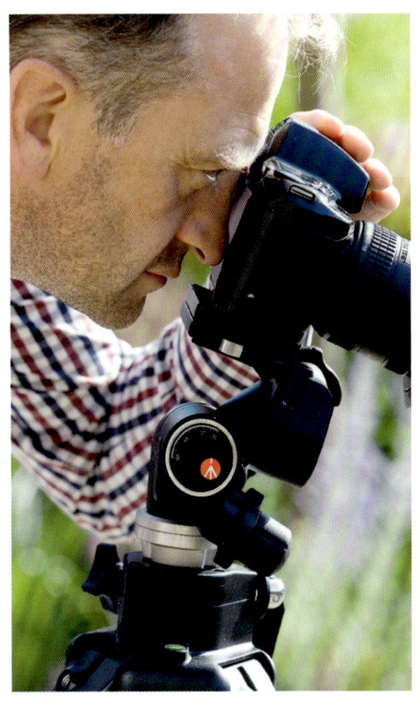

FOREWORD

By Clive Nichols, leading garden photographer and author

Photographing gardens and plants has to be one of the most enjoyable occupations on the planet. And the easiest? After all, plants don't move, they are naturally photogenic, and full of colour – surely all you have to do is point and click?

All the images in this book demonstrate vividly that the opposite is true. The photographer must take time and prepare the shoot; appreciate the plant in all its growth stages, understand the garden in all its moods. They must know instinctively how the weather will affect the images, what time of day is best to photograph, in what season the garden will be at its best. It is an activity that requires contemplation, observation, knowledge – and a determination to accept only the perfect shot.

This collection of photographs celebrates gardens and plants all over the world. It also takes us into the wider plant world with 'Images of a Green Planet'. Life on earth depends on plants. Without them, the Earth would be just another barren rock spinning around the sun. Many plants are under threat from loss of habitat and the ever-increasing demands of a growing population. This book draws attention to the essential part that plants play in our lives all over the globe: as food, as medicine, as bringers of well-being, as wonders of the natural world, and as sanctuaries for insects and animals of all kinds.

Many thousands of people take part in International Garden Photographer of the Year, whether as visitors to the exhibition, as participants in the competition, or in our workshops and lectures. As a competition judge, I see some amazing work and marvel at the sheer variety of approaches to photographing the plant world.

The best of the best can be found on these pages. Some of the images are by professional photographers, some by artists, some by hobby photographers enjoying a weekend stroll around a favourite place. Cameras are very 'clever' these days: they are sophisticated computers with very high quality optics on the front. But these photographs show that it is not cameras that create great photography. It's people.

The images in this book inspire us to develop our own photographic 'eye' and skill – and to use the art of photography to celebrate the fantastic world of plants and gardens.

INTRODUCTION

Professor Stephen D. Hopper, Director (CEO & Chief Scientist), Royal Botanic Gardens, Kew

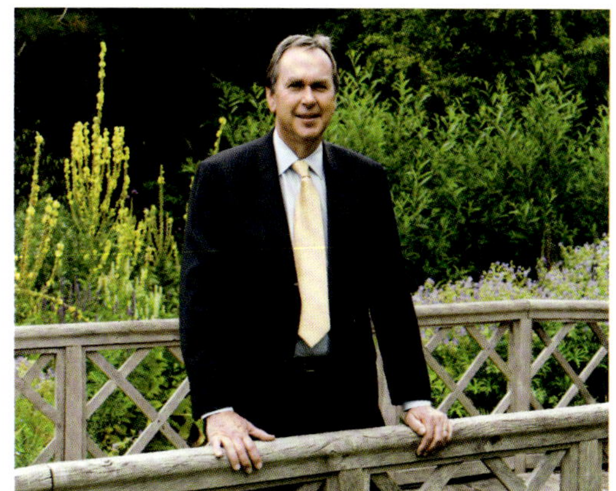

The International Garden Photographer of the Year competition, upon which this splendid book is based, is now in its fifth year. This competition continues to push the boundaries of garden photography, with the help of the thousands of committed and inspired photographers from around the world, from a wide variety of backgrounds, who each year contribute a vast array of astounding images. These not only celebrate plants but show the many ways in which their uses are woven into the fabric of our lives.

The scope of the competition has been broadened this year, with new categories close to the heart of the work of the Royal Botanic Gardens, Kew. These include 'fragile landscapes', which has encouraged photographers to seek and discover plants in their natural settings, bringing attention to habitats and plants under threat; 'greening the city' celebrating plants in urban settings, their ability to bring pleasure and thrive in unlikely places, and 'the bountiful Earth', portraying vividly that many of life's essentials – food, medicines, and much else, comes from plants.

Yet again, the Royal Botanic Gardens, Kew has been pleased to welcome to its gardens, at Kew and Wakehurst Place in Sussex, the exhibition showing the winning photographs seen in the book. This year images from the competition will delight not only our own visitors but also those at botanic gardens around the world with whom we work closely – notably The New York Botanical Garden and the Royal Botanic Garden, Sydney. This is very fitting, since together we strive to highlight the importance of plants in our global environment, to improve the responsible use of plants in our economies, and to cherish and appreciate their aesthetic qualities that enrich our lives.

In conclusion, it is heartening to see that so many of these wonderful images show the positive impact of human activity on the environment and our natural world.

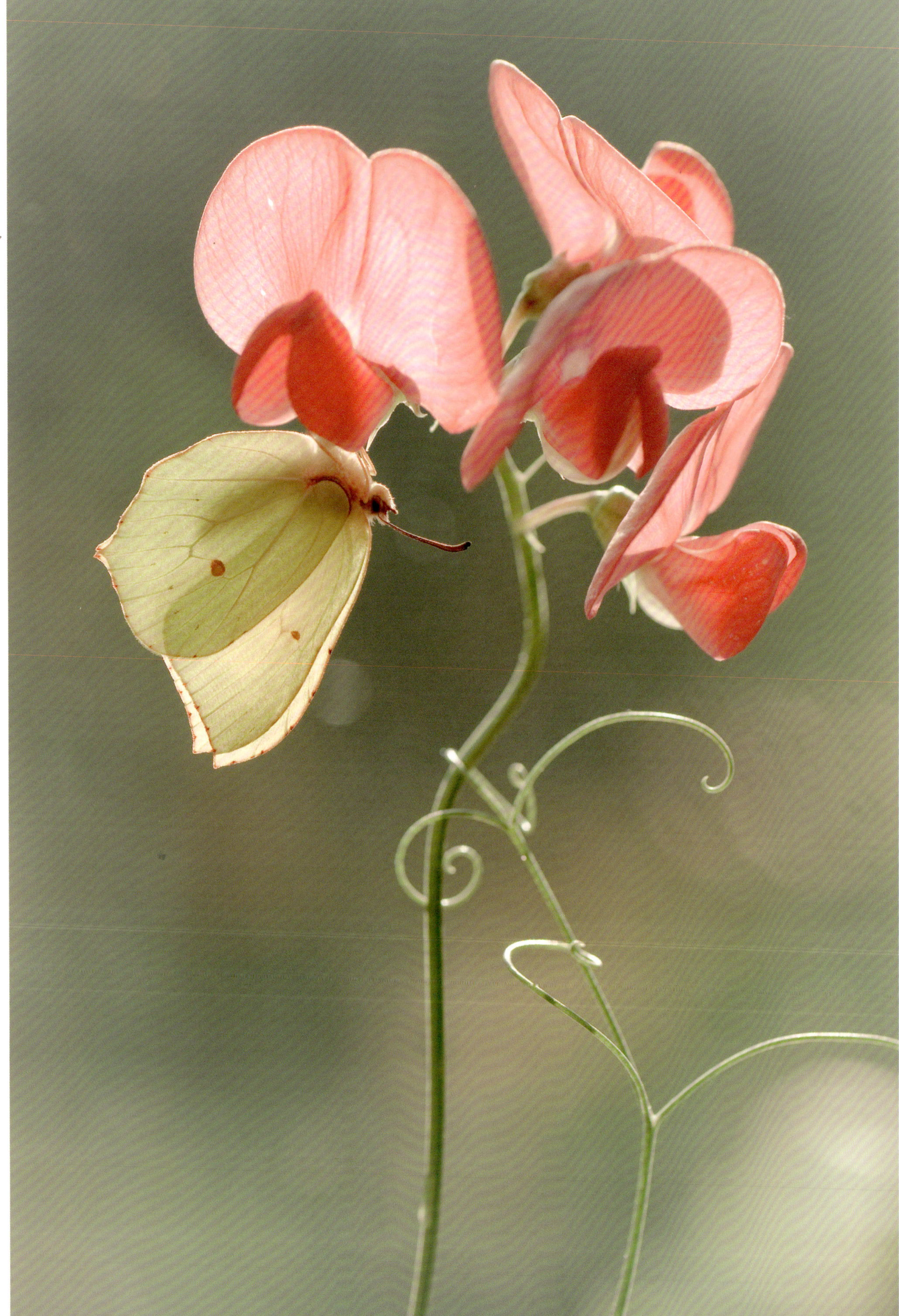

INTERNATIONAL GARDEN PHOTOGRAPHER OF THE YEAR

MAGDALENA WASICZEK

MAGDALENA WASICZEK 1ST PLACE

Upside Down
Trzebinia, Malopolska region, Poland

I grow sweet peas (*Lathyrus odoratus*) to attract these brimstone butterflies (*Gonepteryx rhamni*). This butterfly's wings were beautifully illuminated by the sun. She created a delicate composition with a sprig of sweet pea.

Nikon D300, Tamron 90 lens. 1/640sec at f/5.6. Post-capture: basic colour management.

"I love the subtlety and balletic simplicity of this picture. The brimstone alighting on a sweet pea is a fortuitous event, brilliantly seen. The butterfly and the flower are the perfect complement to each other.

The outlines of the insect's wings are continuous with the lines of the flowers; and the patterning on its wings picks up an echo of the pink colour of the flowers. The negative spaces between the different shapes are particularly beautiful. The pea tendril at the bottom right is an essential part of the composition, creating repetitive shapes and acting as a metaphor for the butterfly grasping onto the flower."

Andrew Lawson

leading garden photographer, artist, author and International Garden Photographer of the Year judge

WILDLIFE HAVENS AWARD SPONSORED BY towergate camerasure

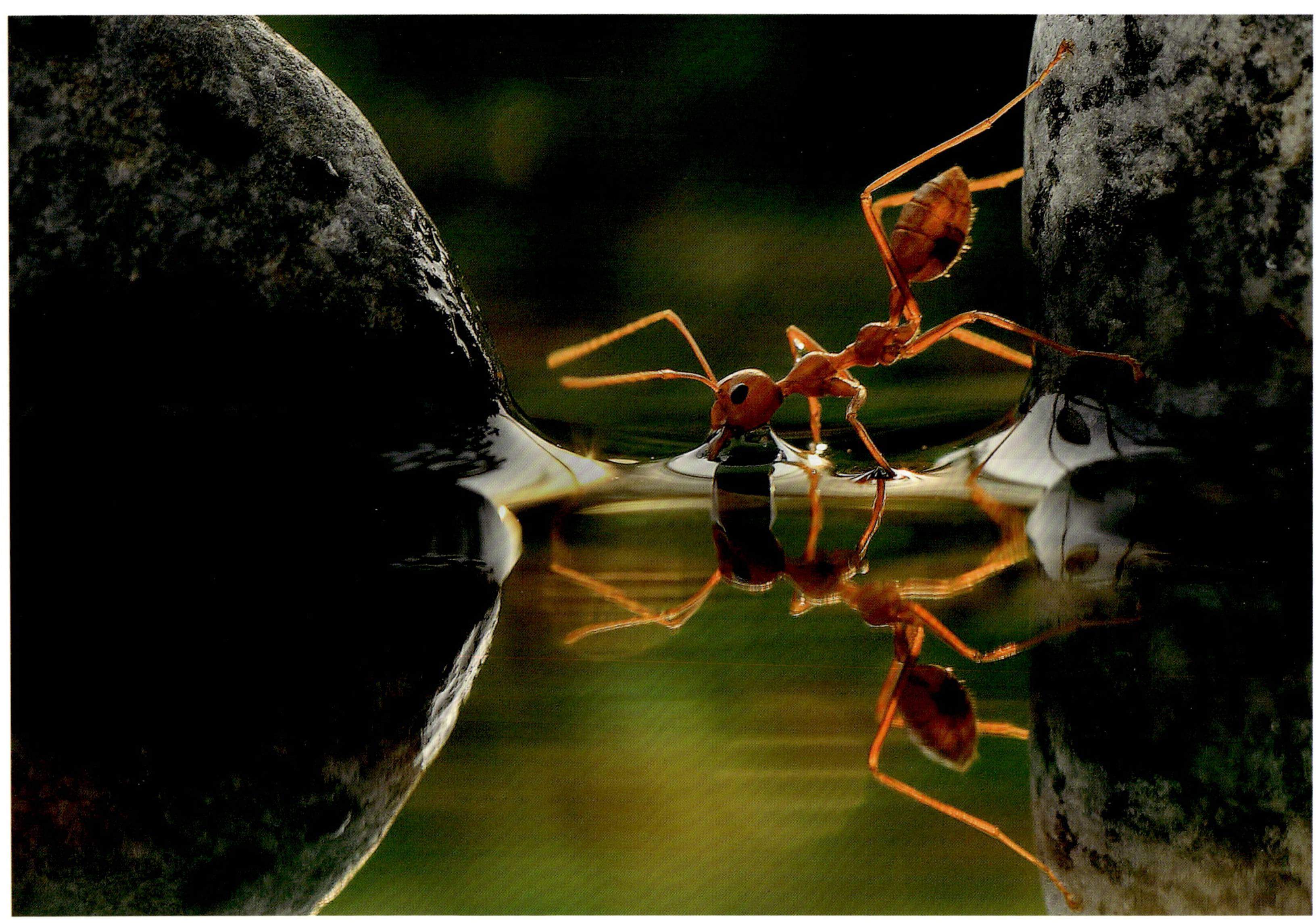

VINCENTIUS FERDINAND 2ND PLACE

Drinking II
Batam Island, Indonesia

I took hundreds of shots to capture this photo, and paid a lot of attention to the behaviour of these ants. The right time to take these shots is the late afternoon, when the light is gentle enough light to produce good backlighting and a perfect reflection.

Canon 7D, 100mm lens. Post-capture: some cropping and levels adjustment.

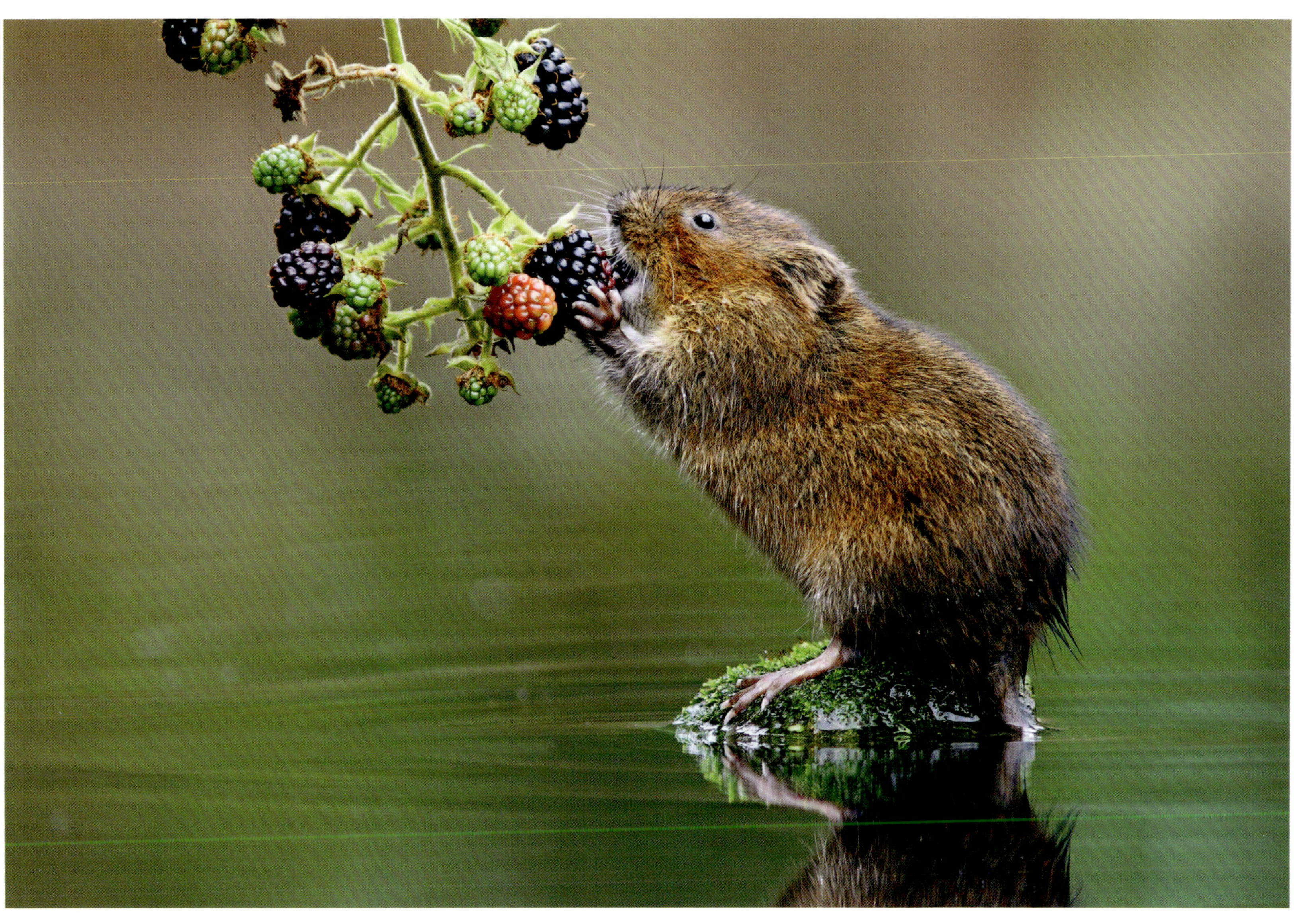

SIMON ROY 3RD PLACE

Ratty Breakfast
Askham Bog Nature Reserve, Yorkshire Wildlife Trust, UK

Water vole eating brambles on a late summer morning. I had observed a water vole attempting to reach overhanging brambles from the edge of a small pond situated in a local nature reserve. I created a natural looking island using a moss-covered rock and positioned it so that a vole could use it to get to the fruit. I then spent many hours lying in the mud waiting for one to try.

Canon EOS 7D, Canon 300mm lens. 1/500sec at f/4, ISO 800. Post-capture: tonal adjustments.

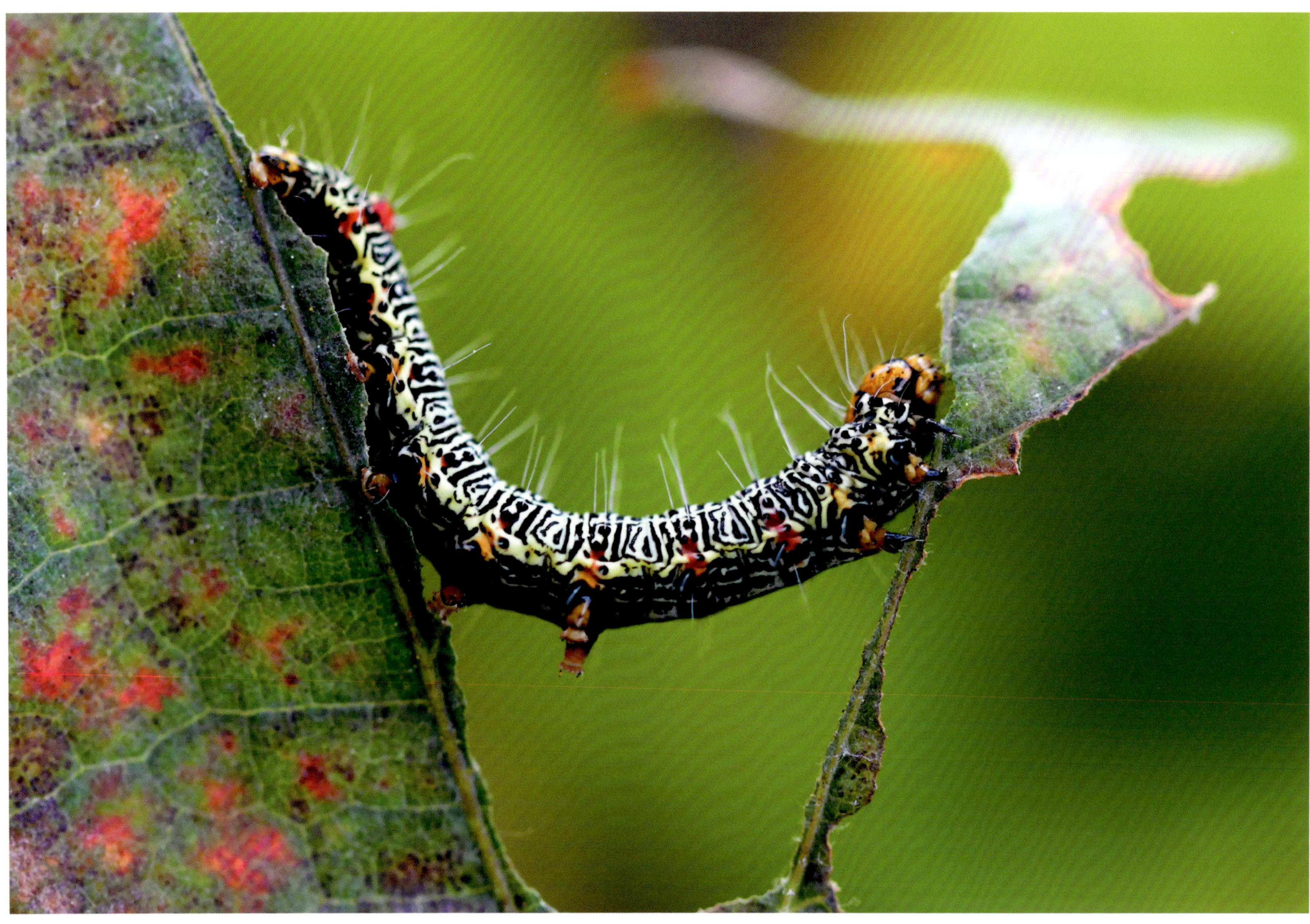

▲ **DEBBIE HARTLEY** HIGHLY COMMENDED

Back-breaking
My back garden, Canberra, Australia

I found this grapevine moth caterpillar feeding on the grapevine leaves in my backyard. The strength and flexibility of these small creatures always amazes me: the leaf was already half gone when I found it! I am always intrigued by nature and the small world of minibeasts, and I am always wandering around my yard inspecting plants for living creatures. The camera was hand held and I used continuous shooting so I could get a sharp picture, as the caterpillar was moving slightly while it ate.

Canon EOS 7D, Canon 100mm lens. 1/40sec at f/2.8. Post-capture: slight colour adjustment and sharpening.

MAGDALENA WASICZEK ► FINALIST

Sinuous
Glichów, Malopolska region, Poland

This is a small elephant hawk moth caterpillar (*Deilephila porcellus*) at a young stage. I think it is one of the most beautiful caterpillars and I was amazed by its size of nearly 9 cm. In this photo I like the layout of caterpillar and stem like an 'S'. This was the first time I had seen this type of caterpillar, and I could not pass up this opportunity to photograph it. I have to admit that she was a top model.

Nikon D300, Tamron 90 lens. 1/250sec at f/10. Post-capture: basic colour management.

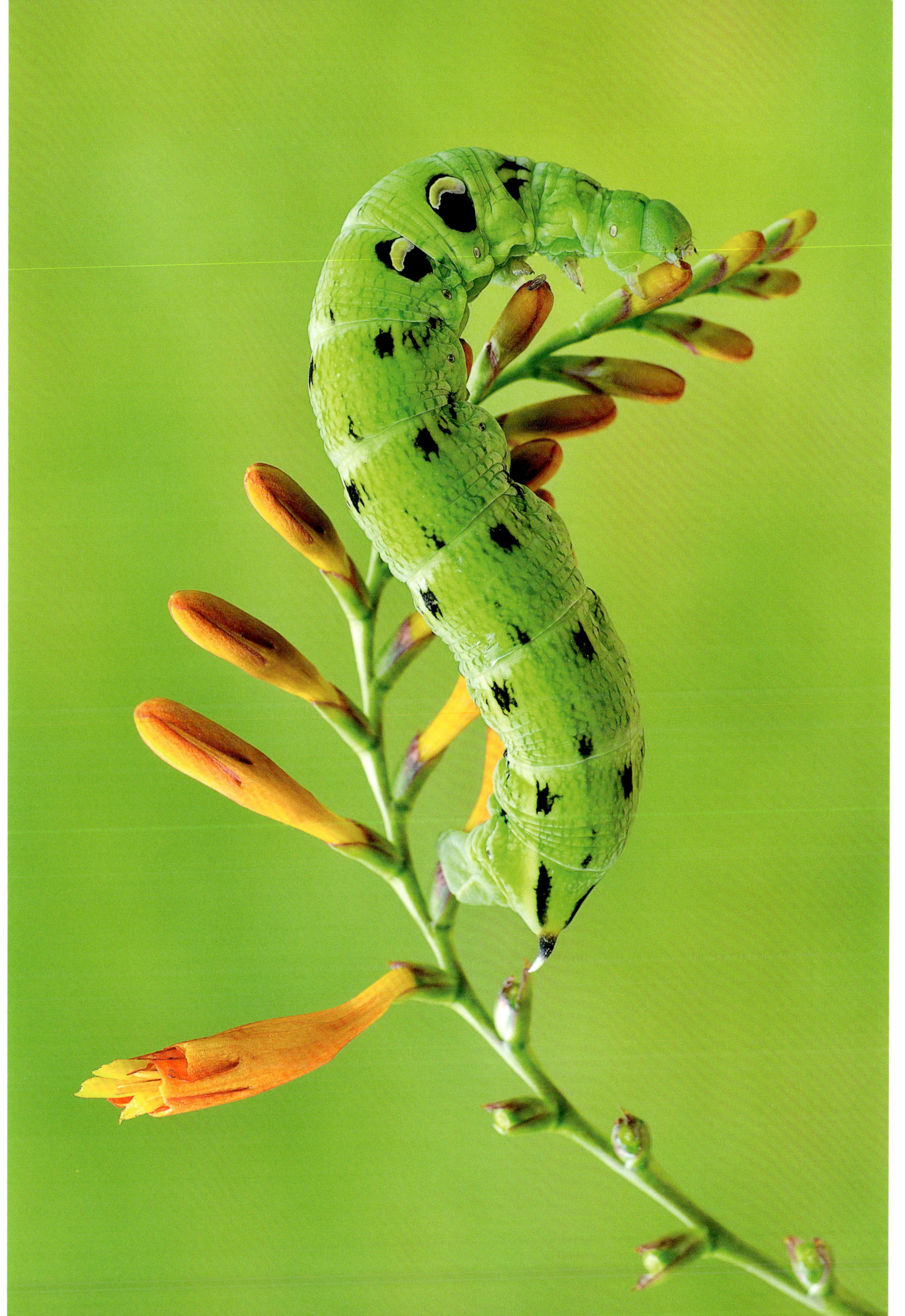

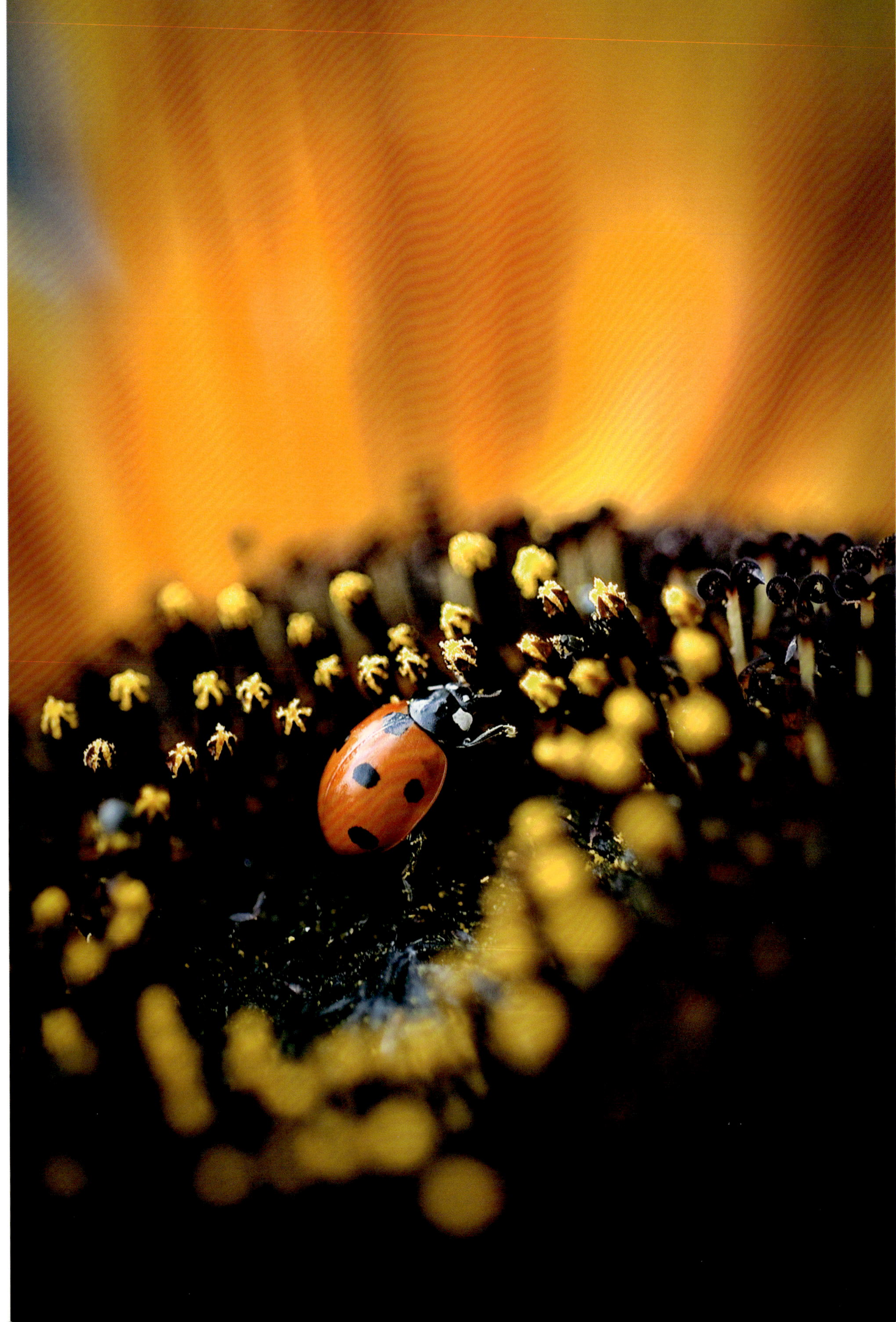

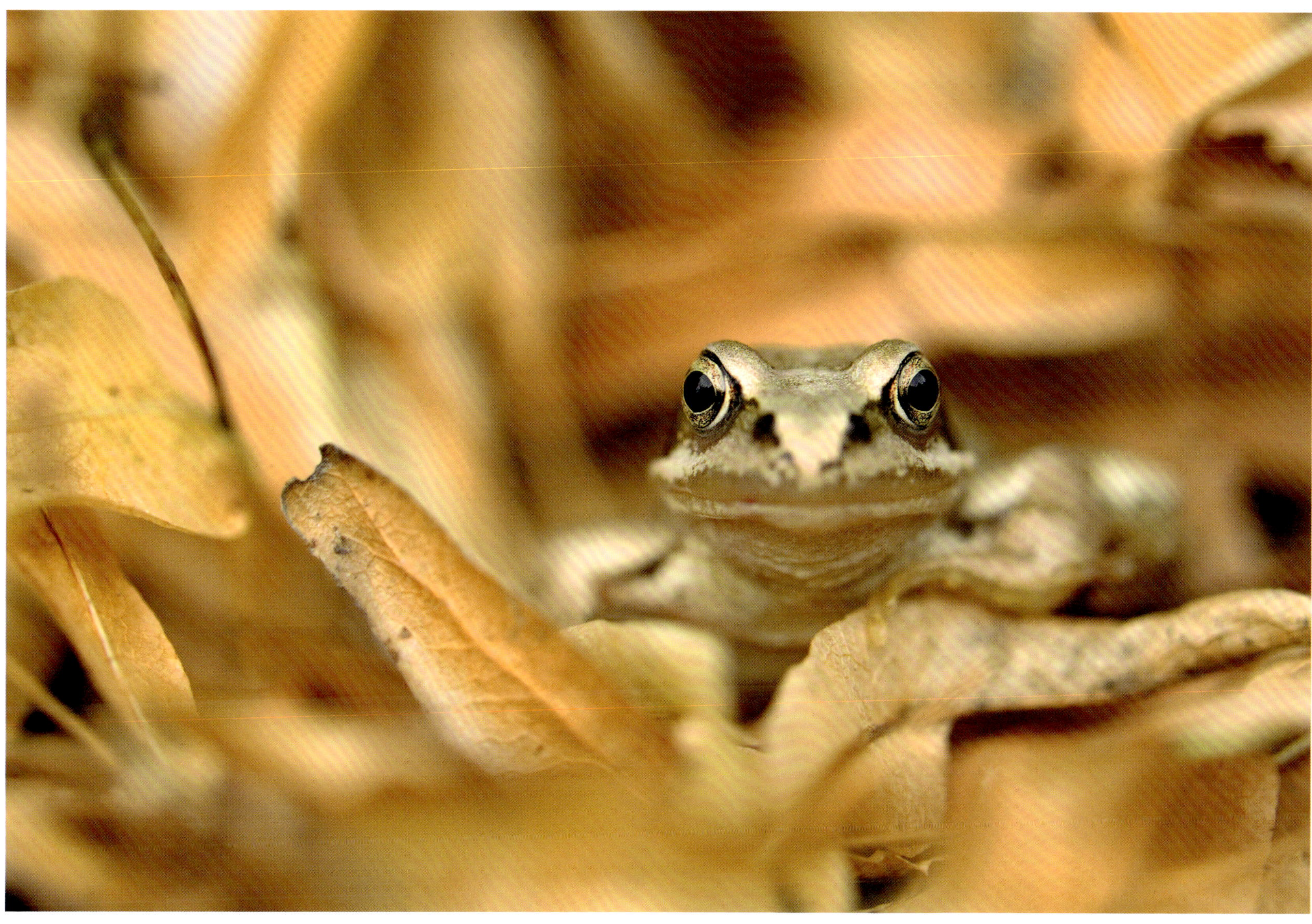

◄ **JEFF EDEN** HIGHLY COMMENDED

Firetrap
Outside the Temperate House at Royal Botanic Gardens, Kew, UK

During a project for '*Kew Magazine*' documenting the Temperate House, I noticed this single ladybird walking over the sunflower and took a couple of shots before it flew away. When I got back to the computer I realised because of the low depth-of-field in the shot, the ladybird looked like it was walking into flames. Sometimes you have to compose fast, especially when photographing insects with a tendency to fly away!

Nikon D300, 60mm lens. 1/250sec at f/4. Post-capture: basic colour correction.

▲ **TIM HUNT** HIGHLY COMMENDED

Among the Leaves
My garden, Barnt Green, Worcestershire, UK

When I was exploring in my garden I heard a rustle from the leaf litter. I did not see anything until a frog suddenly leapt out at me. I liked how the frog and the leaves were a similar colour, and ran to get my camera. The image had to have a shallow depth of field as I only wanted the eyes in focus. I wanted to be eye-level with the subject to create more of the personality in the photograph.

Canon EOS-1D Mark IV, 100mm lens. 1/1000sec at f2.8. Post-capture: the image was cropped slightly.

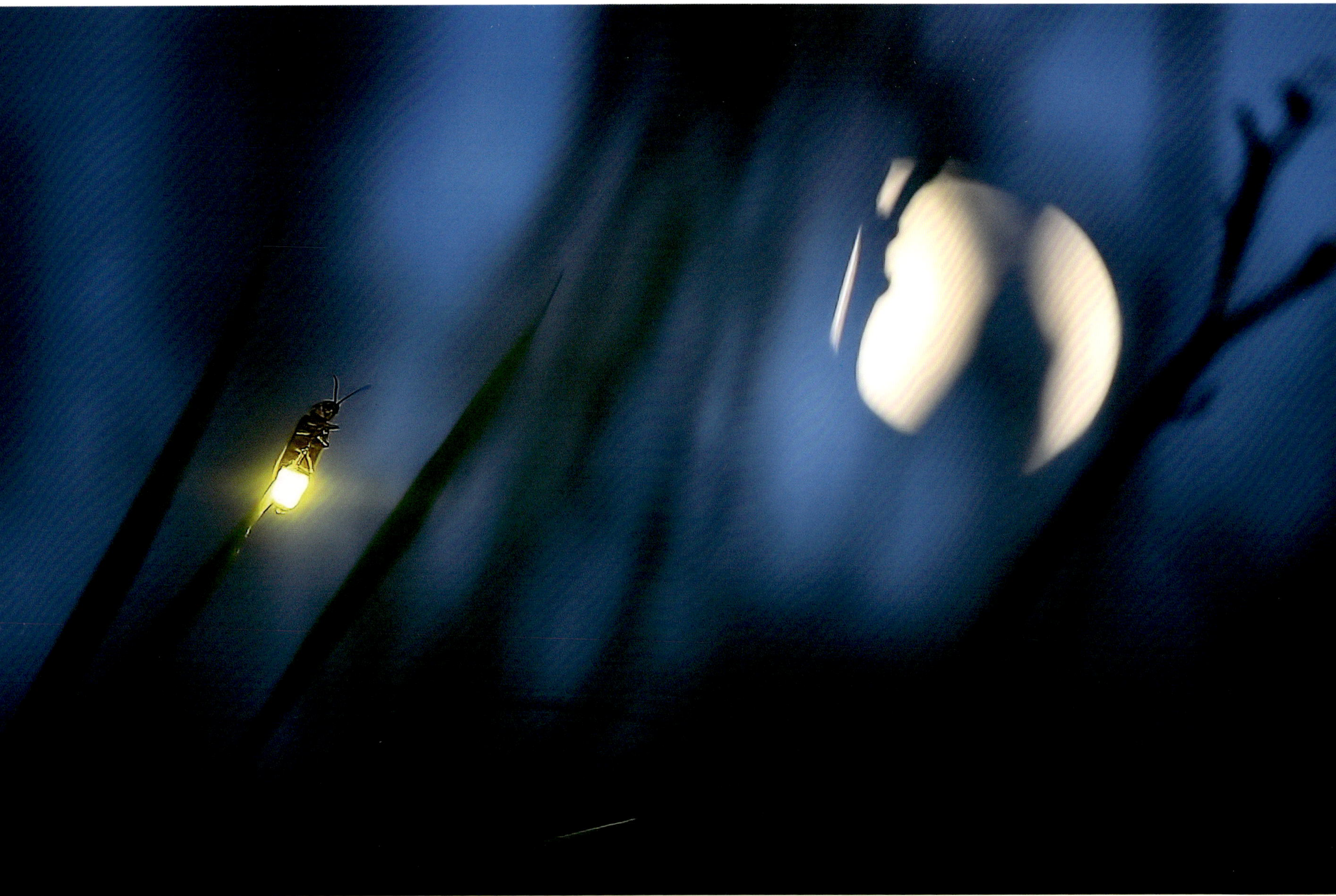

▲ RADIM SCHREIBER FINALIST

Firefly and Moon
Fairfield, Iowa, USA

I took this photograph of a firefly a couple days before full moon. This allowed me to have enough ambient light and to have the moon placed near the horizon. The distant moon appears large and split: an effect of lens bokeh.

Canon EOS 5D Mark II, 100mm lens. 1/30sec at f/2.8. Post-capture: no digital alterations.

MAGDALENA WASICZEK ► HIGHLY COMMENDED

Find Me…
Trzebinia, Malopolska region, Poland

A common blue (*Polyommatus icarus*) camouflaged in iris petals. From a distance, this tiny butterfly looked like the petals. This photo was taken in the evening, and the butterfly did not pay attention to me. I wanted to show the gentleness of the butterfly and flower, emphasise the softness of petals and give the atmosphere of sleepiness. I fell in love with this delicate duo and with the colours of butterfly and iris in harmony.

Nikon D300, Tamron 90 lens. 1/400sec at f/5. Post-capture: basic colour management.

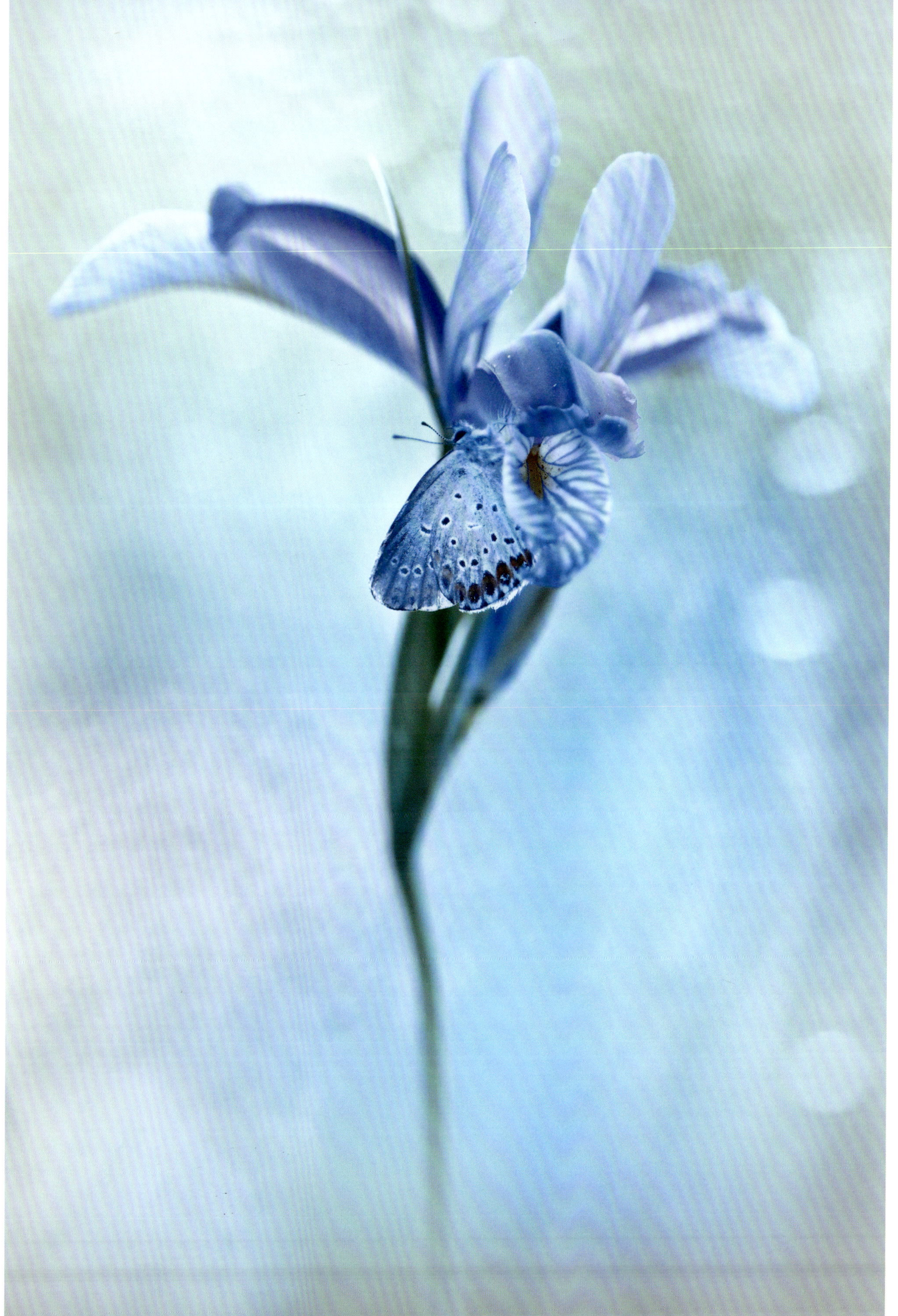

FLEUR ROBERTSON ► HIGHLY COMMENDED

A Place to Rest
Parkland near Guildford, Surrey, UK

These geese used the lake for less than half an hour during their journey south. This was early on a misty late summer morning and I was there to shoot a warm sunrise. The scene looks calm, but it was actually quite noisy: as I approached the lake, I heard the geese. They were far enough away for me to prime my camera in order to capture their flight without blurring their wings. I don't think fast at 5.30am, but their calls gave me fair warning!

Canon 60D 17-55mm at 23mm 1/250 at f/8 Post-capture: no digital alterations.

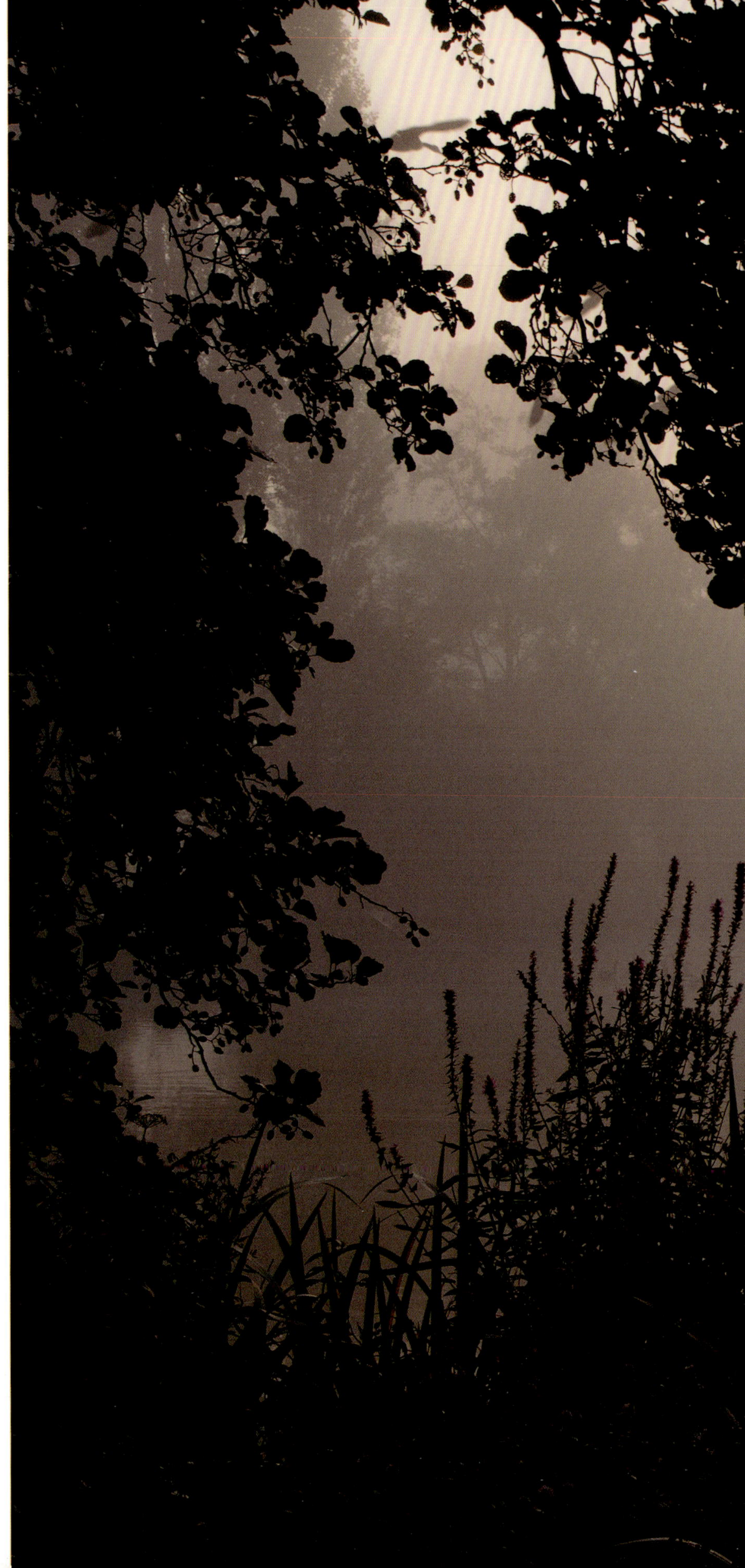

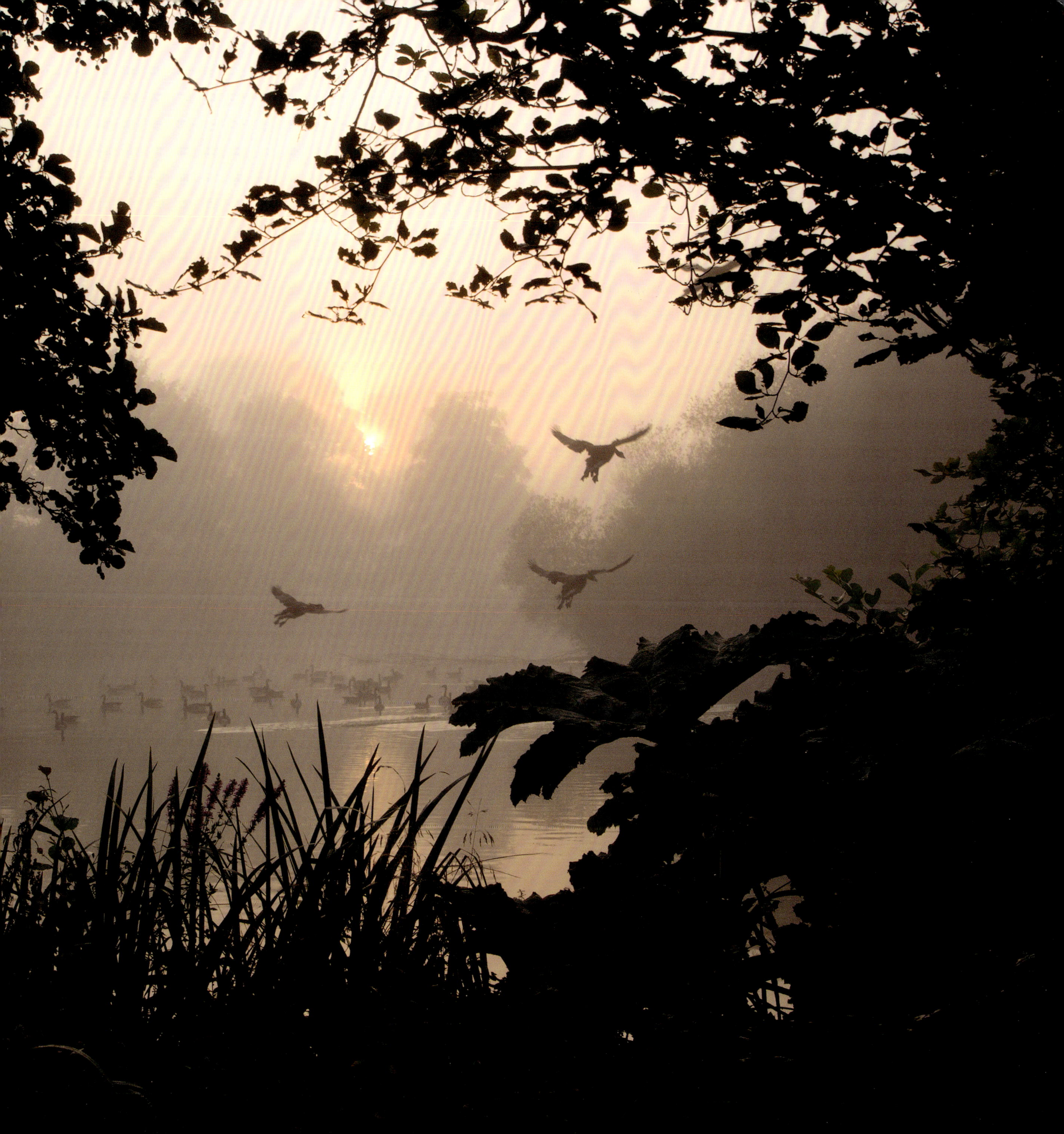

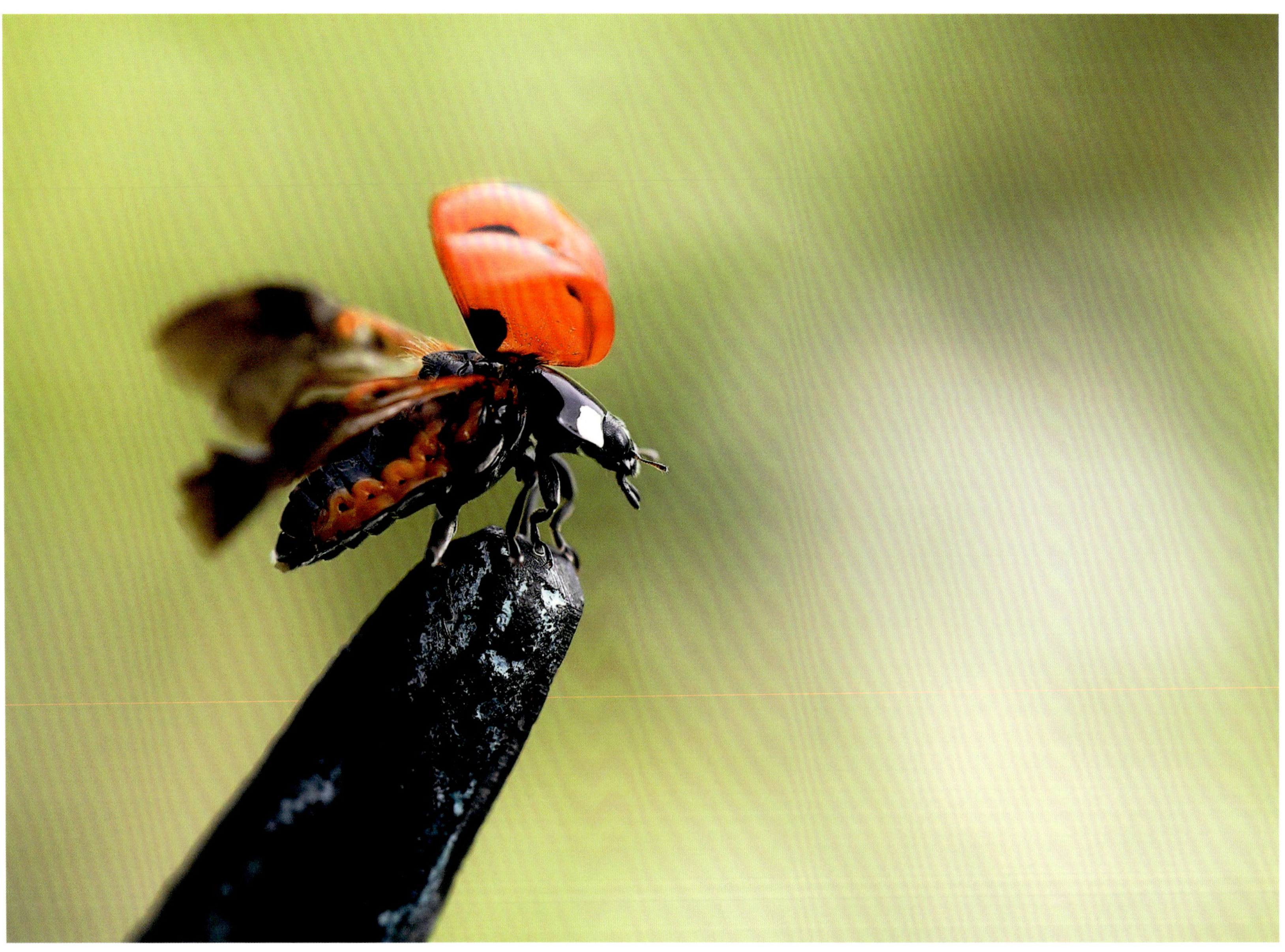

▲ **DAVID HANDLEY** — HIGHLY COMMENDED

Ladybird about to take off
My back garden, Wrexham, North Wales

I noticed this ladybird on the sundial and took photographs as it moved. It climbed up onto the tip of the sundial and started to open its shell and expose its wings. I followed it and was lucky to capture this moment just a split second before it flew away. I was inspired to take this photograph after a number of previous attempts. I wanted to try again and this time it worked. A shallow depth of field has blurred the background and helped keep the focus on the ladybird.

Canon EOS 40D, Canon 100mm lens. 1/640sec at f/6.4. Post-capture: slightly cropped to give a more pleasing composition.

MATT COLE ► — FINALIST

Confused Grasshopper
Lount Nature Reserve, Leicestershire, UK

A lesser marsh grasshopper (*Chorthippus albomarginatus*) perched on top of Devil's-bit scabious. It was starting to rain and I think the grasshopper is wiping a raindrop from its head. I am a keen macro photographer and always on the look out for interesting insect images. This would have been a fairly standard portrait but the grasshopper's behaviour gives it that something extra. It being a cool day, the grasshopper allowed me to get quite close and to set up my tripod in front of it.

Canon 7D, Sigma 150mm lens. 1/100sec at f/9. Post-capture: levels, saturation and other basic adjustments.

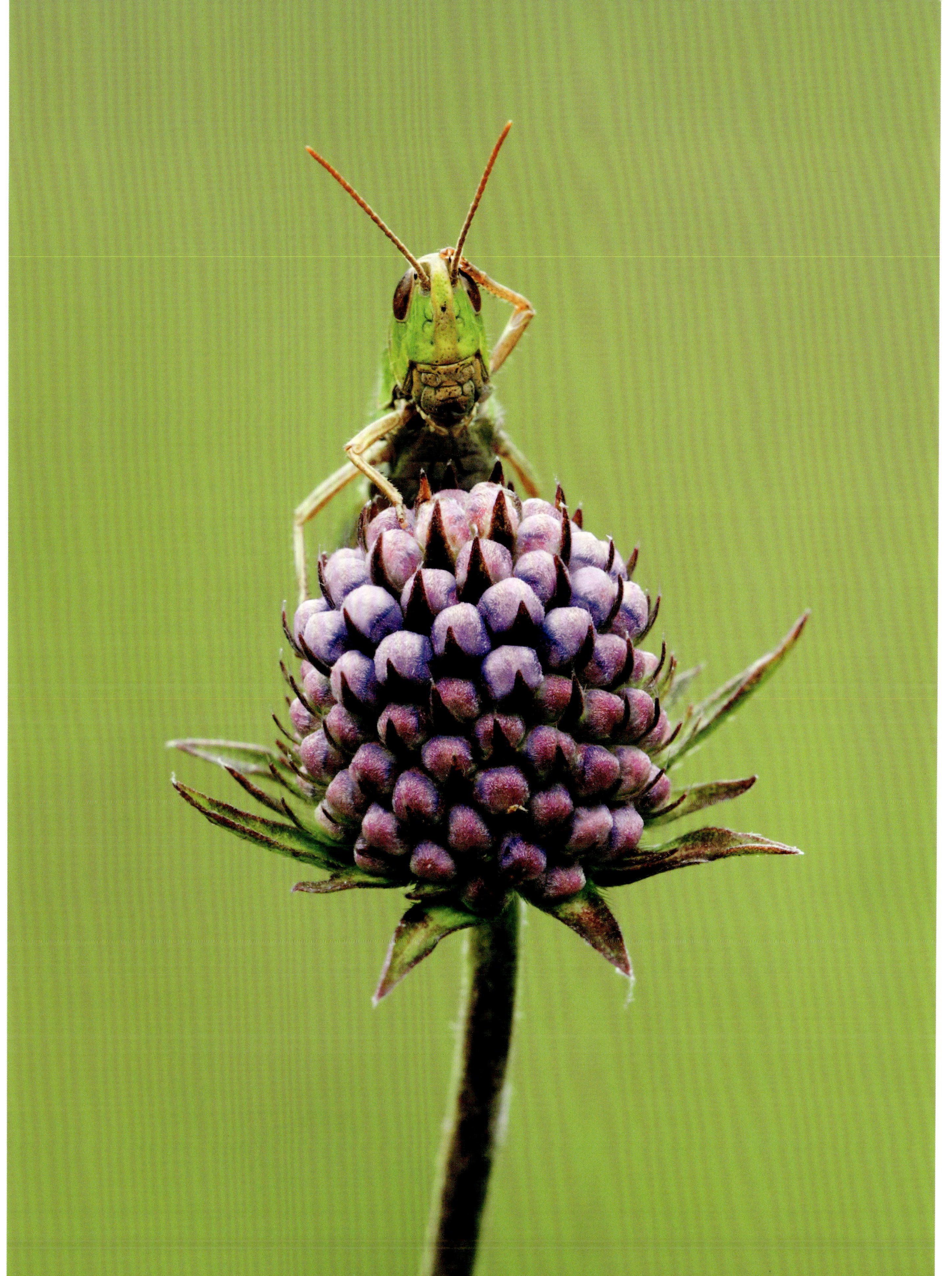

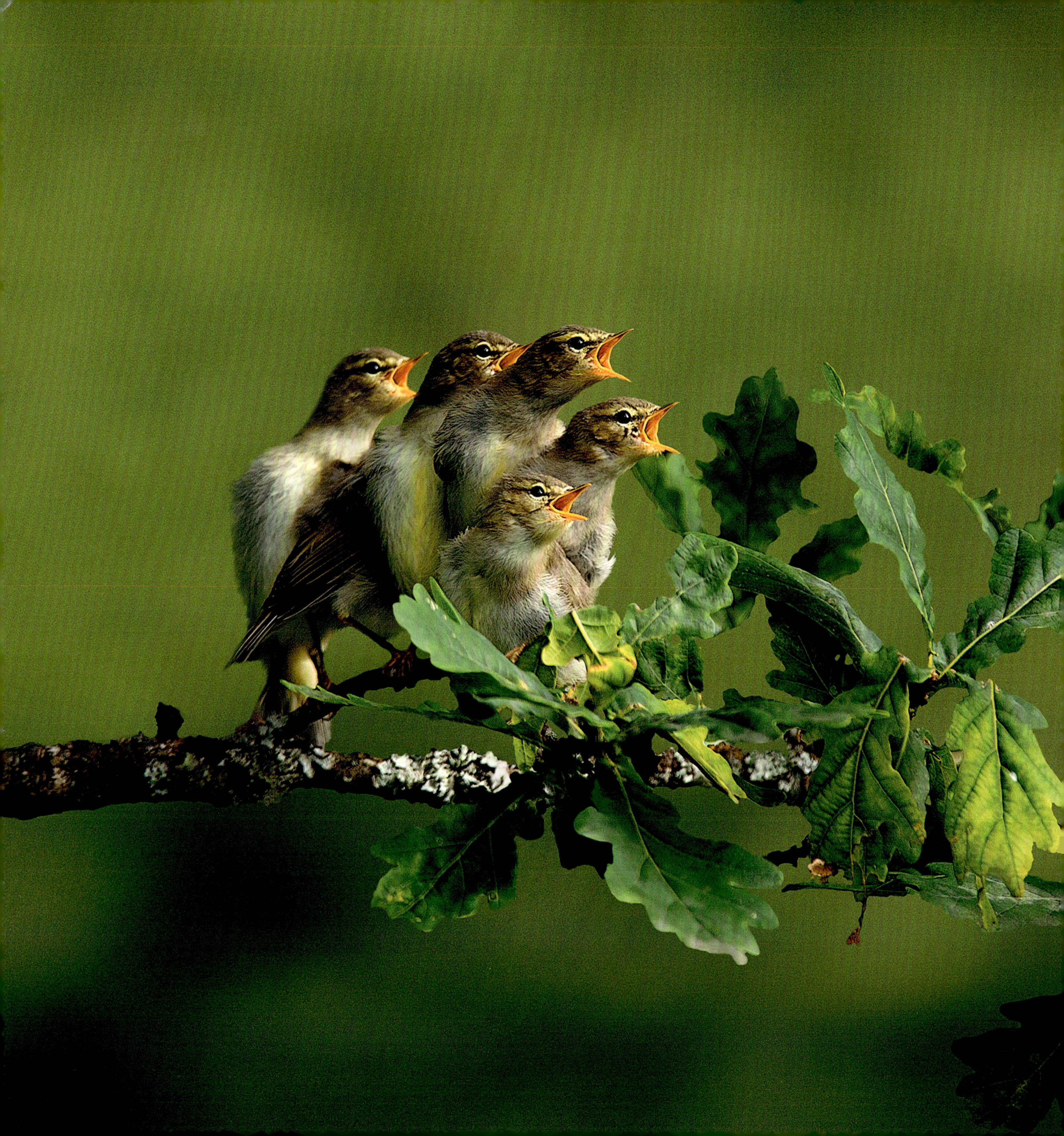

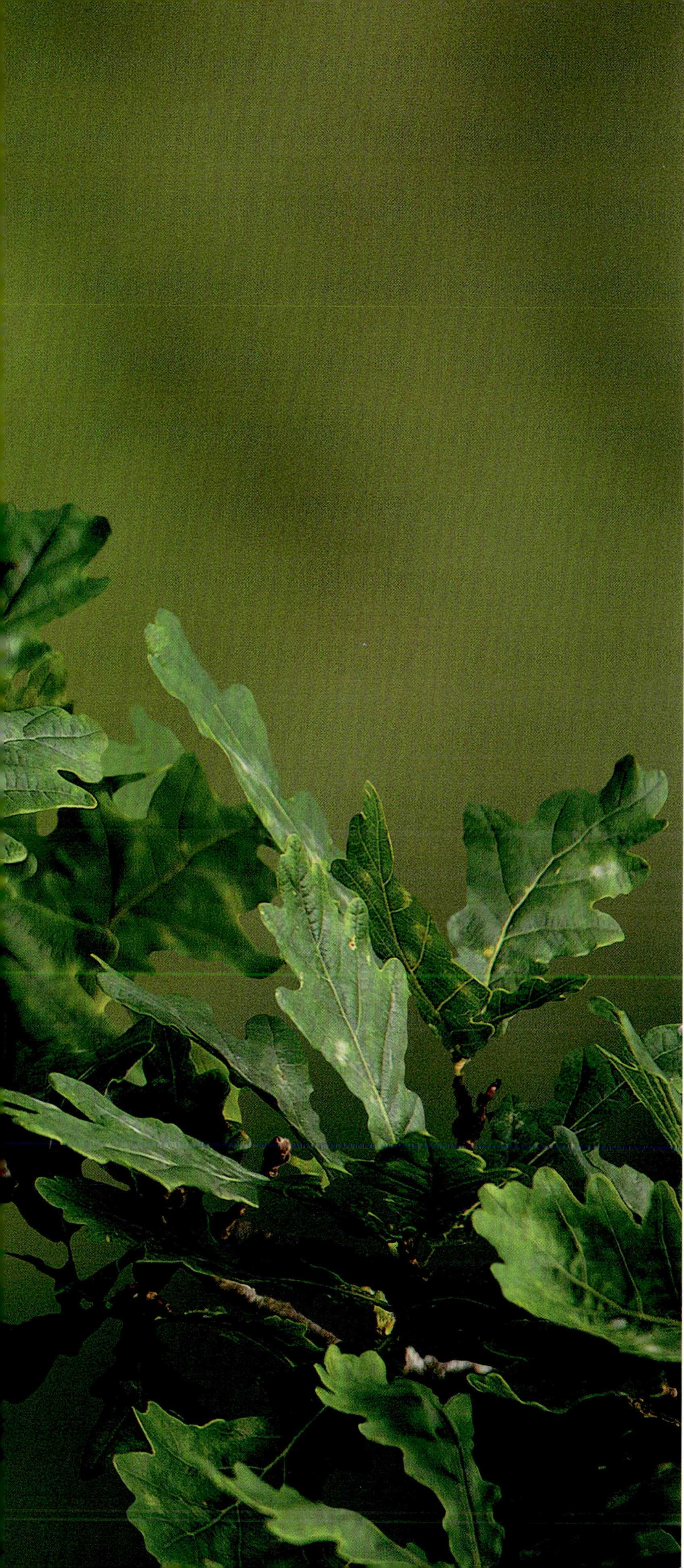

NINA JONSSON FINALIST

The Hungry Bunch
Son, Norway

The young willow warblers' open beaks and stretched necks signalled that they were impatient for insects from their parents. They bunched together and moved restlessly from branch to branch for predator protection.

Digital Canon EOS 5D MK II Canon EF 600 mm F4.0L IS USM + Canon extender EF 1.4 x II 1/200 sec at f/5.6. Post-capture: the background plane was taken from a different photograph of the same tree to achieve more depth of field on the main subject.

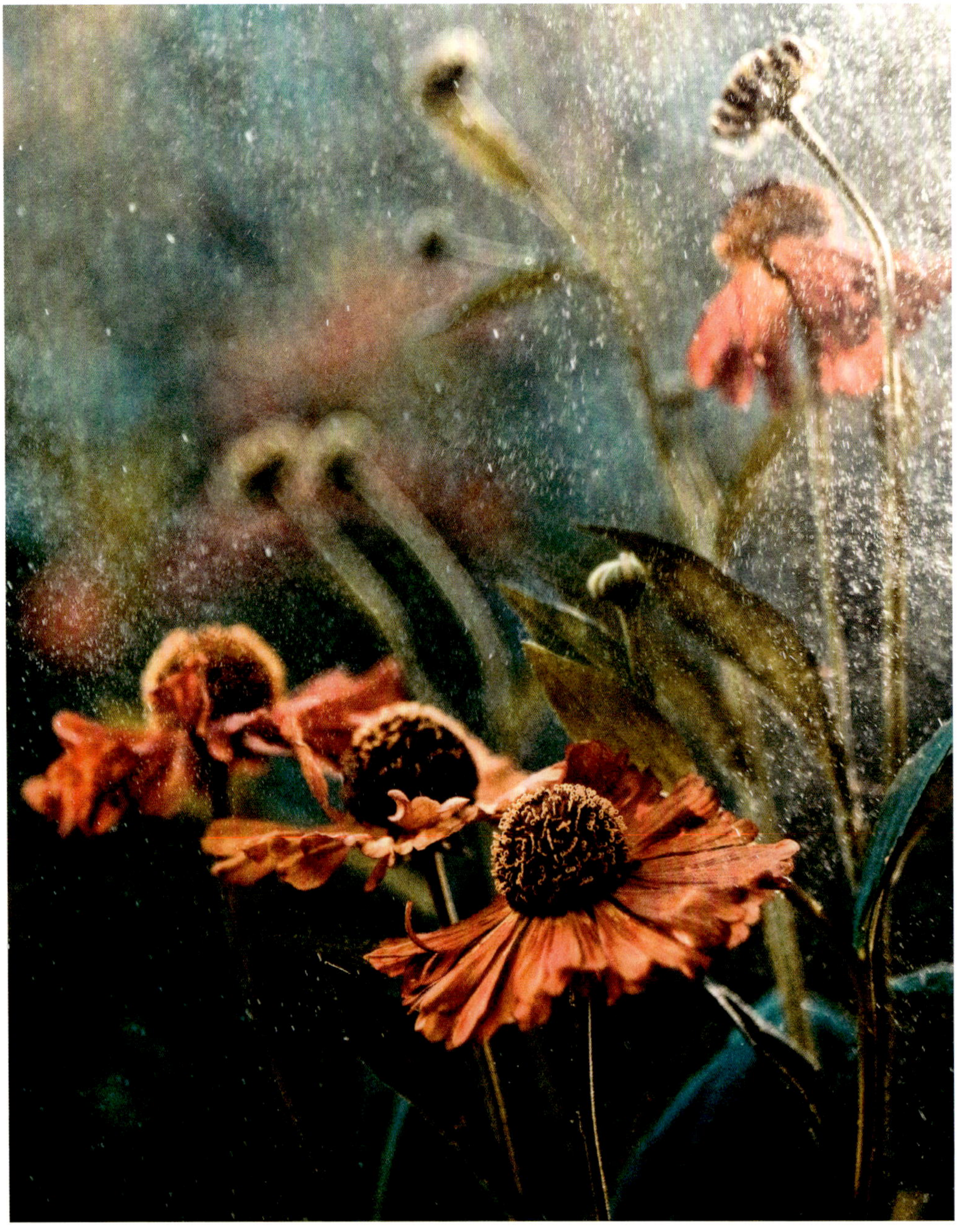

MAGDALENA WASICZEK 1ST PLACE

Summer in Rain
Glichów, Malopolska region, Poland

Every year we spend part of the holidays in Glichów. Because of the abundance and diversity of fauna and flora, it is a true photographic paradise for me. Dzielzan (*Hellenium*) is one of my favourite plants of late summer. My pictures are a record of impression, colours and light effects rather than encyclopaedic documentation. I can walk for hours in the garden and observe the change of lights, shadows and colours.

Nikon D300, Pentacon 50 manual lens. 1/250sec at f/2. Post-capture: basic contrast and colour management, some desaturation.

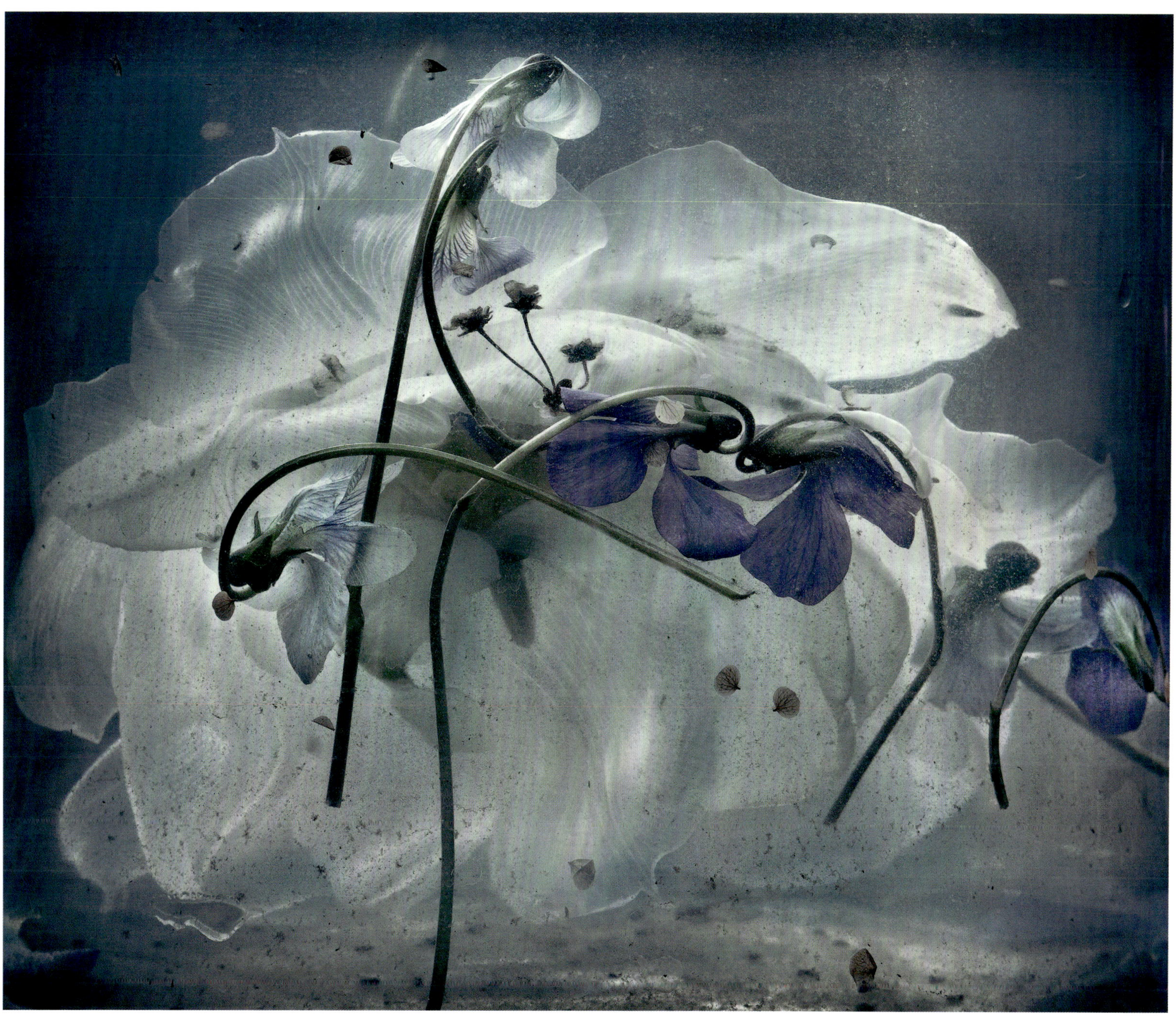

JOHN GRANT 2ND PLACE

Dance
My studio, Virginia, USA

This is an image of decayed white tulips along with fresh violets under water. The flowers were allowed to float in the water for several weeks, making them very delicate. The results of the work can never be predicted; it requires patience and steady observation, along with just the right natural light. All the specimens were grown in my own garden.

Canon EOS 5D Mark II, 100mm lens. 1/60sec at f/8. Post-capture: no digital alterations.

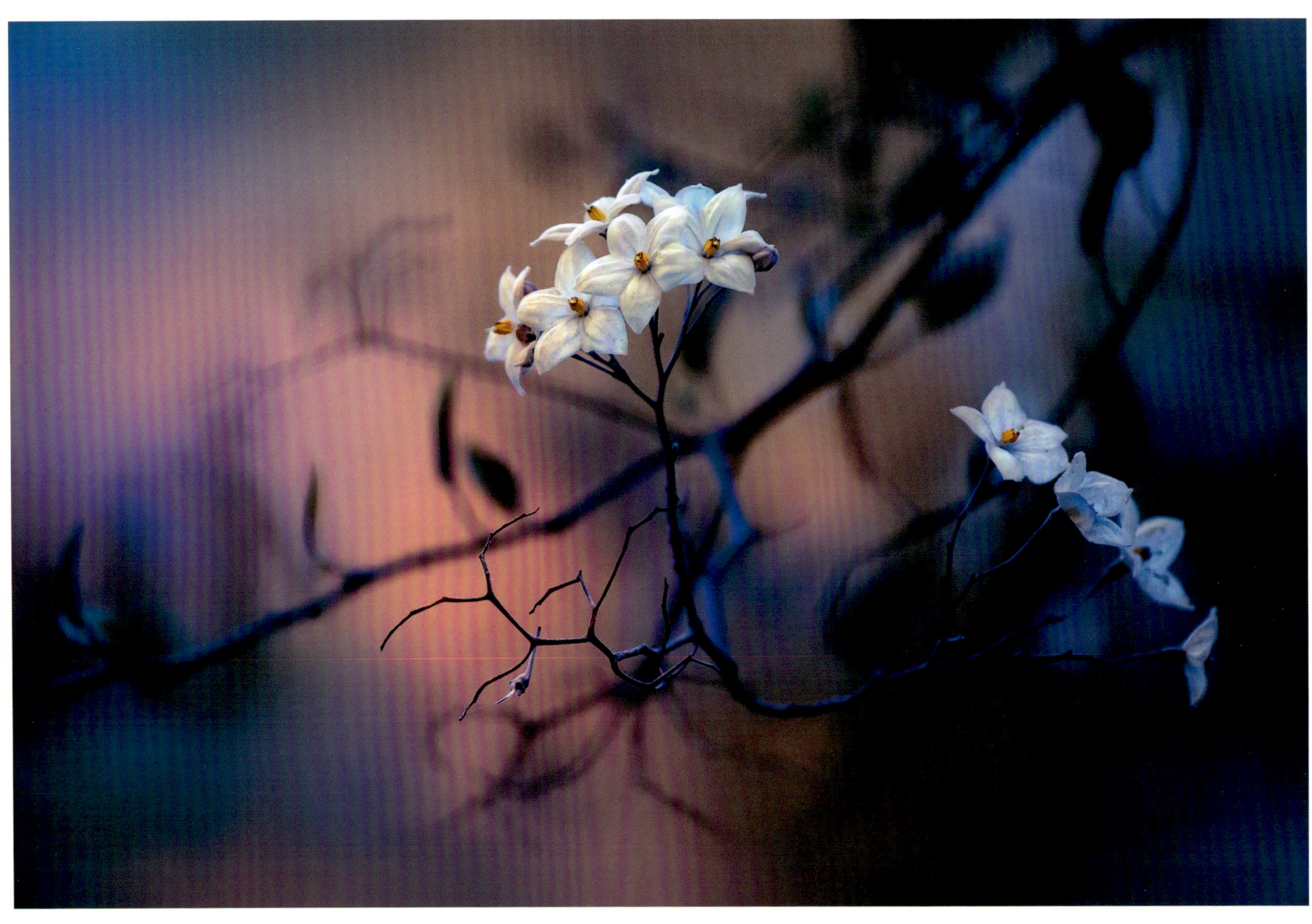

DIANE VARNER 3RD PLACE

Sweet Dawn
San Mateo Coast, California, USA

On this particularly brisk November morning, these fragrant potato vine flowers (*Solanum jasminoides*) seemed to have a presence that invited me to look closer and photograph their beauty. The image was taken with a hand-held camera.

Canon EOS 5D Mark II, 70-200 mm lens. 1/800sec at f/4.0. Post-capture: tonal adjustment.

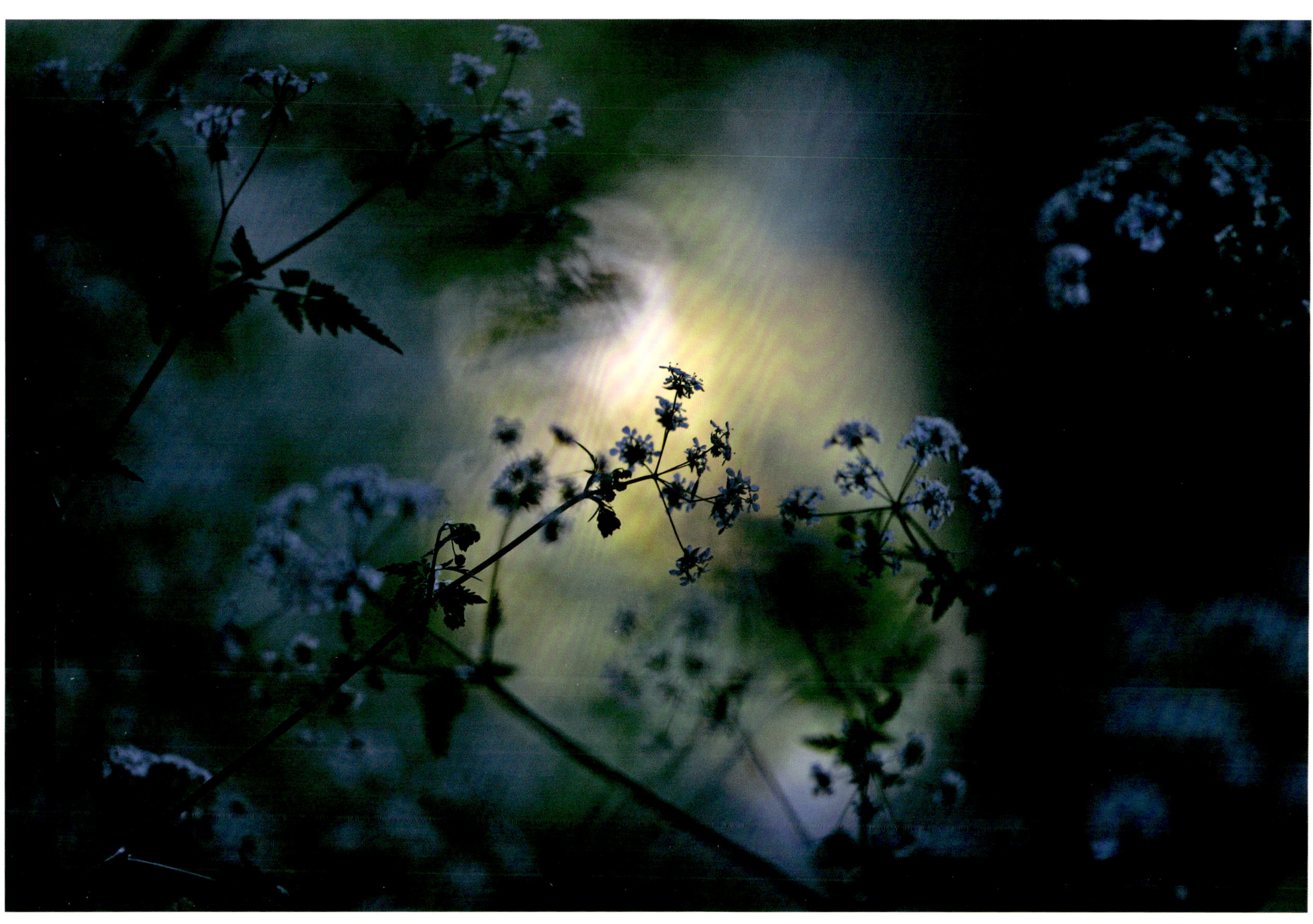

RAJYA LAKSHMI DOWNES FINALIST

Simple Beauty
Deux Sèvres, France

I love the light, feathery, flower heads of cow parsley whenever I see them swaying in the breeze. This photograph was taken on one of my morning walks. The tree-lined avenue makes a wonderful tunnel effect with the early morning sun filtering through at the end. The soft effect of the light captured my imagination.

Canon EOS 20D, Canon 100mm lens. 1/60sec at f/2.8. Post-capture: basic tonal adjustment.

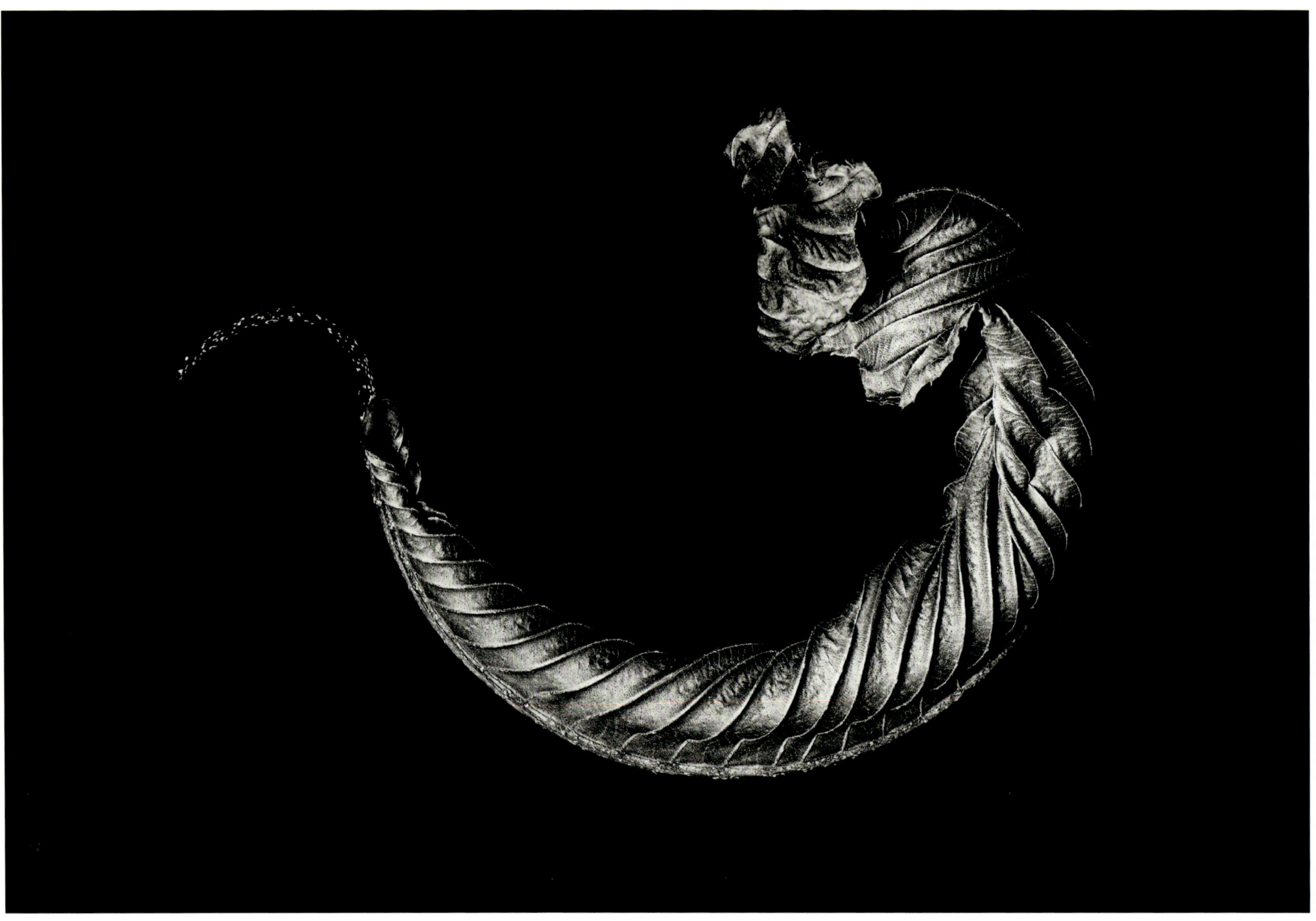

▲ **ANDREW PADDON** HIGHLY COMMENDED

Dried Leaf
Home studio, Cornwall, UK

My kids and I were enjoying the autumn colours and magnificent glasshouses at Kew, and they eagerly collected fallen leaves. Several weeks later, while tidying up, I found the leaves, and this amazing specimen had dried and curled up. It oozed texture, so I set up a makeshift studio - an ironing board and black velvet background clamped to a curtain pole - to photograph it!

Canon EOS 1DS Mark II, Canon 100mm lens. 1/250sec at f/11. Post-capture: image converted to black and white with software. Tones adjusted.

NANCY JOHNSON ► FINALIST

Bat Plant 1
Royal Botanic Gardens, Melbourne, Victoria, Australia

The White Batflower (*Tacca integrifolia*), commonly known as White Bat Plant, is native to India and Malaysia. The plant is large and the batflower is particularly striking with long 'whiskers' that are actually filiform bracteoles (small leaves) that can grow up to 30cm. This is the most amazing flower I have seen. I was absolutely transfixed. It is perfection. I kept finding new aspects and nuances, and was especially taken by the symmetry and the 'whiskers'. I intended to take many photos in the gardens but I could not leave this flower. My photography is intimate, bold and personal. That is my experience with Tacca, and I want you to be surprised, to look more, to explore every detail, look at every aspect, find the secrets.

Canon EOS 5D Mark II, Canon EF 70-200 lens. 1/160sec at f/2.8 ISO 100. Tripod. Post-capture: original colour image converted to black and white in software. Some foliage removed in software to emphasise the drama of the flower.

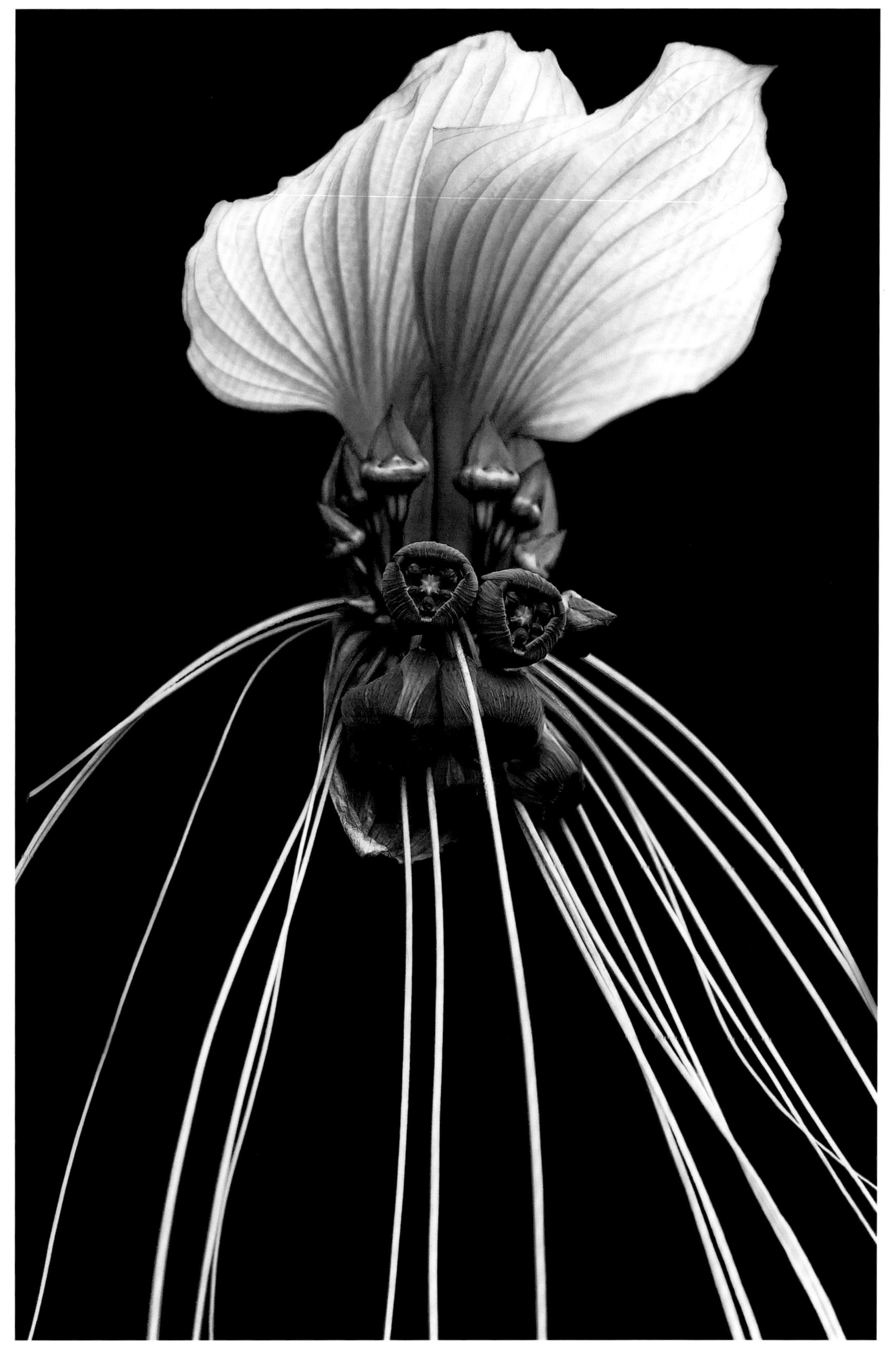

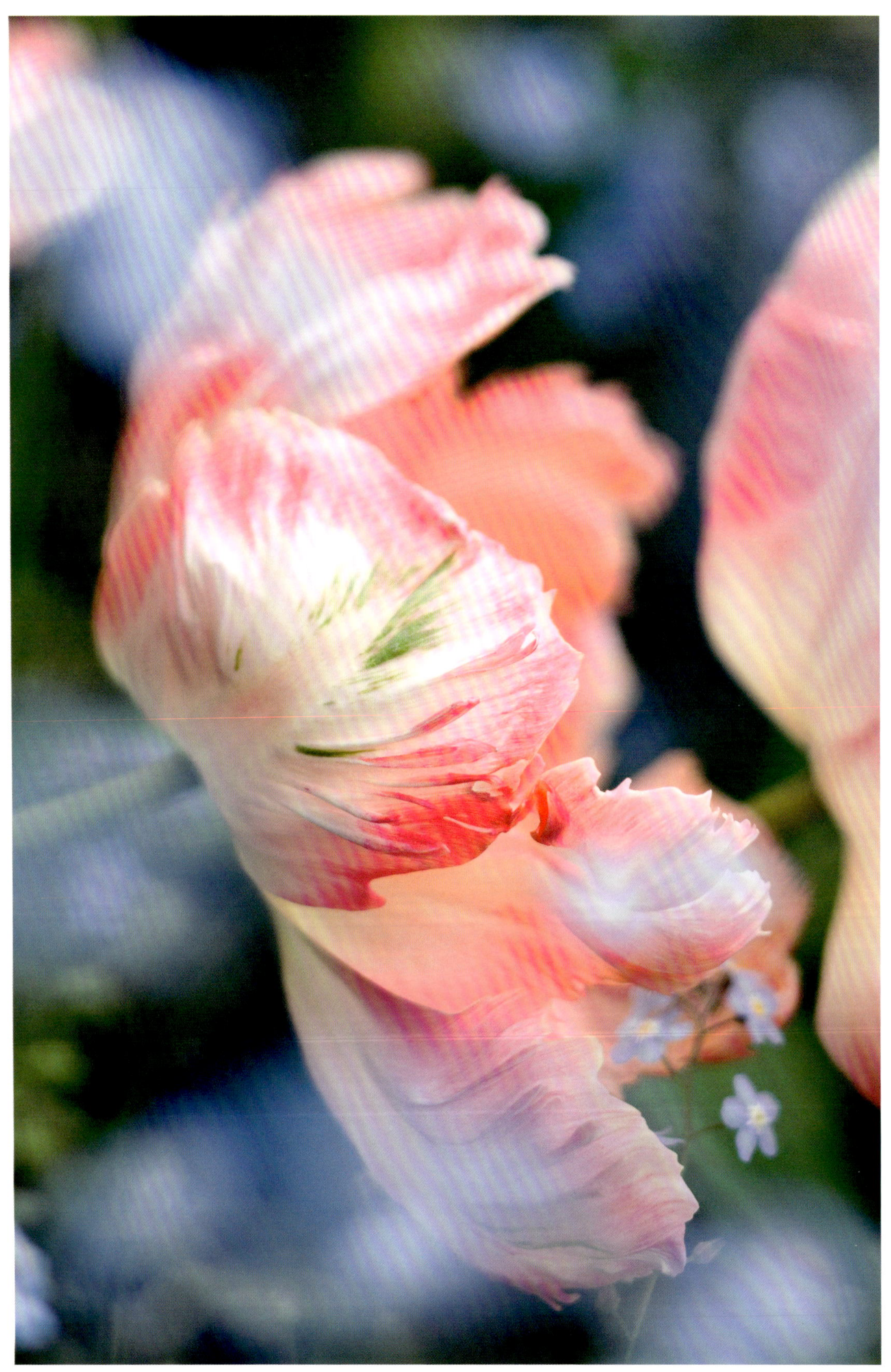

◄ **GEOFF DU FEU** FINALIST

Tulip "Peach Blossom"
My Garden, Norfolk, UK

I was attracted to the lovely pastel colours and a very still evening produced the soft light I needed to bring out their full subtlety. I wanted to show the tulip flower surrounded by clouds of blue so I used a large aperture combined with a tilt-shift lens to define the area of focus.

Canon EOS 40D, TS-E 90mm lens. 1/200sec at f/3.2. Post-capture: no digital alterations.

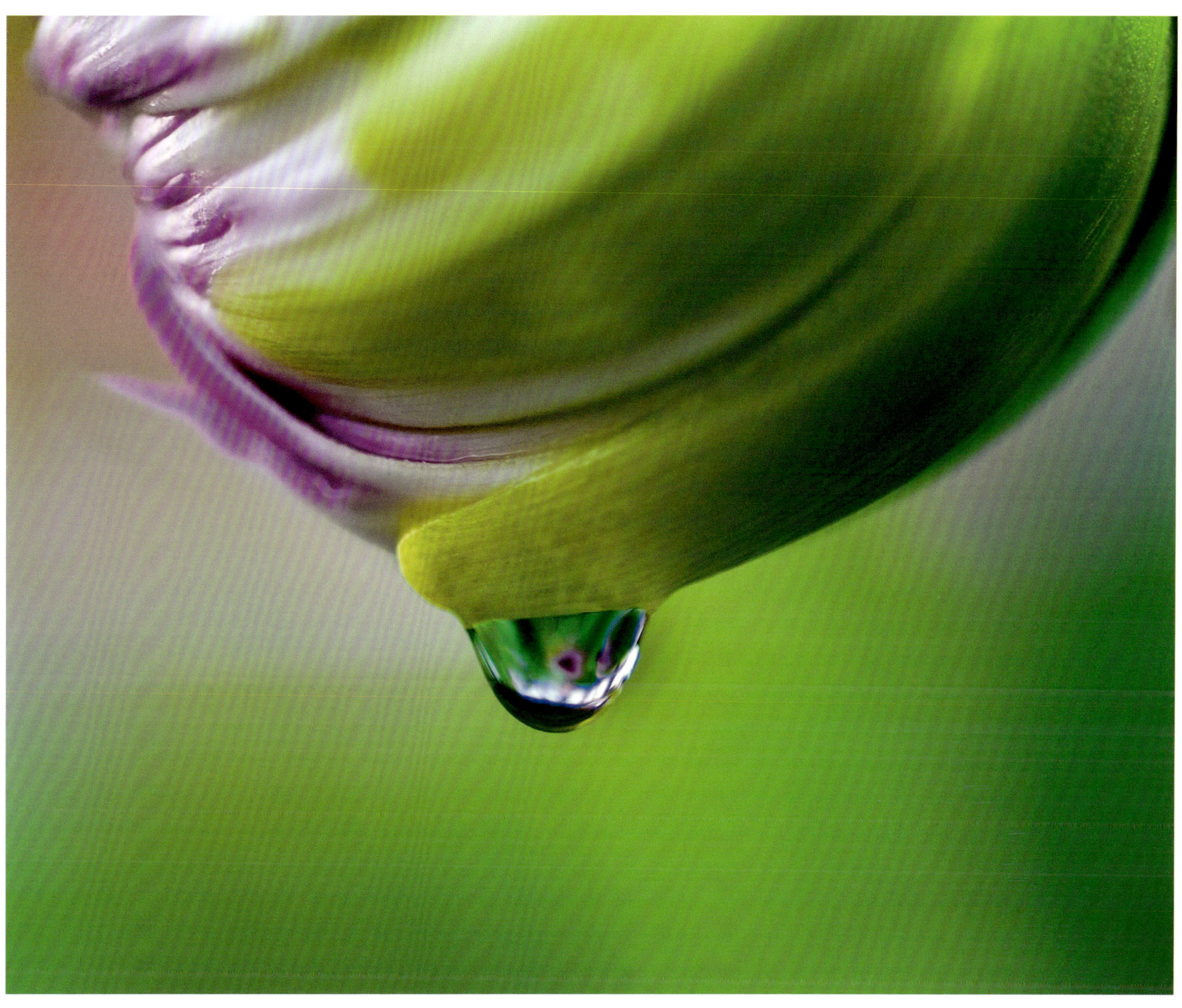

DIANE FIFIELD — Highly Commended

Chrysanthemum Raindrop
Plymouth, Devon, UK

The rain had just stopped so I ventured out into the garden with my camera and macro lens. I wanted to capture raindrops and saw this chrysanthemum bud with one little raindrop about to fall. I quickly set up, focused with a manual setting to give me control, and took the shot. Macro photography shows up all the wonderful details and textures in the flower which normally go unnoticed by the human eye. I edged my way between the dripping wet chrysanthemums until I found just the shot I was looking for.

Canon EOS 400D, Tamron 90mm lens. 1/100sec at f/3.2. Post-capture: some tonal adjustment.

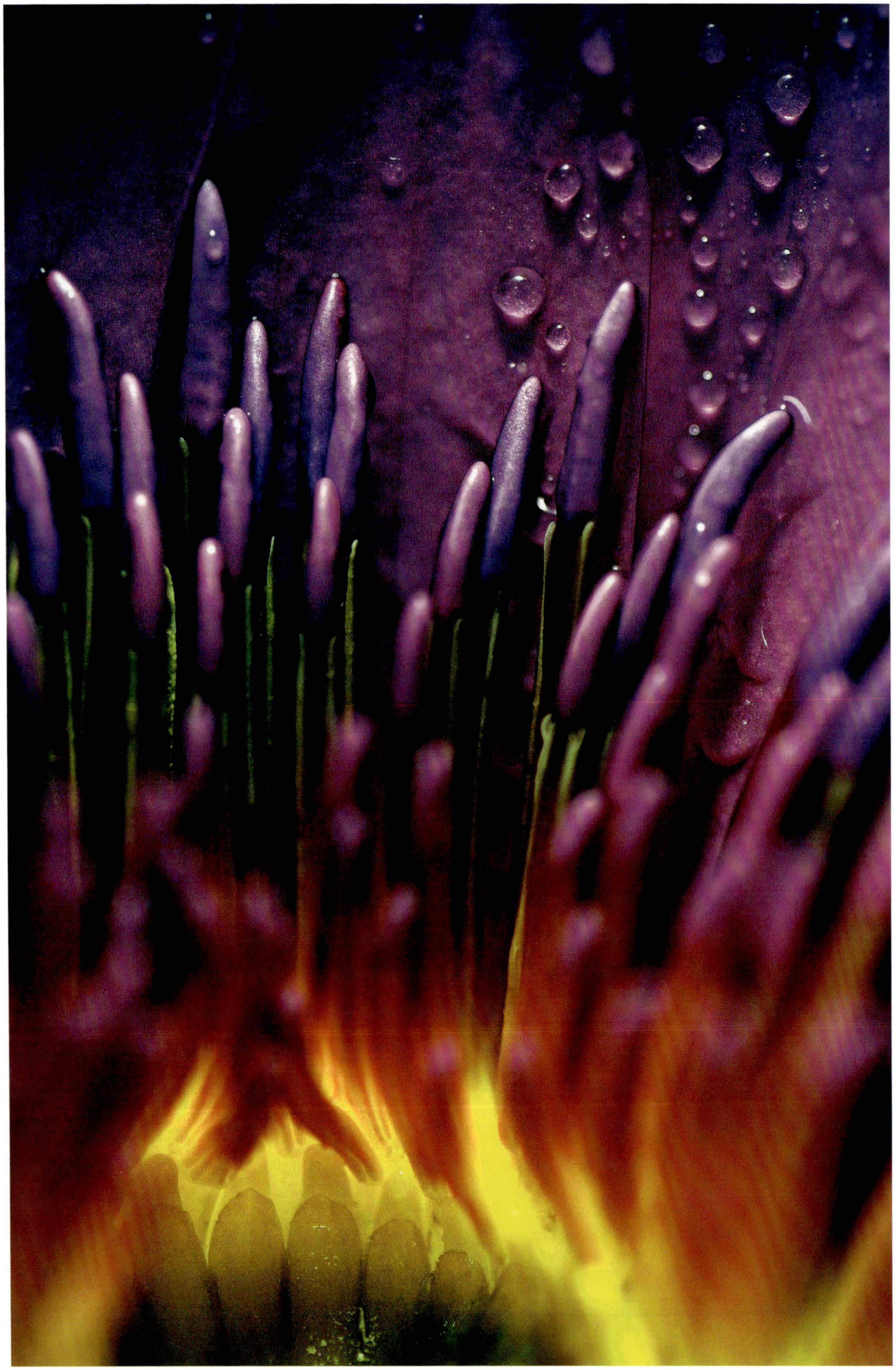

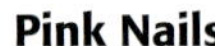

ANNA ULMESTRAND HIGHLY COMMENDED

Pink Nails
My house, Gothenburg, Sweden

I saw this beautiful flower in the supermarket and could not resist buying it. Winter is such a dark time, and this flower made life beautiful again. I had to pull the flower apart to capture all the colours. The light was not the best, but with a tripod I could photograph even at night, indoors and in the middle of winter.

Canon EOS 350 D, Tamron 90 mm lens. 1/40 sec at f/2.8. Post-capture: contrast and tonal manipulation.

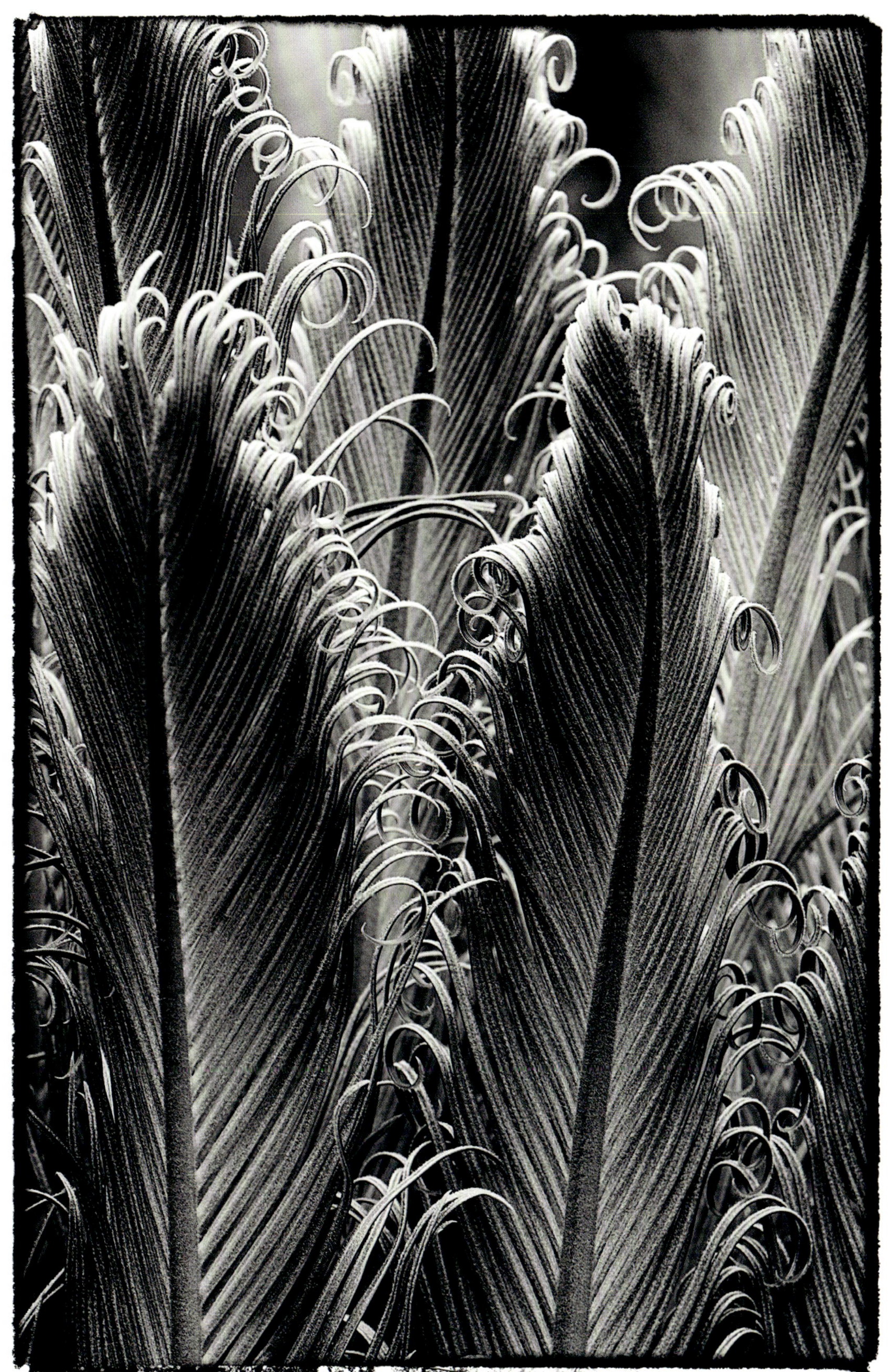

IOANNIS SCHINEZOS AND ROBERTA PAGANO ►

HIGHLY COMMENDED

Cycas revoluta
Kirstenbosch Botanical Gardens, Cape Town, South Africa

I often shoot nature photographs in black and white to lead the observer to the essential components of the picture. Because of the wind, I had to wait with my tripod for a calm moment.

Nikon D300, Nikkor 70-200mm lens. 1/50sec at f/8. Post-capture: the colour original was transformed to black and white with software.

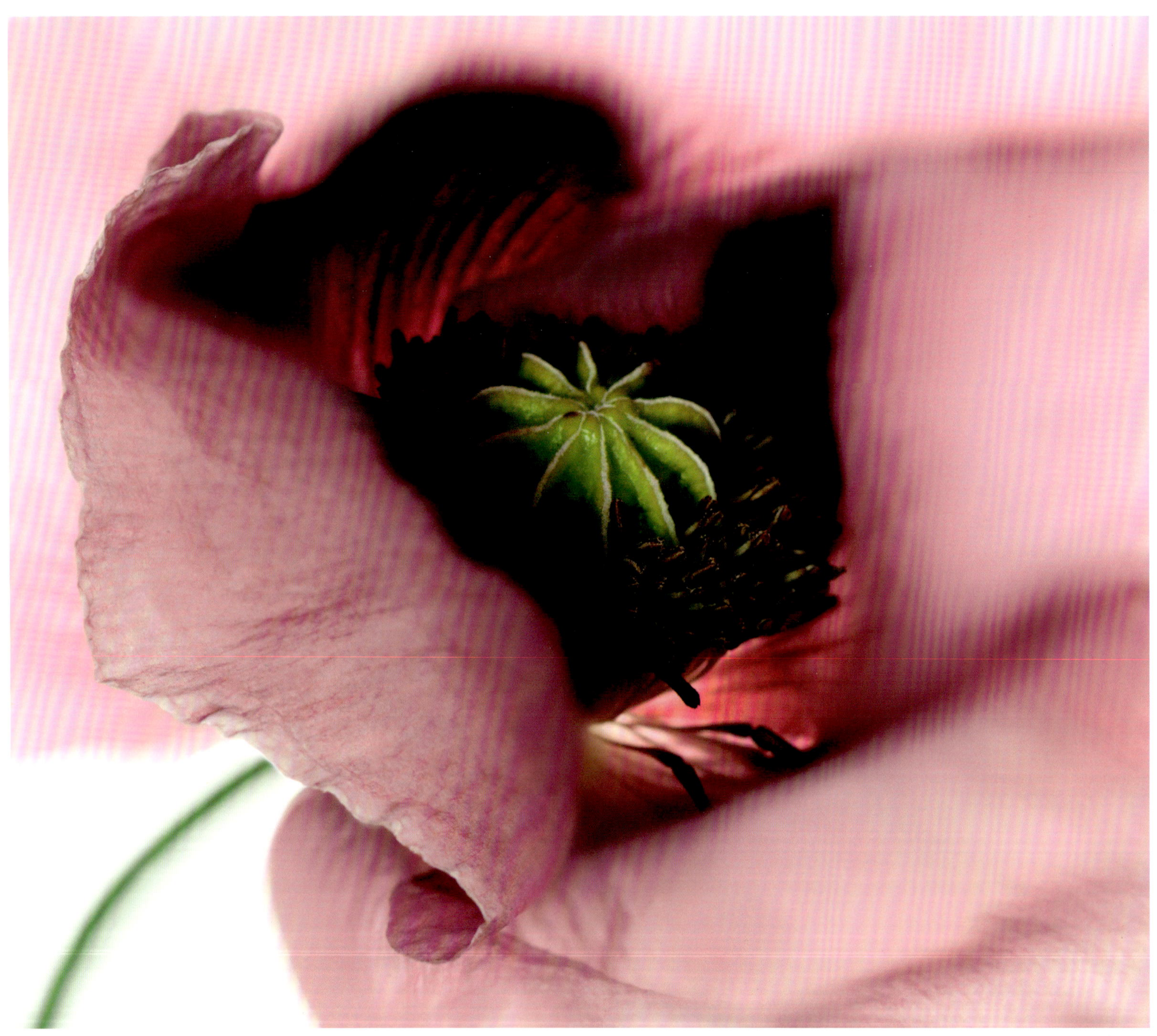

POLINA PLOTNIKOVA FINALIST

Poppy Flower
Home studio, London, UK

As I was passing down a path in my garden, a gust of wind blew over this corn poppy and bright sunlight shone through it, all at the same time. I noticed how tender the petals look as they flutter and, by contrast, how formidable the centre of the plant looks.

Canon EOS 5D Mark II, Canon 100mm lens. 1/125sec at f9/. Post-capture: soft brush tool used to emphasise the selective focus of the shot.

ANNEMARIE FARLEY ► FINALIST

Rainbow Poppy
My garden, Blackpool, UK

Poppies are my favourite flowers and I take many photographs of them during summer. I was taking this picture with the other orange poppies as the background but as I turned to get a different angle I picked up other colours in the garden. They contrasted against the orange of the poppy and produced a kind of 'rainbow' colour effect. I always try to photograph a flower from a different perspective rather than showing the whole of the flower head, so I only showed the parts I was interested in to create an attractive shape. I focused on the centre of the flower and knocked the background and stem out of focus to make all the colours fade in to each other like a rainbow.

Nikon D300, Sigma 105mm lens. 1/400sec at f/4.
Post-capture: no digital alterations.

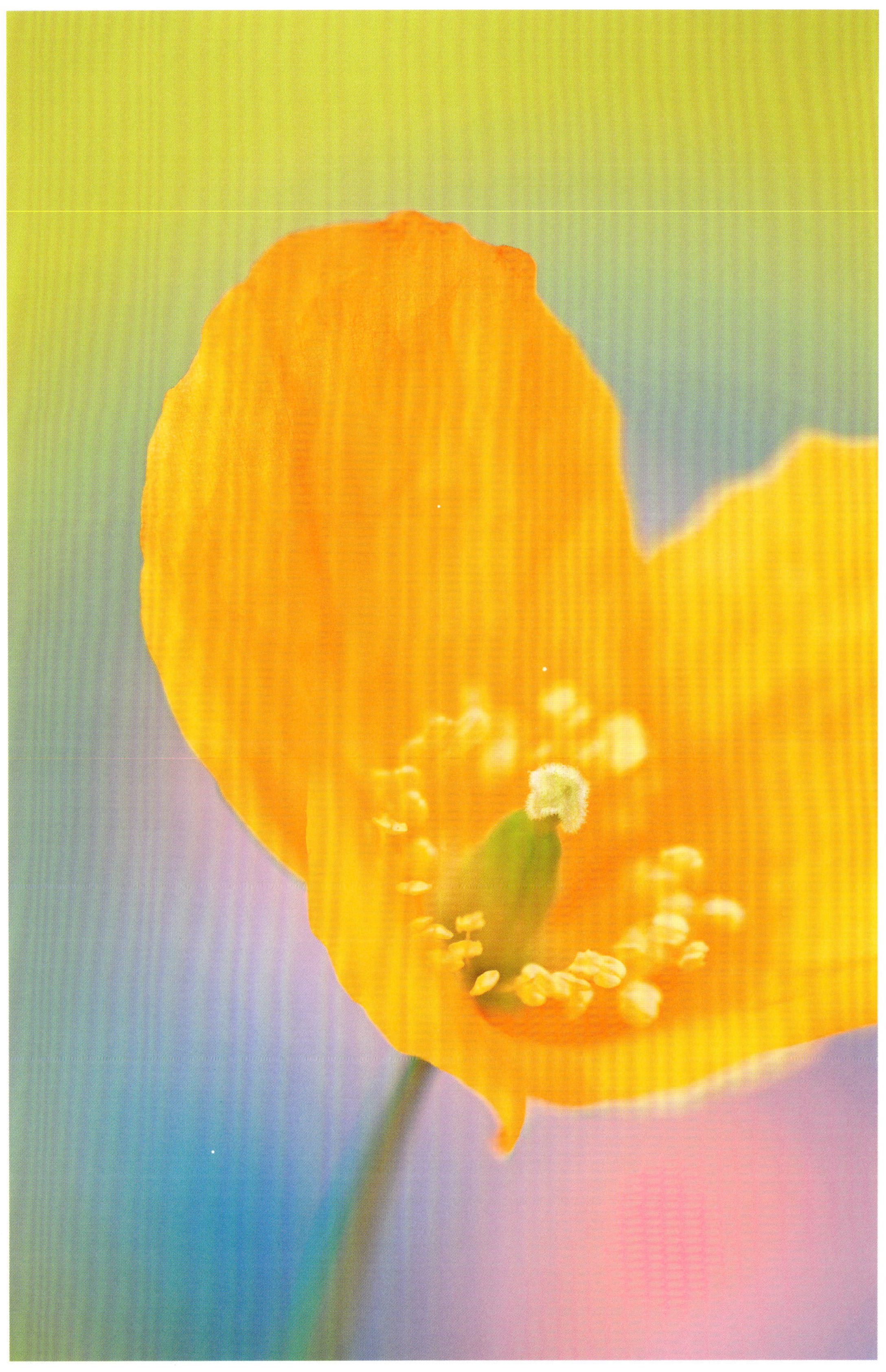

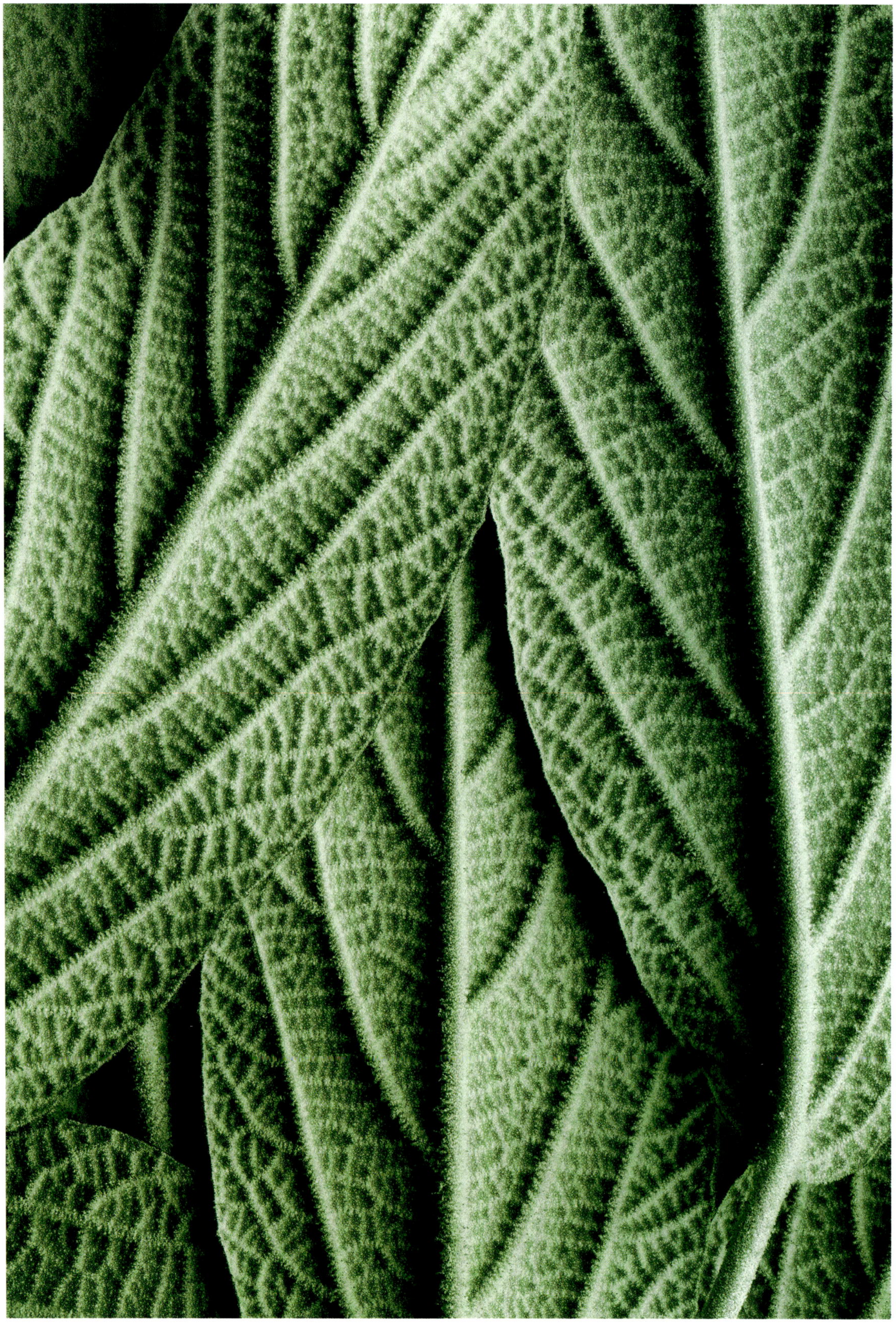

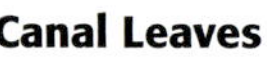

JOHANNA PARKIN HIGHLY COMMENDED

Canal Leaves
Studio, London, UK

Studio shot of a pile of wild-growing leaves picked along the walkway of Regent's Canal, London. The fuzzy veined texture of the underside of these leaves was too graphic and tactile not to photograph.

Film Fuji Velvia 50. Sinar 5x4 format, 150mm lens. Post-capture: no digital alterations.

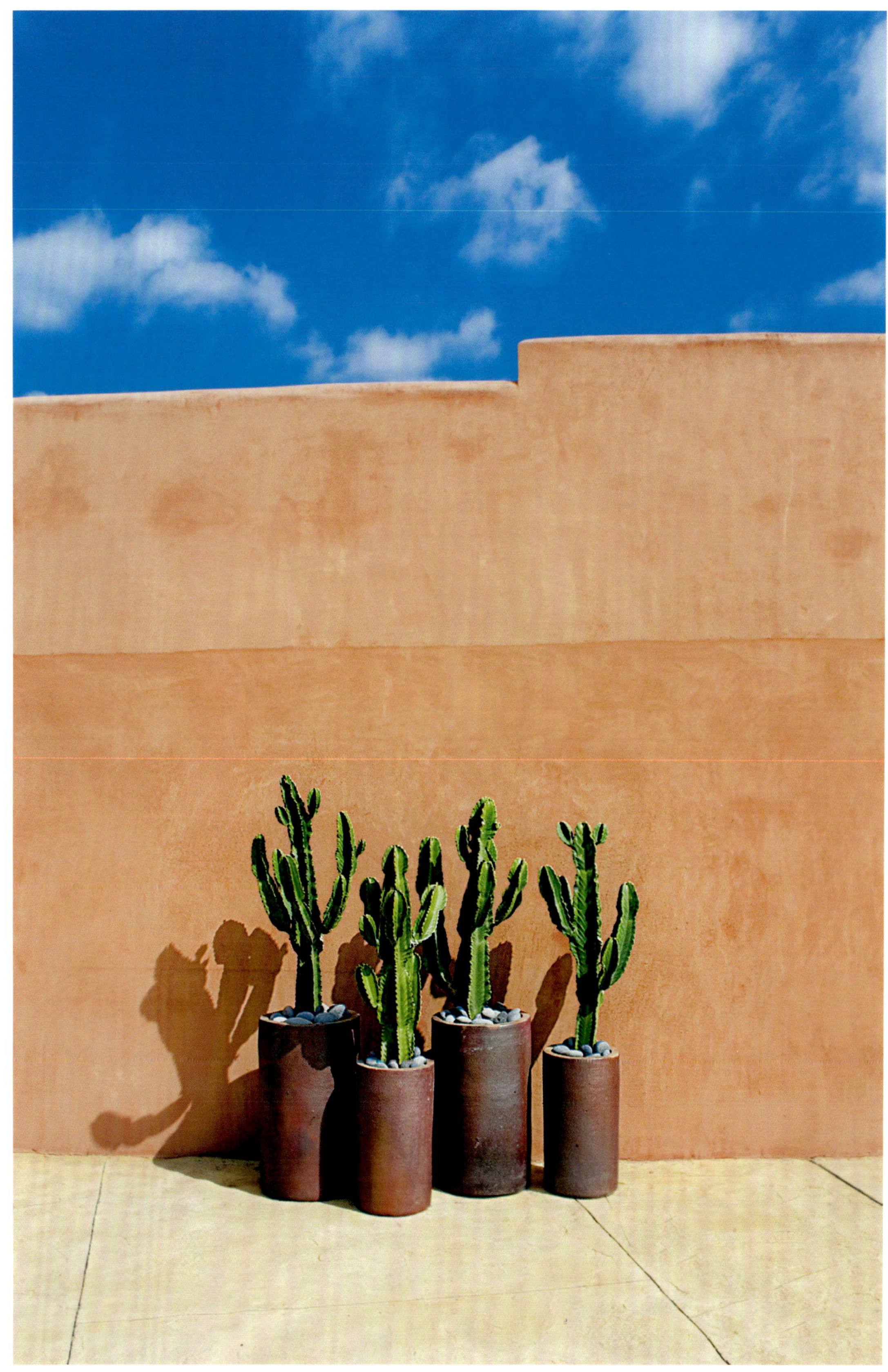

KATHRYN WEST ► HIGHLY COMMENDED

Heat

Los Abrigos, Tenerife, Canary Islands, Spain

These four potted cacti are typical examples of the cacti and succulents that flourish in Tenerife's sub-tropical climate. I wanted to capture the feeling of heat by showcasing the ornamental beauty potted cacti offer, as opposed to shooting them in their wild environment. I decided to include background details, especially the bright sky, and I lined my subject at a point where I could frame it in a portrait format.

Canon EOS 450D, Canon EF 18-55mm lens. 1/320sec at f/8. Post-capture: no digital alterations.

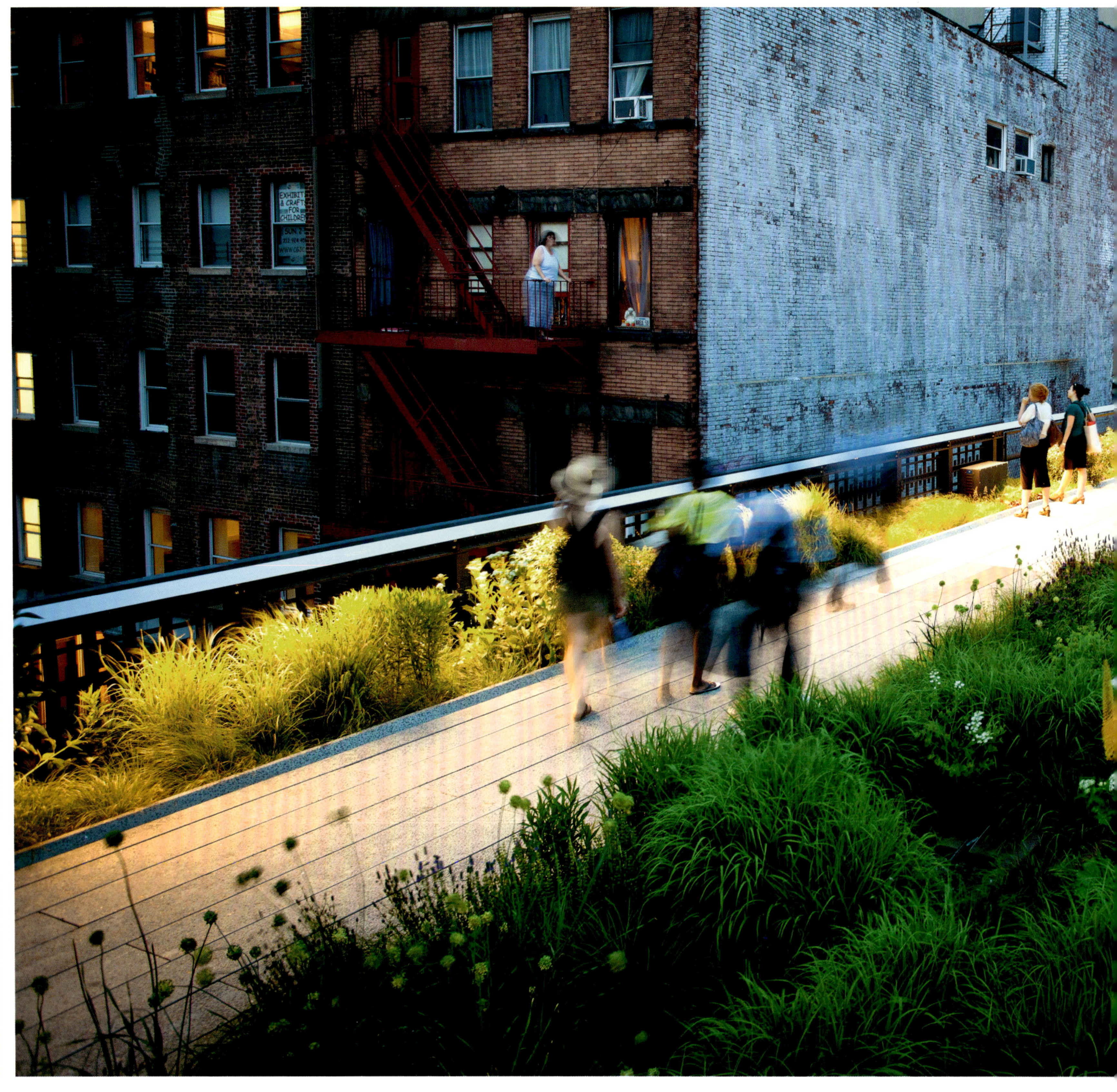
EXHIBIT
& CRAFT
FOR

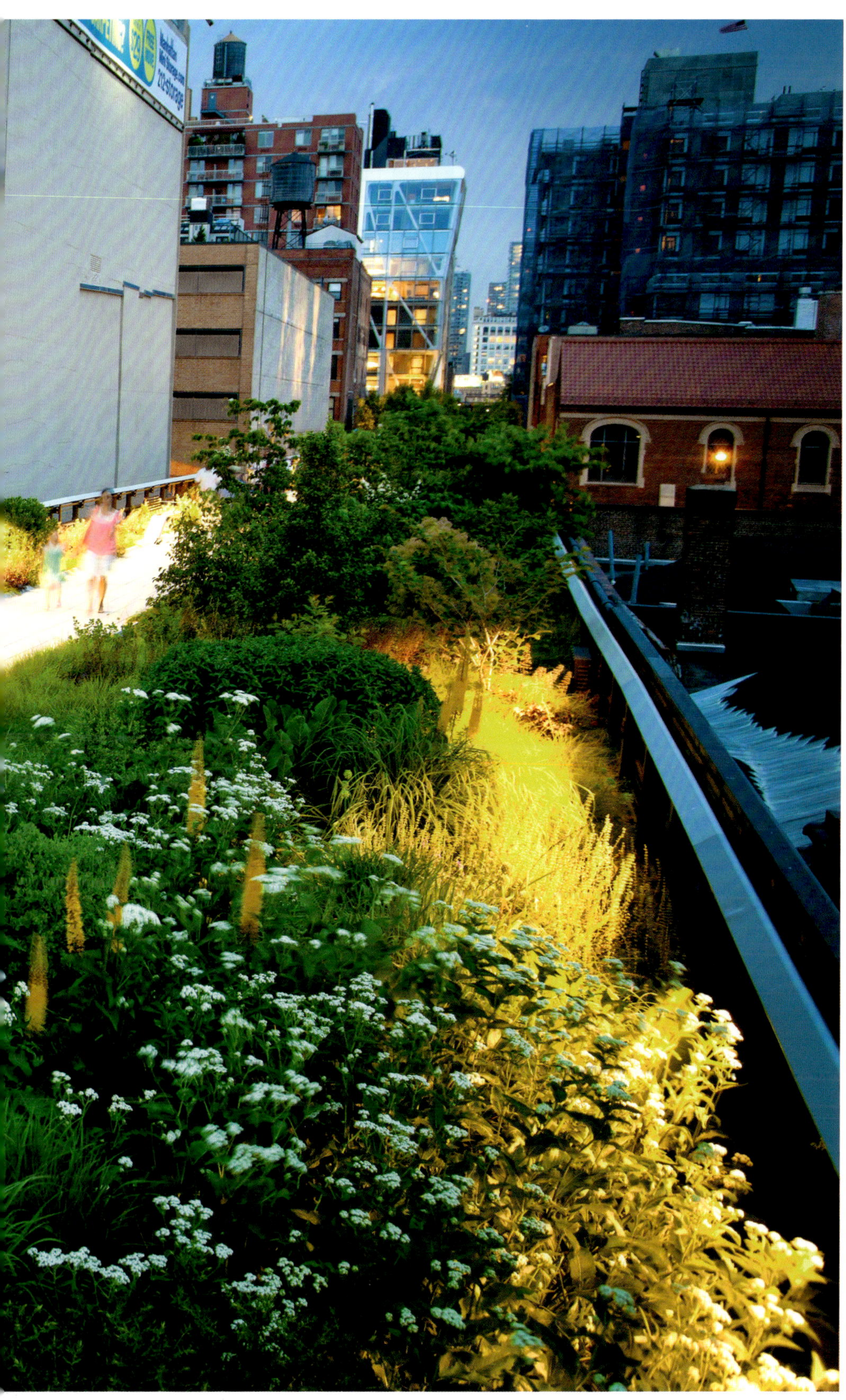

CLAIRE TAKACS 1ST PLACE

Conversations from a Balcony at dusk along the High Line
The High Line, New York, USA

I was photographing the High Line for a magazine. This was my first visit and I absolutely loved it, especially at dusk when this was taken. The human interaction was something I wanted to capture. I think there is something really special about this wonderful green space: I am sure it means so many things to so many people and results in so many daily exchanges.

Canon EOS 5D Mark II, 17-40mm lens. 0.8 sec at f/5.6. Tripod, remote shutter release. Post-capture: no digital alterations.

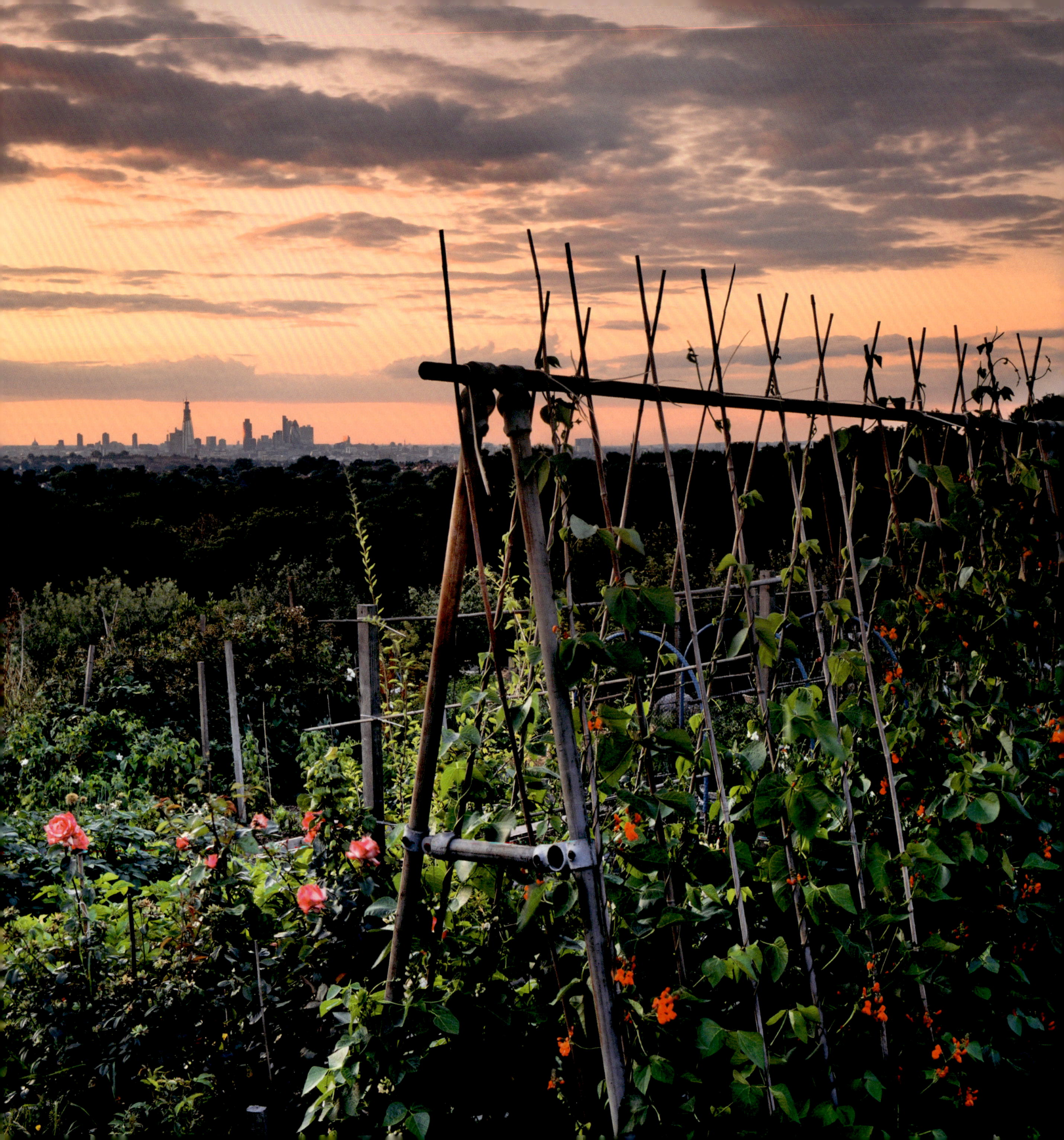

◄ MAX RUSH 2ND PLACE

Beans and the City
Sydenham Hill, South London, UK

A hillside allotment near Dulwich in late summer. This site is a little-known outside the area, but its gardeners have the privilege of one of the greatest views in London. This view of climbing beans against the backdrop of the city of London is from the first summer of a project which has already proved inspiring and exciting.

Fuji Velvia 50 film, 120 Bronica SQAi, 80mm lens. 4 sec at f/22, with 0.6 neutral density graduated filter to balance exposure between sky and land. Post-capture: minor tonal adjustment.

MALCOLM BOYD ► 3RD PLACE

City against Nature
La Défense, Paris, France

In the battle for space, trees and plants often lose to buildings, and this photograph puts both on the same scale and is a plea for more green areas in urban sites. I work in the business district of La Défense in Paris, so the area is a kind of photographic playground for me. I have taken numerous shots of this building and the surrounding trees. The camera was hand held and the shot is slightly underexposed to keep the details in the sky.

Canon EOS 5D Mark II, 24-105mm lens. 1/160sec at f/5. Post-capture: cleaning, cropping and white balance adjustment.

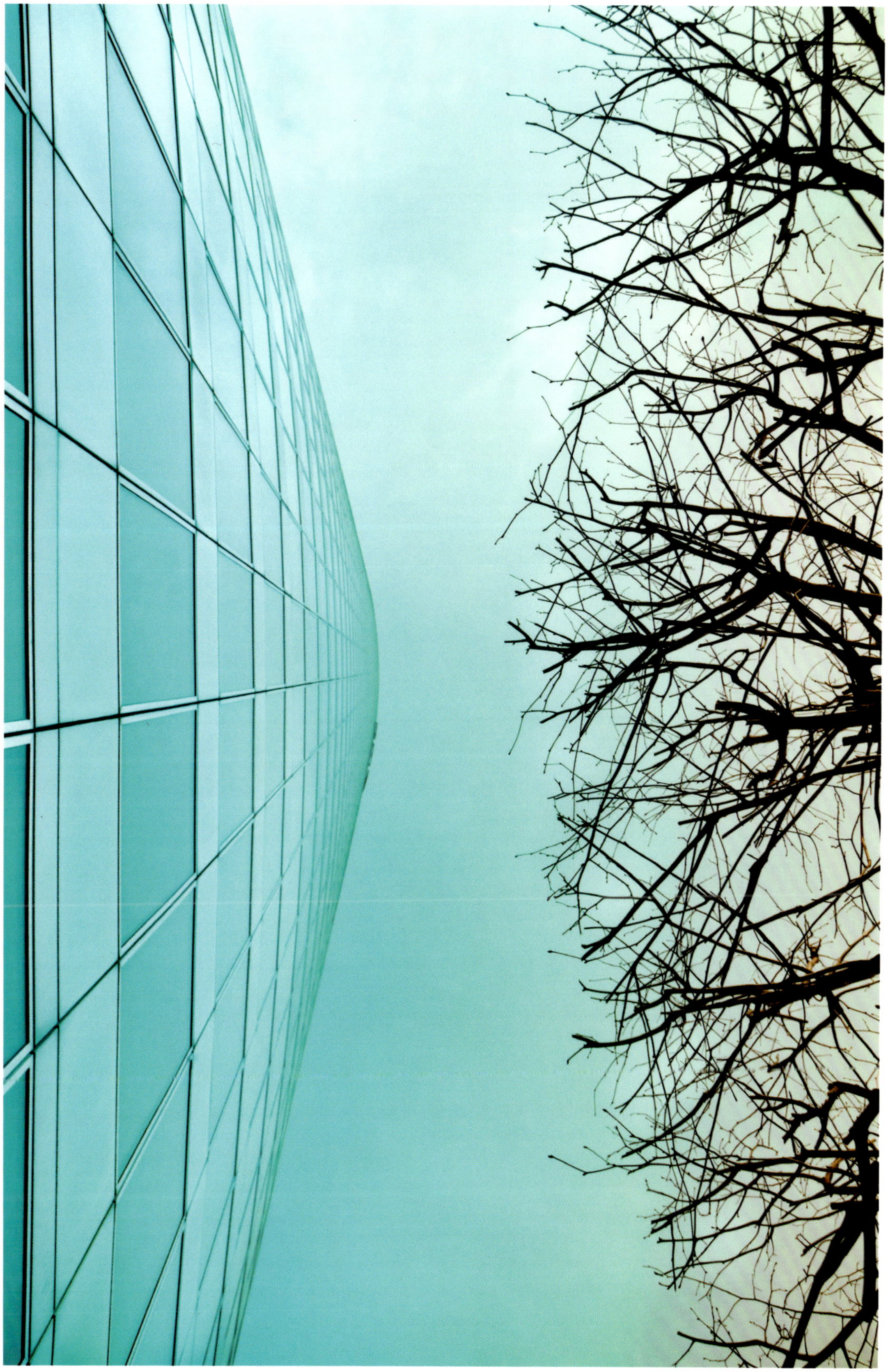

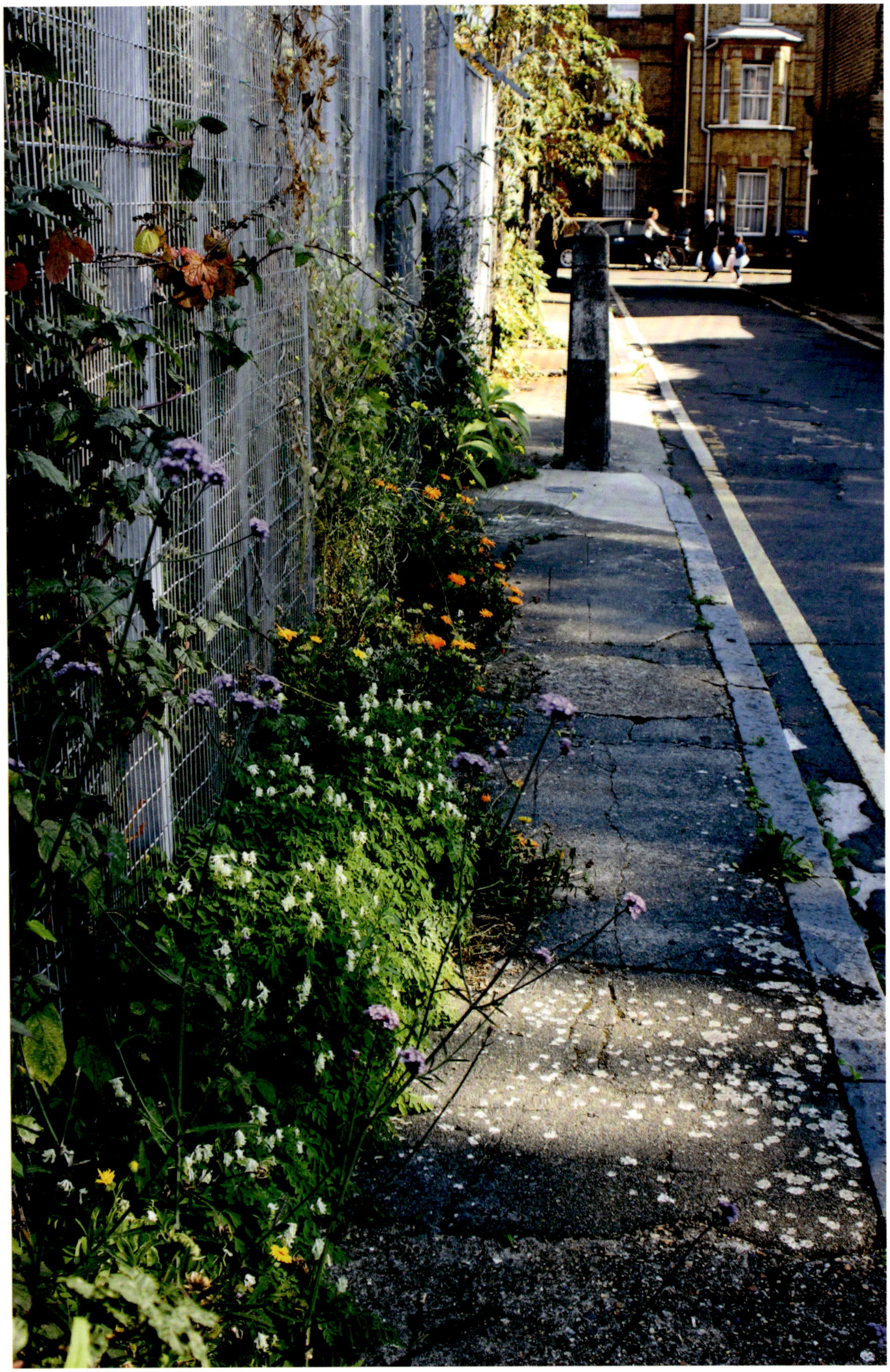

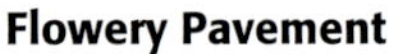

◄ **CANDACE WRIGHT** FINALIST

Flowery Pavement
Elephant and Castle, London, UK

We grow flowers on the allotments behind the fence for the beneficial insects. These ones have sown themselves outside the fence and we leave them for the pleasure of passers-by. *Verbena bonariensis*, *Calendula officinalis* and *Corydalis ochroleuca*, with blackberry leaves on the fence - all self-sown. This view gives me pleasure every time I turn the corner into this street.

Canon EOS 500D, Sigma 28-300mm lens. 1/100sec at f/5.6. Post-capture: no digital alterations.

SAM KIRK ► FINALIST

A Brockley Street
Brockley, London, UK

I like taking images from a different perspective and I focus on the smaller things that add that touch of greenery to city surroundings. Here, small moss plants enhance a built up urban environment if you look for them. I often stop to touch these tactile floras and wonder how many people notice them and what the streets would look like without these soft, feathery little plants.

Canon EOS 400D, 50mm lens. 1/125sec at f/4.5. Post-capture: tone adjustment.

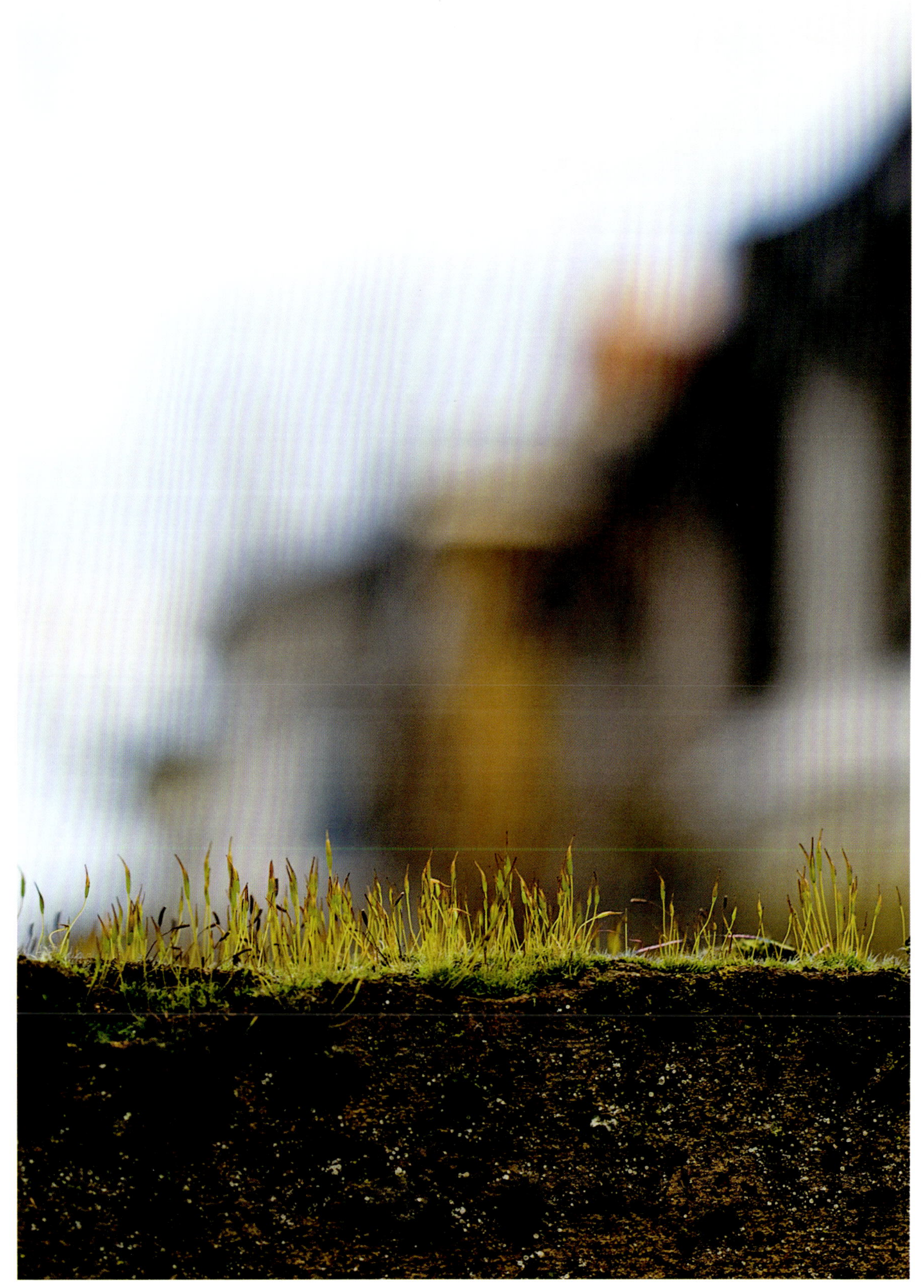

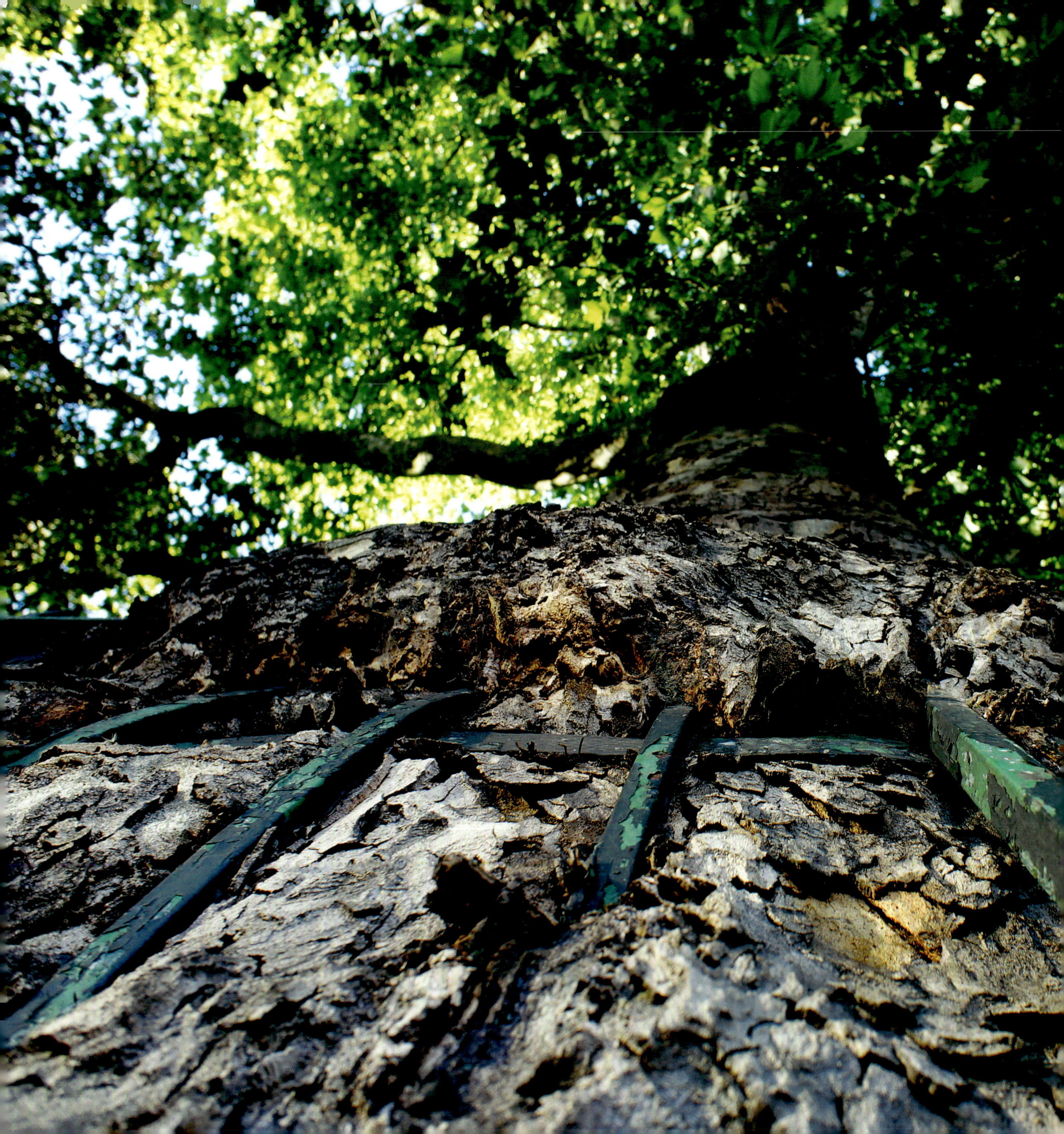

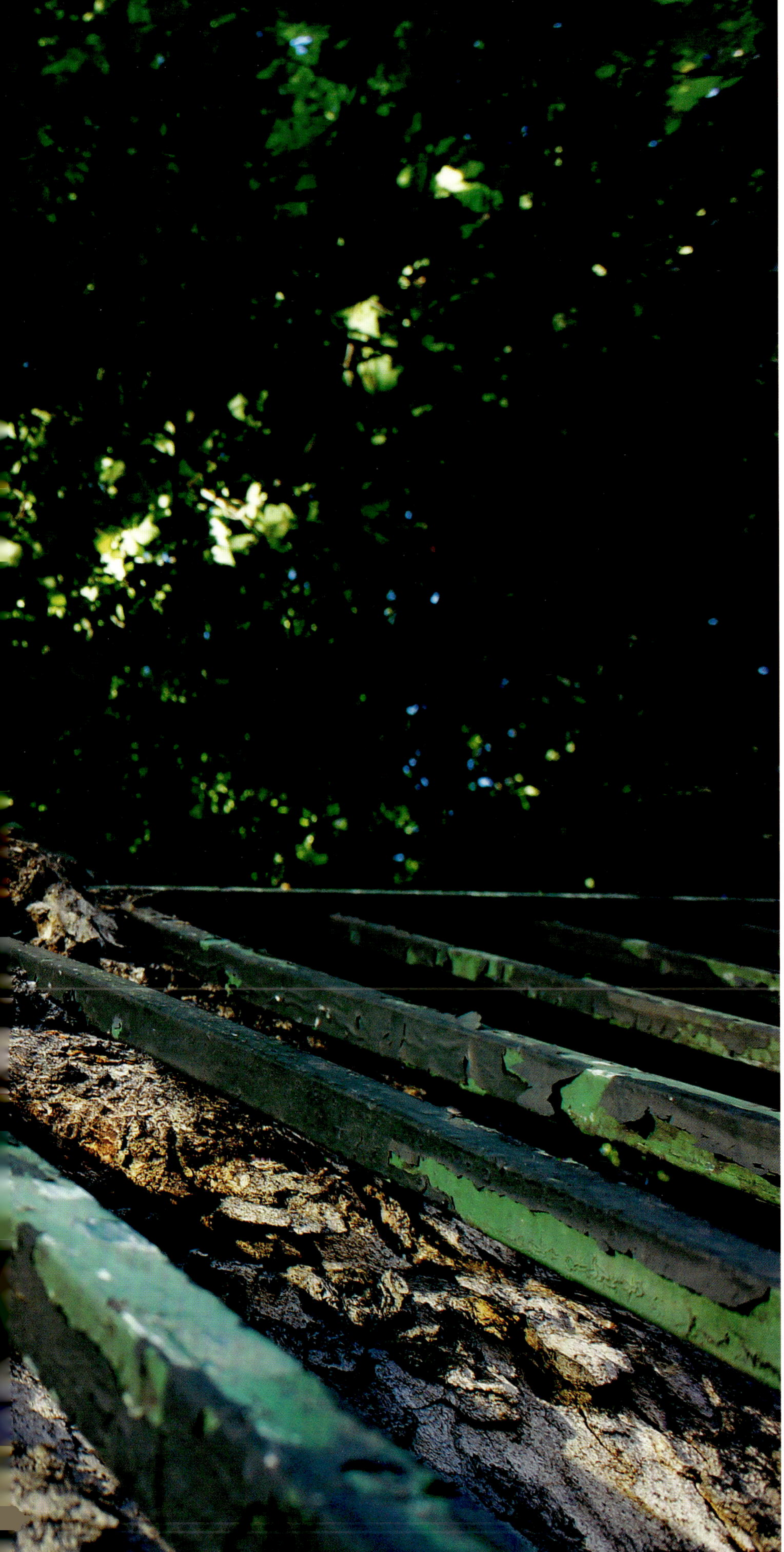

◄ **GREG SMITH** FINALIST

The Battle
Putney Bridge, London, UK

The tree and railings seem to be fighting for survival but the tree is winning.

Sony NEX-3, 16mm lens. 1/50sec at f/5.6. Post-capture: rotated by a few degrees clockwise.

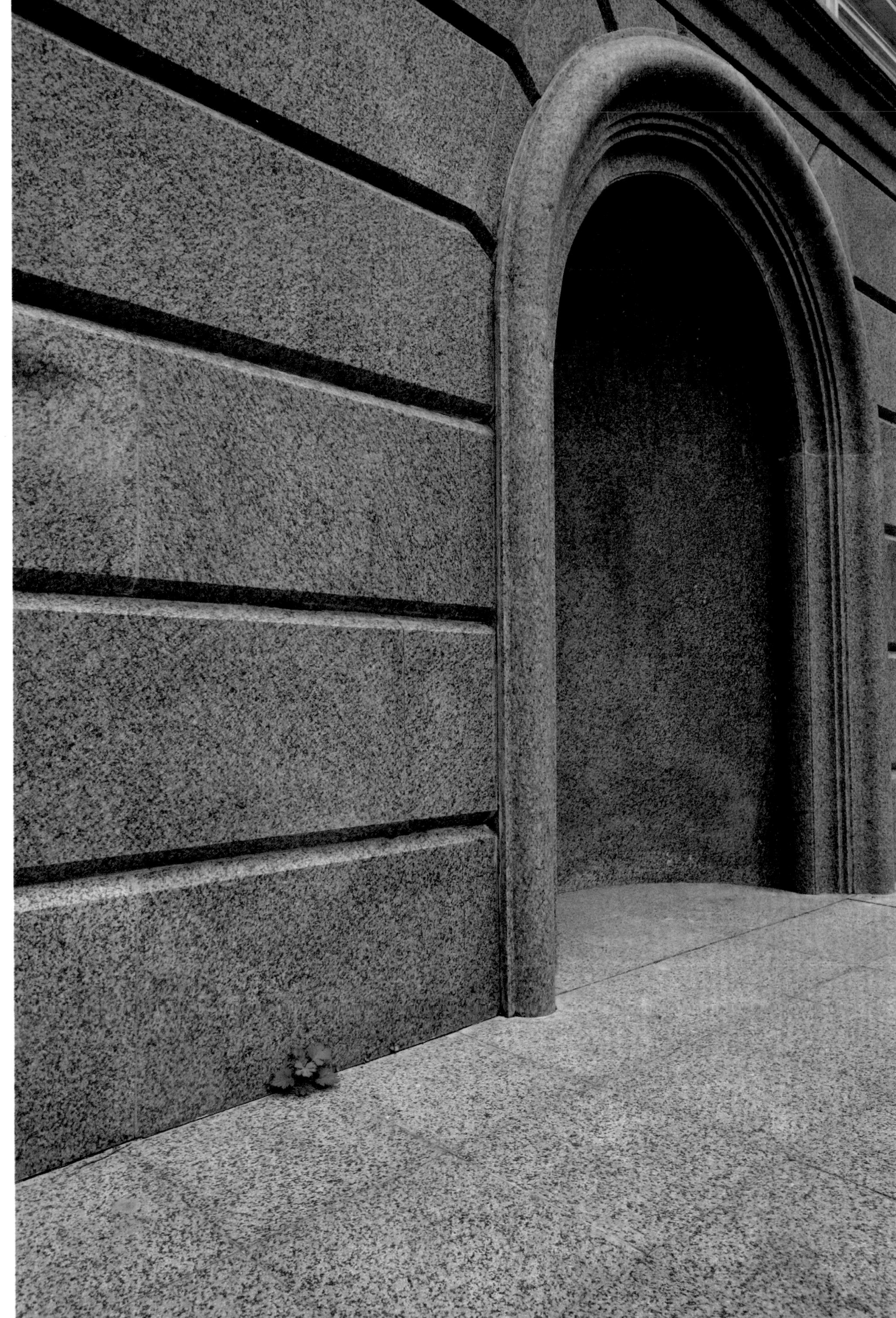

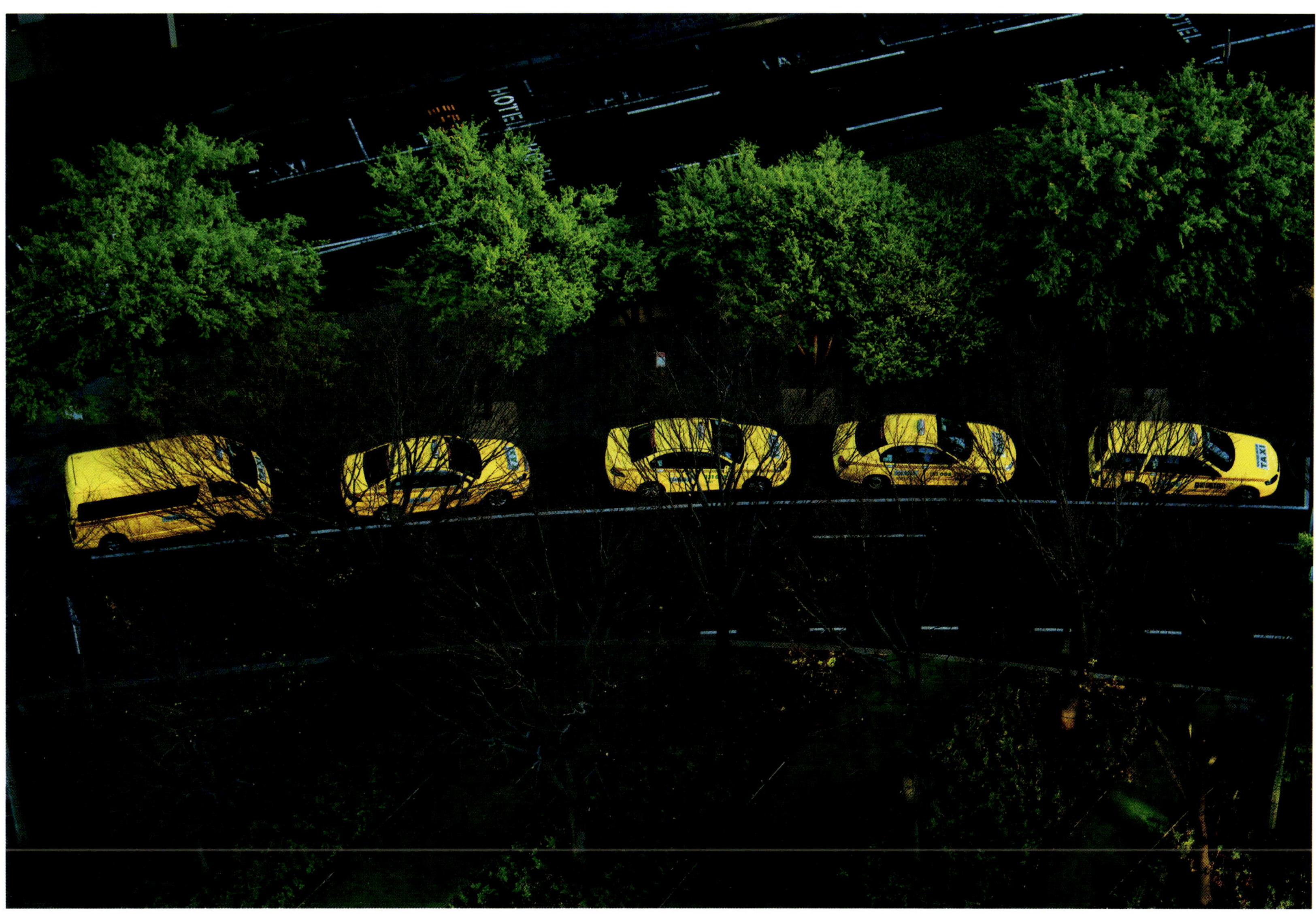

◄ **SERGEY KAREPANOV** — Highly Commended

Fragility and Defencelessness
Government building, Vienna, Austria

These shoots grow for only a few hours before cleaners see them and shred them, but there were plants here thousand of years before the city was built.

Canon EOS-1Ds Mark III, Canon 16-35 mm lens. 1/250sec at f/10 Post-capture: no digital alterations.

▲ **KERRY MARTIN** — Highly Commended

Melbourne
Southbank, Melbourne, Victoria, Australia

I was staying overnight in a hotel in Melbourne. In the morning I looked from my window to this interesting view: Melbourne's yellow taxis waiting along a tree-lined street. Only half the trees have their spring growth. Using the zoom, I composed this to focus on the trees, the roads and the yellow taxis. I was careful to avoid other surrounding elements of the city.

Canon EOS 5D Mark II, Canon EF 70-200mm lens. 1/160sec at f/4. Post-capture: colour balance adjustment.

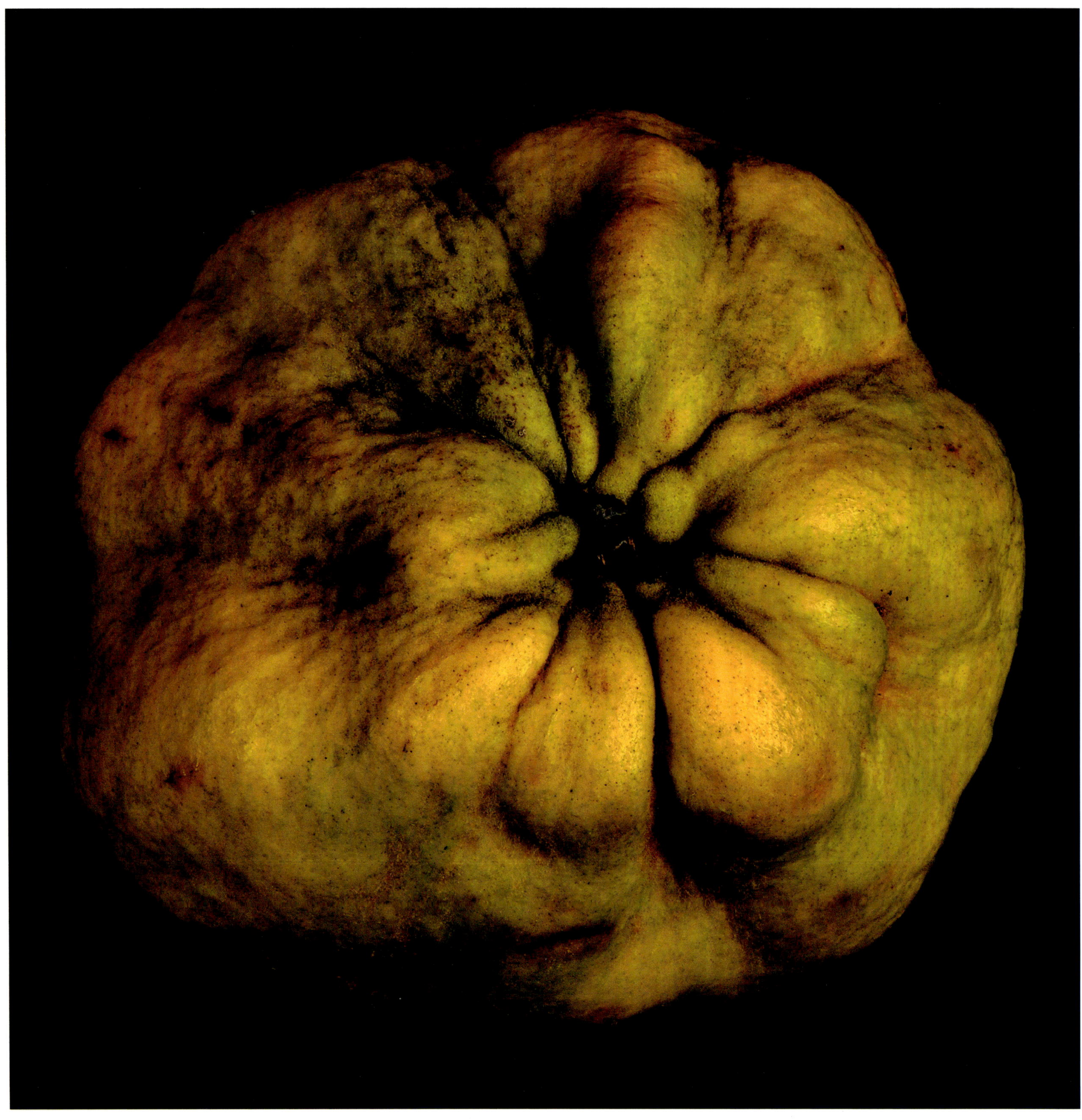

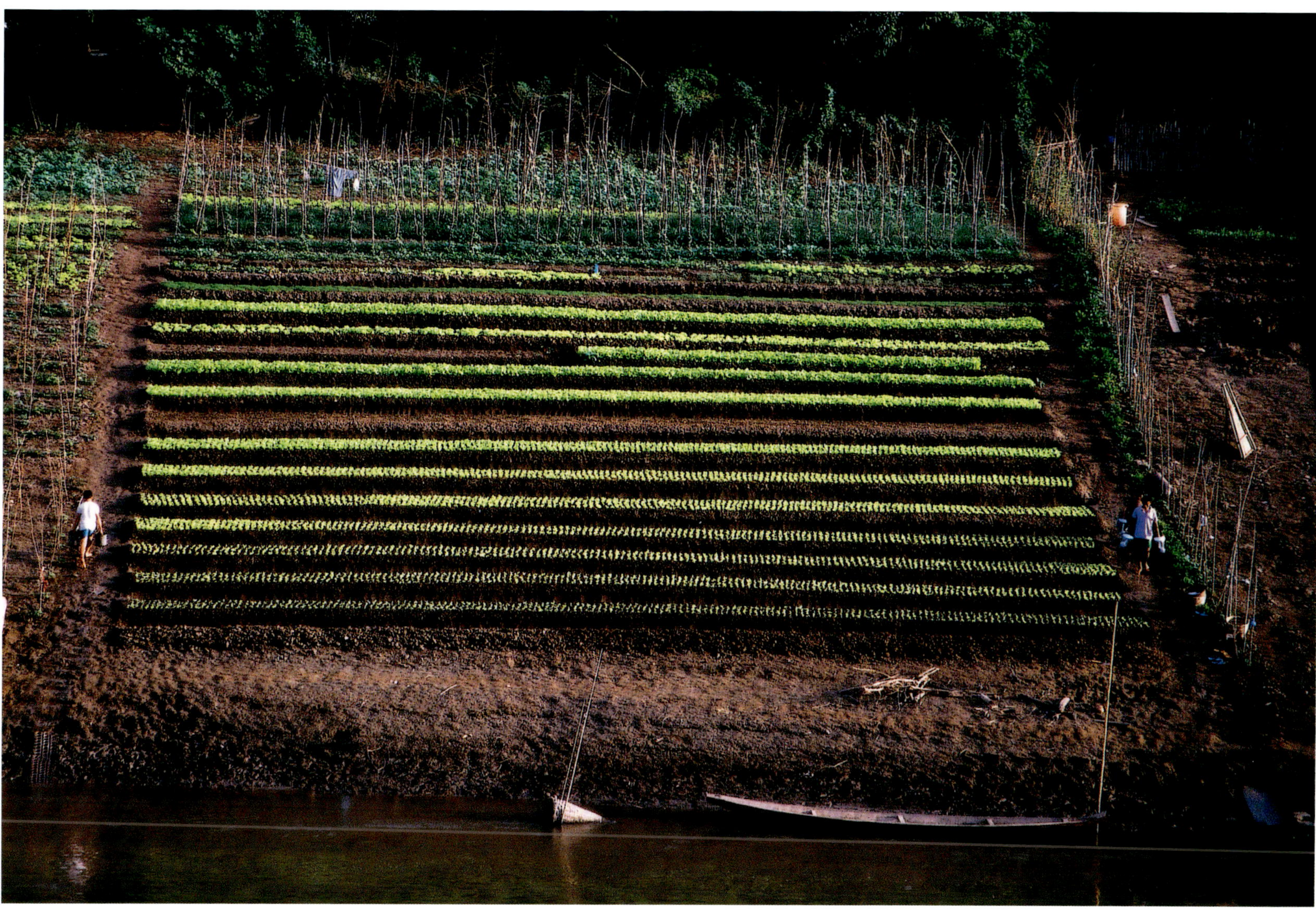

◄ **HENRIQUE SOUTO** 1ST PLACE

Quince
Studio, Lisbon, Portugal

I have been photographing fruits and vegetables especially for the aesthetic value that some of them have. I wanted to bring out the roughness of the fruit, and I used two flash units positioned on opposite sides of the fruit, with a slight underexposure to bring out the colour. This photo is part of an ongoing series.

Nikon D300, Nikkor 60 mm lens. 1/125sec at f/20. Post-capture: image cropped to a square format. Adjustments to colour and contrast.

▲ **DAVID THURSTON** 2ND PLACE

Mekong Garden
Mekong River, Luang Prabang, Laos

When the river level begins to recede in late summer, slow-growing crops such as legumes are planted. A succession of salad crops follow as the water level continues to fall. They grow quickly and are harvested. There is still time before the upriver snow melts for a second crop, aided by the warmth and fertility of the riverbank soil.

Fuji Provia film. Canon EOS 5, 70-200mm lens. 1/125sec at f11. Post-capture: no digital alterations.

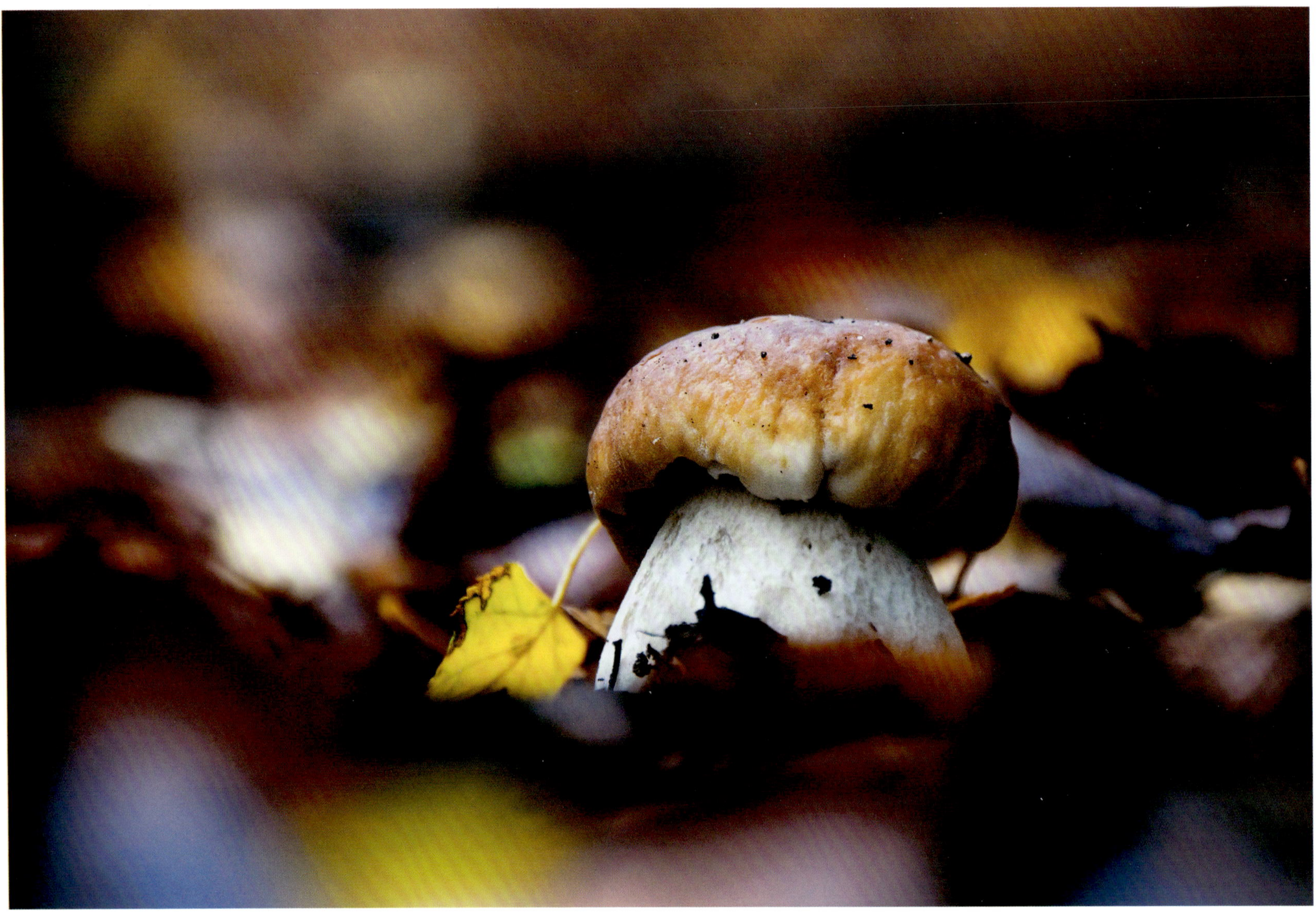

MAGDALENA KNIECICKA — 3RD PLACE

Delicious Porcino
Kent, UK

Boletus edulis, or porcino, is the king of edible mushrooms because of its aromatic, earthy-chestnut flavour. They are the colour of fallen leaves and are easy to overlook, so finding one is an exciting moment. This particular porcino was just a few hours old, untouched by snails. I love its distinctive texture, shape and colour. I gathered leaves to create a stable base for my camera to minimise any movement, and used very shallow depth of field to make the porcino stand out.

Nikon D80, Tamron 18-270mm lens. 1/13sec at f/6.2. Post-capture: I merged two shots to improve depth of field and sharpness.

DAVID BALLANTYNE — HIGHLY COMMENDED

Red Pear Square
My home, Calgary, Alberta, Canada

I had purchased a few red pears with the intention of photographing them indoors as it was early winter and not much was happening outdoors in the snow-covered garden. I liked the colour of the pear against the blue wall and added the wrapping paper as a third colour to the composition. I placed the pear near a window and used the north light to light the pear. I felt a square crop created better balance in the final composition.

Fujifilm Velvia 50. 4x5 Cambo SC 135mm. Post-capture: cropped to square format.

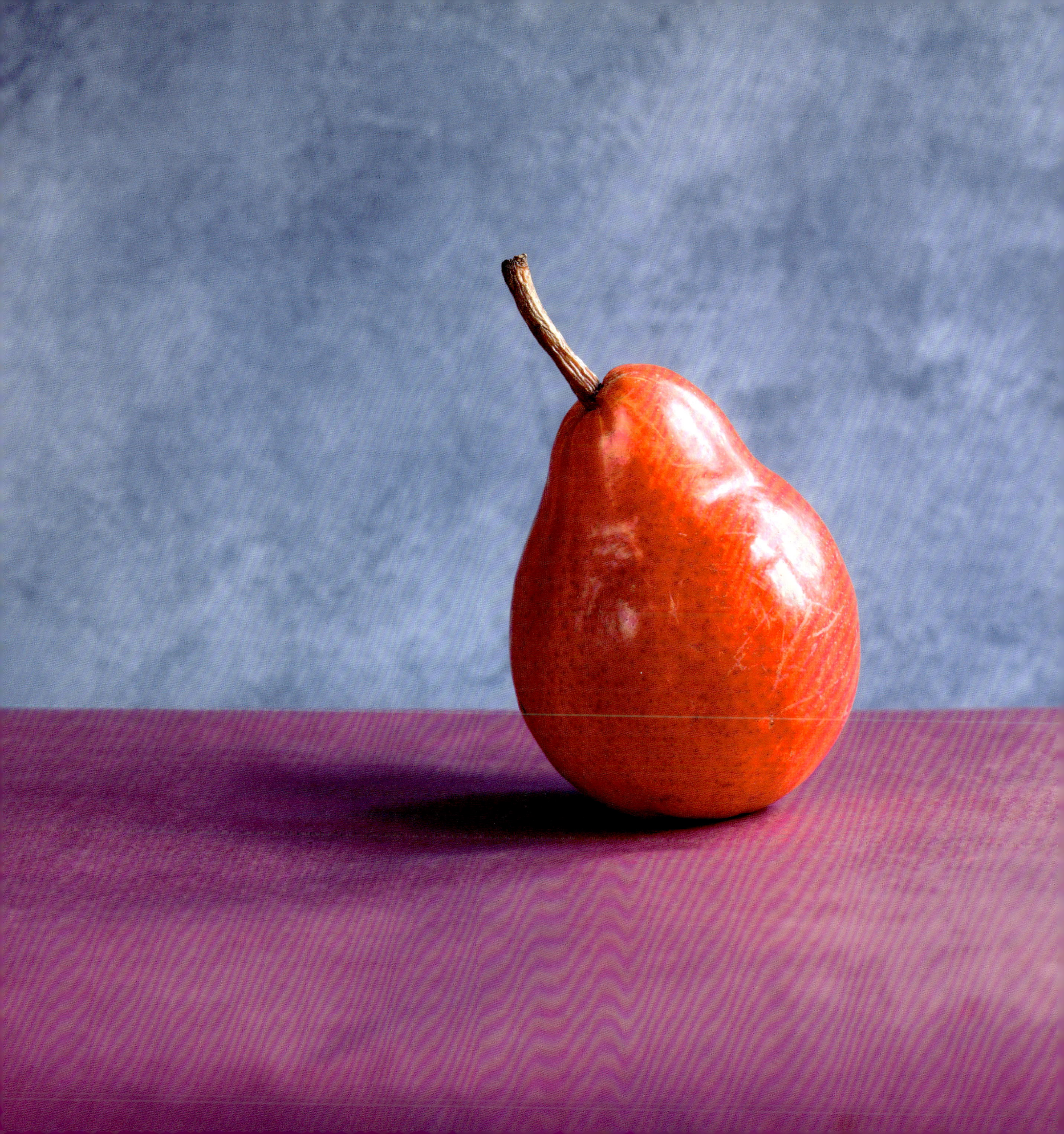

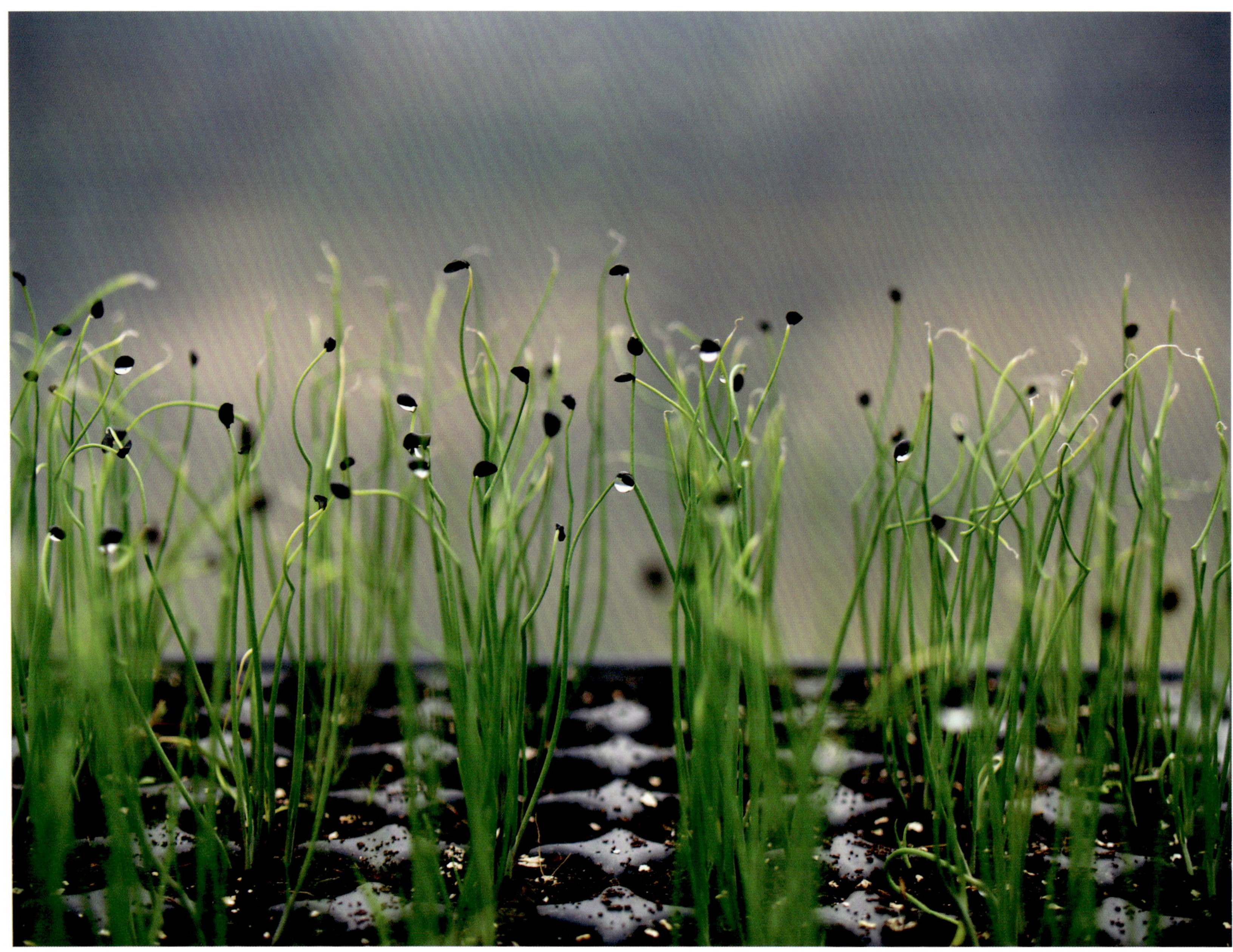

▲ **MARIA SANTOS** HIGHLY COMMENDED

From small beginnings, great things grow
Walled garden of Newbold House, Forres, Scotland

The inspiration for this photograph comes from the beauty and vulnerability of the tiny green onion shoots. The tray was sitting on a table inside the polytunnel. I held the camera in my hands and positioned it at the same level as the table and got as close as I could to the seedlings for the close-up shot.

Olympus E 500, 14-45 mm lens. 1/30sec at f/5.6. Post-capture: no digital alterations.

DIANNA JAZWINSKI ► HIGHLY COMMENDED

Home
New Forest, Hampshire, UK

The rows of the lavender provided the perfect lead in to the beehive. I wanted the beehive as the focal point with the rows of lavender leading the eye towards it.

Canon EOS 5D, 24-105mm lens. 0.3sec at f/16. Post-capture: no digital alterations.

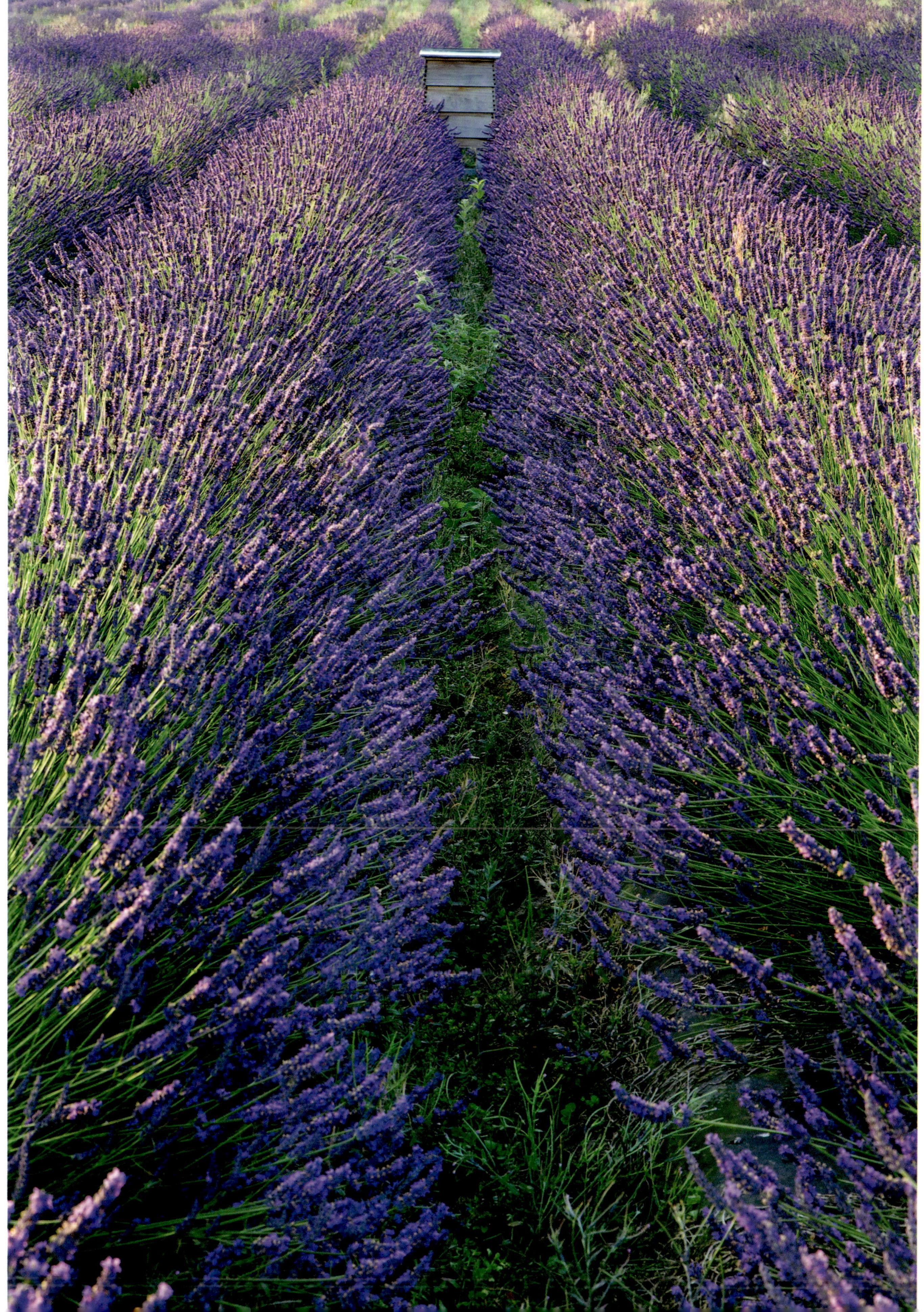

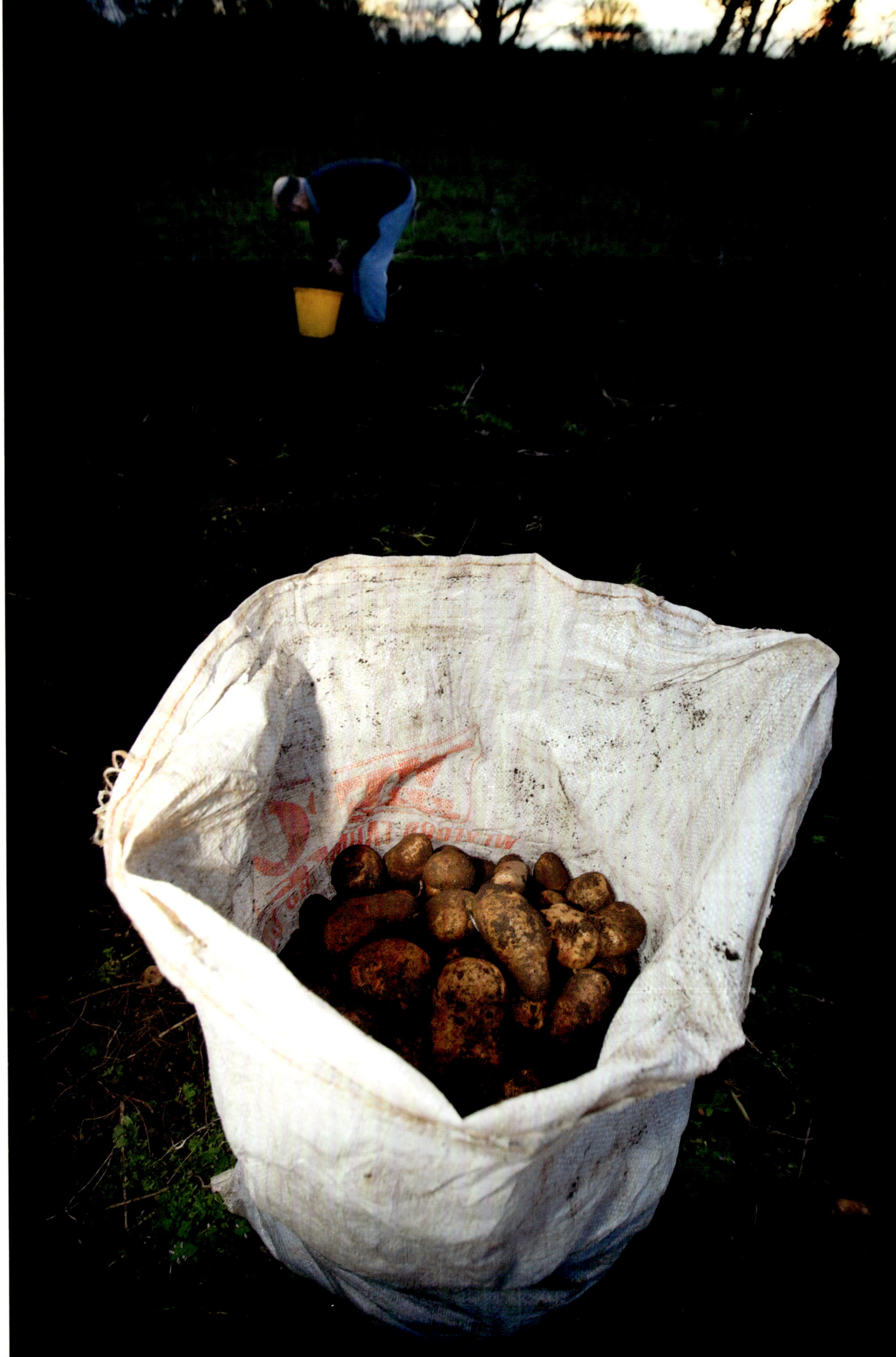

◄ ALAN MAHON — FINALIST

The Last Crop
Rathmacknee, Killinick, Co. Wexford, Ireland

It was a late November afternoon when I took this photo of my friend Richard in his garden. He was gathering up his last crop of potatoes for the season. He decided to retire from gardening at the end of that year so not only was it the last crop of the year, but also the last crop for Richard. I got a phone call from my friend to say that he was digging the last of the season's potatoes and I brought the camera to record the moment. I used on-camera flash to light the potatoes in the sack.

Canon 5D Mark II, Canon EF 16-35mm lens. 1/30sec at f/5, ISO 400.
Post-capture: some contrast and tone adjustment. Slight vignette added.

CAROL SHARP ► — FINALIST

Medicinal Herbs
Studio, London, UK

Medicinal herbs including *Calendula officinalis*, *Lavandula officinalis*, *Achillea millefolium*, *Artemisia absinthium*, *Borago officinalis* and *Urtica dioica*. I was inspired by the array of different colours and textures of herbs and their medicinal powers. I gathered the herbs and arranged them in layers on sheets of glass in my studio. A soft box light was put underneath to bring out the translucent colours, and I added strong side light to accentuate the edges.

Film Fuji Velvia 50. Sinar F 5x4, Sinaron 210 lens. 1/125sec at f/22
Post-capture: some tonal adjustments.

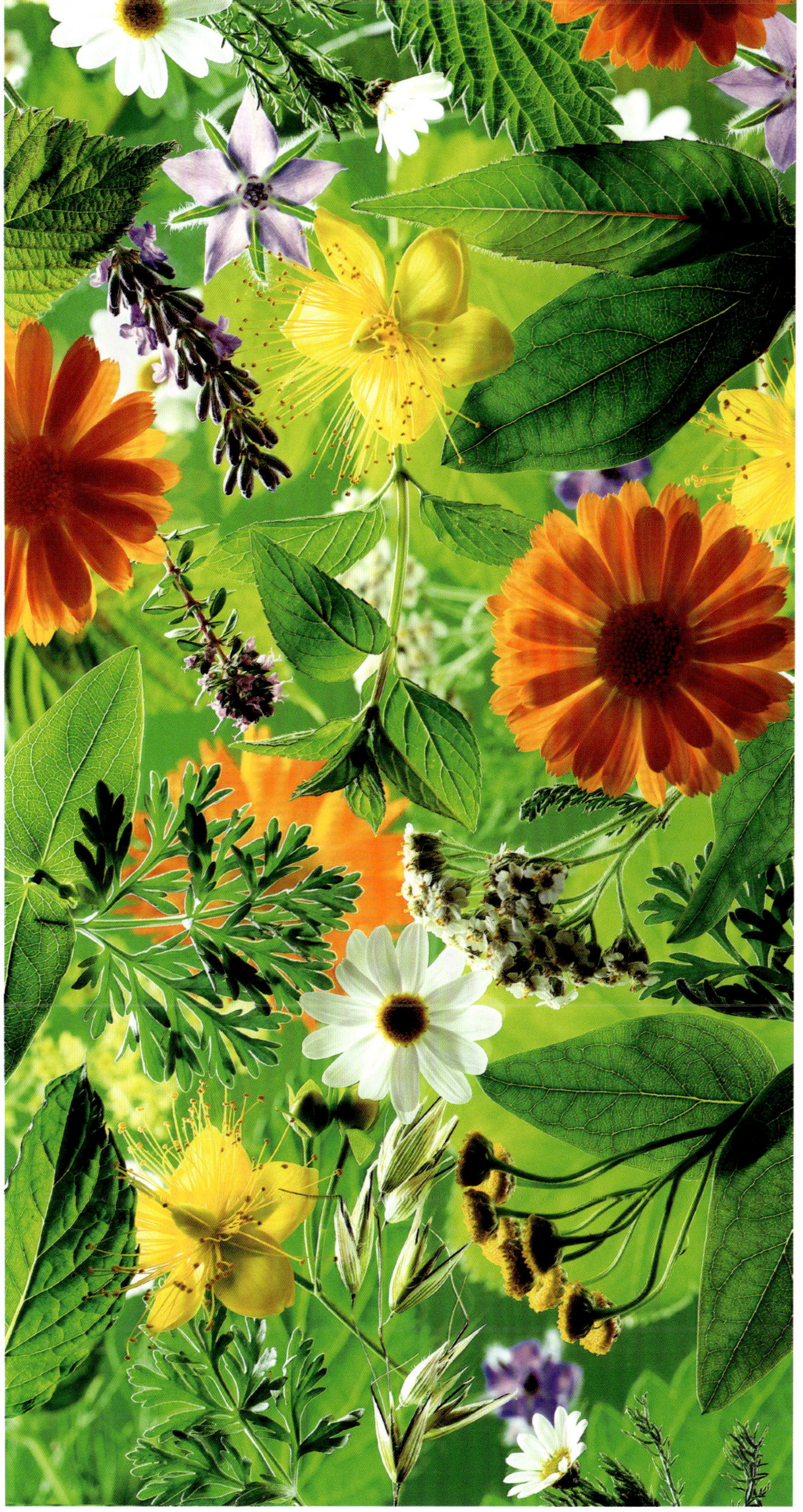

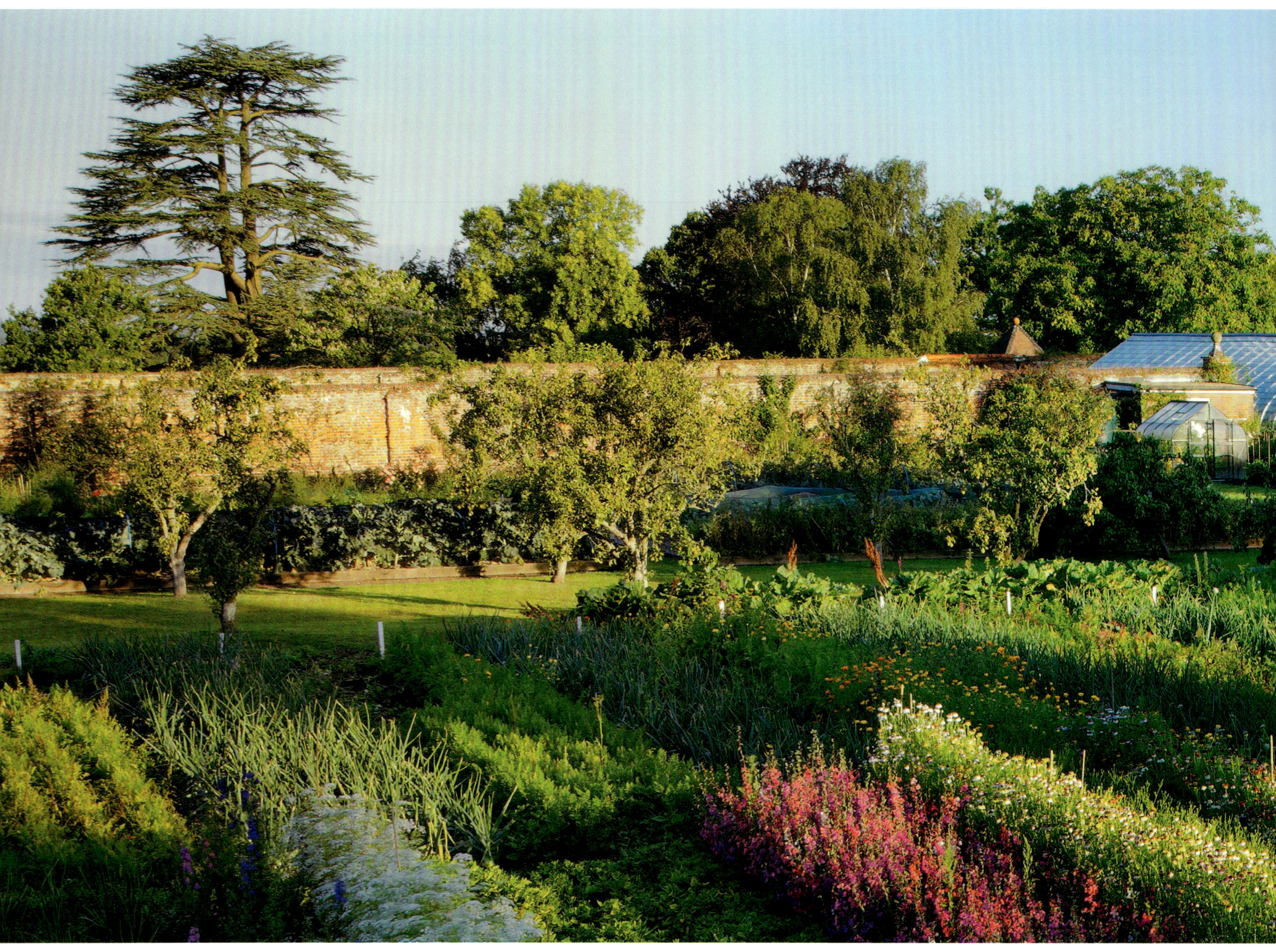

▲ **NIGEL BURKITT** HIGHLY COMMENDED

The Walled Kitchen Garden at Claydon
Claydon Estate Gardens, Middle Claydon, Buckinghamshire, UK

In the last six years, this two-acre kitchen garden has been returned to full productivity, growing organic vegetables, fruit from heritage trees and exquisite flowers, including many unusual varieties not seen on supermarket shelves. This view across the kitchen garden is top of my favourites and I can imagine it was not so different in Victorian times. I know the position where the sun rises and sought to catch the early morning light coming through surrounding trees. A ladder against the wall gave me convenient elevation.

Canon 5D Mark II, Canon EF 24-105mm lens. 0.6sec at f/20. Post-capture: basic adjustments.

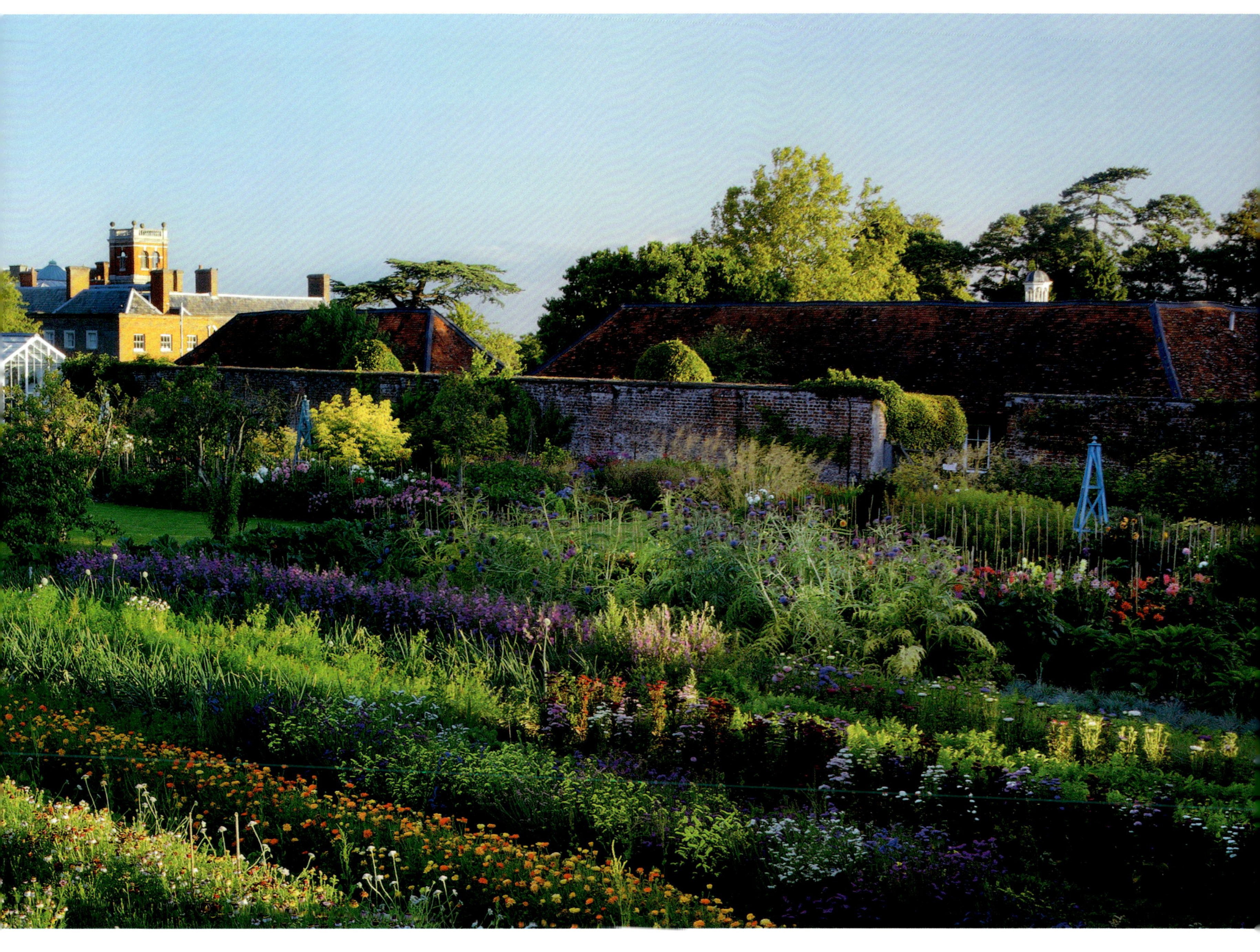

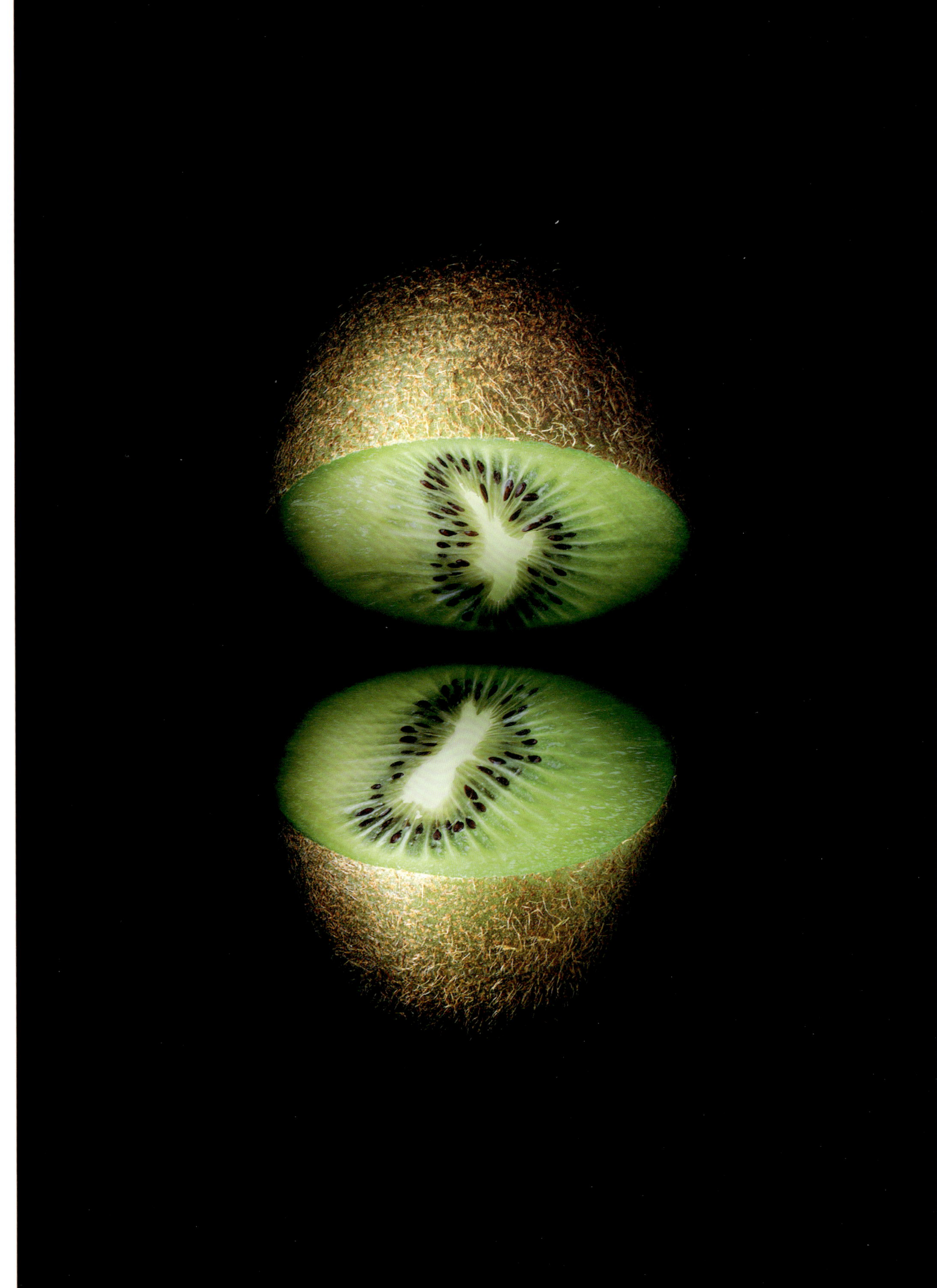

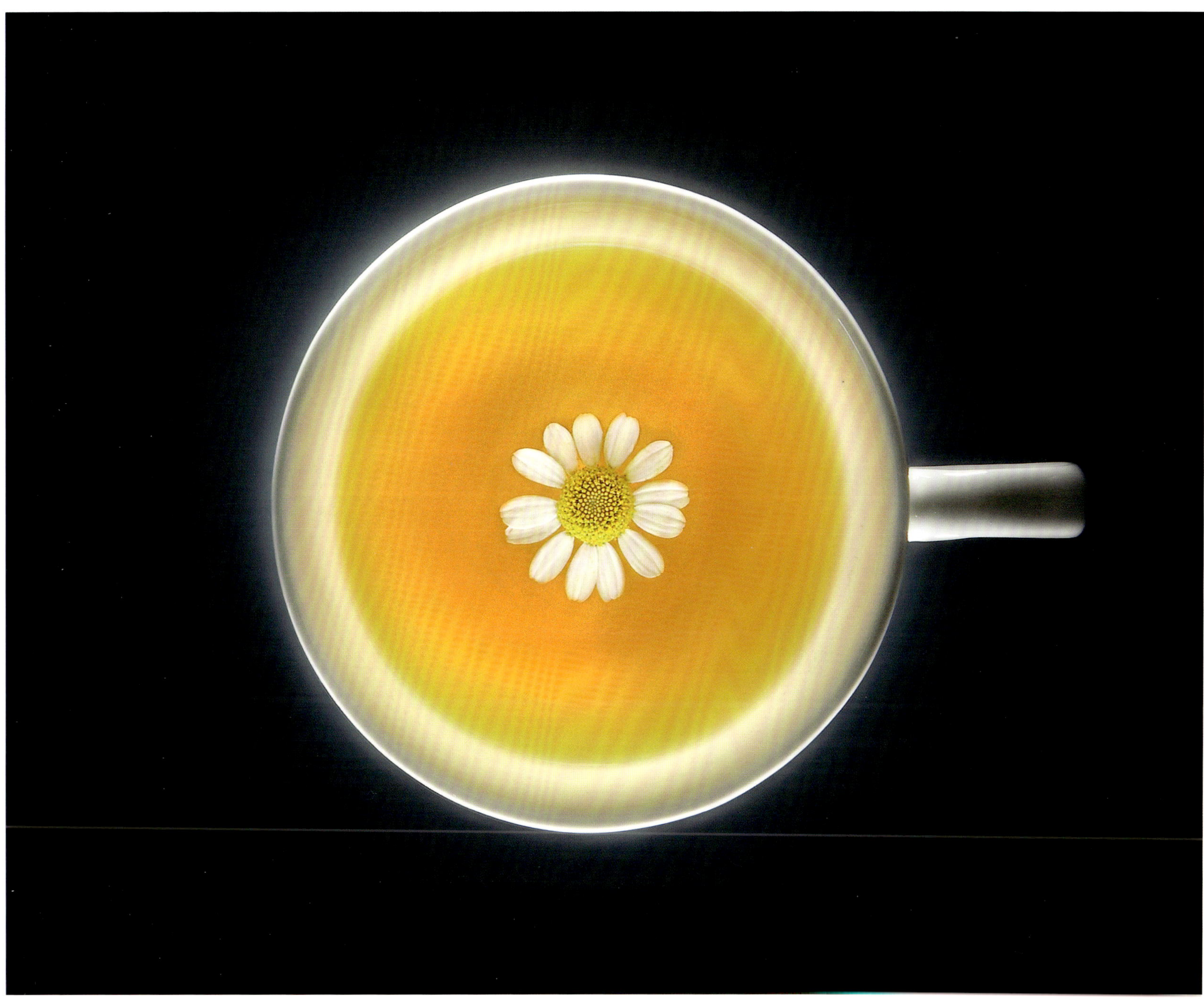

◄ **JOHANNA PARKIN** HIGHLY COMMENDED

New Zealand Kiwi fruit
Studio, London, UK

Being both a proud New Zealander and a lover of our national fruit, I was excited when I saw the potential to create the map of New Zealand out of the kiwi fruit centre.

Film 5x4 Velvia transparency film. Sinar 180mm lens. Post-capture: the map of New Zealand in the centre was created by manipulating the natural centre of the fruit using imaging software.

▲ **JOHANNA PARKIN** FINALIST

Chamomile Flower
Studio, London, UK

The symmetries of the round chamomile flower with the teacup and the yellow flower against the warm colour of the tea appealed to me.

Canon EOS 400D, 50mm lens. 1/125sec at f/20. Post-capture: no digital alterations.

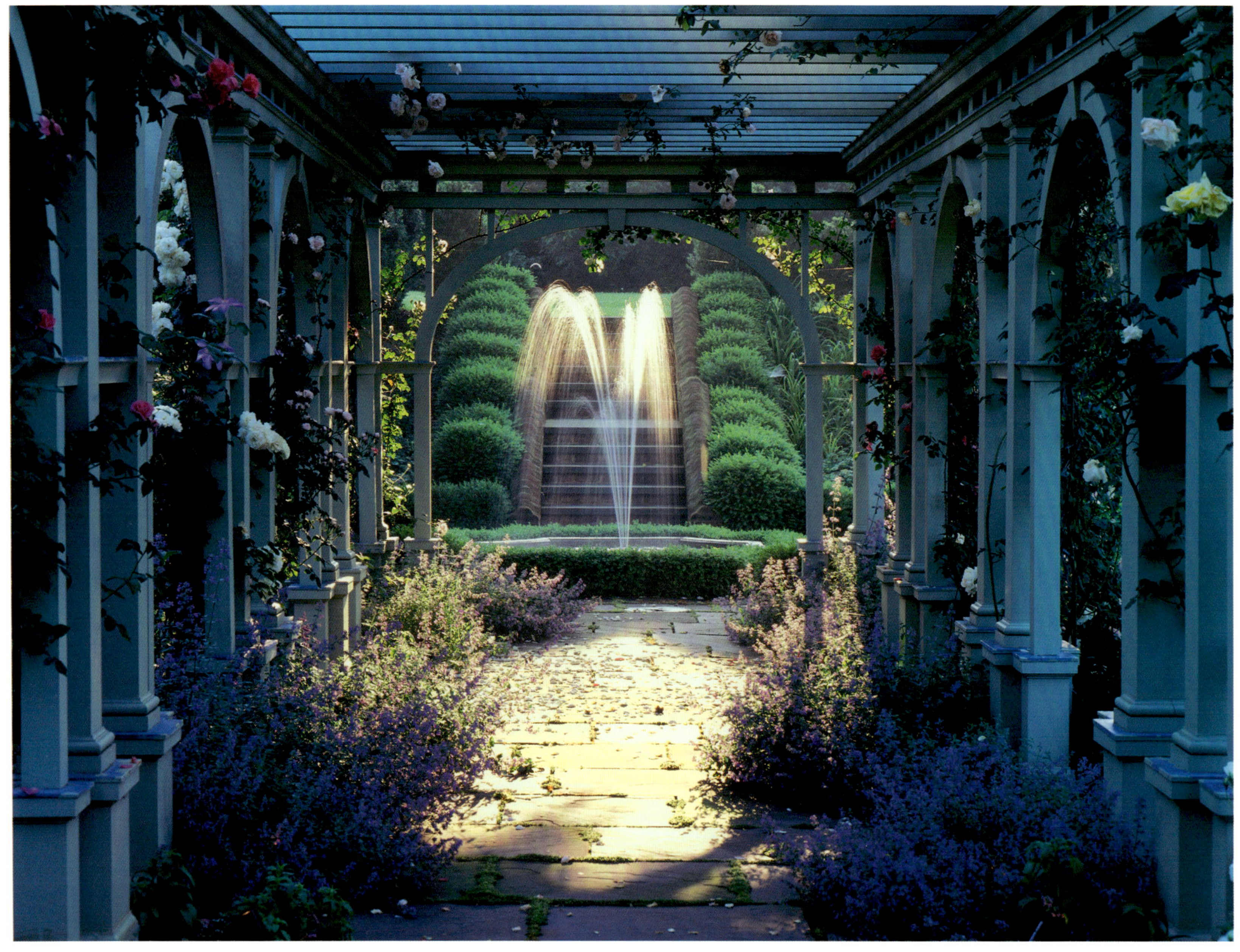

ROGER FOLEY 1ST PLACE

In the Garden of the Four Seasons
Mount Sharon Farm, Virginia, USA

Designed by landscape architect Charles Stick, the rose-laden pergola frames the small fountain at its end, lit up by the late afternoon sun. The garden gets its name from its Italian statues of The Four Seasons. I was inspired, as always, by the light. I loved the intensity of the highlights on the paving, and the way the fountain was lit up as if by a spotlight. In the late afternoon, the sun slanted through the overhead canopy of an immense black walnut, making a play of light and shadow. I was searching for a way to combine the architecture of this large pergola with the sense of mystery from being inside it.

Fuji Velvia 100 film. Contax 645 film camera, 120mm lens. 1sec at f/11. Post-capture: scanned with a Nikon Coolscan 8000.

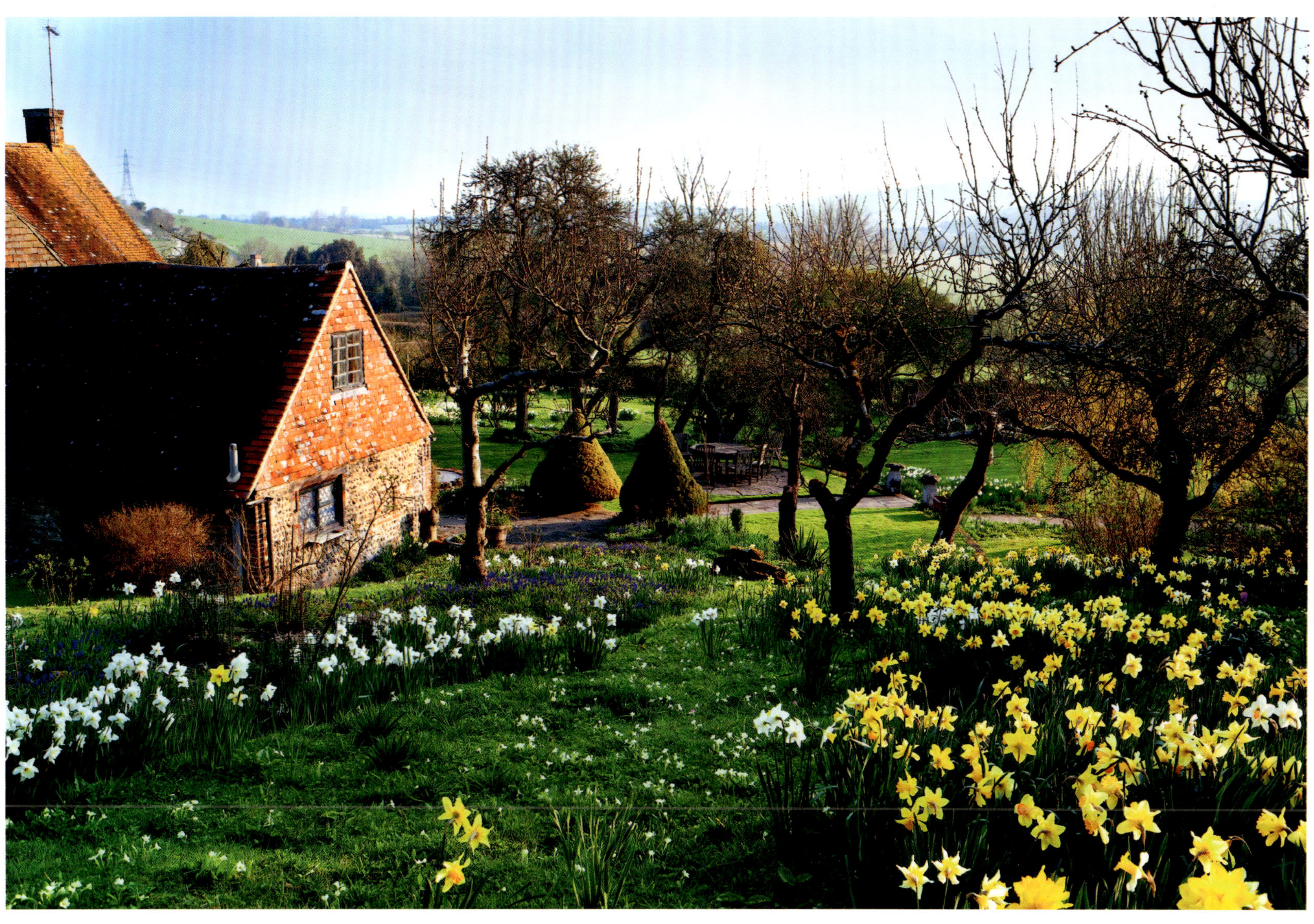

RACHEL WARNE 2ND PLACE

Old Rectory
Coombes, South Downs, UK

The remote Old Rectory has been a part of the landscape for hundreds of years. The Reeves moved in thirty-four years ago and turned it into a family home. It was refreshing to see so much colour in early spring. After scrambling up the hill, I wanted to capture the sense of spring bulbs en-masse and show the garden in its full glory.

Canon 5D Mark II, 24-70mm lens. 1/125sec at f/7. Post-capture: digitally processed. No special treatment.

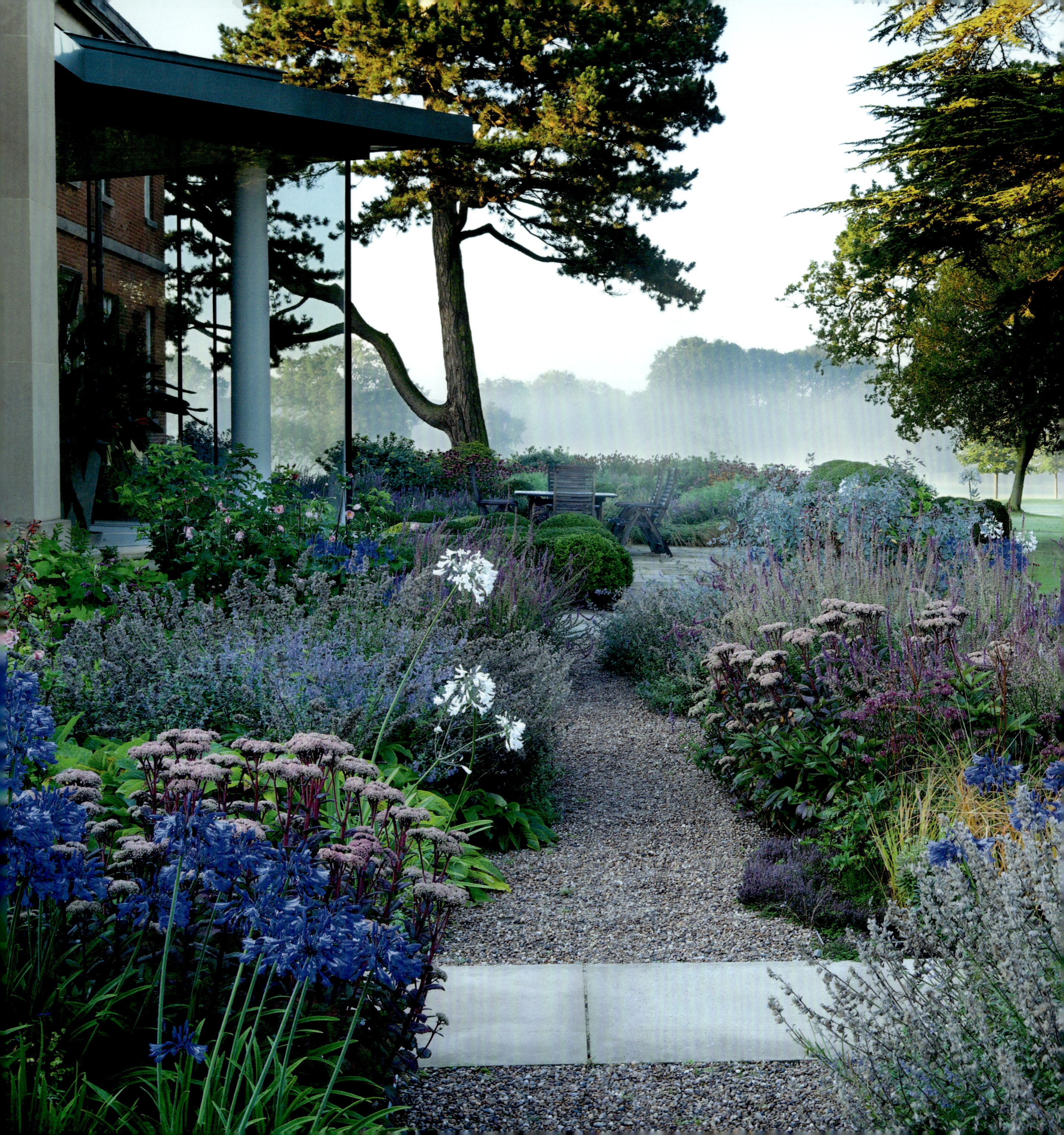

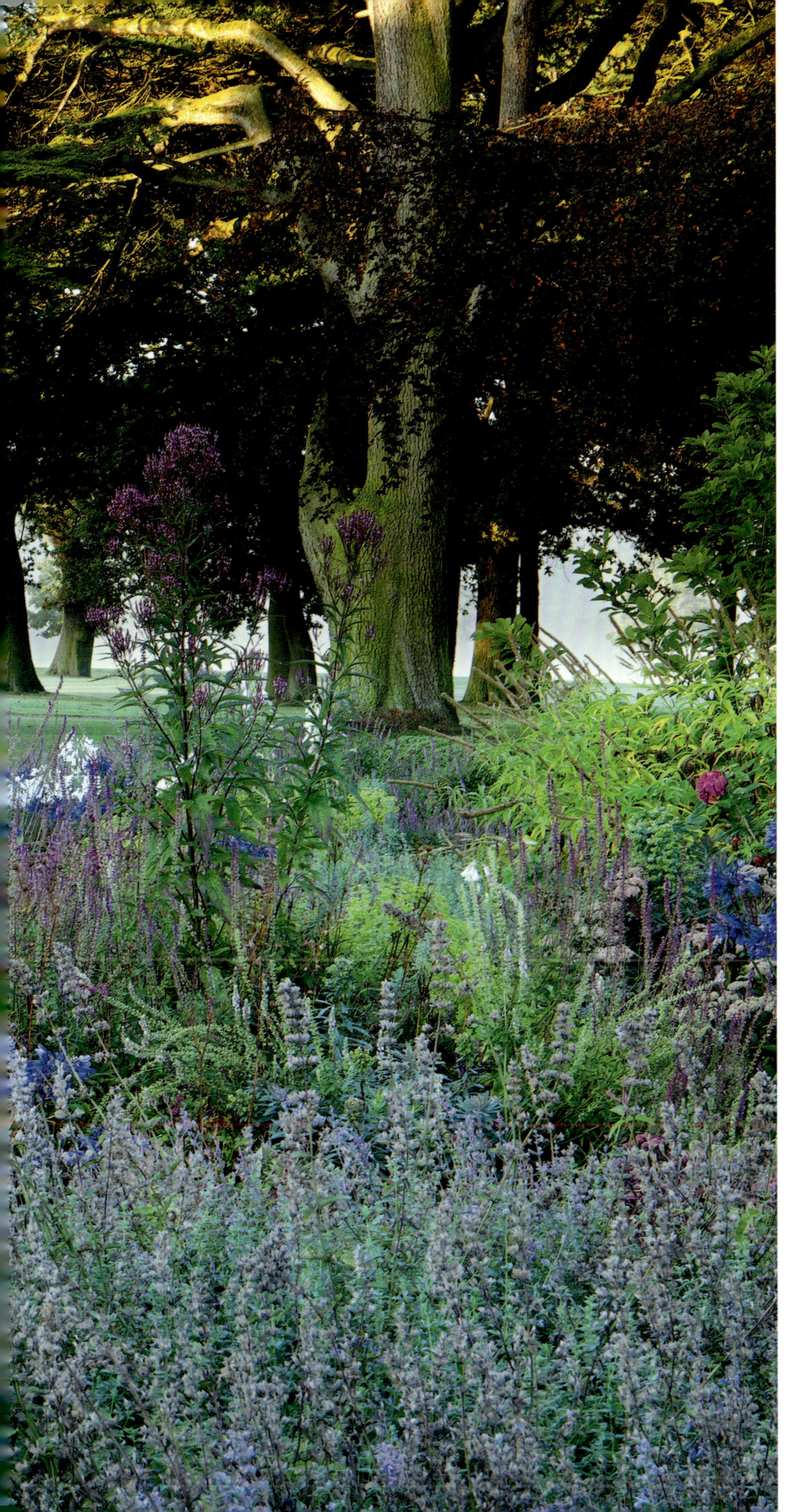

MARIANNE MAJERUS 3RD PLACE

Blue Dawn
Private garden, Cheshire, UK

The morning holds its breath for a fleeting moment before the sun rises. The photograph is about anticipation: the meeting of night and day. It was taken a few moments before the garden is transformed by sunshine and the distant mist has disappeared. This delicate balance is echoed in the interaction between the contemporary architecture and planting and the traditional parkland beyond.

Canon EOS 5D Mark II, 24-70mm lens. 1/10sec at f/16. Post-capture: no digital alterations.

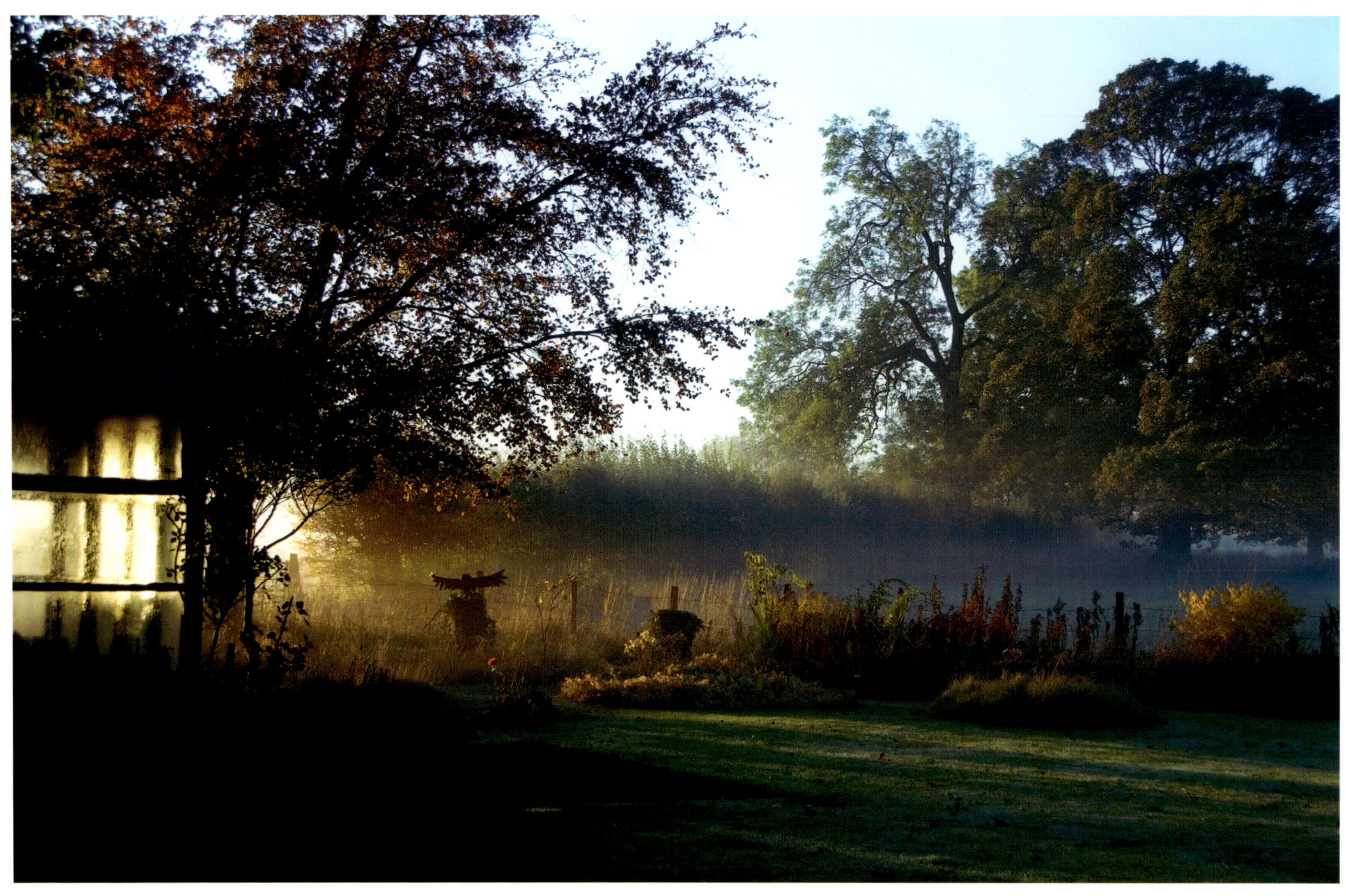

STEFFIE SHIELDS — HIGHLY COMMENDED

The Glow
My country garden in Welby, Lincolnshire, UK

Early morning light swept across my garden last October when all was quiet and I was still in dressing-gown and slippers! Low sunrays set the summerhouse alight and catch a last red rose. The terrific light and mist were changing by the second and the light would soon move away from the owl's wing-tip. My other concern was to keep the summerhouse vertical to avoid distraction. I crouched for this photograph to catch the low sunlight on the fiery dogwood.

Nikon D200, Nikon 18-200mm lens. 1/90sec at f/5. Post-capture: some adjustment of brightness, more of contrast to give depth, and a very slight increase in saturation to enhance autumnal colour and warmth before sharpening. I applied a healing brush for a few distracting speckles of light, particularly on the dewy grass. The most significant manipulation was to use a clone tool to remove a distracting snail trail from the glass panes of the summerhouse!

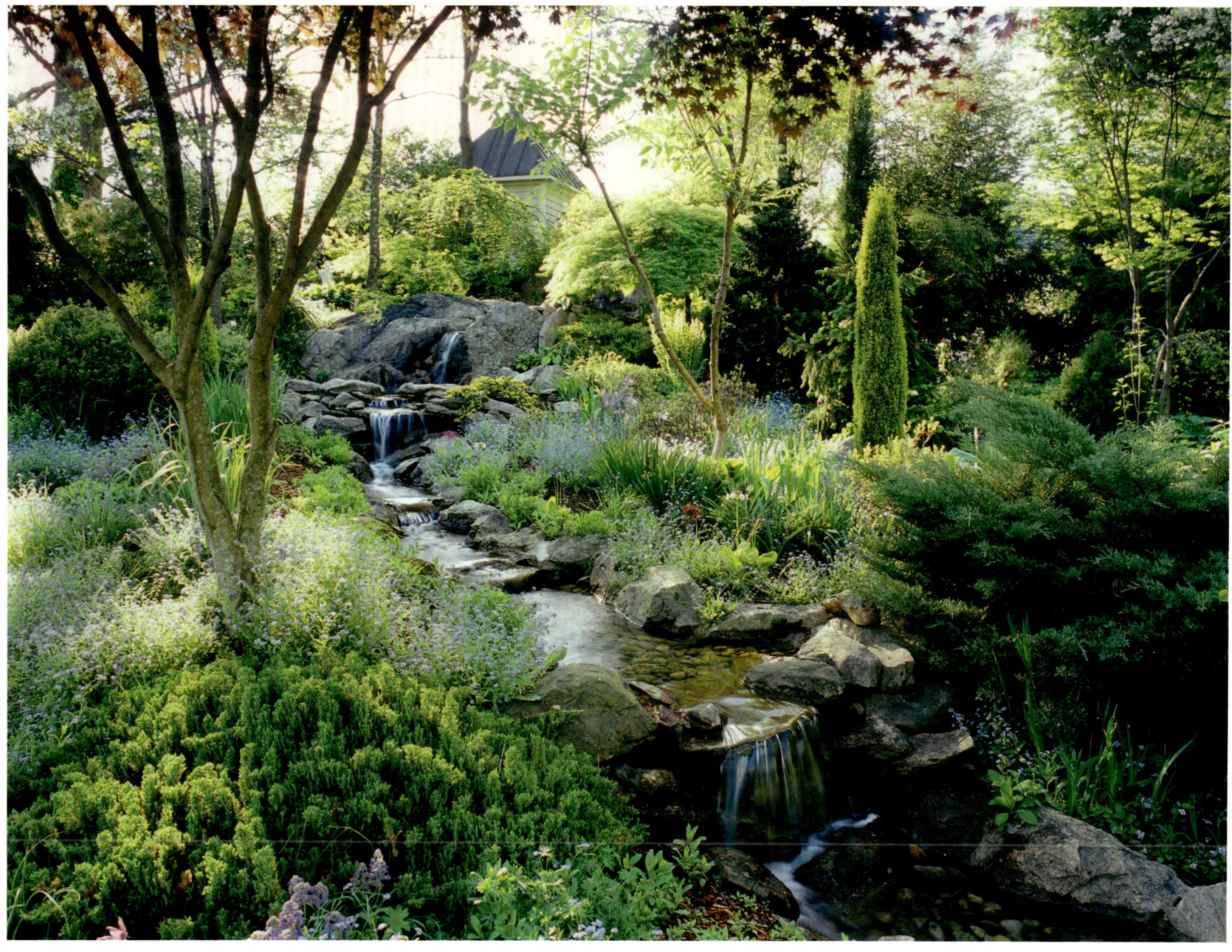

ROGER FOLEY HIGHLY COMMENDED

Highland Spring
Highland Spring, Middleburg, Virginia, USA

Highland Spring is a three-acre garden designed and maintained by its owner, Donna Hackman. The design takes inspiration from a rock outcropping at the top of a hill on the property. There was just enough sunlight at the scene to create a sense of a three-dimensional space. I wanted the viewer to feel they were within the picture and almost hear the stream.

Fuji Velvia 100 film. Contax 645 film camera, 45mm lens. 1sec at f/11 Post-capture: scanned with a Nikon Coolscan 8000.

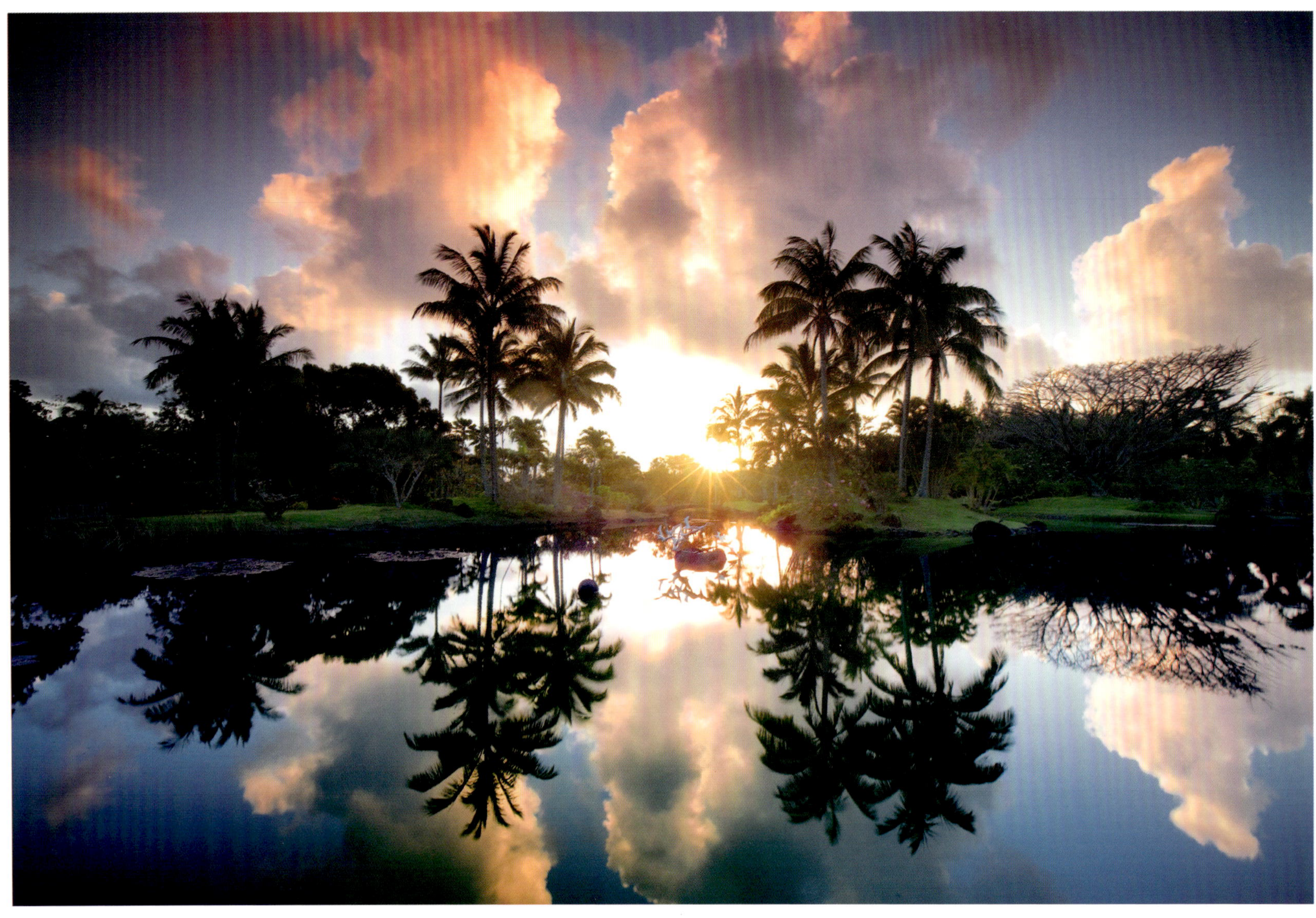

DENNIS FRATES FINALIST

Tropical Garden Sunrise
Na Aina Kai Botanical Gardens, Kauai, Hawaii

This shot was taken at sunrise. The shot was made before the gardens opened to the public, so all was peaceful and calm. This type of morning cloud is not uncommon in tropical environments, but they especially lit up this morning.

I like how there is something of interest in every part of the image. I contacted the nursery months in advance and arranged a sunrise visit: it normally doesn't open, even for guided tours, until way after sunrise.

Canon 1DS Mark III, Canon 16-35mm lens. 1.3sec at f/14. Post-capture: tone and colour correction.

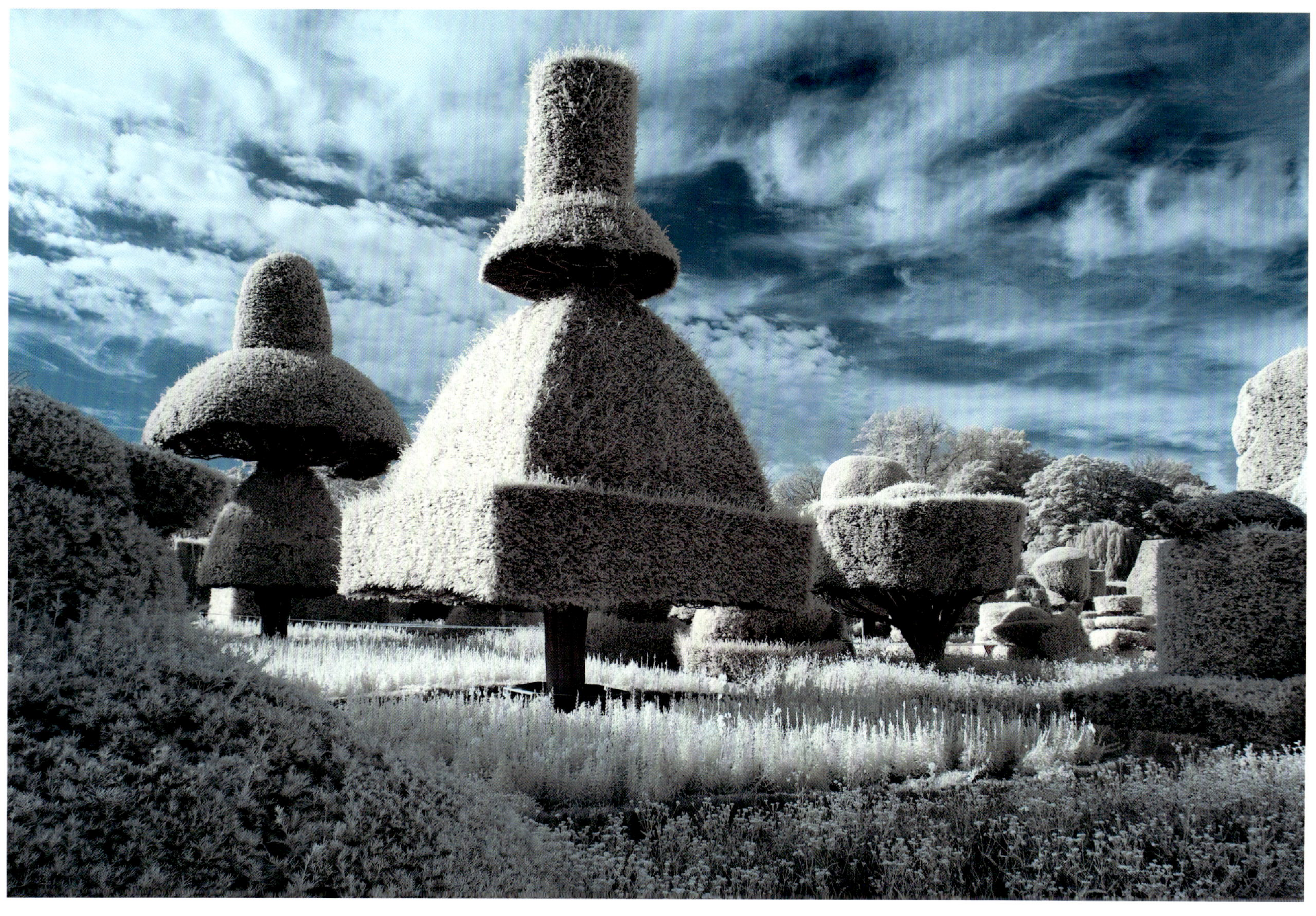

JOHN WHITAKER — HIGHLY COMMENDED

View in a Different Light
The Topiary Garden, Levens Hall, Kendal, UK

Some of the finest and oldest topiary in England can be seen at Levens Hall Gardens in Cumbria. The low angle of the mid-morning sun enhanced the various shapes and I decided that an infra-red image would be dramatic, particularly with a blue sky and the interesting cloud pattern. The yew trees (*Taxus baccata*) have been trimmed and shaped over the years but the patterns remain unchanged.

I arrived early for good side illumination, visualizing the shapes as white images. I considered that the sky would be shown to advantage by changing the red colours to blue. A wide-angle lens avoided a cramped picture, giving space and depth to produce an unusual and surreal picture.

Canon EOS 350D. Sensor fitted with an IR filter 720nm, which allows some near infra-red to pass through, giving more picture creativity. Canon 17-40mm lens. 1/200sec at f/8. Post-capture: I made the usual minor corrections to exposure, plus some changes to Clarity values. Following the instructions in 'Digital Infra Red Capture and Workflow' by Clive R Haynes FRPS, I used channel swapping in layers, changing reds to blues. This was followed by Auto Levels and Auto Contrast, as I preferred the effect these gave rather than manual controls.

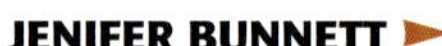

JENIFER BUNNETT FINALIST

Inside Out

Worplesdon, Surrey, UK

The sun in the window first caught my attention, and then I noticed the cobwebs, paraphernalia in the shed and reflections of what was outside. With the ripe fruit and the handle of the spade, I thought this combined to portray a happy family garden.

The branch is hanging down from a Williams' Pear tree (*Pyrus "Williams Bon Chrétien"*). I was photographing the nearby apples into the setting sun and looked round to see what it was I kept knocking. The pears were in my way! Then I saw the sun in the glass, and knew there was a good picture there for the taking. I planned the shot in advance, seeing where the tripod and camera needed to be placed to achieve the right composition and avoid glare. I chose an f-stop to give good depth of field on both sides of the glass. I was not completely happy the first time and was relieved to see another clear sunset the following night when I got what I was after.

Pentax K20D, Pentax 35mm lens. 1sec at f/13. Post-capture: I shot this picture at the correct exposure and also under and over exposed, then combined the exposures afterwards to help bring out the details in the deep shadow and the highlight areas.

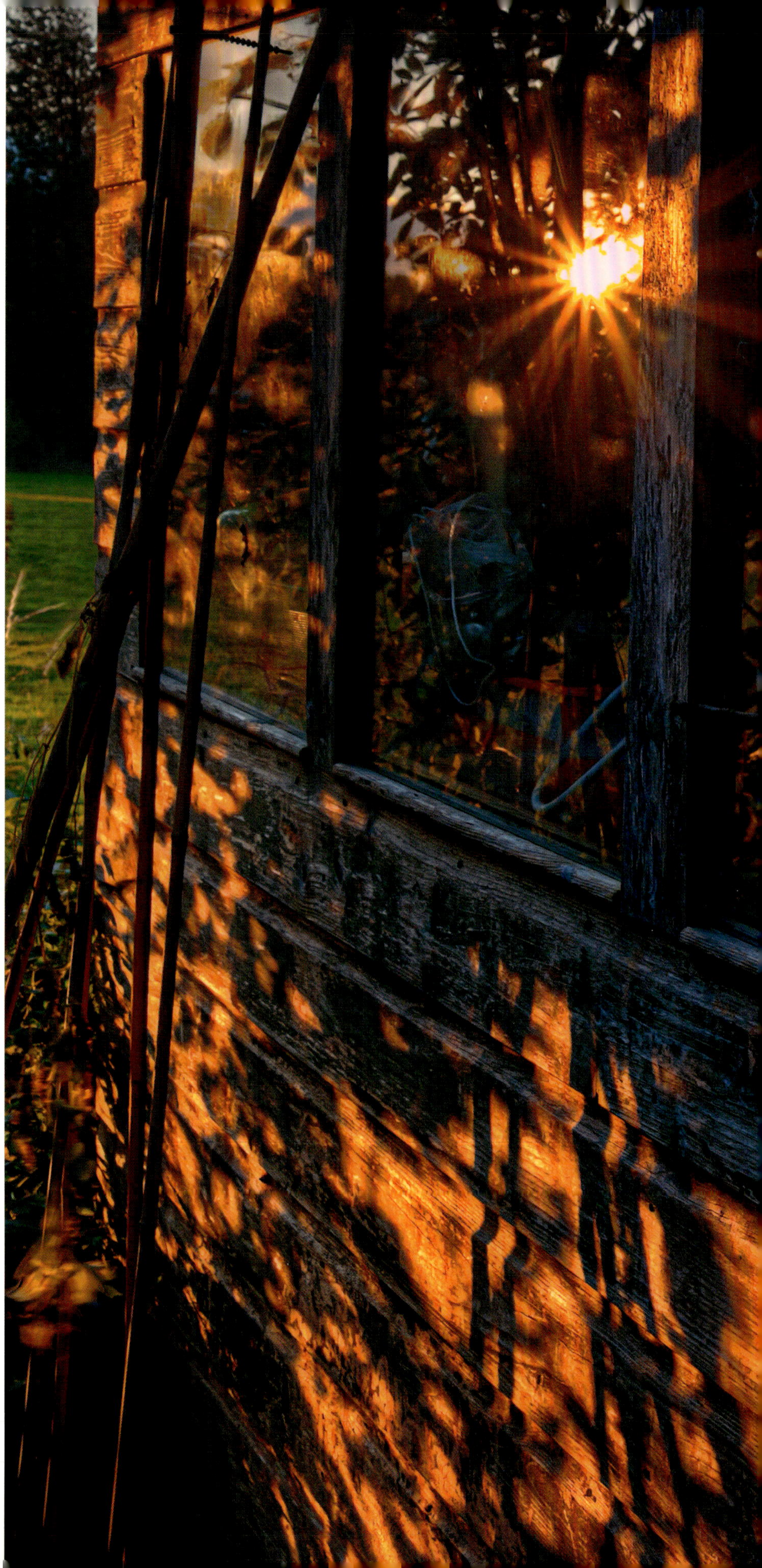

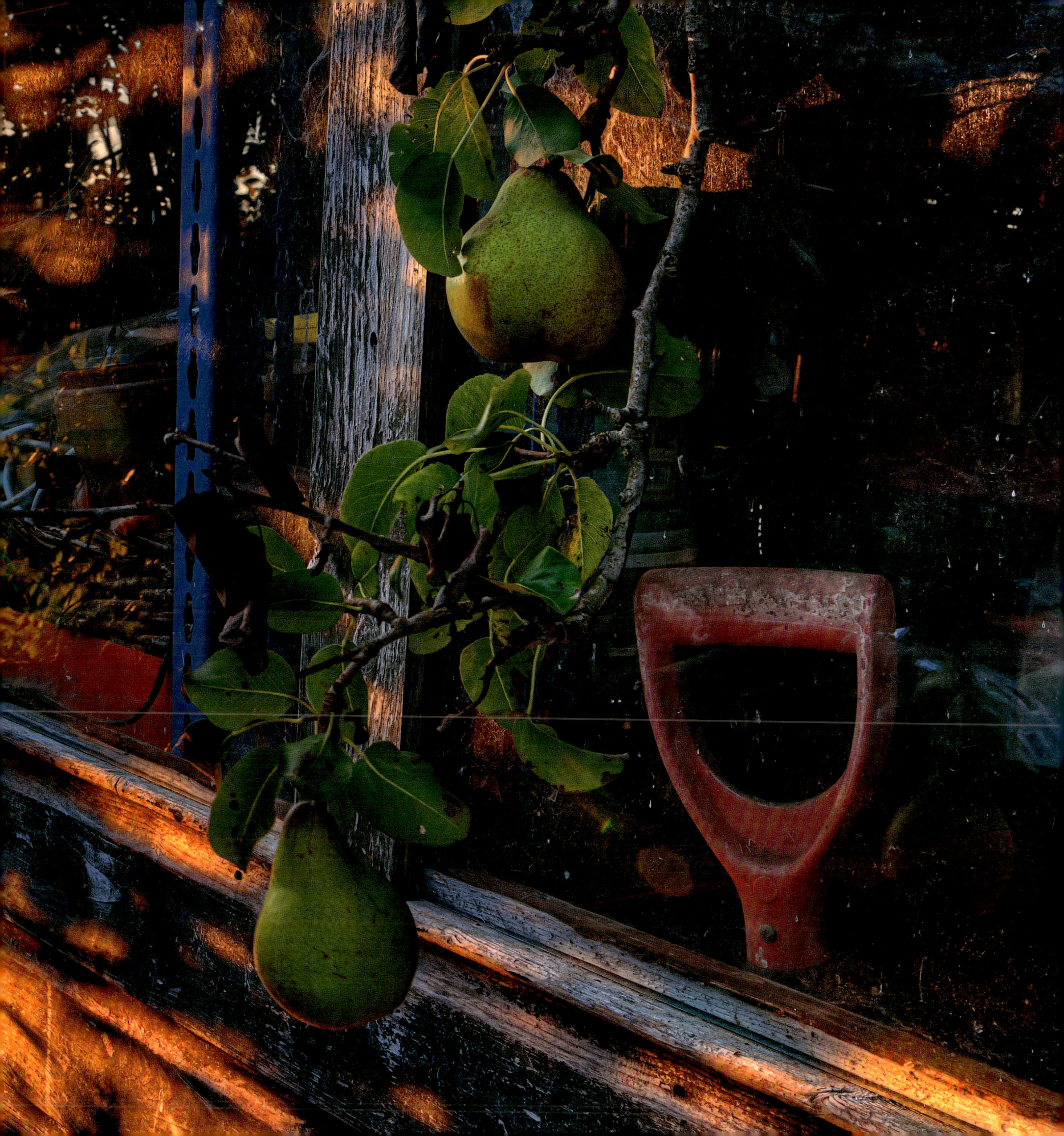

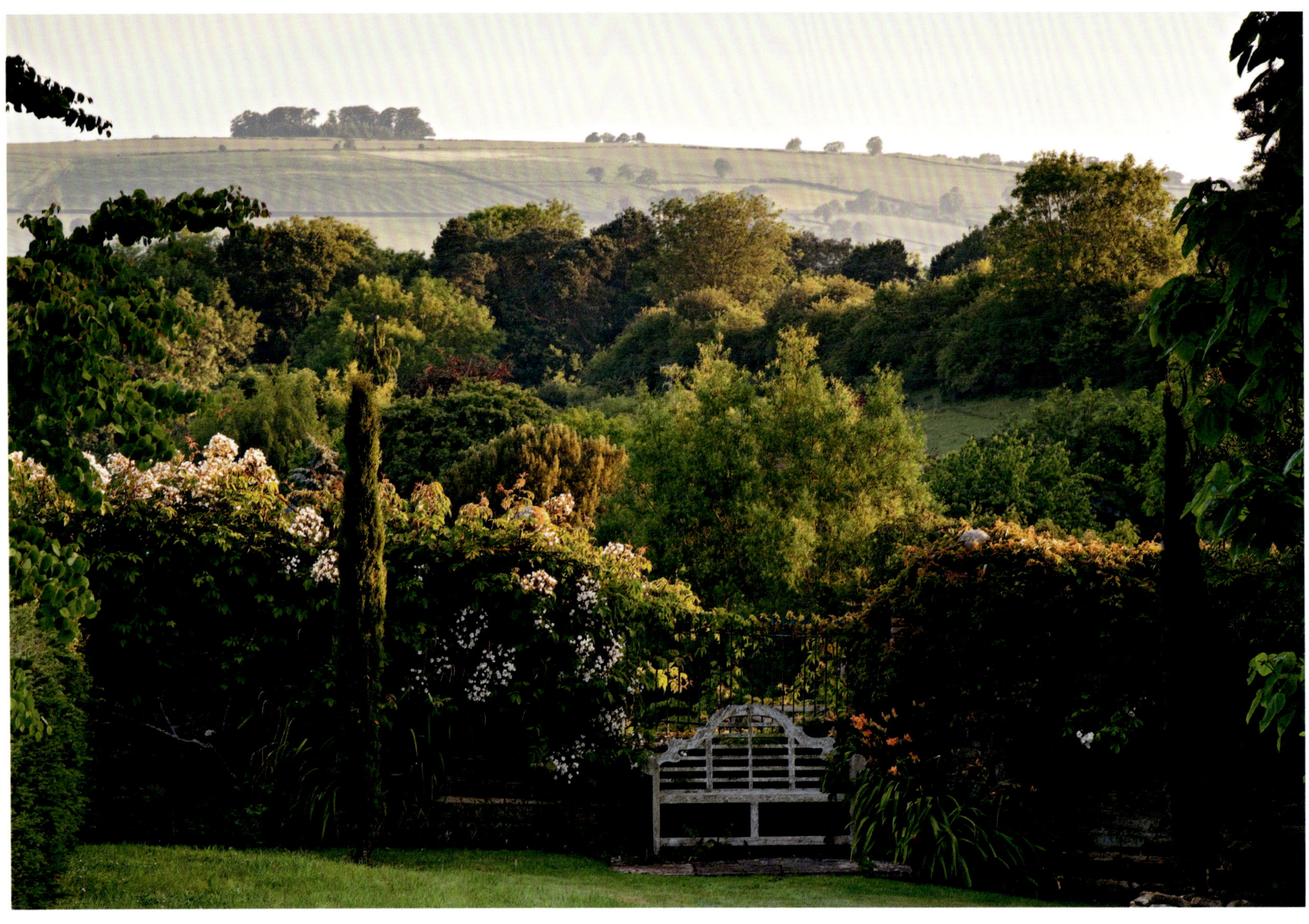

JAMES KERR FINALIST

Borrowed View
Whichford House garden, Warwickshire, UK

This is the main focal point of the garden at Whichford. It is a borrowed view beyond the garden that carries the eye to a distant focal point; in this case the clump of trees on Brailes Hill, a well-known local landmark. I took this photograph very early just as the mist started to lift. All that was required was to wait for the moment when the sun had risen enough to catch the foliage. I used a telephoto lens to isolate the part of the view I found most interesting, and took several frames over a five minute period to ensure the light was perfect.

Canon 1DS Mark III, 70-200 mm lens. 1/8sec at f/16. Post-capture: minor adjustments to lift shadows and bring up contrast.

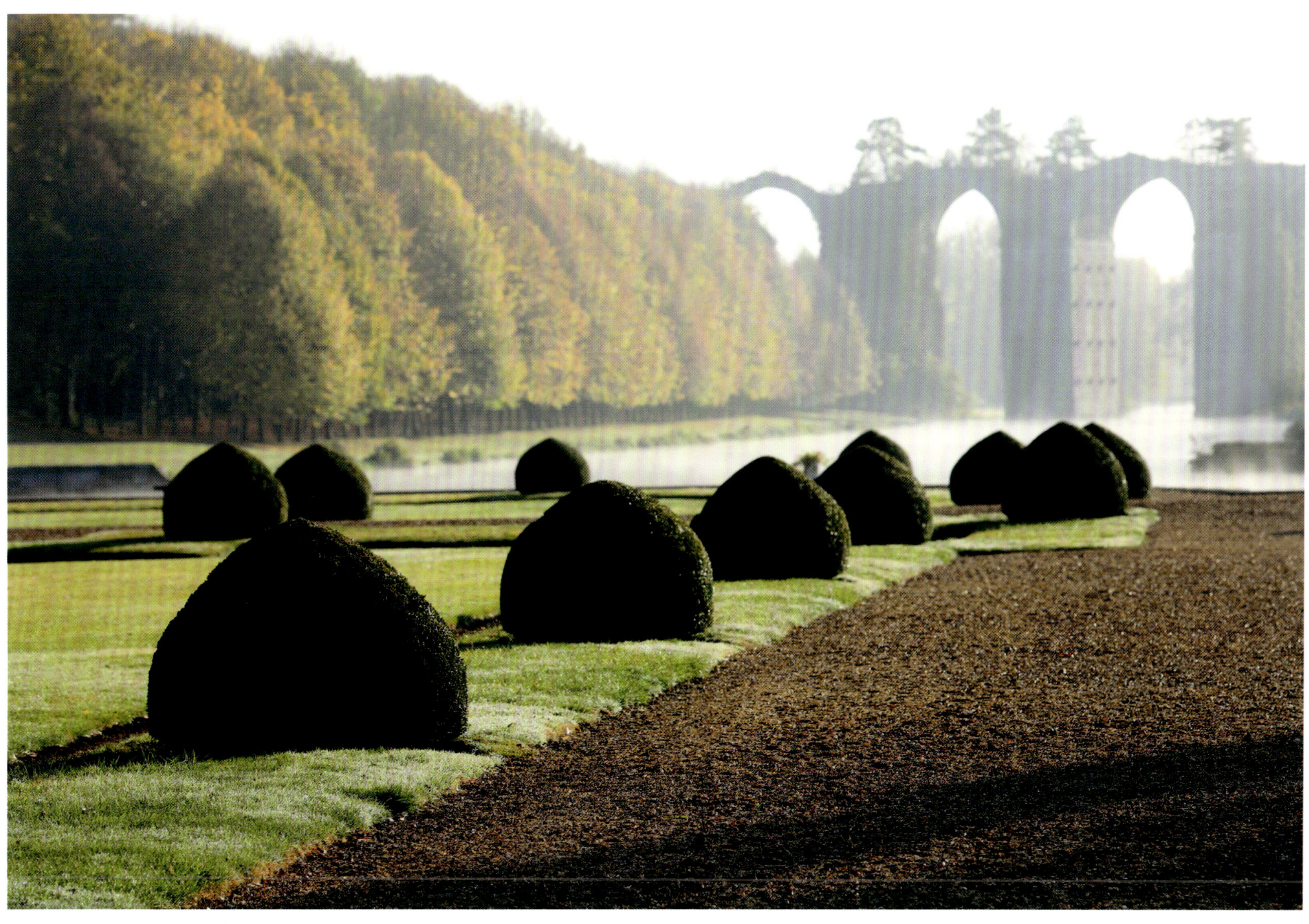

SERGEY KAREPANOV HIGHLY COMMENDED

Early Morning
Château de Maintenon, Eure-et-Loir, France

This garden was designed by André Le Nôtre. The aqueduct in the background was used for water delivery to Versailles gardens. There are three geometric correlations in this composition: the form of the shrubs, the form of the arches, and the parallel row of trees on the other side of the canal.

Canon EOS 5D, Canon EF 135 mm lens. 1/500sec at f/5. Post-capture: no digital alterations.

FÁBIO CLAUDINO ► HIGHLY COMMENDED

Morning in The Garden

Parque de Monserrate, Sintra, Portugal

Photograph taken in autumn morning in the gardens of Monserrate, Sintra, Portugal. This is the granite ladder marking the beginning of the Valley of Ferns. I enjoy shooting against the sun and I liked the arrangement of the elements. The photo was taken at ground level and I used the articulated screen to get my camera close to the ground to achieve the composition I wanted.

Canon 600D, 18-55mm lens. 1/10sec at f/11. Post-capture: basic adjustments to tone and colour balance, saturation, brightness and contrast.

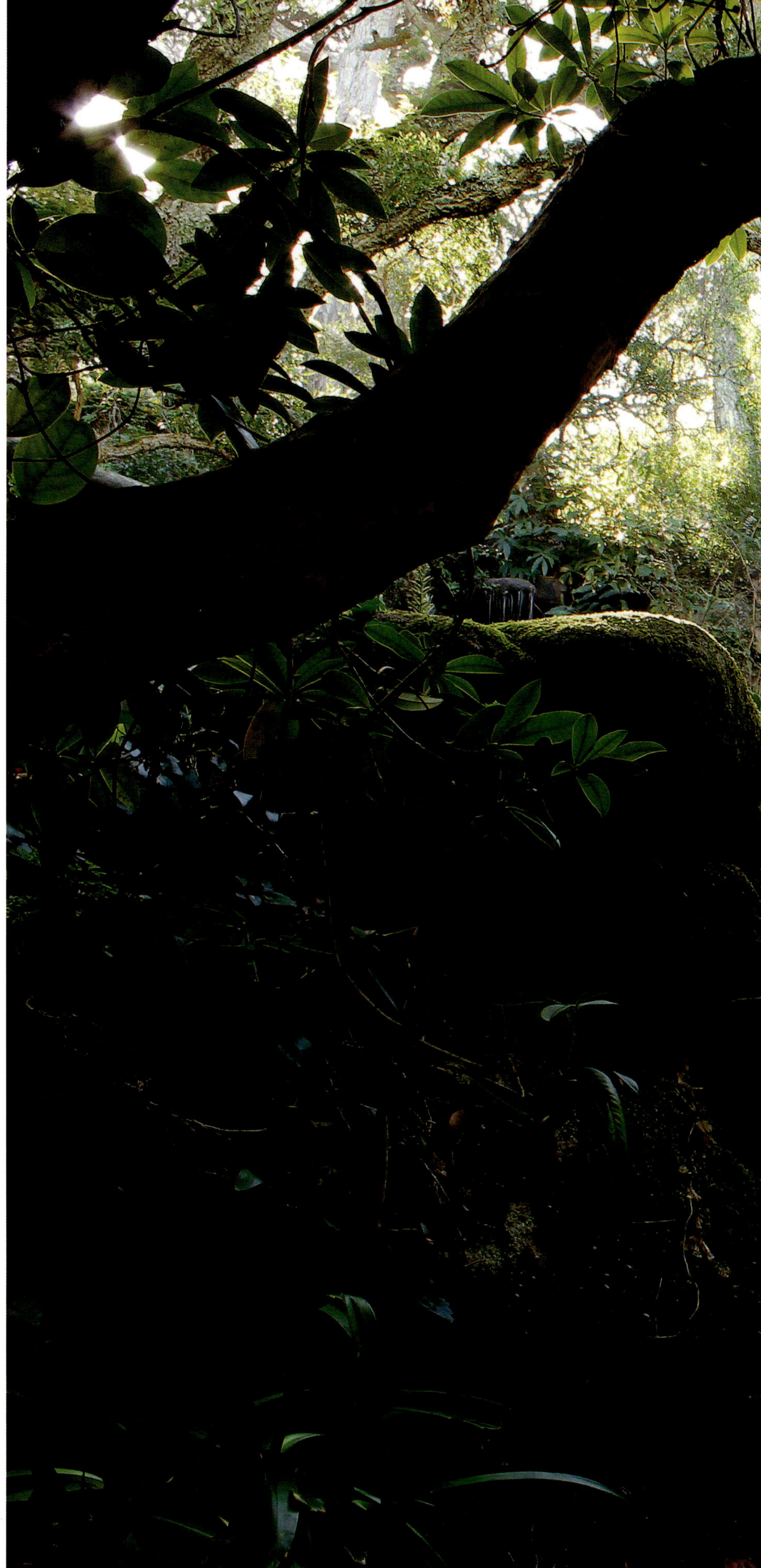

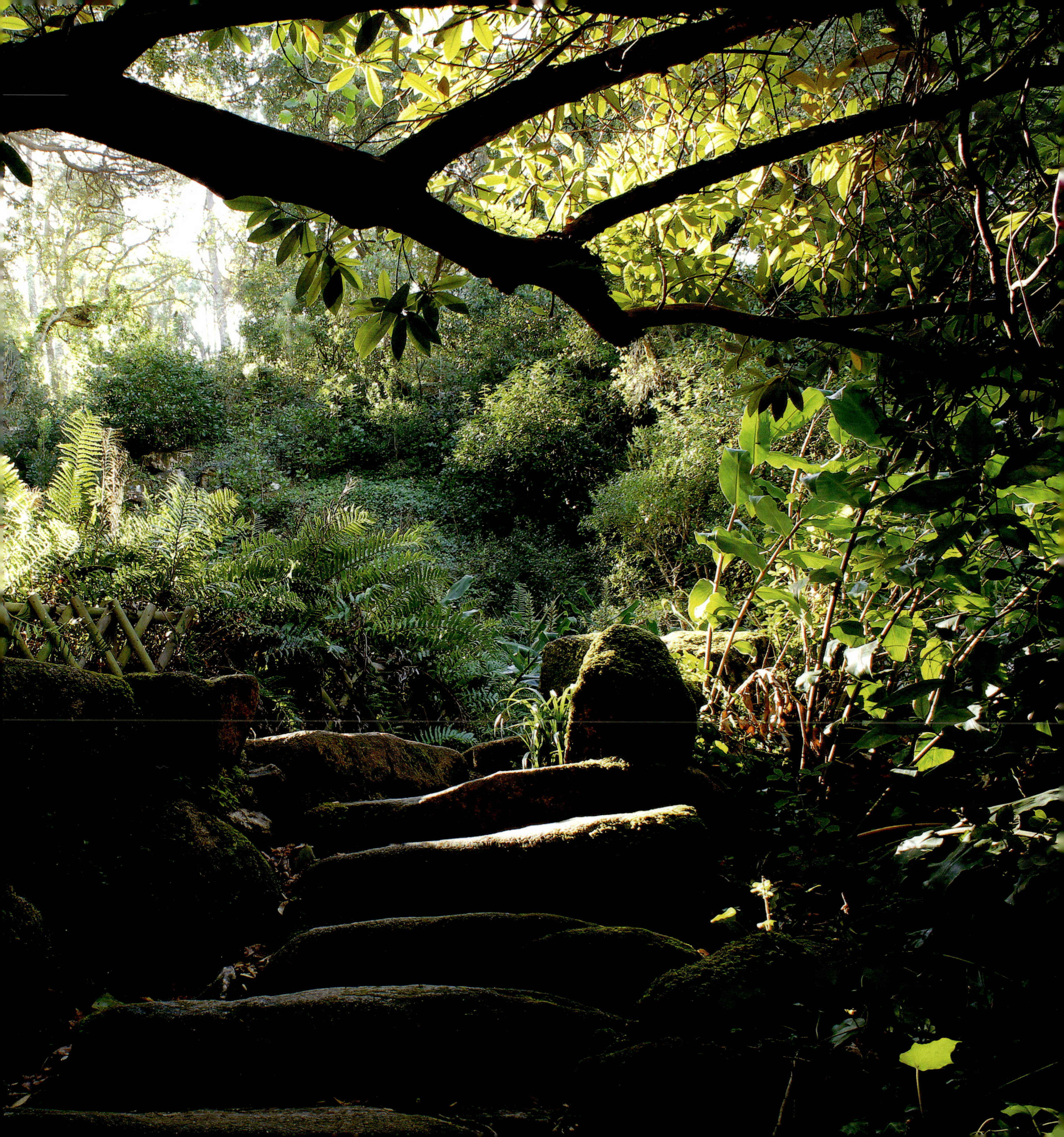

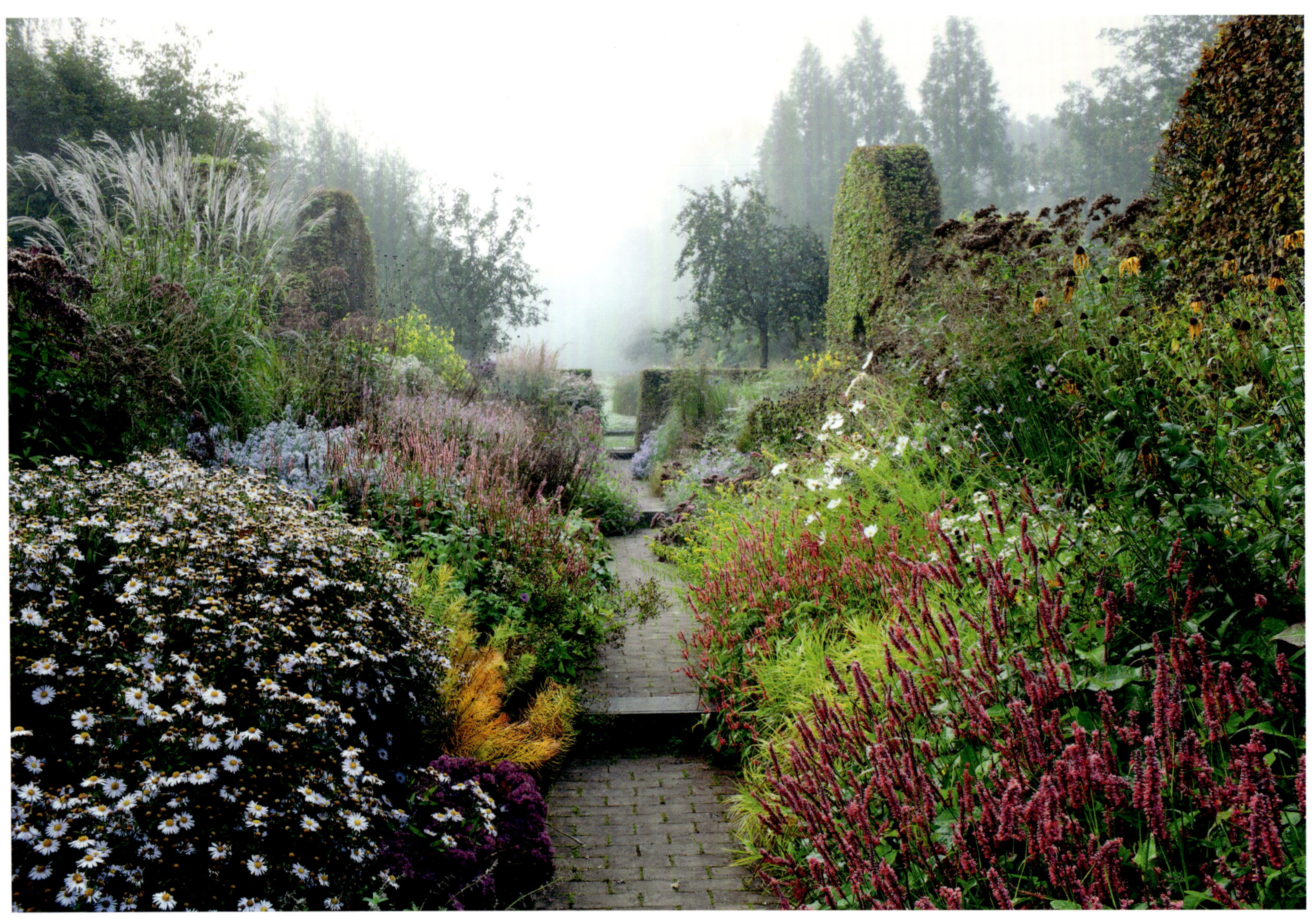

MARIANNE MAJERUS HIGHLY COMMENDED

Enclosed Exuberance
Belgium

The late summer colours of persicaria, kalimeris, cosmos and helianthus punctuate the mist which shrouds the distant fields.

Canon EOS 5D Mark II, 35mm lens. 1/5sec at f/16. Post-capture: no digital alterations.

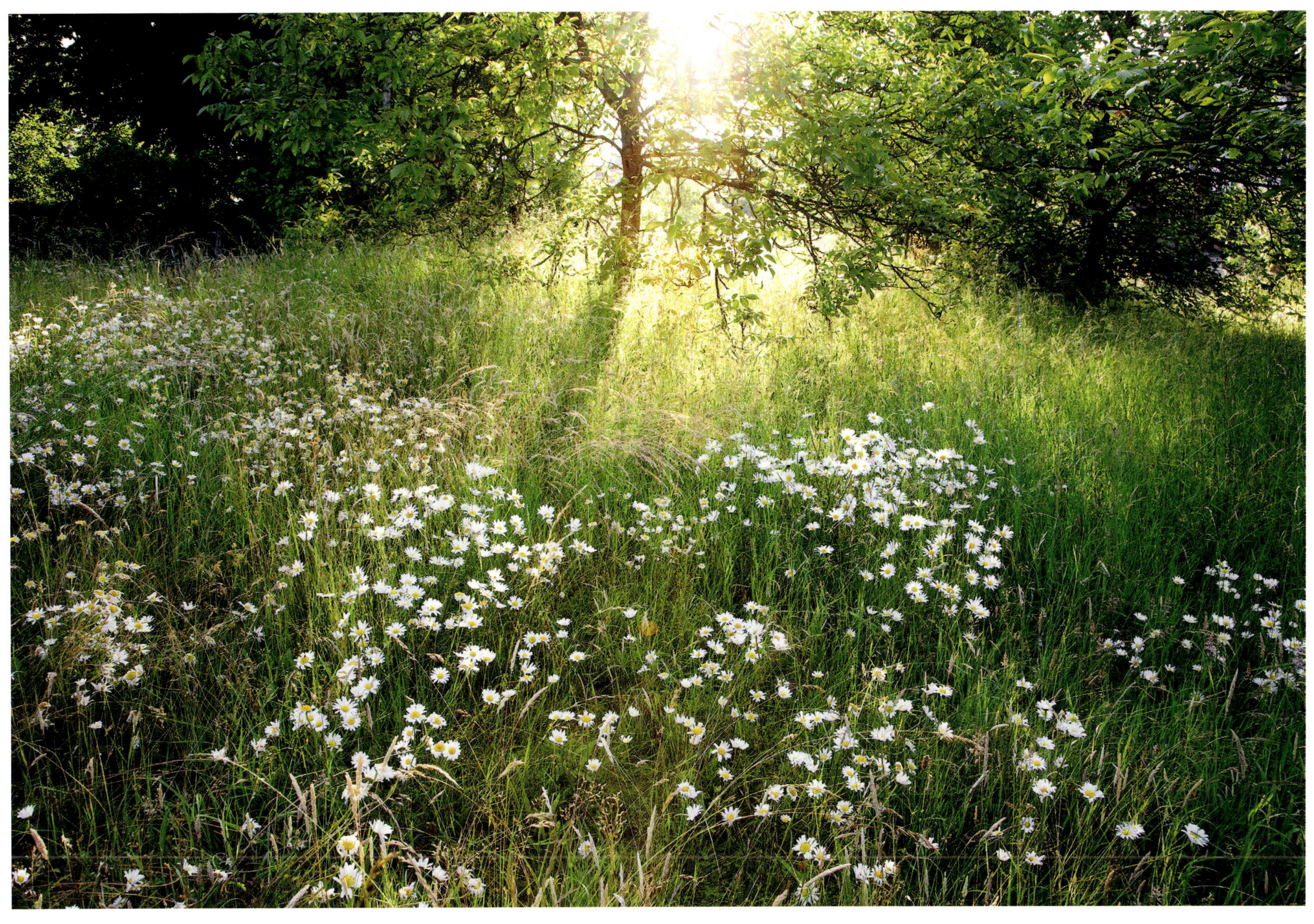

ABIGAIL REX FINALIST

Morning Glow
The Wild Garden at The Manor House, Upton Grey, Hampshire, UK

This image was taken early on a warm June morning. This garden was originally designed by Gertrude Jekyll and restored by the current owners. Naturalistic planting includes mixed grasses and *Leucanthemum vulgare*. I loved the tranquillity, stillness and dreamy light within the garden. This shot enables me to remember the moment perfectly.

Canon EOS 5D, 24-105mm lens. 1/50 sec at f/11. Post-capture: the image was tinted with a warming filter before contrast and saturation adjustments.

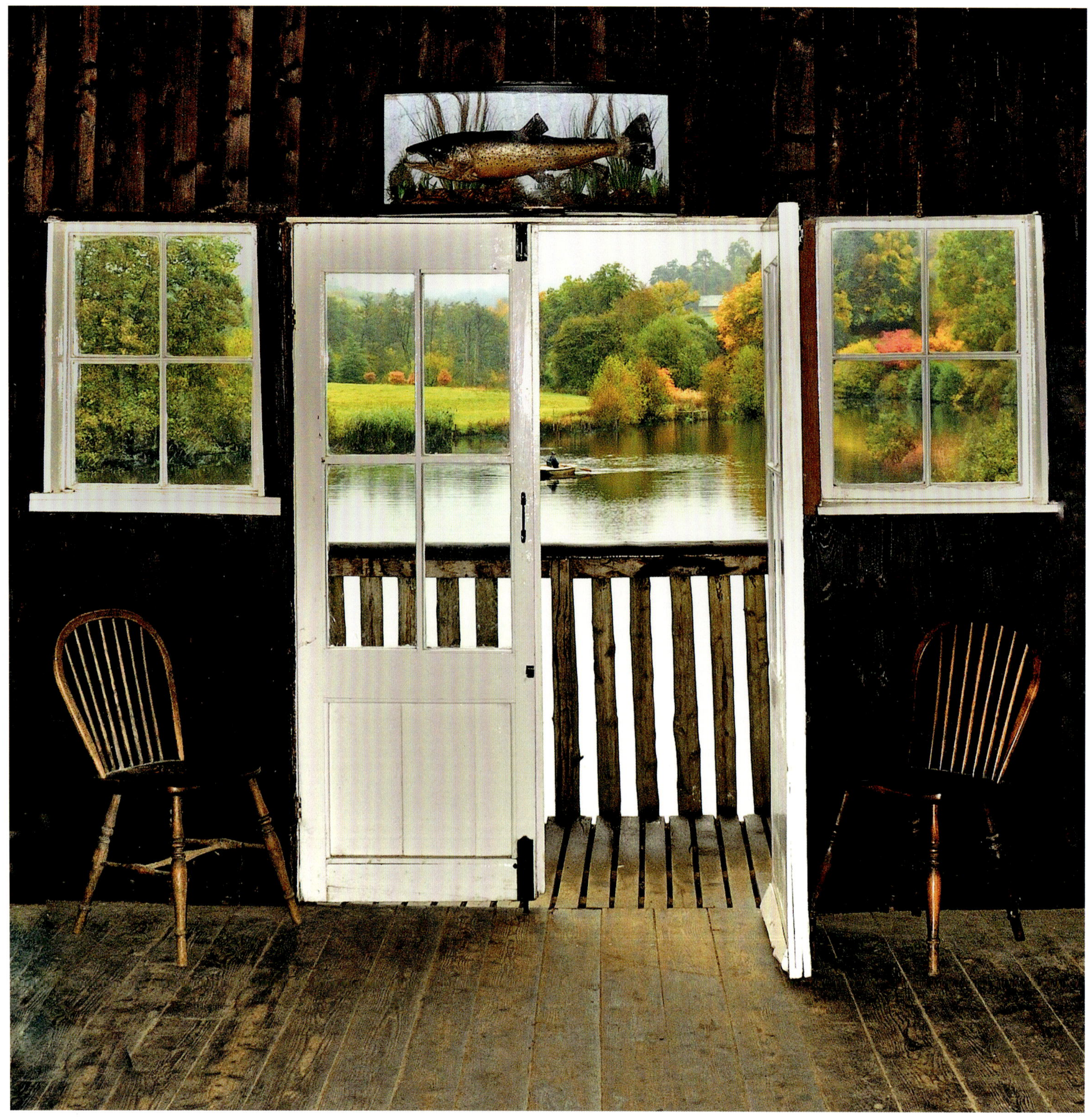

AWARD SPONSORED BY **THE NATIONAL TRUST**

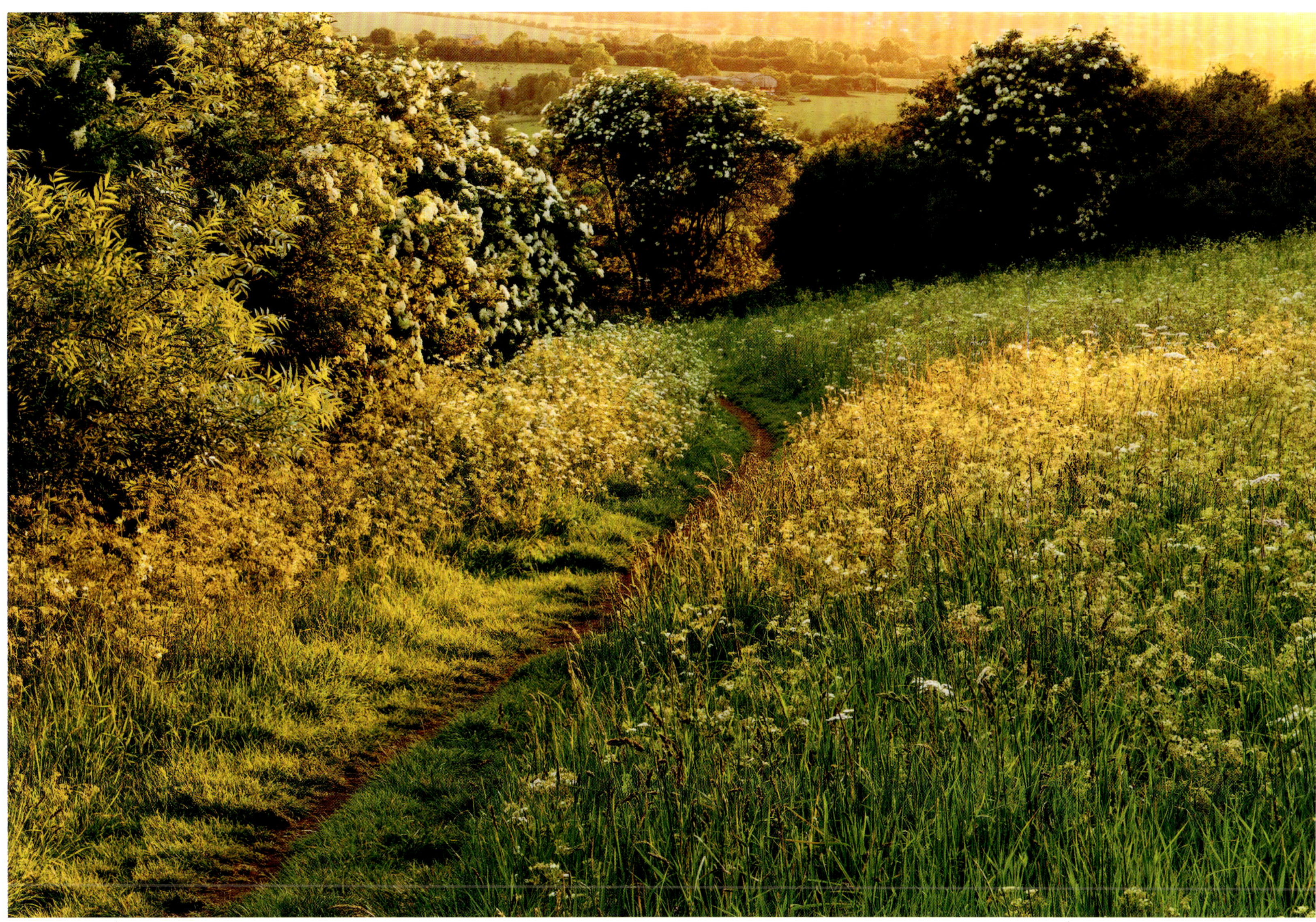

DACE UMBLIJA 1ST PLACE

Boat-house
Winkworth Arboretum, Surrey, UK
By kind permission of the National Trust

The old wooden boat-house sits comfortably at the end of the lake at the Winkworth Arboretum, providing atmospheric views whatever the weather or season. The view from inside the boat-house looked like four colourful framed pictures. I used flash and tripod, since it was quite dark inside.

Nikon D300, 18-200mm lens. 1/60sec at f/8. Post-capture: tone and colour adjustment.

ANDREW BASKOTT 2ND PLACE

Evening Gold
Brampton valley near the village of Brixworth, Northamptonshire, UK

On a late May evening, the setting sun casts a warm glow over the grassland meadow. The vital ingredient for the shot was to this golden light, but I had just a five-minute window in which the sun's angle was just right. This required a pre-planned shot which includes the narrow path and gives a hint of the valley beyond the hedgerow.

Nikon D300, Sigma 28-70 lens. 1/3sec at f/18. Post-capture: minor white balance adjustment.

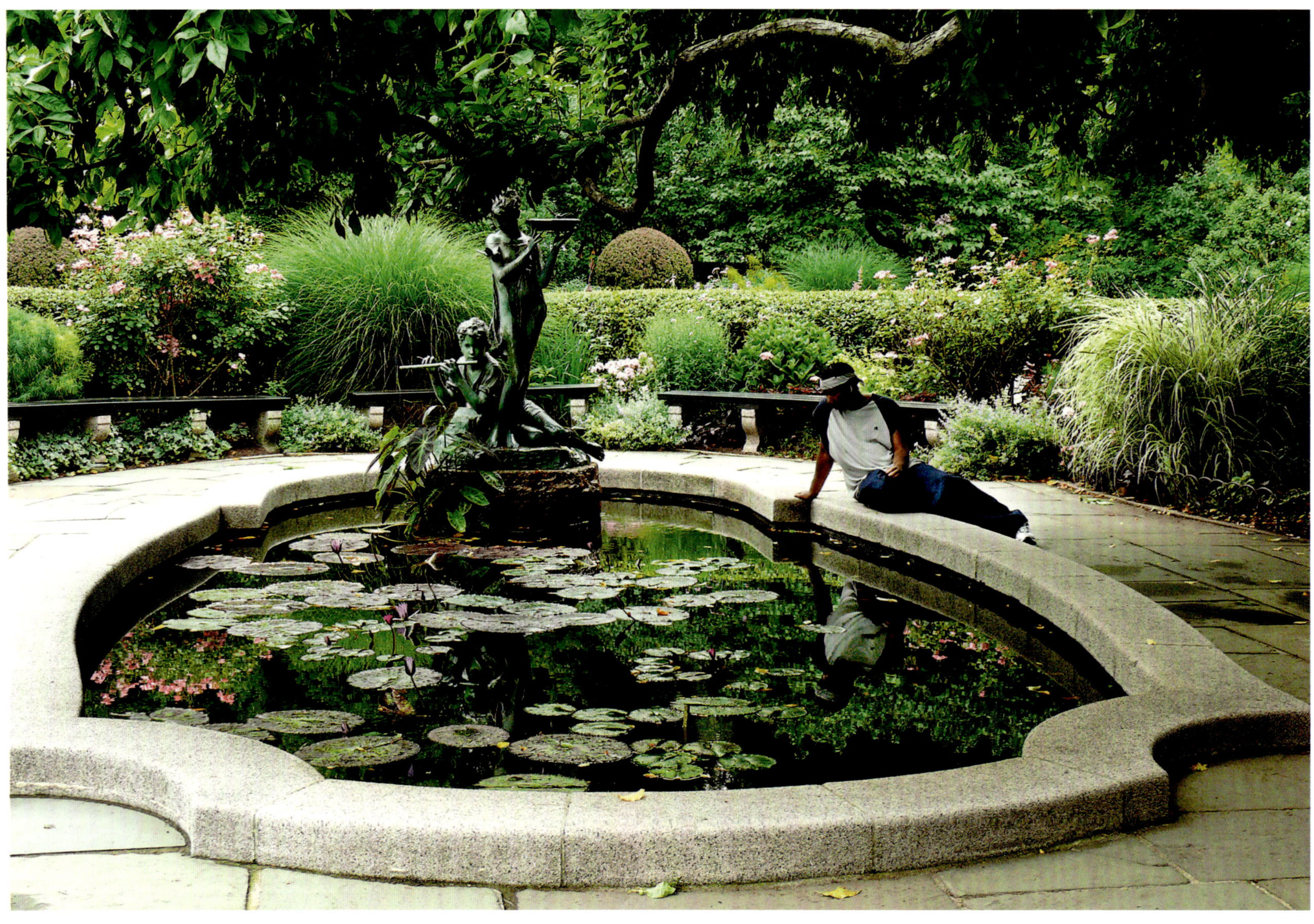

GERHARD PIRNER — 3RD PLACE

Orpheus

Conservatory Garden, Central Park, New York, USA

The northern part of Central Park in New York was a dangerous place for many years. However, the old Conservatory Garden was restored and it has become a safe area for people from Harlem to take a break.

Leica V-Lux 1, Leica DC Vario-Elmarit lens. 1/100sec at f 3.6. Post-capture: basic colour management.

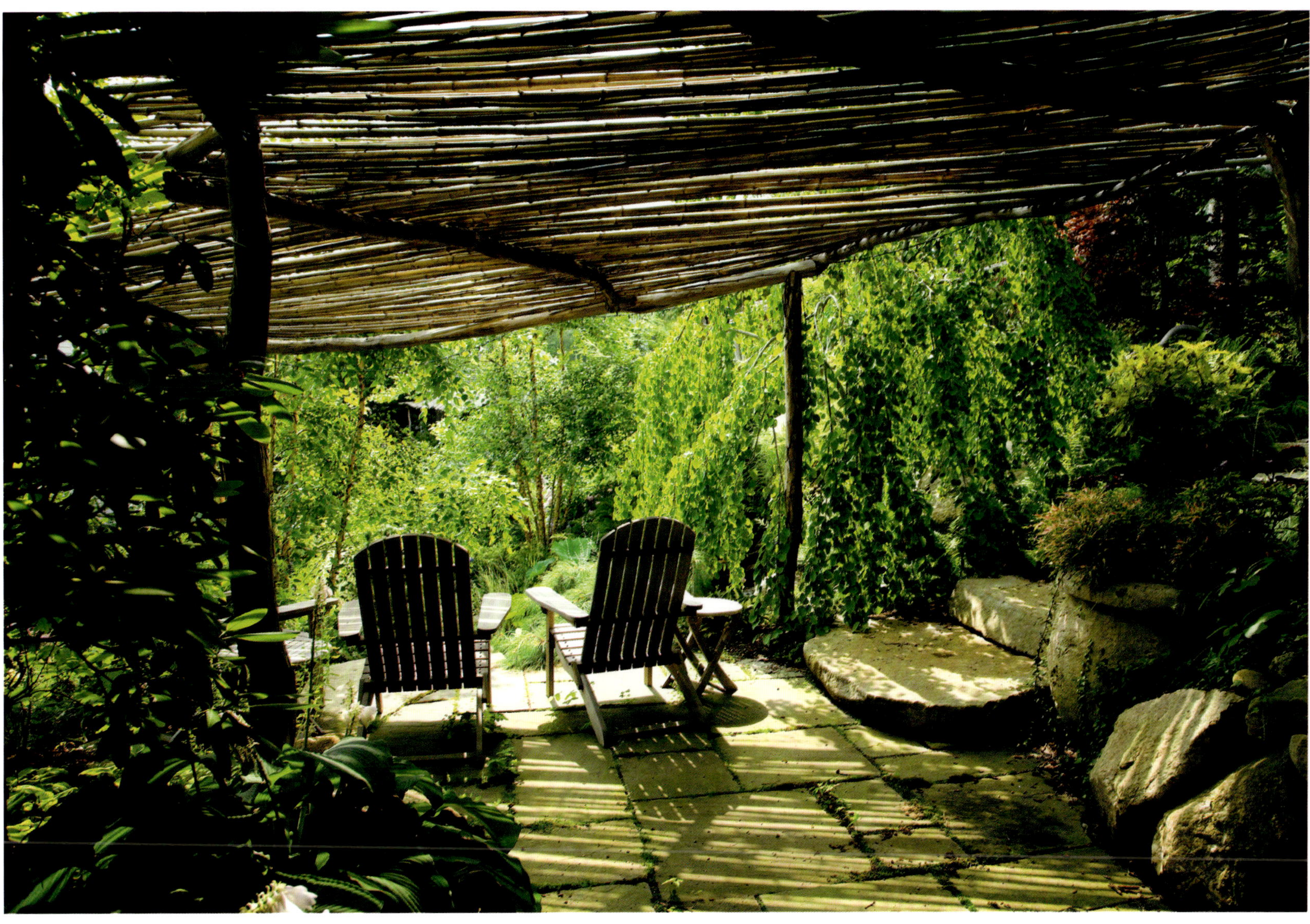

ERIC ROTH HIGHLY COMMENDED

Sunny Shady Perch
Cape Cod, Massachusetts, USA

This lovely spot was created by gardener Paul Miskovsky. The combination of streaming sunlight and back-lit foliage is very compelling to me. I wanted to capture enough of the terrace and its surroundings to show how delightful it was to be there, while being close enough to retain the intimacy of this cosy enclosure. My visit was very early in the morning to capture the dawn light. I used a polarizing filter to minimize glare and get great saturation in the foliage.

Canon EOS 5D, Mark II, 24-105mm lens. 1/50sec. Post-capture: no digital alterations.

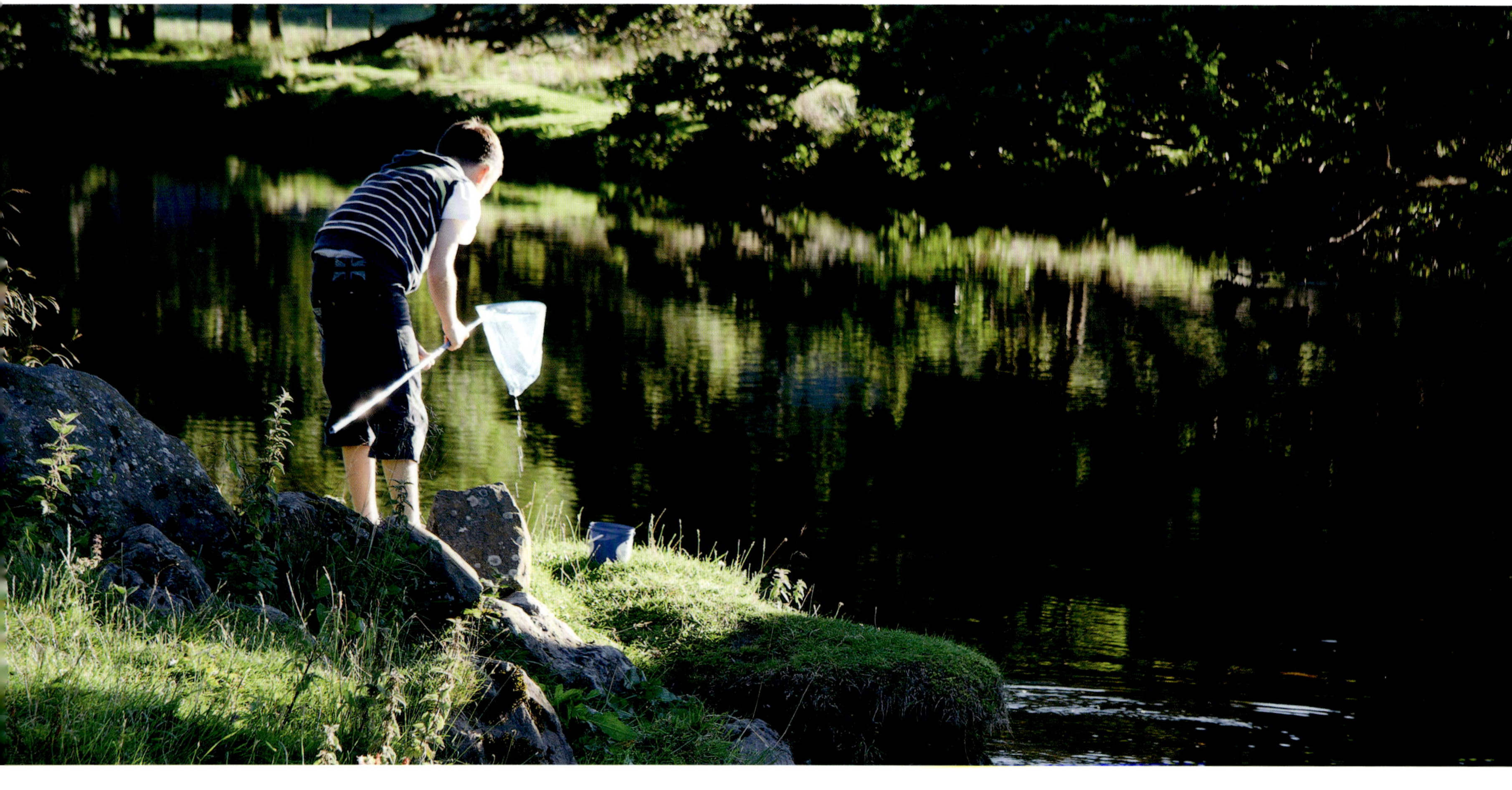

CLARE FORBES FINALIST

The Catch
River Derwent, Lake District National Park, Cumbria, UK

After spending a warm, sunny day exploring, our feet were tired. We decided to relax on the bank of the River Derwent so my son could enjoy catching sticklebacks and counting them in his bucket before releasing them back into the river. To emphasize how engrossed he was in his fishing, I used a relatively shallow depth of field to make him sharp against the softened background. I positioned myself so that side lighting would illuminate his activity and cropped the image to lead the eye along the river.

Canon EOS 400D, Canon 17-85mm lens. 1/50sec at f/5.6. Post-capture: the image was slightly sharpened and cropped.

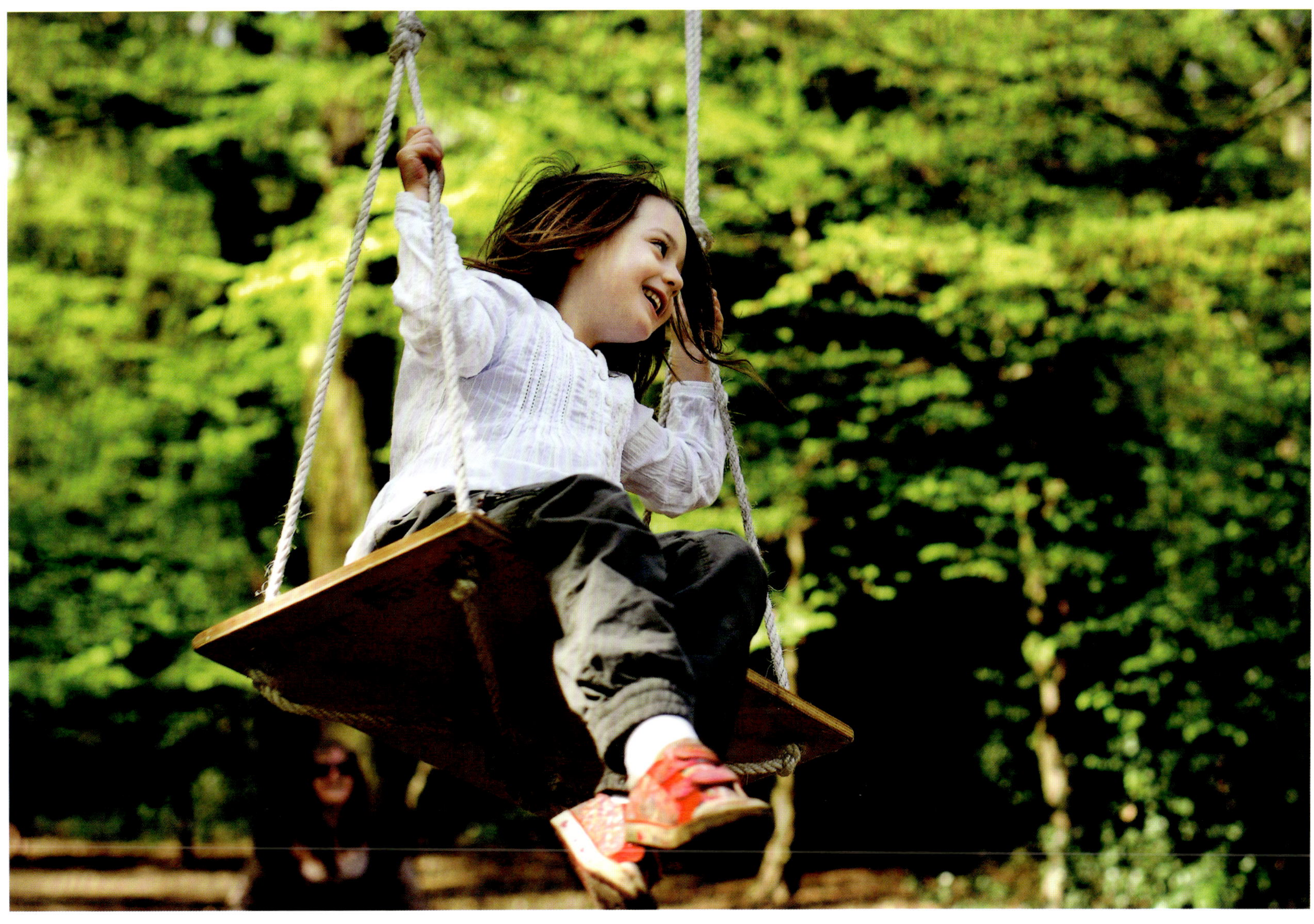

JANI SHEPHERD HIGHLY COMMENDED

Freedom
Queen's Wood, Muswell Hill, London, UK

One of Georgie's favourite 'Breathing Spaces'. On my last visit to the UK to see my sister and her family it became apparent to me how important breathing spaces are in work-driven urban environments. Where back gardens are limited, London's beautiful parks and woods play an important part in any family's life as places to enjoy the fresh air and re-energise in nature.

Nikon D200, Nikkor 50mm lens. 1/400sec at f/2.8. Post-capture: basic colour adjustments.

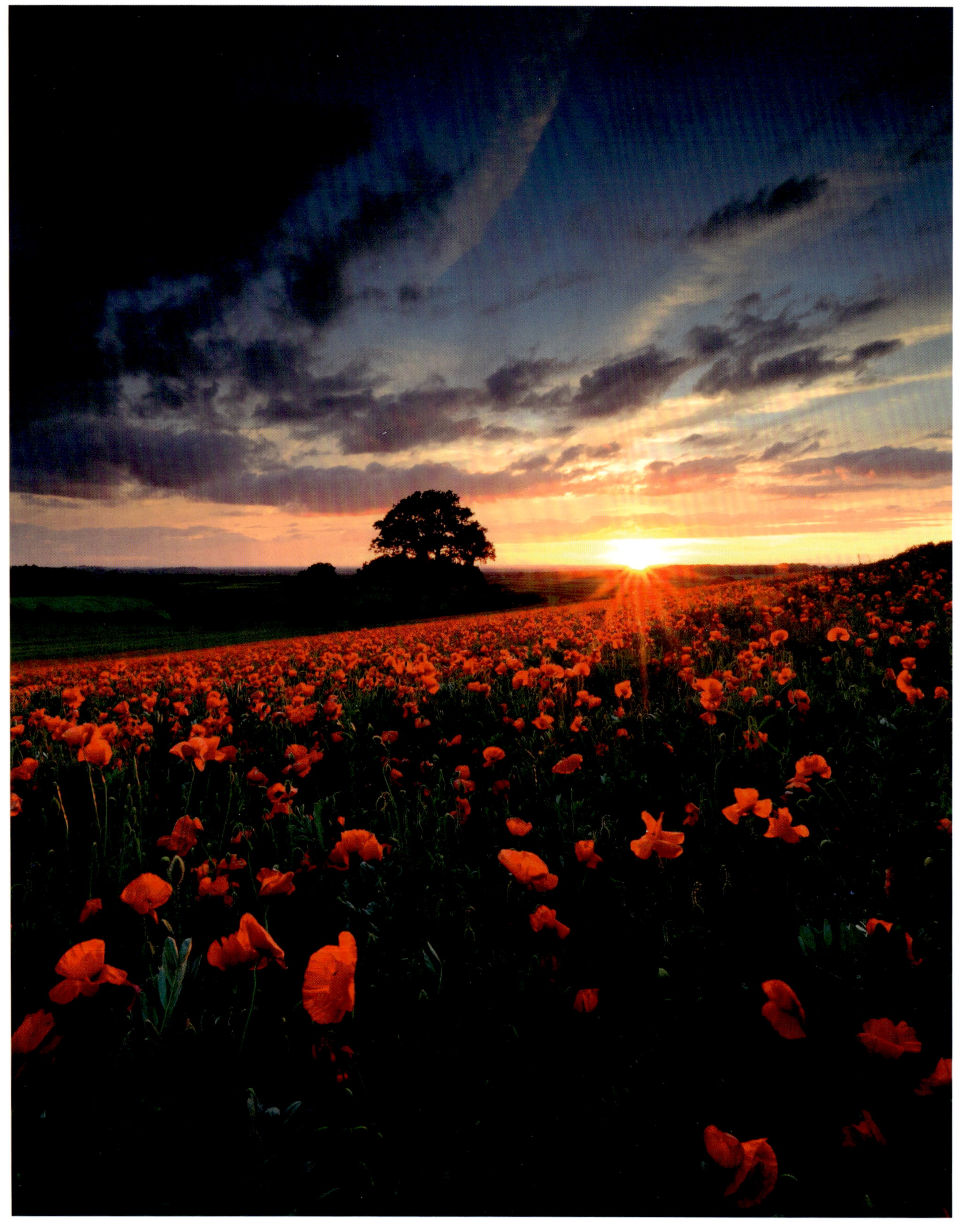

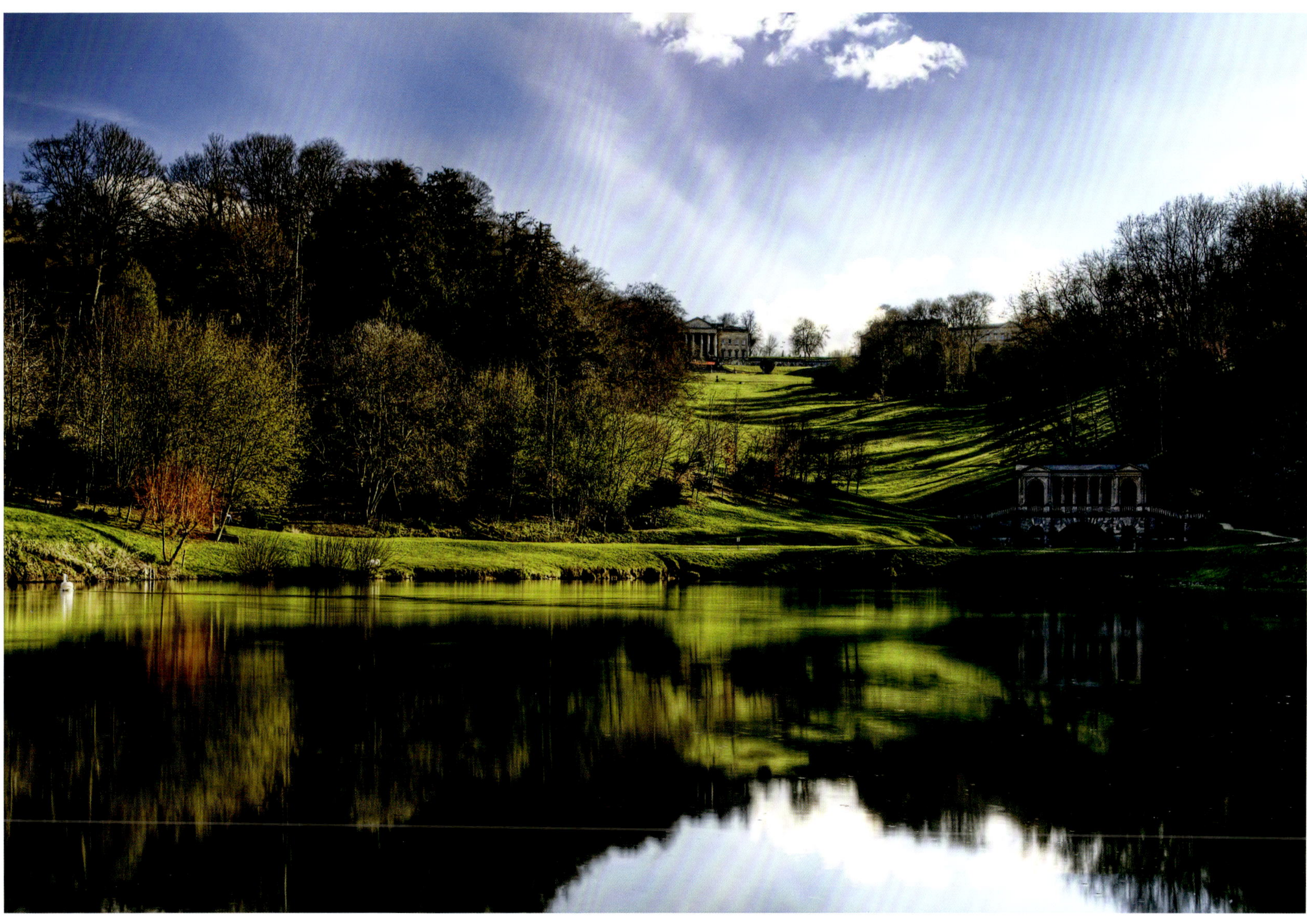

◄ **RENATA ARPASOVA** FINALIST

Sunset Poppies
Badbury Hill, Oxfordshire, UK

Poppies are at their most beautiful when illuminated by the setting sun. I used a tripod and neutral density graduated filter for this image.

Canon EOS 5D Mark II, 17-40mm lens. 4 seconds at f/22. Post-capture: I blended two exposures, one for the sky and one for the ground, to achieve a natural looking scene.

▲ **ARRON GENT** FINALIST

Prior Park
Prior Park, Bath, UK
By kind permission of the National Trust.

This was taken on a brief visit to Bath. I went to Bath specifically to see this park having seen it in the book that came with my National Trust membership. I used HDR technique with three different exposures.

Canon EOS 550D, 18-55mm lens. Post-capture: surface marks in the water erased.

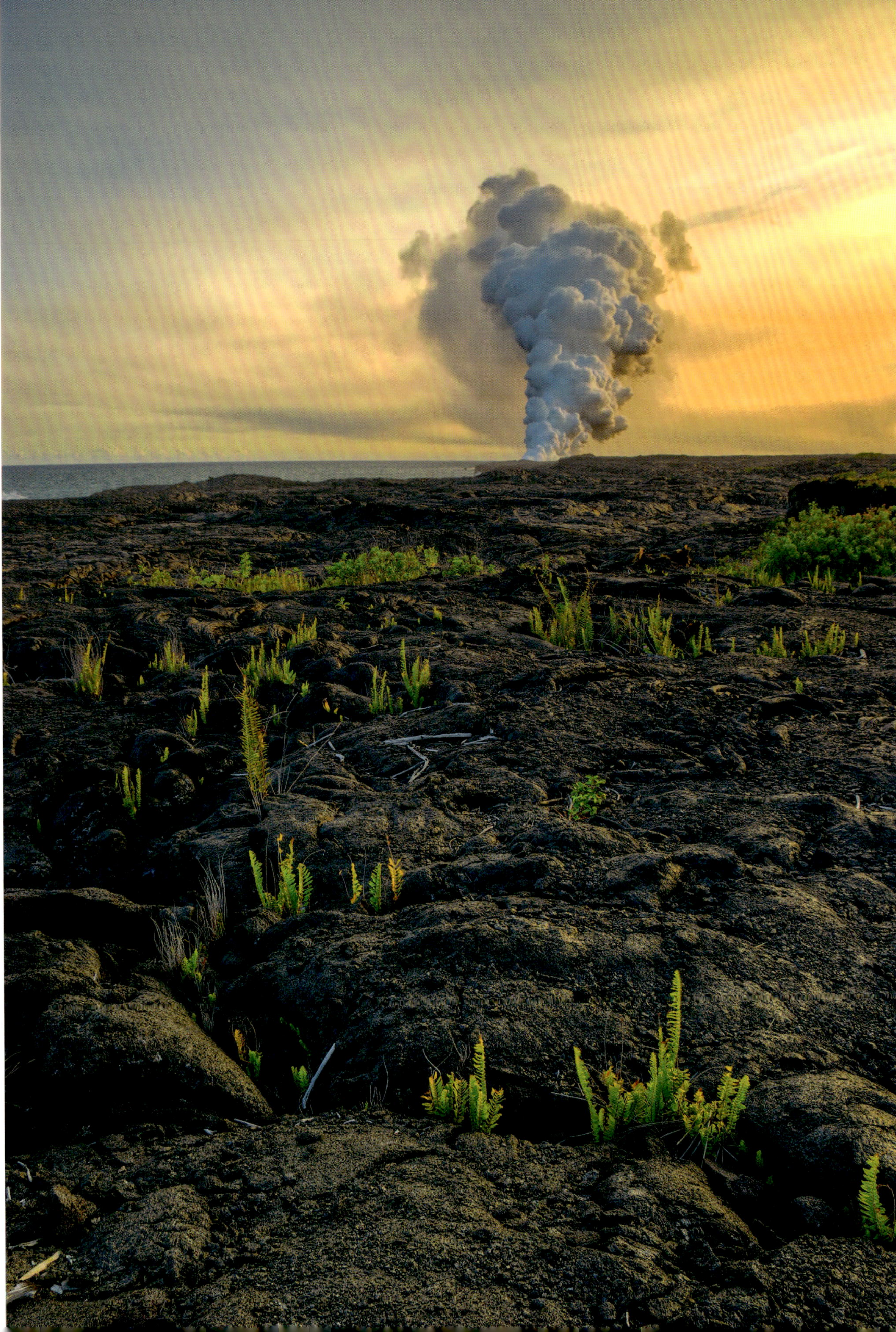

◄ STEVE NICHOLLS 1ST PLACE

Lava Ferns
Kalapana, Big Island, Hawaii, USA

Bright green lines of the fern *Polypodium pellucidum* outline the patterns of cracks and crevices on a recent flow of pahoehoe lava on Hawaii's Big Island. This variety characteristically grows on windswept lava flows, and is among the first life forms to colonise newly-cooled lava flows. I particularly like the linear arrangement of these ferns as they take root in cracks in the lava. I waited until sunset so the steam plume was more softly lit and showed more contrast. The low angle of the sun made the ferns glow with an almost unnatural brightness.

Nikon D200, Nikon 18-200 zoom lens. 1/15sec at f/8. Post-capture: the black lava and bright sunset sky presented a huge tonal contrast, so I took two exposures, one to bring out details in the lava and the other to pick out the sunset colours. I combined the two images using a mask along the horizon.

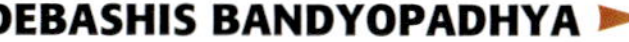

DEBASHIS BANDYOPADHYA ► 2ND PLACE

A Summer Sunrise
Hay Tor, Dartmoor National Park, UK

I made a trip to Dartmoor in August, knowing that the heather would be in full bloom. I scouted for locations and found that the flowers were in abundance near Hay Tor. Next morning I was out before sunrise and ready for the right light when it happened. On this morning, the sun seemed to disappear under a blanket of cloud, but looking at the cloud patterns it was evident that the sun would emerge soon and the presence of clouds made exciting light all the more likely. I had my camera ready on tripod with a 3-stop graduated neutral density filter in place. Sure enough, soon there was this splendid sunburst which I could make the most of as I was all set up.

Canon EOS 350D, Canon 18-55 mm lens. 0.6 sec at f/22. Post-capture: adjustments to saturation, white balance and contrast.

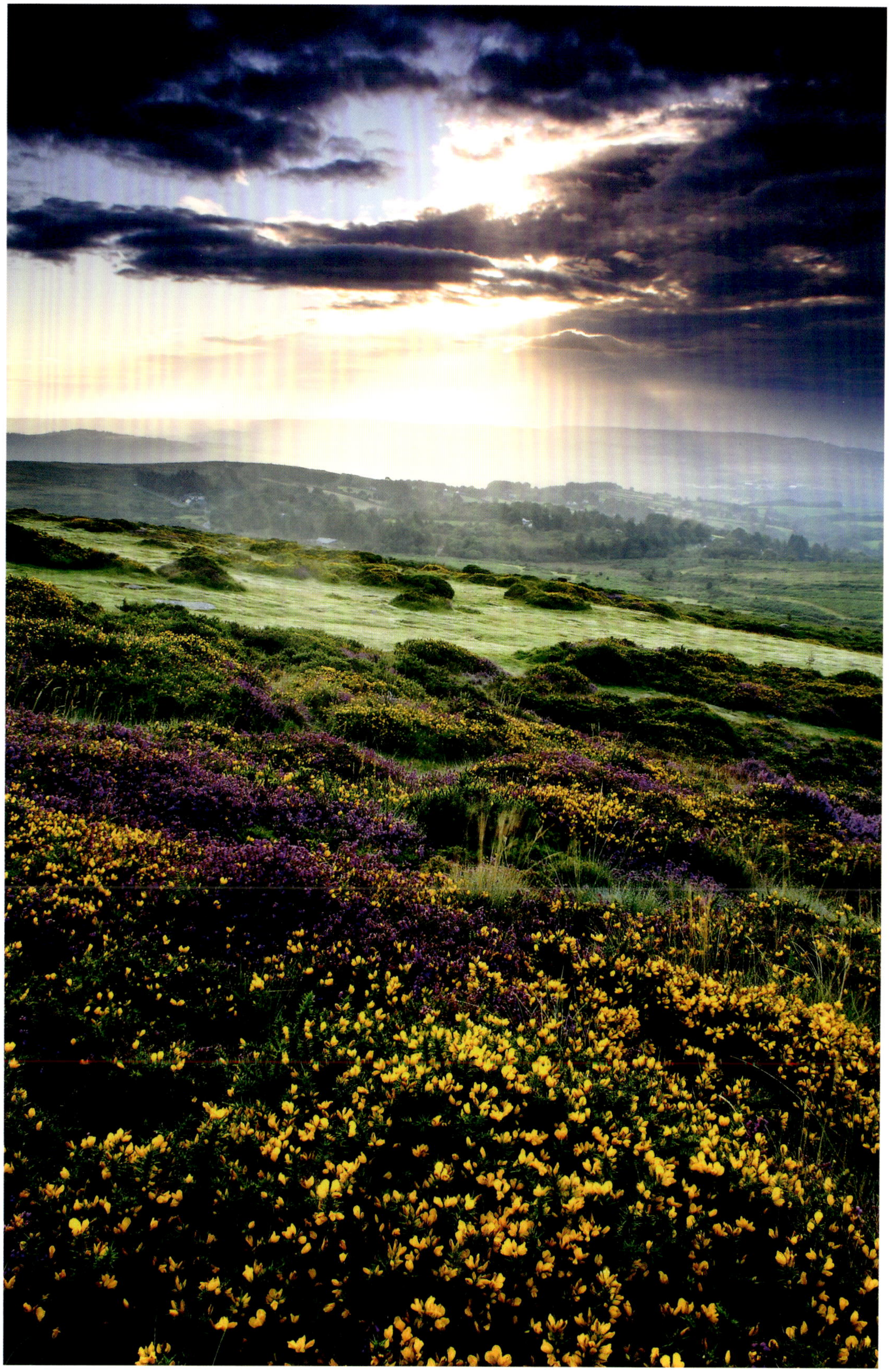

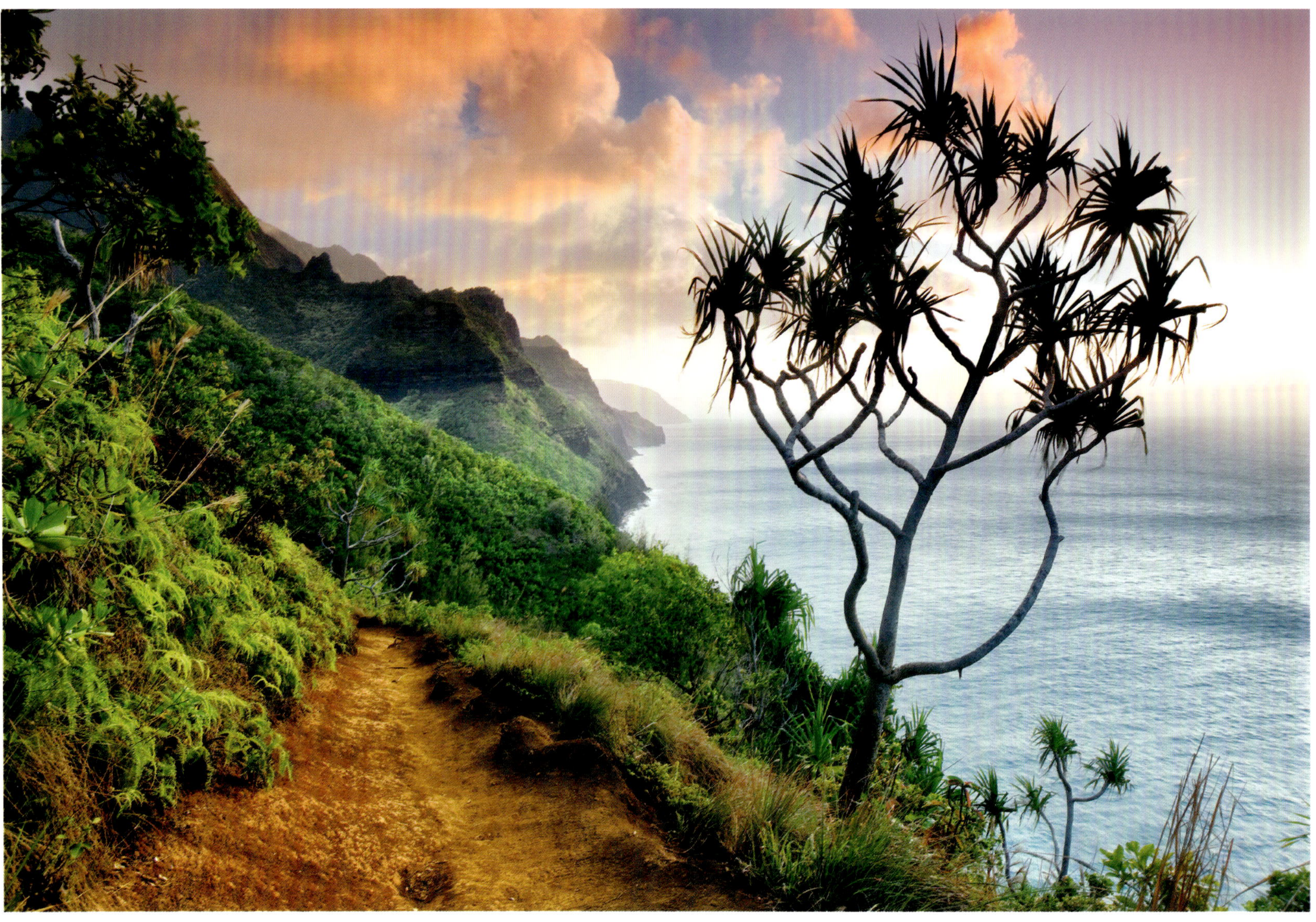

DENNIS FRATES 3RD PLACE

Napali Coast at Sunset

The Napali Coast Trail, Kauai, Hawaii

This shot was made between tropical showers just before sunset, on a trail considered one of the top hiking trails in the world. It leads to some fantastic, secluded beaches not accessible to most travellers. I hiked out with a small flashlight down some very steep slopes for two miles. By then the sun had set and the trail was almost pitch black. A couple I did not know who had passed me on their way out before sunset were worried about me and stayed at the trail's end until I came out. I was very impressed by their thoughtfulness.

Canon 1DS Mark III, Canon EF 16-35mm lens. 0.8sec at f/16. Post-capture: tonality and colour correction.

ROSS BROWN HIGHLY COMMENDED

Sea Pink

Trevone Bay, Cornwall, UK

While on a family walk, I discovered this stunning carpet of thrift close to the South-West coastal path near Trevone Bay. I took a sketch on my digital camera and returned a few days later at sunset to capture the scene in optimal light. The best light was after the sun had set as this softened the foreground colours and avoided too much contrast. The pink glow just above the sea complemented the colour of the thrift and gave balance to the photograph.

Ebony SW45 large format camera Schneider Apo-Symmar 150mm. 16 seconds at f/22. Post-capture: large format transparency film scanned using Epson V750 flatbed scanner. Minor digital adjustments to bring out the detail in the cliff rock.

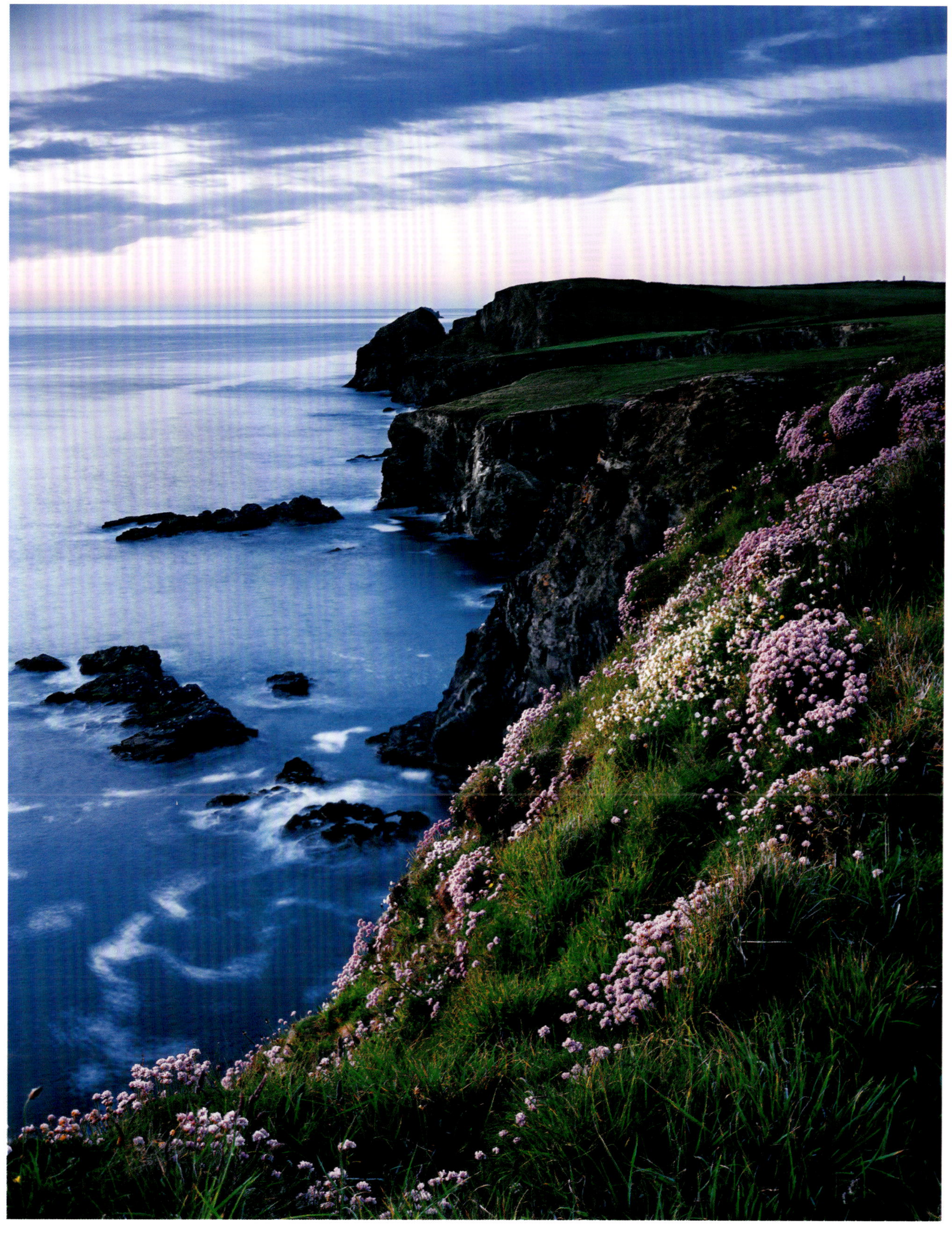

JILL WELHAM ►

HIGHLY COMMENDED

Barn and Buttercups
Swaledale, North Yorkshire, UK

I travelled to Muker in Swaledale to photograph the traditional wildflower meadows. The species-rich meadows provide perfect habitats for butterflies and insects; they are cut once during the summer months to make winter feed for livestock. Each field has its own barn providing shelter for the animals; these traditional methods of farming are rapidly disappearing. Shortly before I made this photograph, RAF jets flew down the valley and created the contrails in the sky. I took a number of photographs but this one stood out, capturing a disappearing landscape and way of life. I made sure that I stayed on the flag-paved path to avoid damaging the wildflowers and waited until no people were visible, as I wanted to capture the peace and tranquillity of the landscape. I used a tripod to maintain image stability and a circular polarising filter to enhance the blue sky.

Nikon D300S, Nikkor 16-85mm lens. 1/15sec at f/16. Post-capture: no digital alterations.

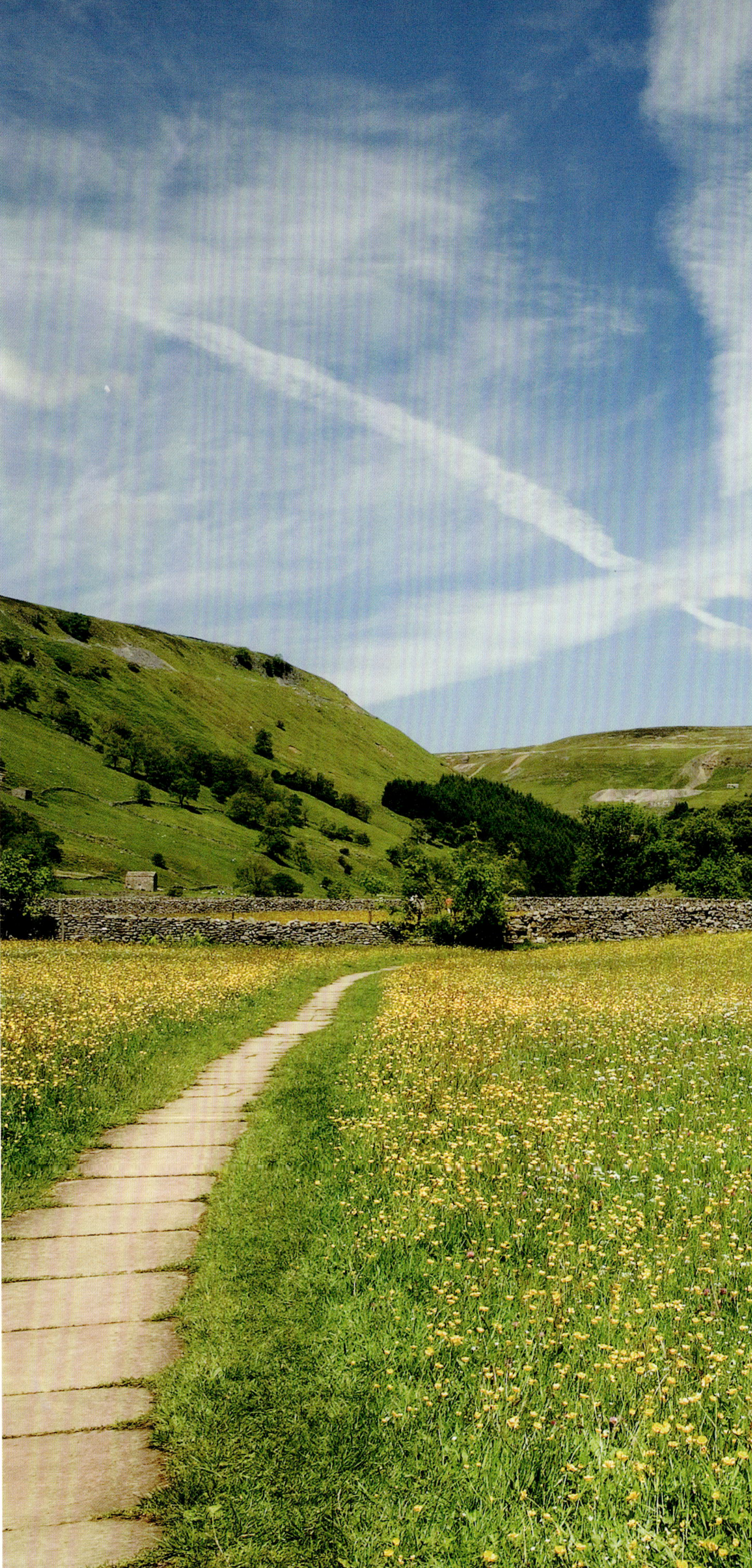

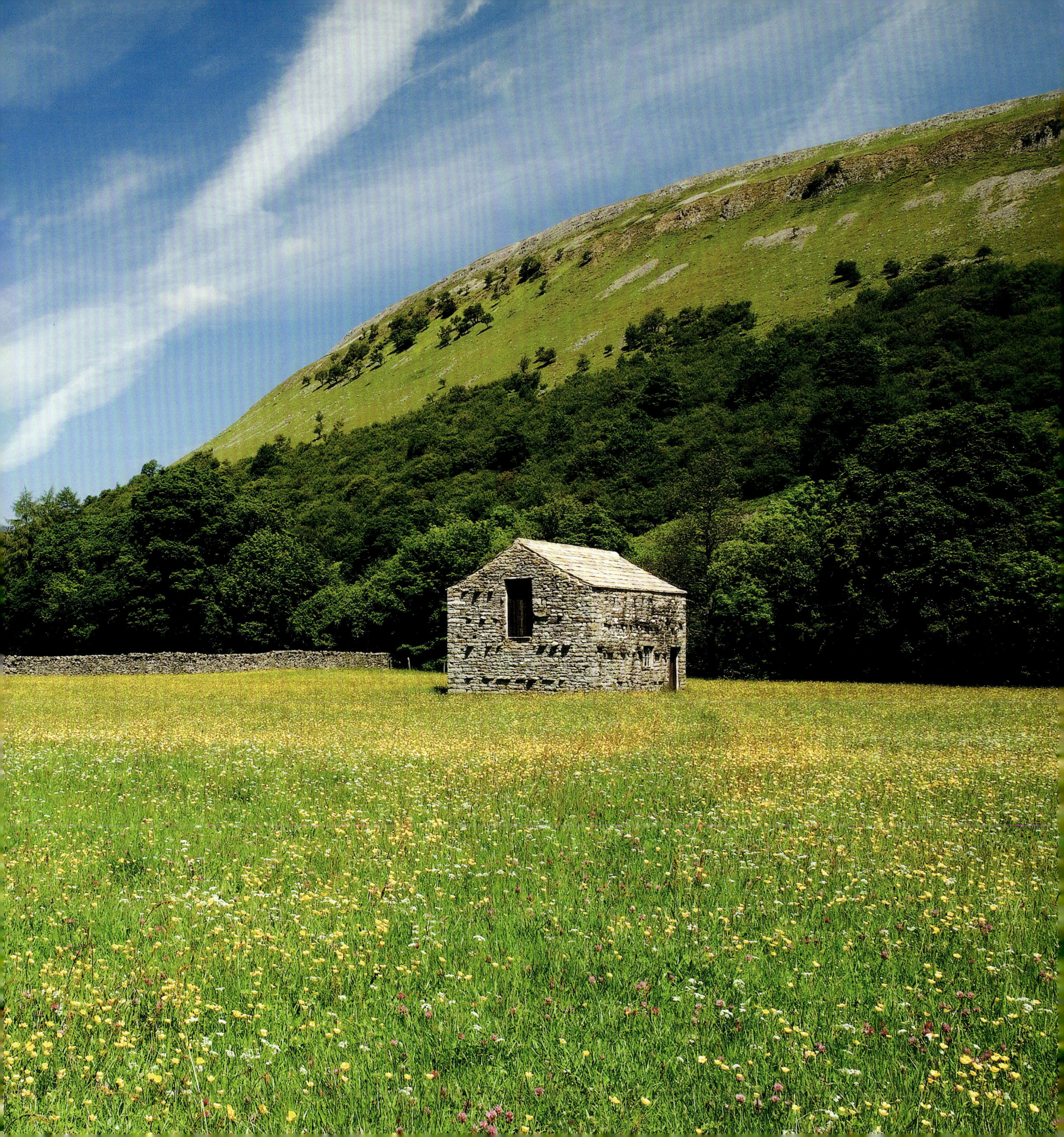

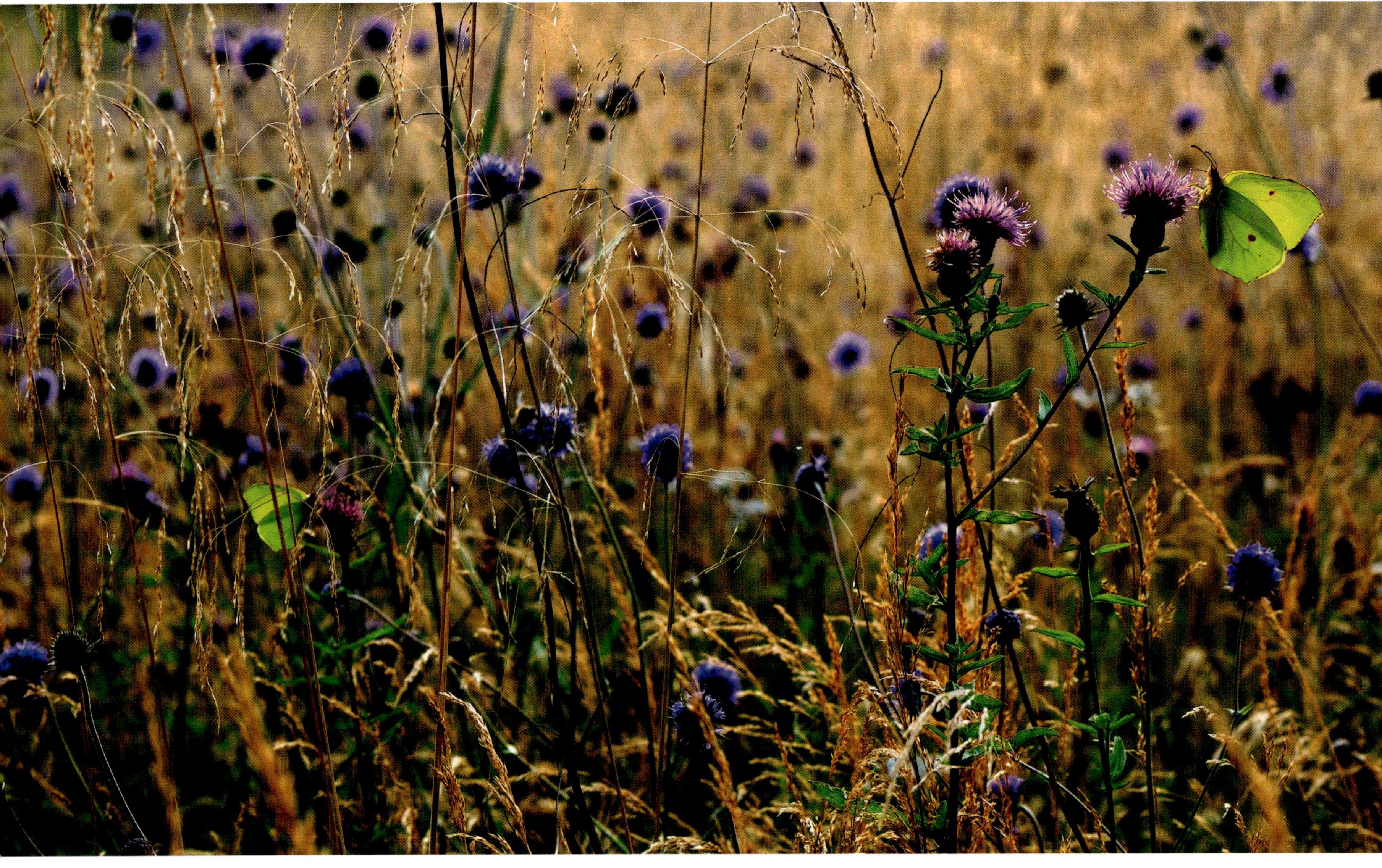

DANNY BEATH — HIGHLY COMMENDED

Scrubs Wildflower Meadow
Chambers Farm Wood, Lincolnshire, UK

This is a rare example of an undisturbed wild flower meadow with many associated scarce flowers and insects. It is a relic from a once much larger meadow that is now situated in a clearing in Chambers Farm Wood. I sat in the meadow for several hours before I finally got this composition.

Nikon D80, Sigma 70-300 macro lens, 1/300sec at f/10, ISO200. Post-capture: no digital alterations.

DANNY BEATH — FINALIST

Silver-studded Blue Habitat
Prees Heath Reserve, North Shropshire, UK

I had waited several years for the right day to take this photograph. I photographed these silver-studded blues (*Plebeius argus*) on, a nature reserve specially set up for these rare butterflies. The butterflies have a symbiotic relationship with the black meadow ant, which is only found in this type of dry acid heathland. I used a slow shutter speed to convey a sense of motion. Sitting low down in the heather, I quietly clicked away all through the calm, sunny afternoon as the butterflies displayed to each other on the clump of heather.

Fuji Velvia 50 film. Nikon FE2, Nikkor 55mm lens, 1/60sec at f/11. Post-capture: original slide scanned. Basic cropping and cleaning.

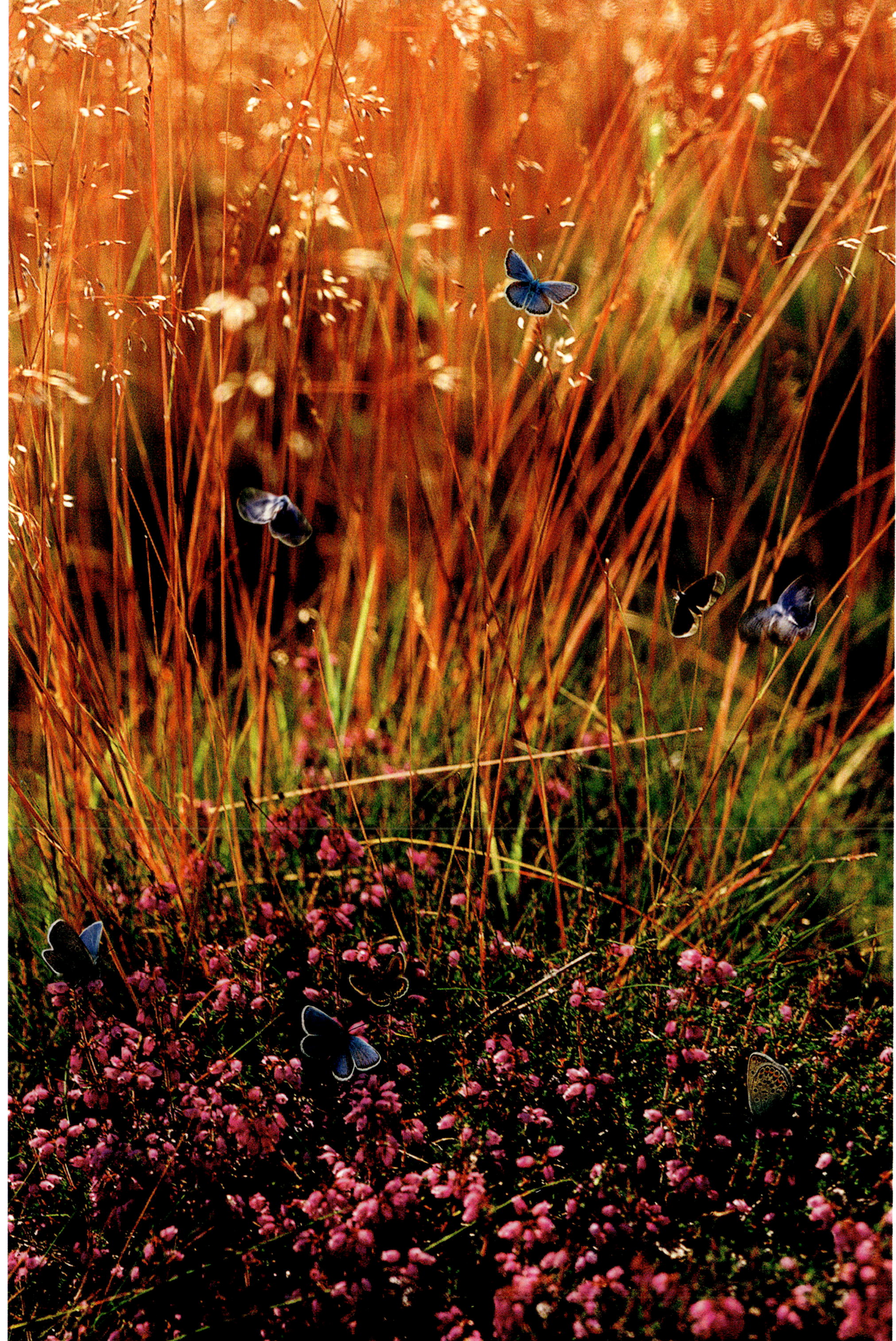

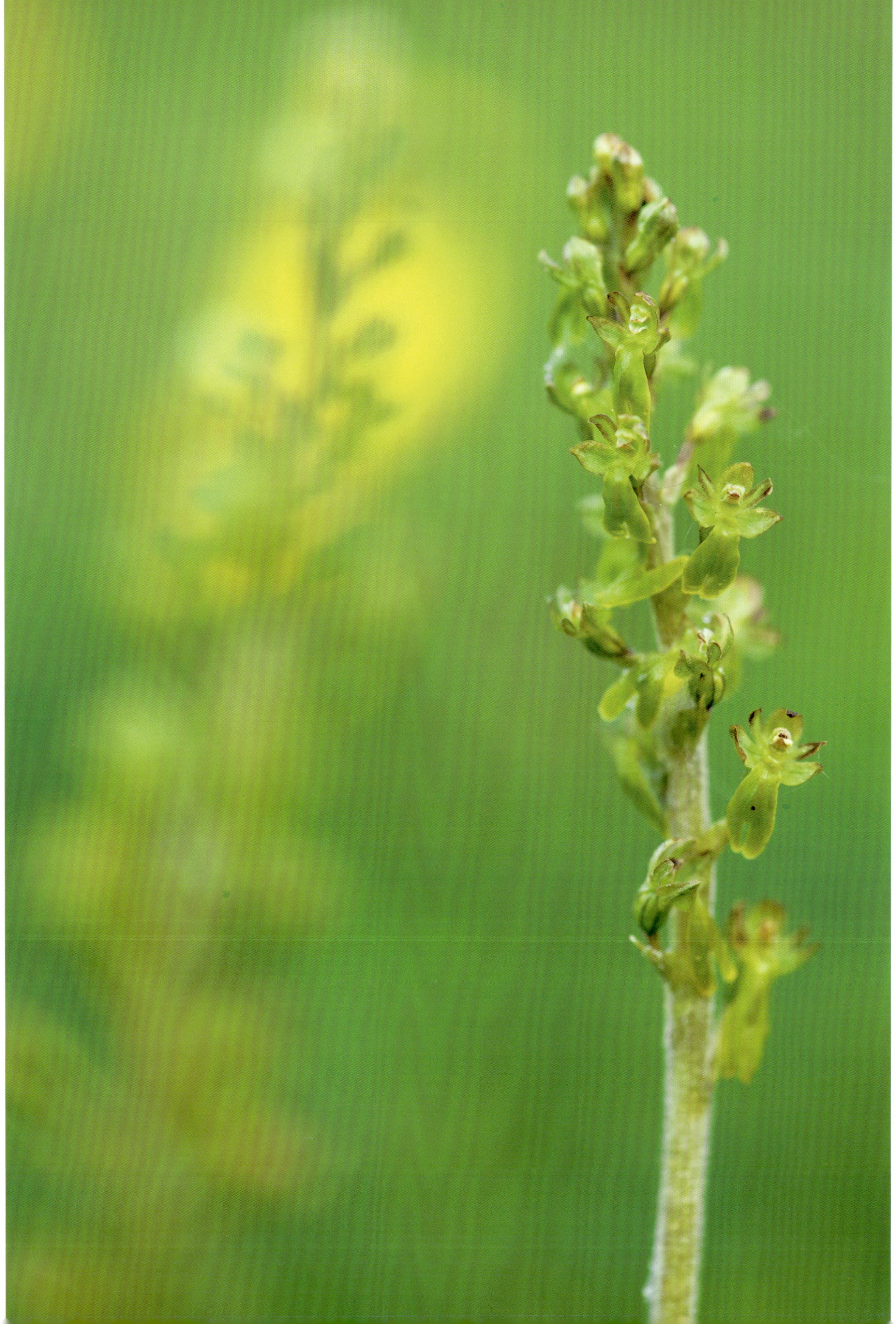

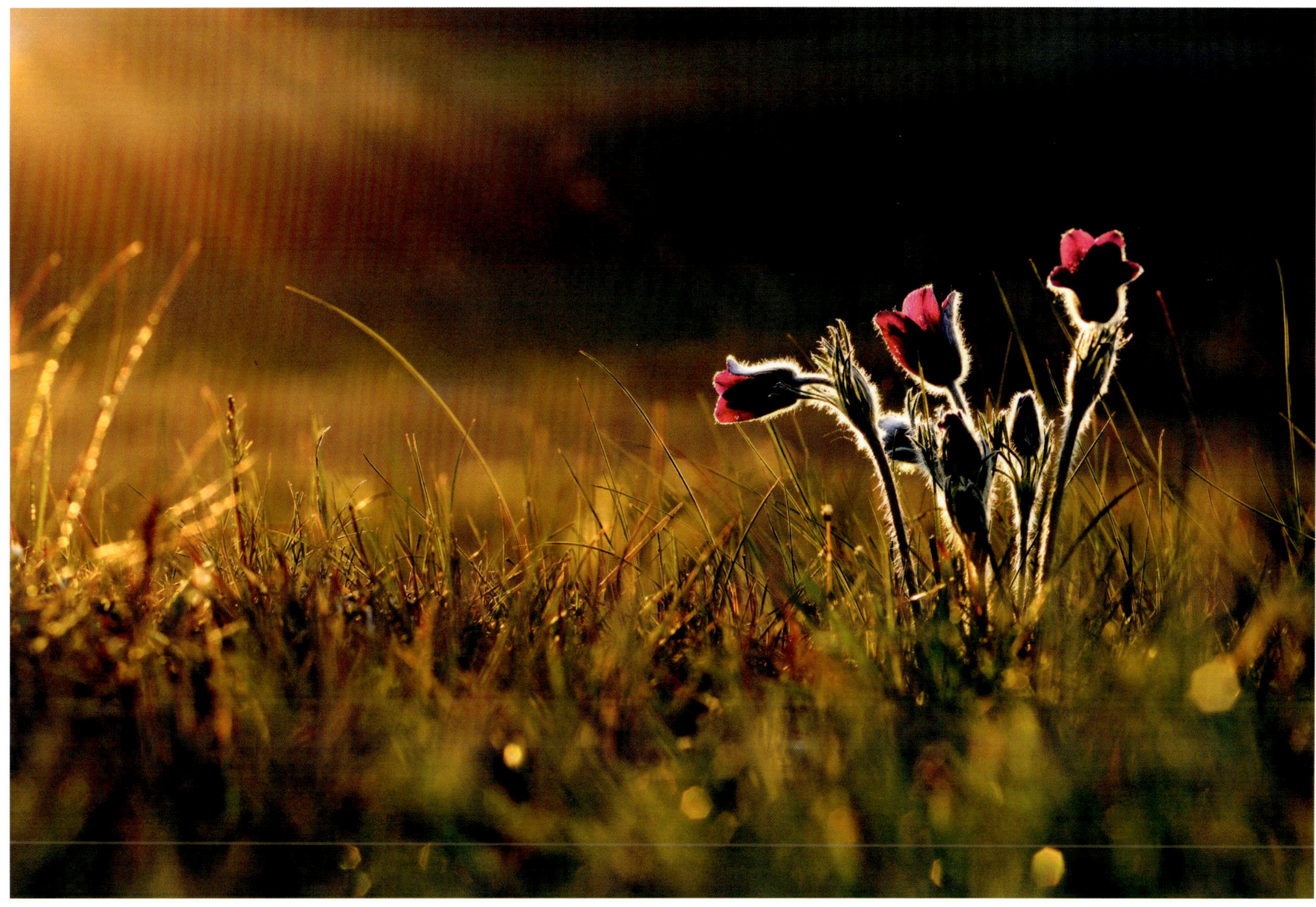

◄ **KIN CORNING** HIGHLY COMMENDED

Common Twayblade
Park Gate Down (Hector Wilks Reserve), Kent, UK

The chalk downlands of Kent where this photograph was taken, Surrey where we live, and other counties of southeast England are rich in orchids and I have been working to photograph them for the past several years. This photograph was taken from a low perspective at a moderately wide aperture, creating the smooth green background. Flower photographs need something extra to be interesting, and in this case it is the silhouette of the second twayblade framed by the yellow of a buttercup.

Nikon D3, Nikkor 105mm lens. 1/160sec at f/5. Post-capture: tone and levels adjustment.

▲ **JEAN DU BOISBERRANGER** HIGHLY COMMENDED

Pulsatilla vulgaris
Causse Méjean, Cévennes National Park, Languedoc Roussillon, France

I was taking pictures for a book about wild flowers in Cévennes, showing the great diversity of plants in this area, and the dry Causse Méjean plateau which is covered with hundreds of different plants. The bright red colour of the *Pulsatilla vulgaris* makes it for me the symbolic flower of this area. As I wanted to show the magnificence of this flower in its environment, I had to lie on the ground among the thistles. I faced the last ray of sun to get this gold colour to match the flower's feathery edges and colour.

Nikon D300, Nikon 105mm lens. 1/160sec at f/8 using a tripod. Post-capture: no digital alterations.

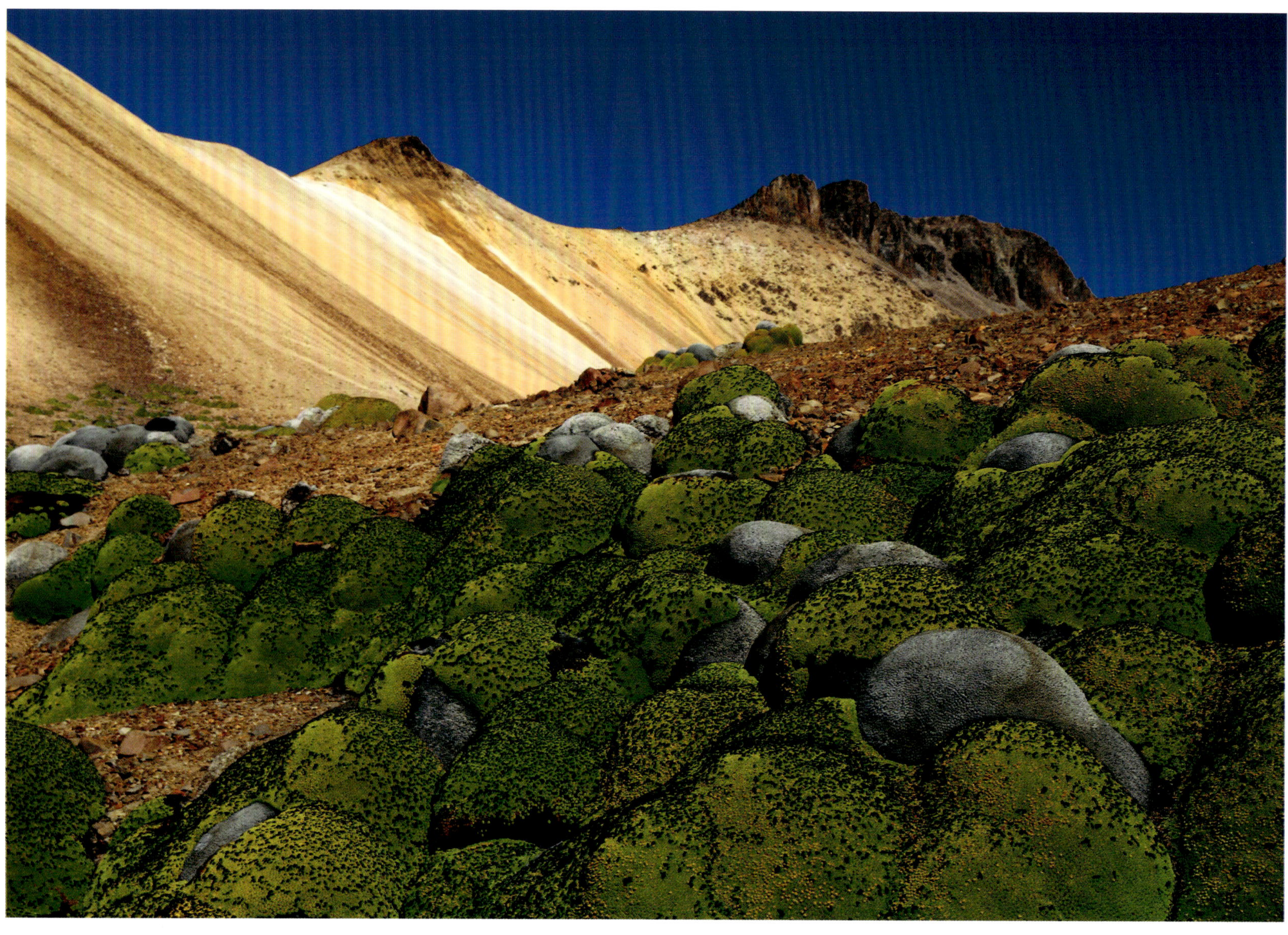

ANGELA ROWLANDS — HIGHLY COMMENDED

Altiplano Landscape Cushion Plants
Parque Nacional Lauca, Chile

This plant is *Azorella compacta* known as yareta: the Andean cushion plant. As I drove up the rough gravel track, the terrain became more and more stony. I came to this area with an expanding mass of these cushion plants: the vivid green contrasting against the blue sky. I got down low on the ground to show the cushion nature of the plant. I took it as a landscape to see the numbers of plants and the fantastic pattern they made in the landscape.

Canon 5D Mark II 24-105 f/4 zoom lens at 58mm. 1/30 sec at f/18 ISO 100. Post-capture: basic colour management.

ALAN MAHON — HIGHLY COMMENDED

The Approaching Storm
Bannow Bay, Co. Wexford, Ireland

It always amazes me how sea thrift ekes out a living, sometimes growing on bare rock without any sort of shelter. I took this photograph during the May thunderstorms. The approaching storm emphasizes what these plants endure during their lives.

Canon 5D Mark II, Canon EF 16-35mm f2.8L lens (at 16mm), 1/500 sec at f/8 ISO 100 using a 0.9 graduated neutral density filter. Post-capture: some tonal adjustment.

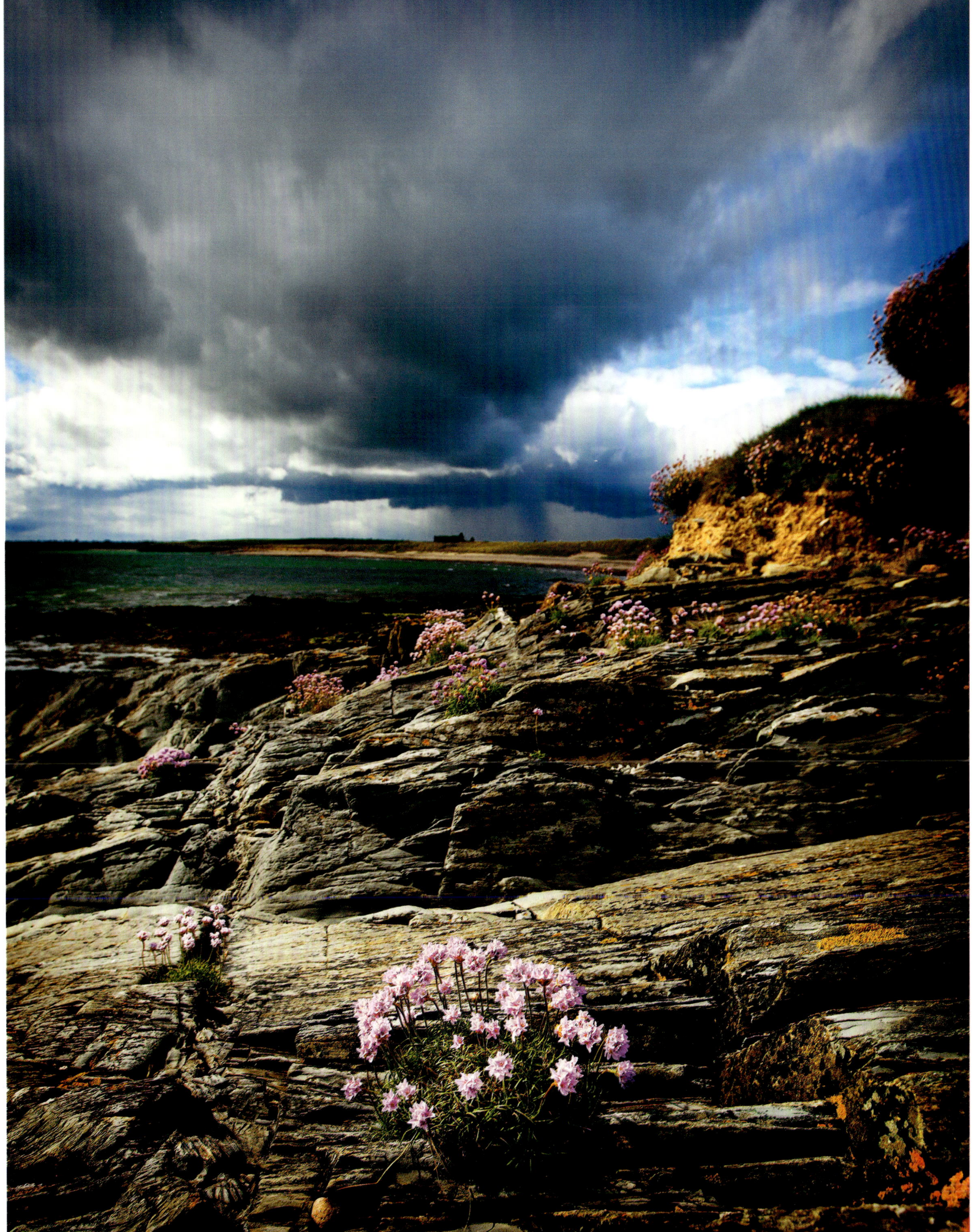

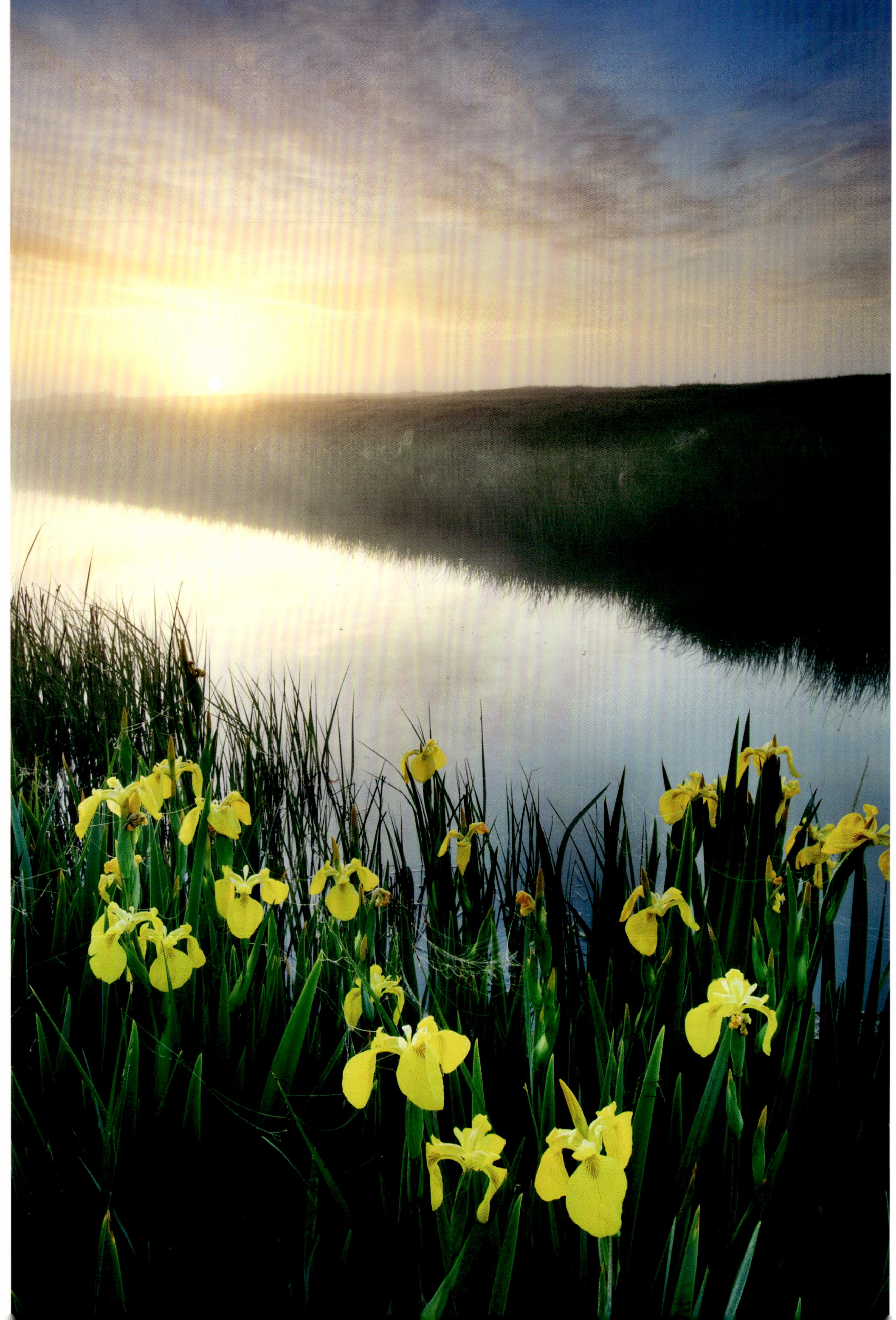

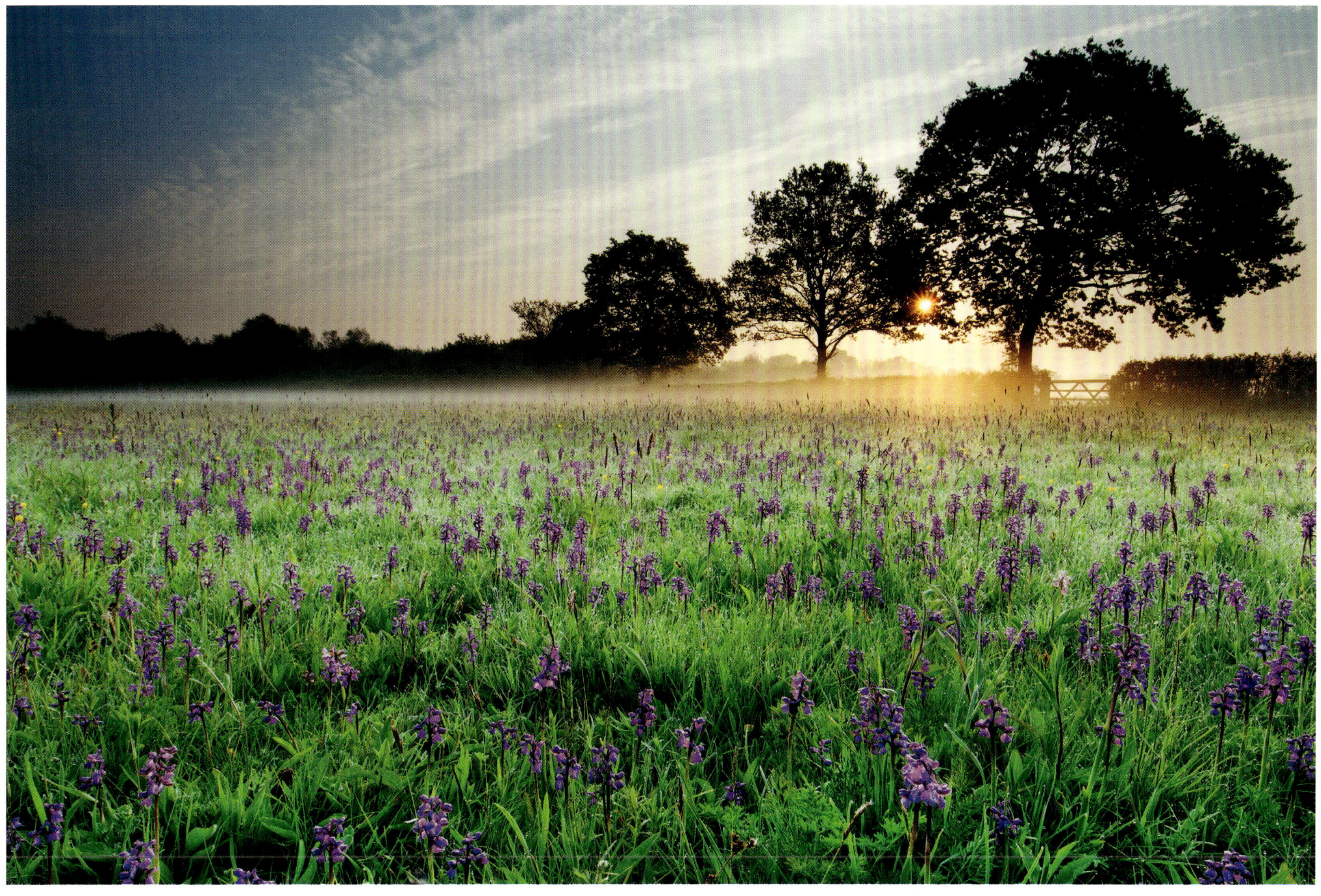

◄ **ROBERT CANIS** HIGHLY COMMENDED

Marsh Sunrise
Elmley Marshes, Kent, UK

Marshes are generally quite monotonous so when I came across this group of irises the colour leapt out at me, as did their isolation on this vast expanse of marshland. It was a perfectly still morning where both the cloud formation and dissipating mist enhanced the atmosphere. I initially spotted them a few days prior to making this image and really wanted to capture their isolation and atmosphere of the marshes in spring. I arrived at dawn following a clear, still night, set the camera up on the tripod and waited for the mist to gradually clear. In order to retain detail in both the foreground and sky, I took two exposures a few seconds after one another to create a neutral density graduated filter effect.

Nikon D2X, 12-24mm lens at 18mm. 1/5 sec at f/16. Post-capture: exposures merged.

▲ **ROBERT CANIS** HIGHLY COMMENDED

Meadow Sunrise
Marden Meadow, Marden, Kent, UK

Each year thousands of green-winged orchids can be seen flowering in Marden Meadow. There are few places left in the UK where thousands of orchids grow in such a small area and I wanted to convey this. I visited the site on three consecutive mornings, each time seeking out a viewpoint to do the scene justice. On the third morning, the conditions were perfect and I found the composition I had been searching for. A neutral-density graduated filter was used to reduce the exposure in the sky.

Nikon D2X, 12-24mm lens at 14mm. 1/8 sec at f/16. Post-capture: removal of a distant distracting grass seed head.

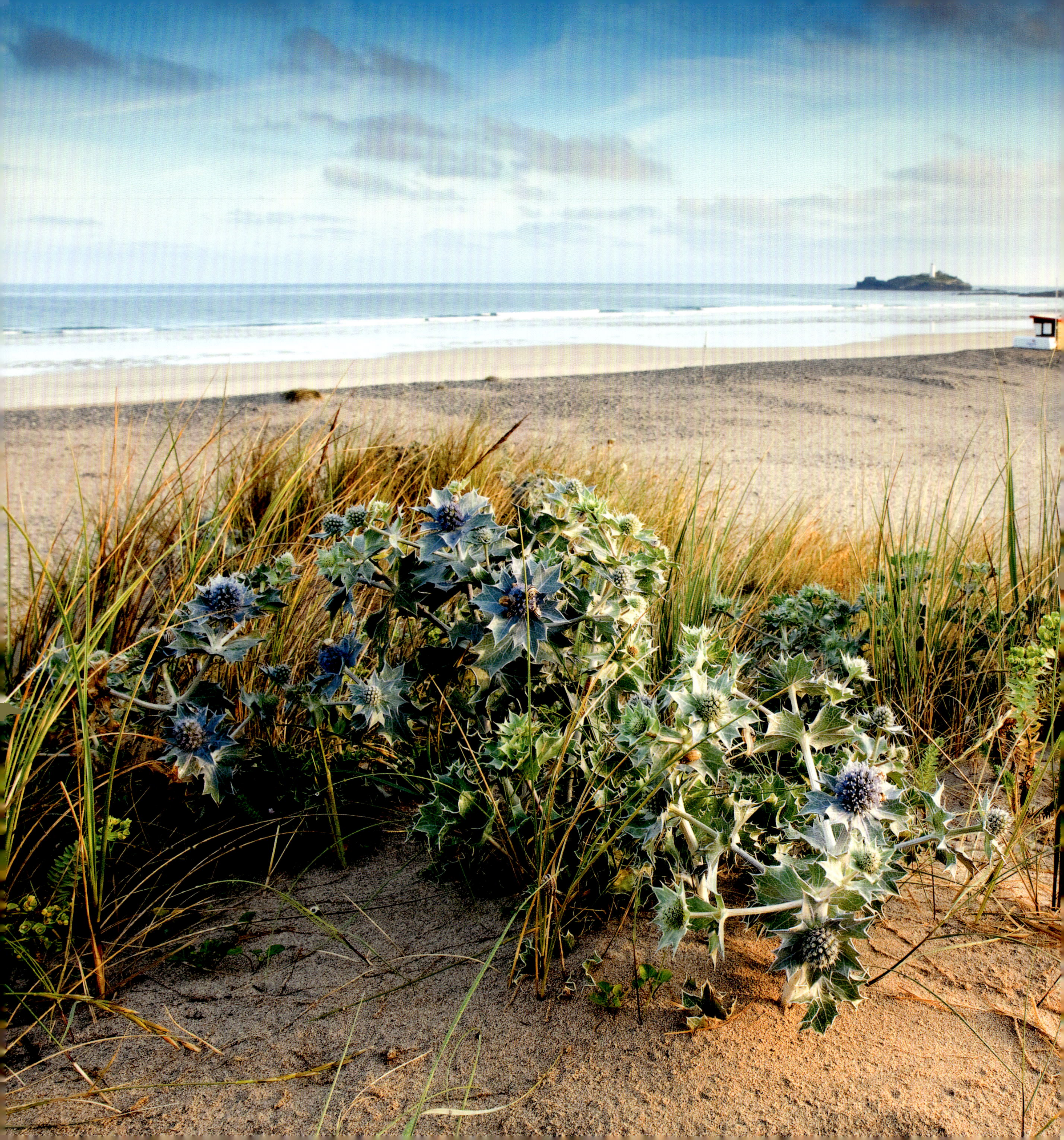

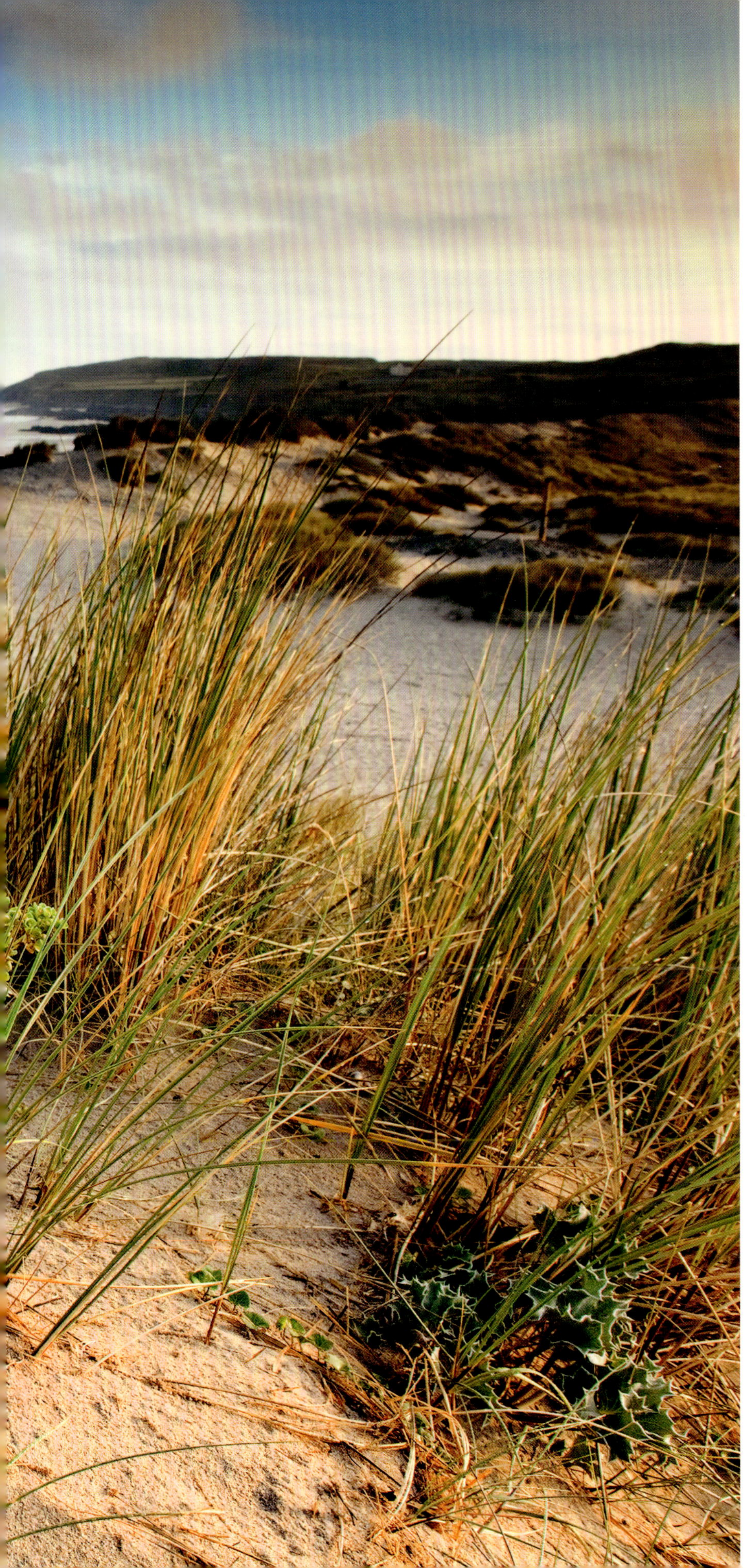

◄ **DAVID CHAPMAN** FINALIST

Sea Holly

St Gothian Sands, near Hayle, Cornwall, UK

I went regularly to this location until I found some sea holly in flower on top of the dunes. Having found the right plant, I returned early in the morning to make best use of the light. I positioned the camera on a tripod close to the plant, focusing on the plant but leaving enough space to allow some detail of its environment to be included. I also used the lighthouse to give a distant focal point.

Canon EOS 5D Mark II, 24mm lens. 1/20sec at f/16. Tripod. Post-capture: basic colour management.

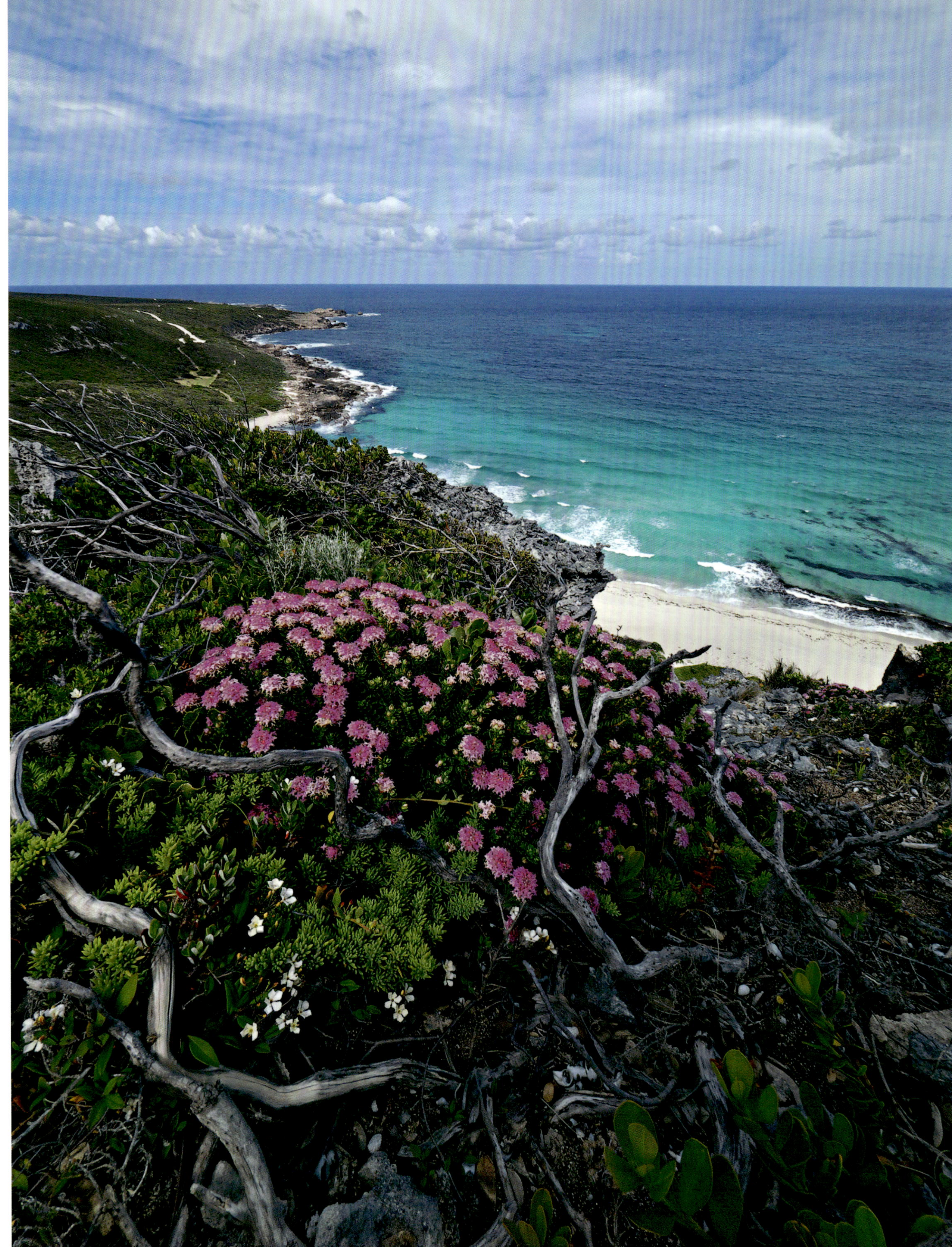

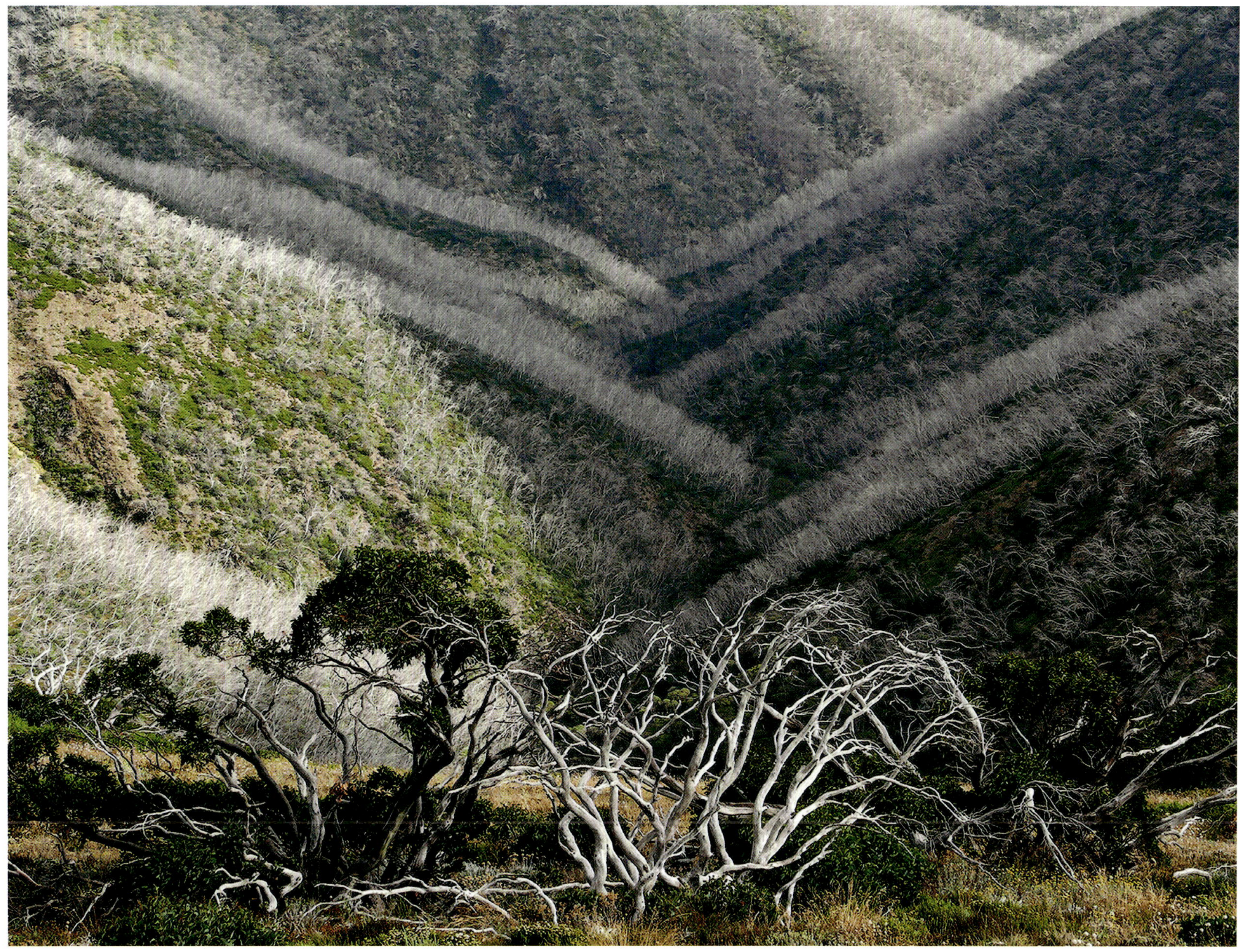

GARY STEER HIGHLY COMMENDED

On the Edge
Leeuwin-Naturaliste National Park, Australia

Though the coast is rugged and the seas wild, the vegetation on this edge of the continent can be fragile. One of the biggest threats is severe summer bushfire. In the foreground is the rice flower (*Pimelea ferruginea*). I had heard much about the Cape to Cape Walk, particularly the profusion of wildflowers in spring and summer, so I decided to do the walk to take photographs of the area. The concept was to get an image of a beautiful, delicate plant in its challenging habitat.

Panasonic DMC - G3 Lumix, G Vario 7-14 mm ASPH lens, 1/80 sec at f/18. Post-capture: small amount of cropping.

GARY STEER FINALIST

Snowgums after the Fires
Mount Feathertop, the Alpine National Park, Victoria, Australia

While a severe fire can kill what is above ground, this plant has the ability to regenerate from lignotubers underground that have been protected from the heat. This form of regeneration can be seen sprouting in the foreground. I wanted to capture the very unusual pattern of the ridges and at the same time show the cause of it in the foreground trees.

Panasonic DMC FZ50, 1/160 sec at f/6.3. Post-capture: no digital alterations.

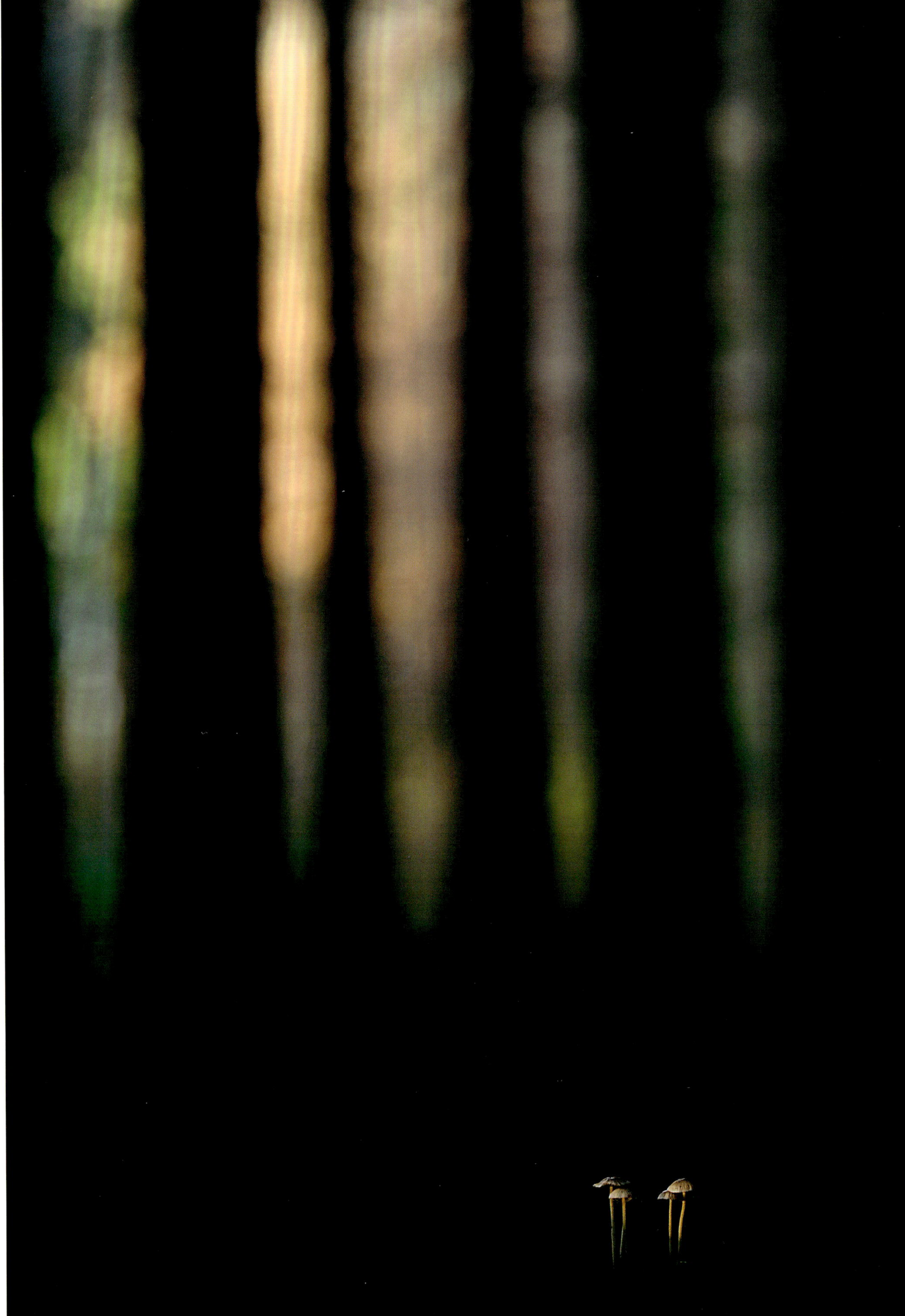

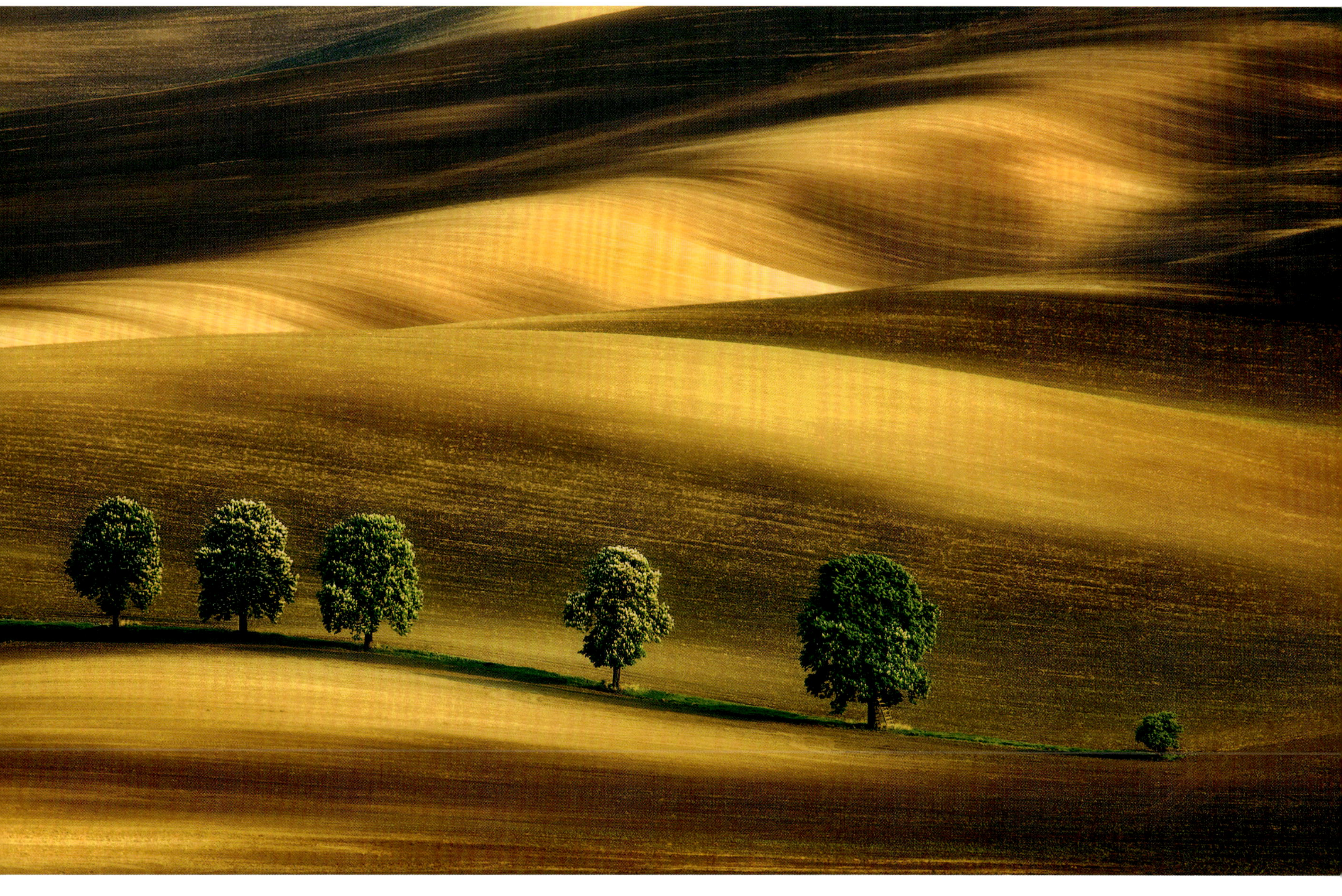

◄ **KERERES ISTVÁN** 1ST PLACE

Forest Dwellers
Salzkammergut, Austria

This pine forest is in the Salzkammergut region of Austria. Just as I was sitting on the ground I noticed a small group of fungus ("*Mycena*"). I lay on my stomach and looked for a suitable composition.

Nikon D3, Nikkor 80-400 mm lens. 1/100sec at f/4.8. Post-capture: sharpening, a little cropping, and slight lightening.

▲ **KRZYSZTOF BROWKO** 2ND PLACE

Six…
Kyjov, Southern Moravia, Czech Republic

The colourful patches on the soil are caused, most probably, by erosion. This phenomenon, which is characteristic of this region, is often mistaken for shadows cast by clouds. The undulating landscape of Moravia is perfect for me to get the results I want.

Canon EOS 5D Mark II, Canon 100-400mm lens. 1/6sec at f/18. Post-capture: adjustment of crop and levels.

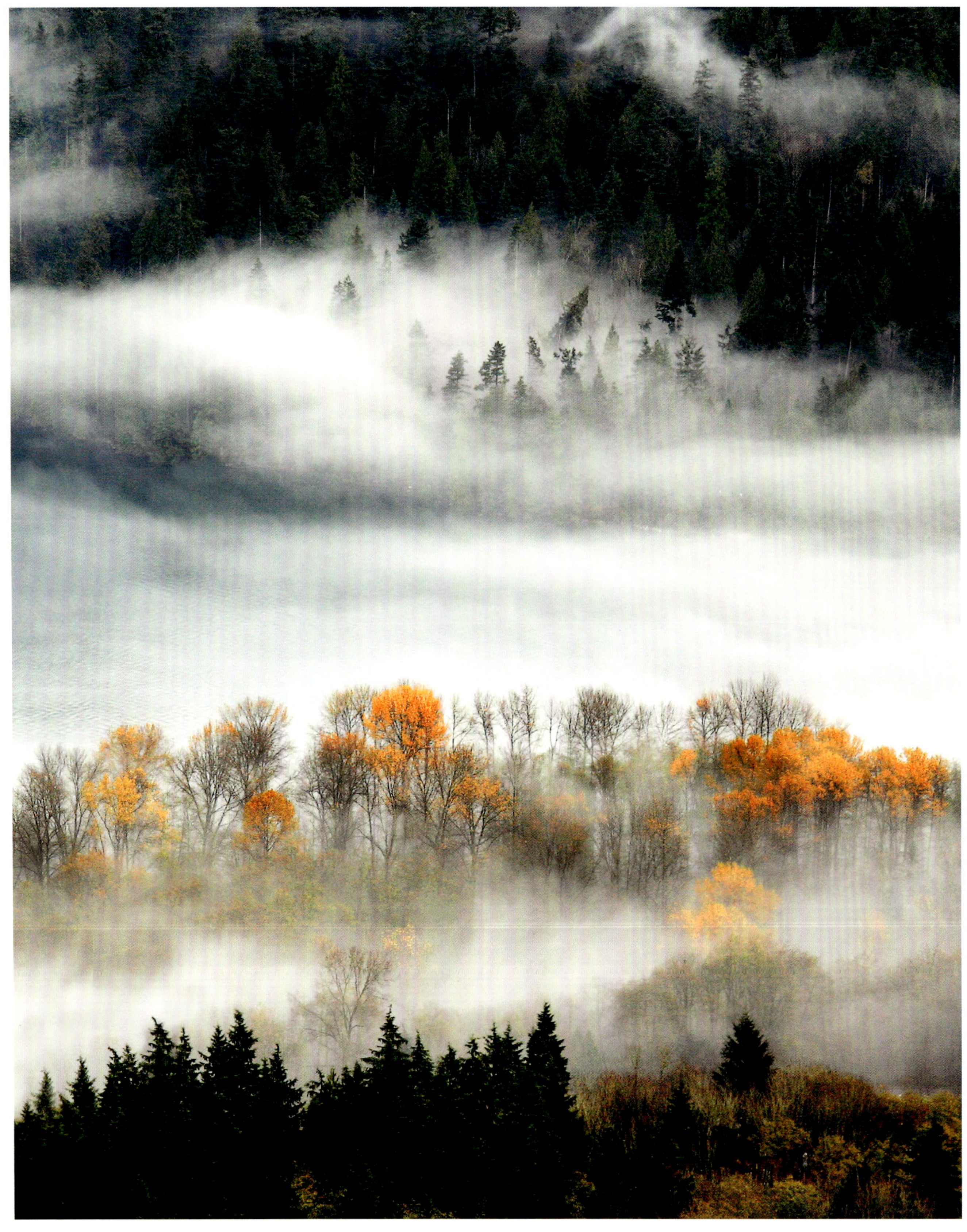

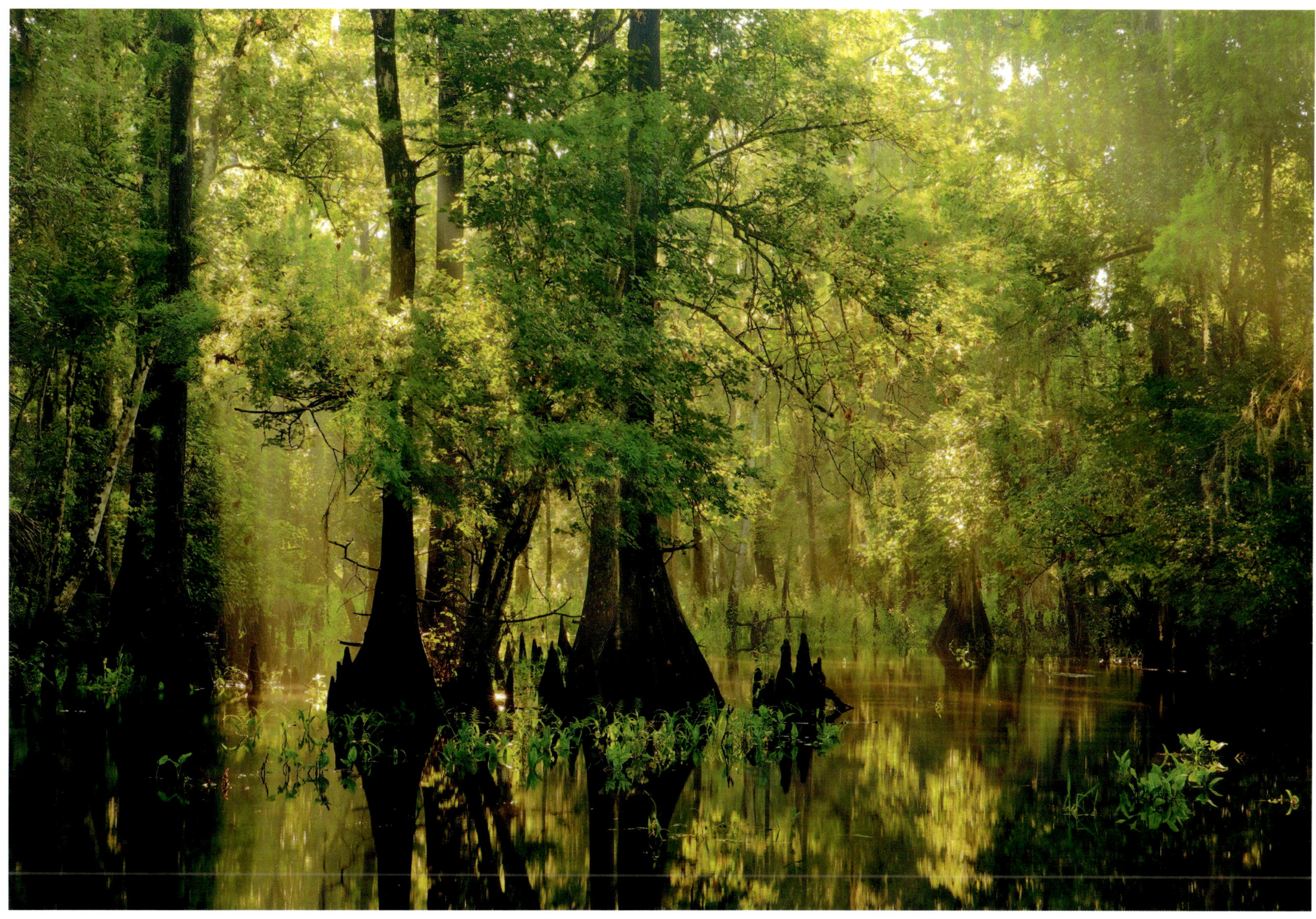

◄ **GLORIA KING** 3RD PLACE

Trees in the Mist
Burnaby Mountain, British Columbia, Canada

I had been up to Burnaby Mountain many times. With the weather forecast for fog clearing by midday, I made my way up, camera in hand. Initially the fog was a white blanket, covering everything at the lower levels. I waited as the scene evolved and this image emerged.
The scene was dynamic - the fog and light drifting and changing. An extra challenge came from photographing from behind a security fence and finding a clear view through bushes and trees.

Canon EOS Digital Rebel XT, Canon 17-85 mm lens. 1/650sec at f/5.6. Post-capture: cleaning, cropping and levels adjustments.

▲ **PAUL MARCELLINI** FINALIST

Fisheating Creek Backwaters
Fisheating Creek, Florida, USA

Fisheating Creek is the last free flowing stream to feed Florida's big Lake Okeechobee. Truly 'wild Florida', it offers a great opportunity to escape amongst the flooded cypress and take in all the forest has to offer. After the thunderstorm had passed, the added humidity diffused the light as it streamed through the trees. Standing waist deep in dark water was a bit daunting, but I took the time to compose around the 'island' of isolated trees and bracketed three exposures to handle the tonal range of light. I took several compositions, but this showcased the best parts of the scene.

Canon 5D Mark II, Tamron 28-75 lens. 2, 1.2, and .5 second exposures at f/16. ISO 200. Post-capture: I took three exposures that were then blended together by hand using luminosity masks. This helped control the dynamic range and allow for more detail in the highlights and shadows. After that, a bit of contrast work and a slight vignette to focus the eye on the center of the image.

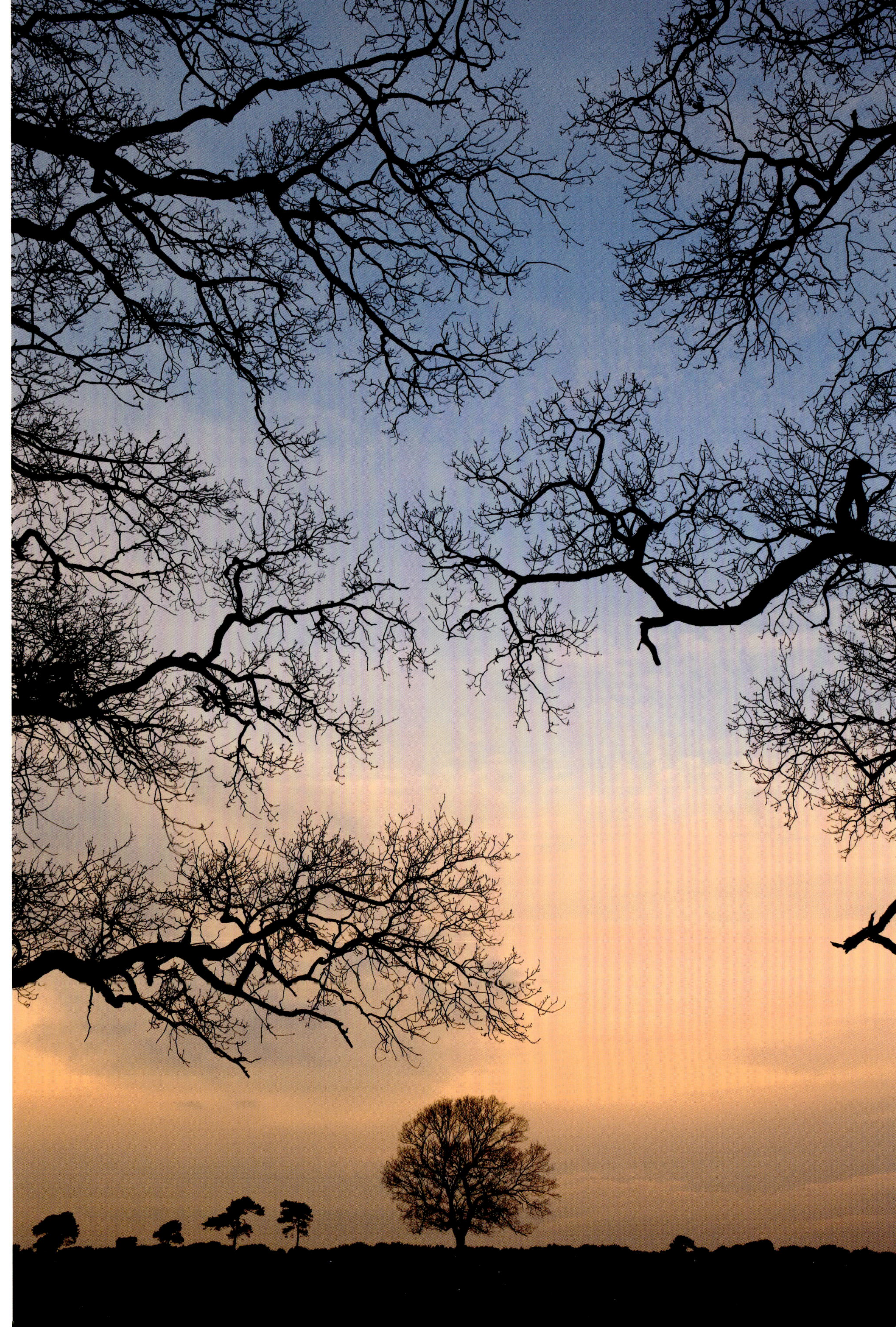

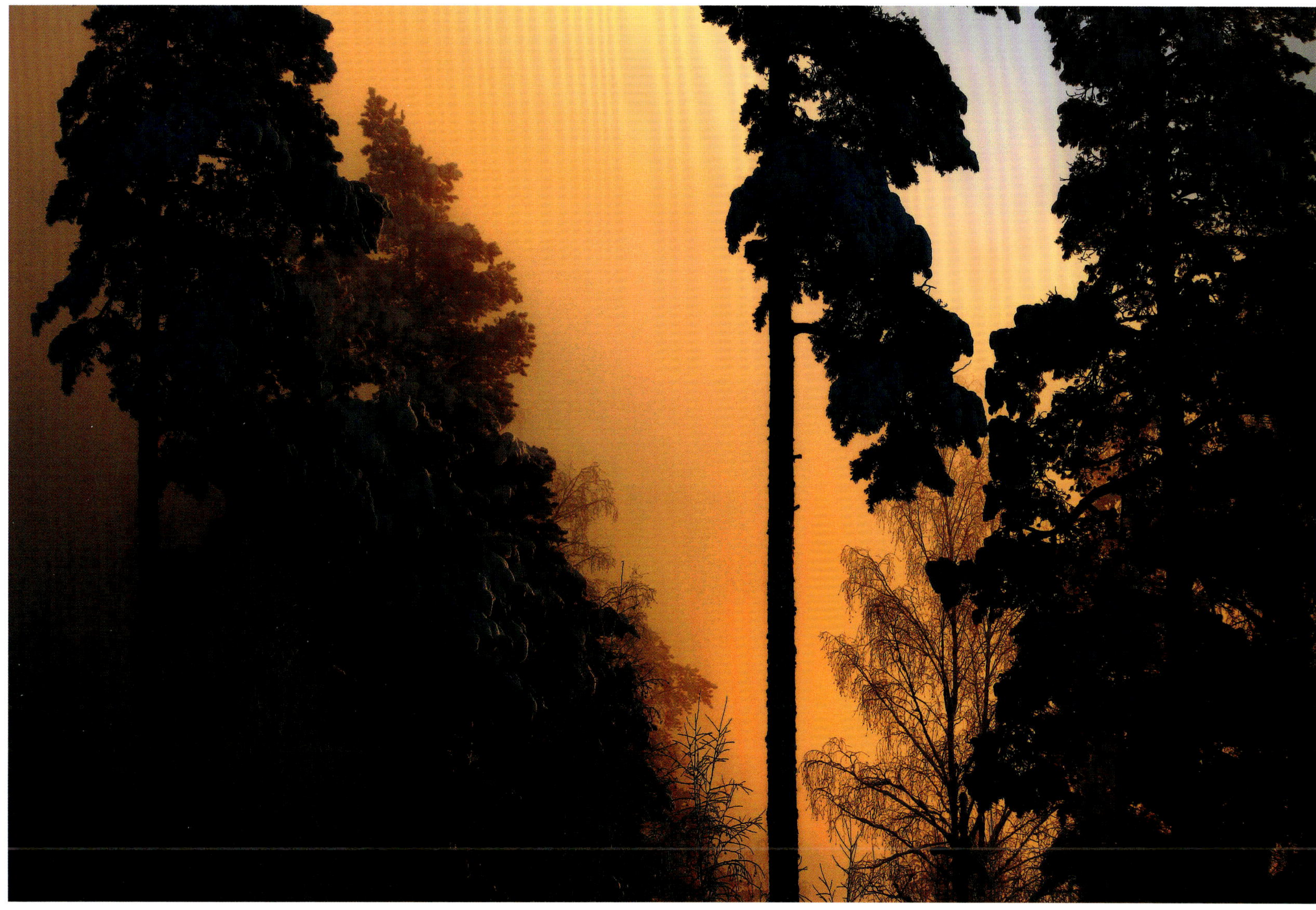

◄ **ADAM BURTON** HIGHLY COMMENDED

Striving for Perfection
New Forest National Park, Hampshire, UK

I have visited and photographed Backley Plain in the New Forest many times over the years, so on this occasion I was looking for something fresh and new. I decided to move in low and close to two mature oak trees. I fitted a wide angle lens and stood almost directly below the branches, tilting the camera up to make the most of the branches. I spent a few minutes refining my position until I could find a composition where the branches fitted together like a jigsaw, yet not touching.

Canon EOS 1DS Mark III, Canon 24-70mm lens. 1/6 sec at f/19. Post-capture: no digital alterations.

▲ **BROR JOHANSSON** HIGHLY COMMENDED

Golden Light
Avesta, Sweden

It is very cold in midwinter and the trees are snow-covered. To the right the sky is clear, but fog is emerging. The sun is setting and the sunlit fog is getting more colourful: that is why I like this scene so much.

Canon EOS 20D, Canon EF 75-300 mm lens. 1/320sec at f/6.3. Post-capture: colour balance adjustment.

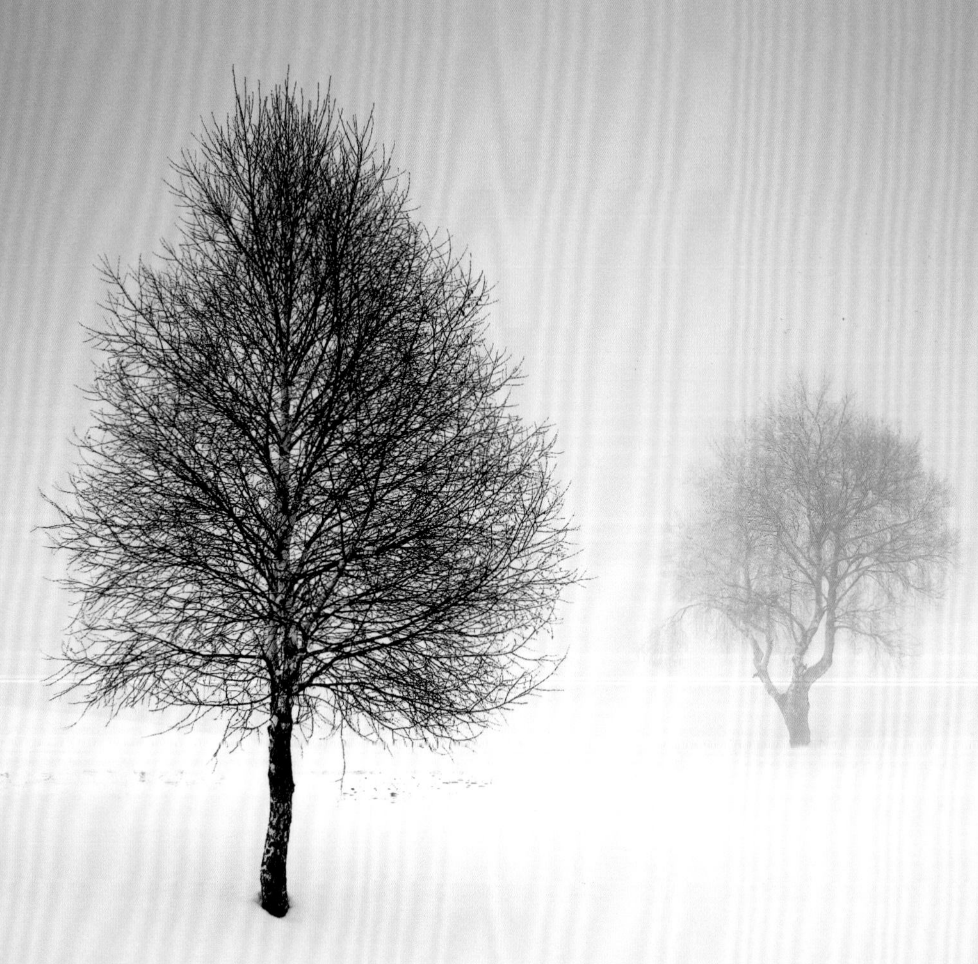

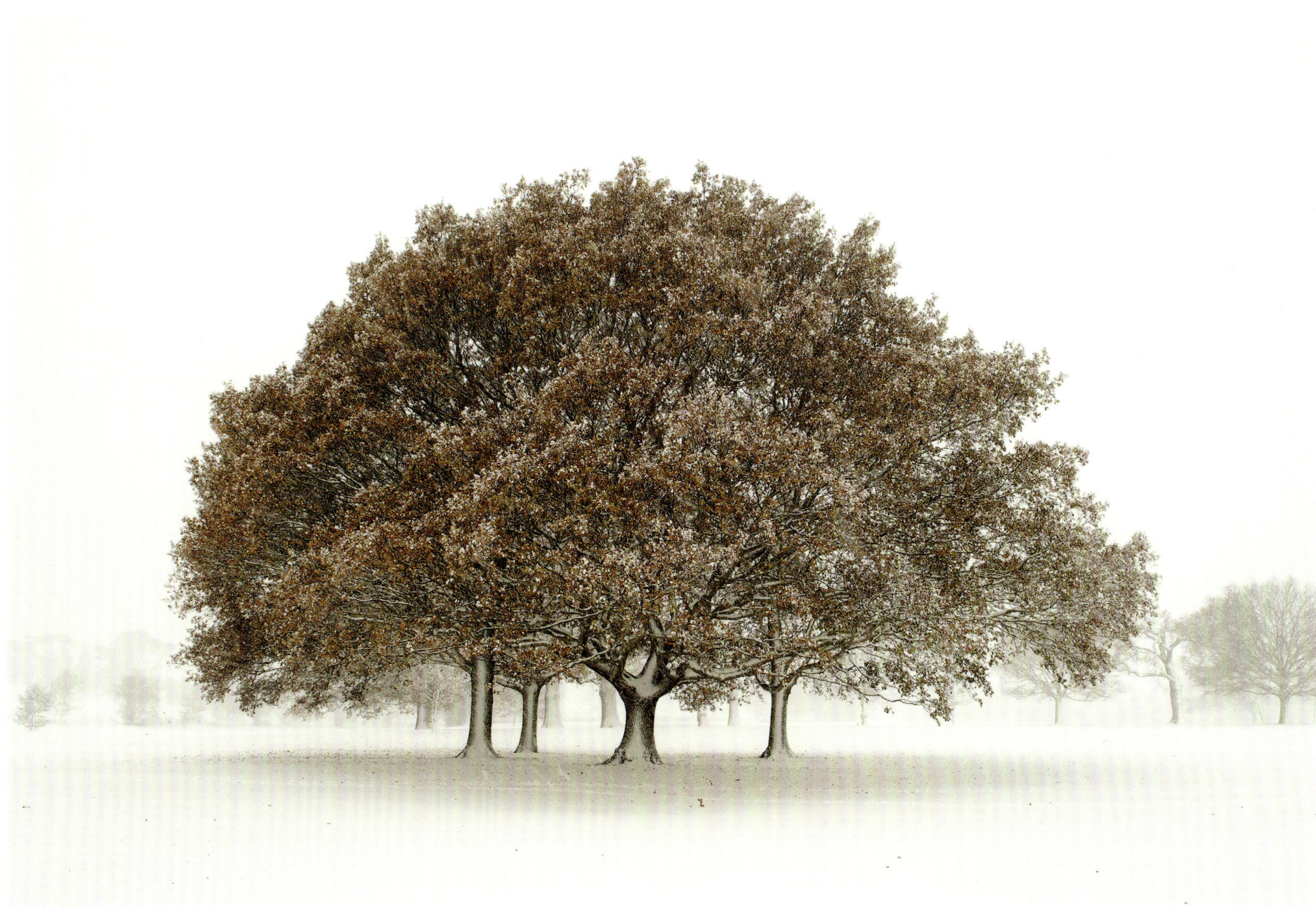

◄ **PIERRE PELLEGRINI** HIGHLY COMMENDED

Trees in Fog II
Capriasca, Ticino, Switzerland

A winter landscape expresses a great sense of peace and quiet. The trees in the snow are wrapped in fog and cold, but in reality are more alive than ever. At first I just wanted to try the first shot because the weather changed quickly. Then I turned around to the subject, being careful to leave no tracks in the snow. It is amazing how you can find many compositions in the same subject.

Hasselblad 503CW with Phase One P20, Hasselbald Distagon 4/40mm lens. 1/8sec at f/16. Post-capture: black and white conversion.

▲ **PETER STEVENS** HIGHLY COMMENDED

Early Snow 2
Rothamsted Park, Harpenden, UK

Branches form a semi-circle, set against the recession of tones in the background. I spent some time moving around the subject to separate and balance the main elements in the composition. I was keen to minimise the overlap between the main tree and those in the background. The lighting was very bright so the exposure had to be carefully handled.

Nikon D700, 24-70mm Nikkor lens, 1/125sec at f/8. Post-capture: no digital alterations.

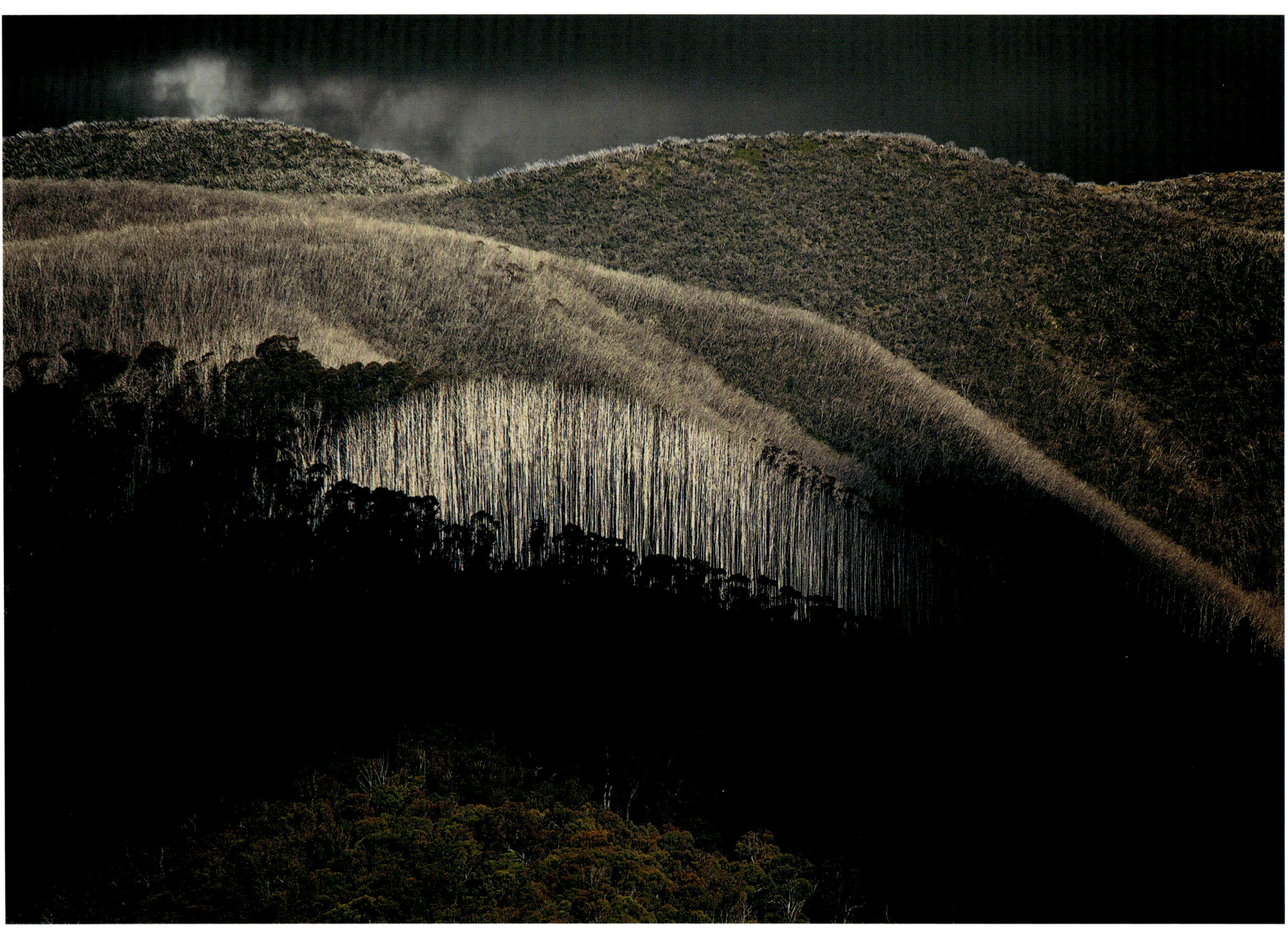

GARY STEER HIGHLY COMMENDED

Ash in the Alps
Mt Hotham, in the Alpine National Park, Victoria, Australia

Alpine ash (*Eucalyptus delegatensis*) is a sub-alpine or temperate tree of south-eastern Australia. In suitable conditions it can grow to heights of over 90 metres. Parts of this forest were burnt by bushfires. Because I was in the valley, a long way from the effect of the light, I used a tele-zoom at its longest focal length, 500mm.

Canon EOS 5D Mark II, Sigma 50-500 mm lens. 1/320sec at f/9. Post-capture: some slight sharpening.

SERGEY KAREPANOV FINALIST

Breaking
Parc de Sceaux, Paris, France

Avenue of trees in the Parc de Sceaux. It reminded me of a zipper. I lay down on my back and took a picture at maximum wide angle – wishing I had a fish-eye lens with me.

Canon EOS 5D, Canon 16-35 mm lens. 1/320sec at f/7.1. Post-capture: no digital alterations.

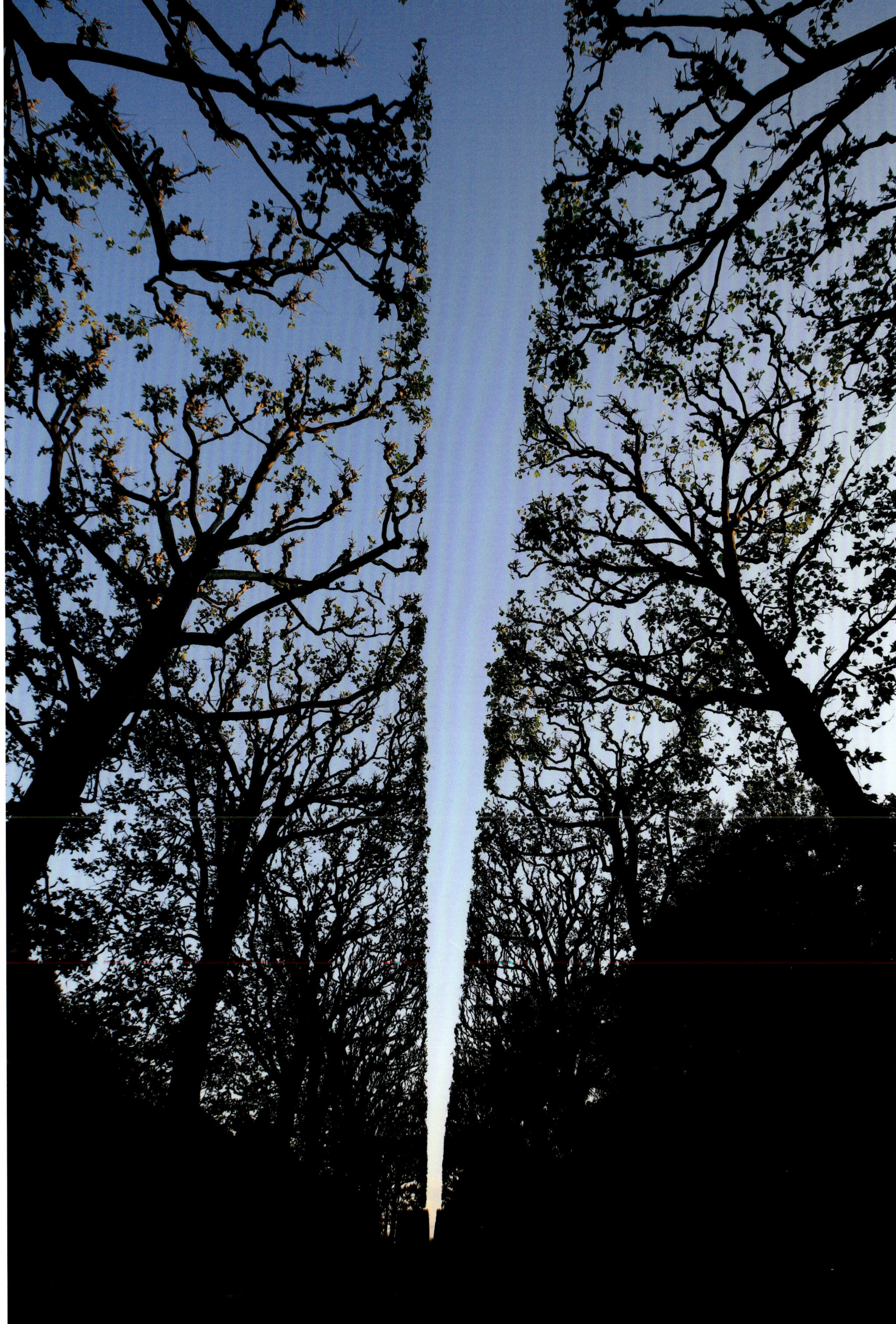

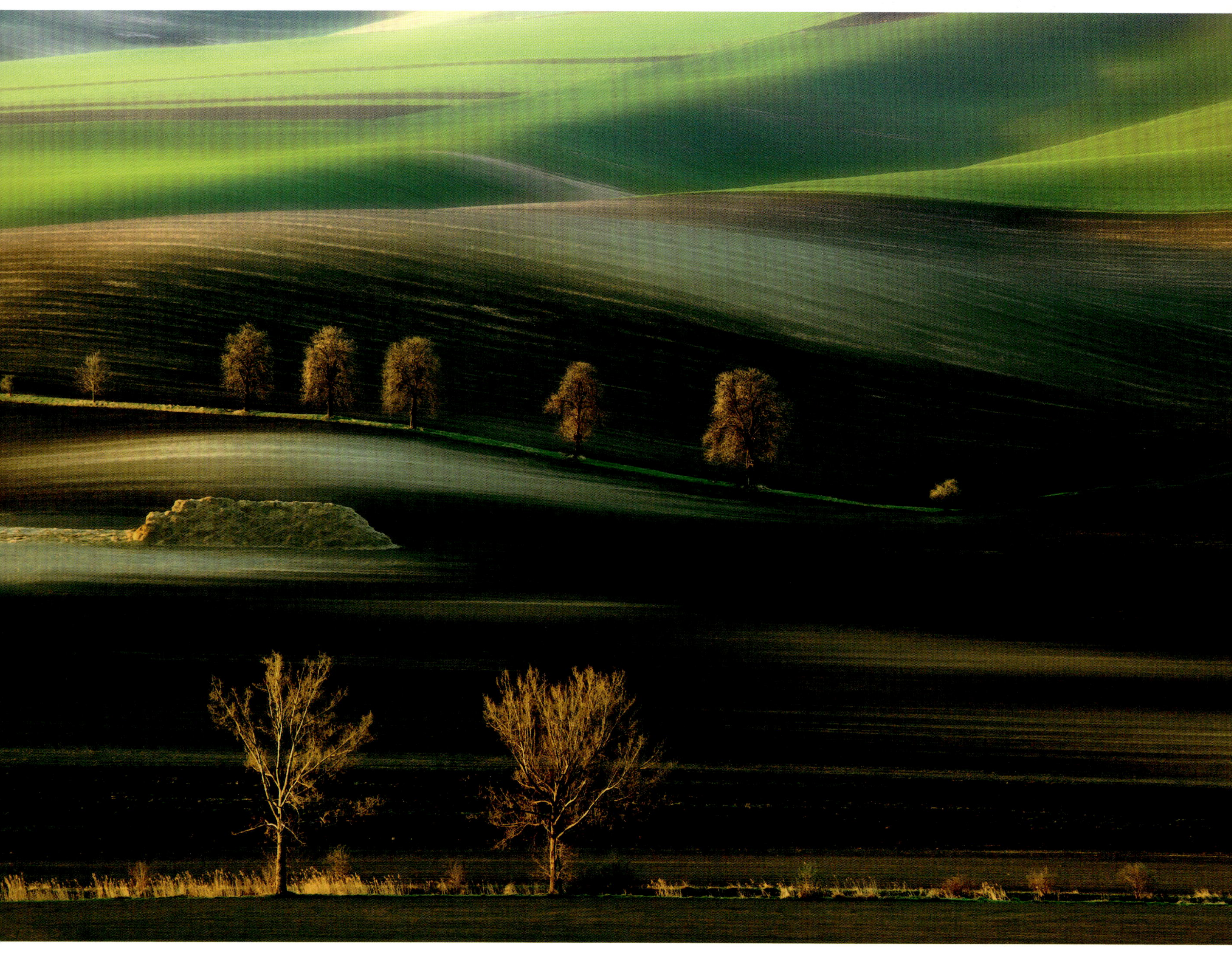

▲ KRZYSZTOF BROWKO HIGHLY COMMENDED

Ten...
Kyjov, Southern Moravia, Czech Republic

The rolling rural countryside is one of my favourite places to photograph. With a focal length of 100mm and more, you can spot some interesting parts of the landscape and at the same time shorten the perspective.

Canon EOS 5D Mark II, Canon 100-400mm lens. 1/10sec at f/16. Post-capture: adjustment of crop and levels.

IOANNIS SCHINEZOS AND ROBERTA PAGANO ► FINALIST

Pinus Texture
Naples Botanical Gardens, Italy

Sometimes barks offer lovely abstract textures but it is not always easy to find the exact scale for a nice composition. In this case I framed the bark of a Pinus sp. very closely by using a macro lens to register an abstract image.

Nikon D300, Nikkor 200mm lens. 1/80sec at f/18. ISO 200. Post-capture: no digital alterations.

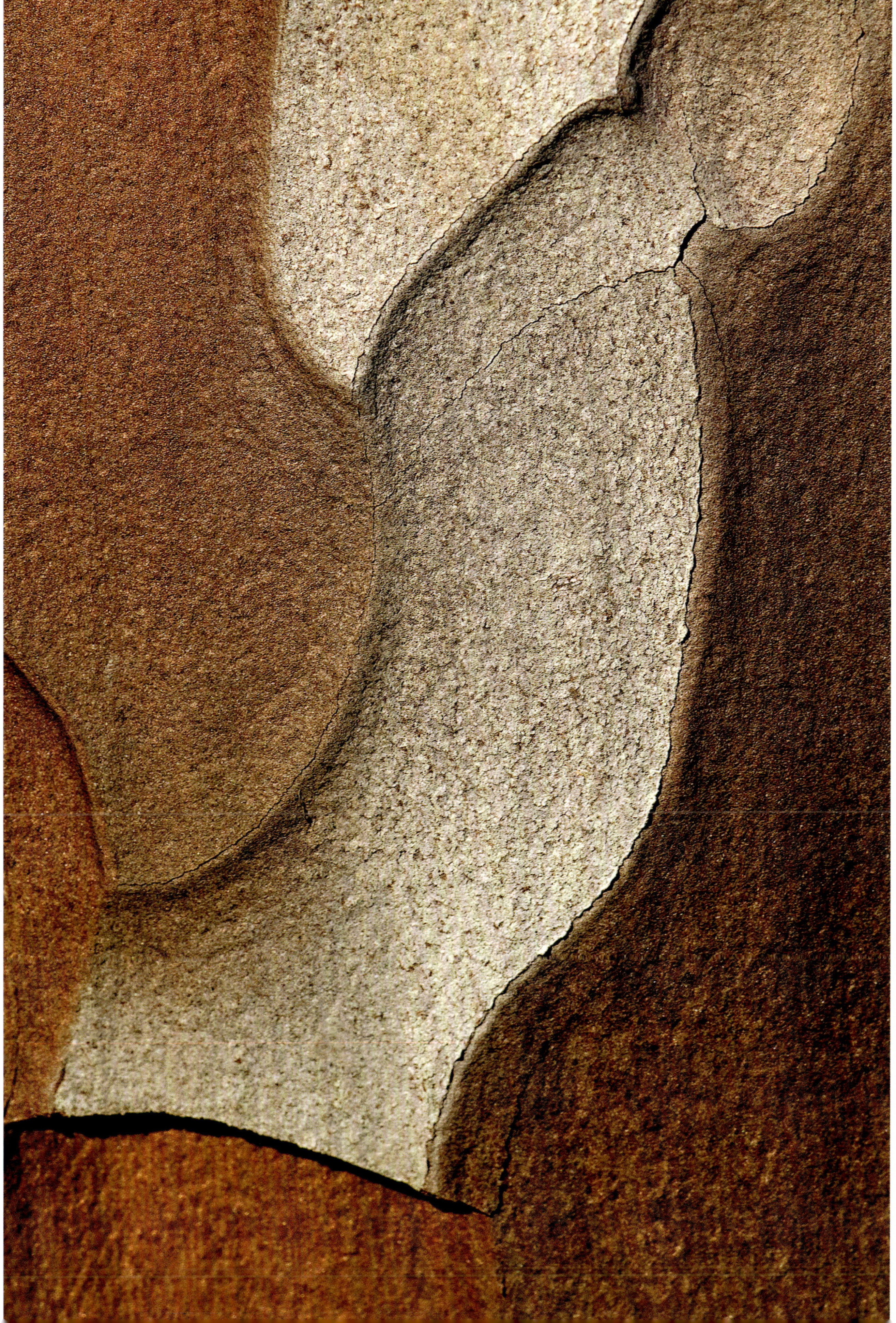

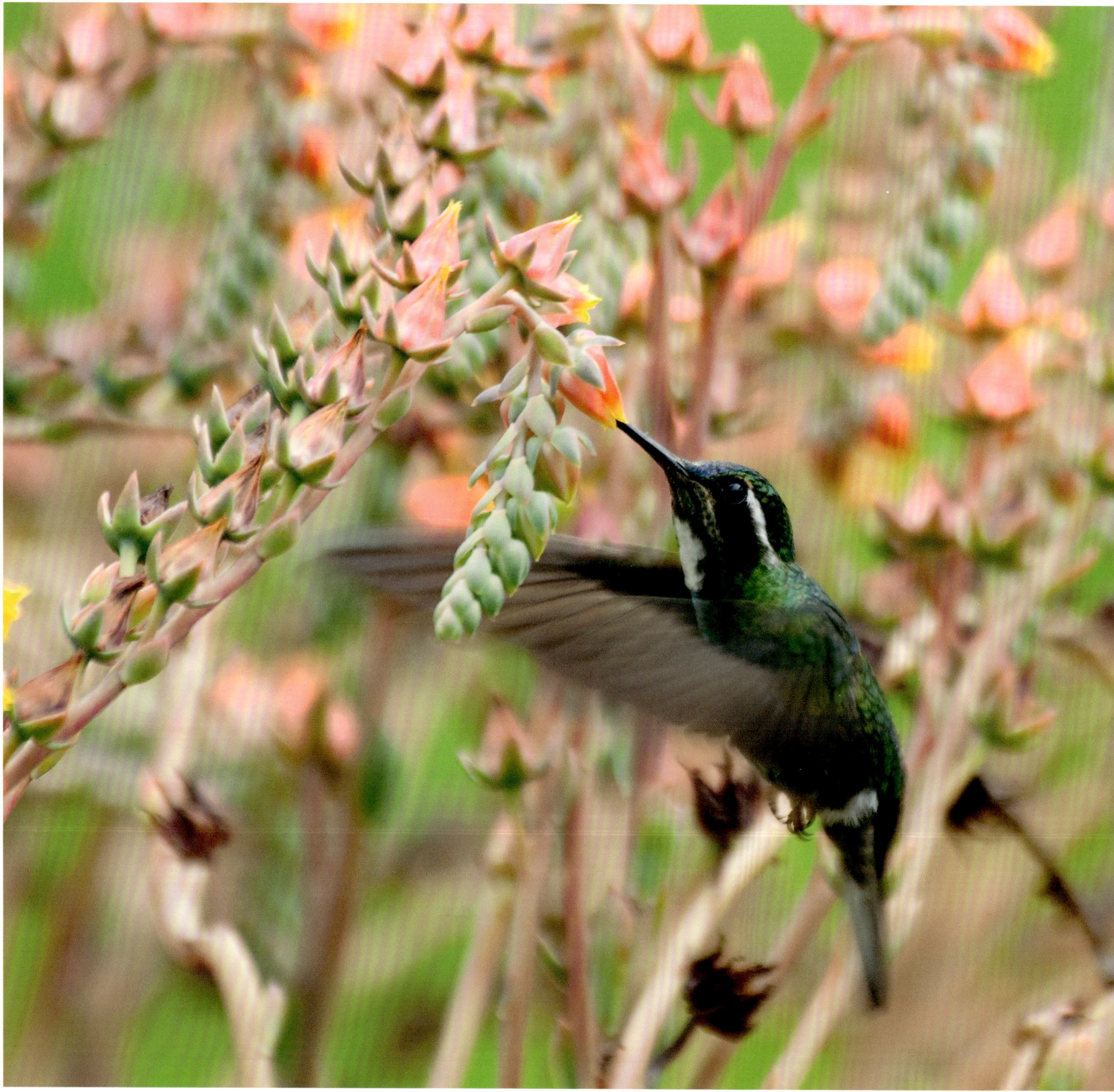

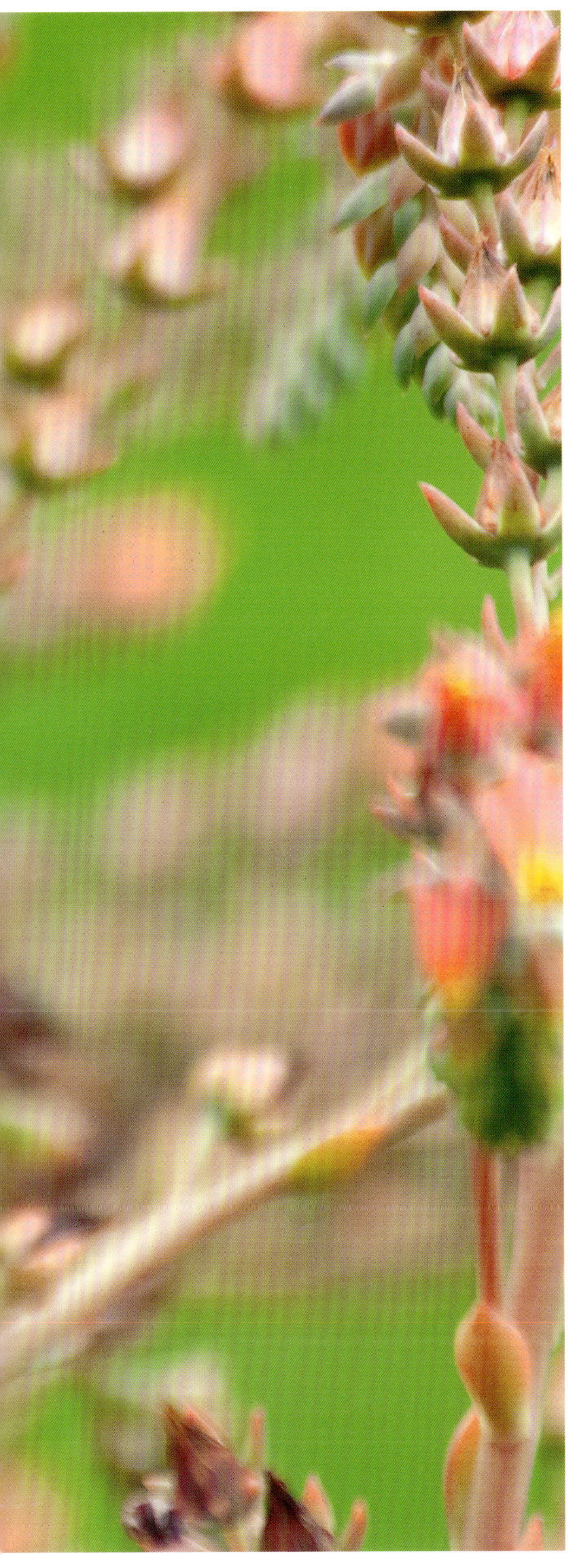

YOUNG GARDEN PHOTOGRAPHER OF THE YEAR

PATRICK CORNING

◄ **PATRICK CORNING – AGE 15** 1st Place, Wildlife Havens

Hummingbird (Grey-tailed Mountaingem)
Cordillera de Talamanca, Costa Rica

This hummingbird is a male Grey-tailed Mountaingem, shown feeding from garden flowers in the Cordillera de Talamanca mountain range in Costa Rica. I noticed that this bird was returning regularly to the same patch of cultivated flowers in the grounds of the lodge where we were staying, so I set up my camera and shot whenever the bird hovered in one place to feed.
This species is fairly common in the Cordillera de Talamanca, the major mountain range in the south of Costa Rica stretching to the Panama border. I enjoy all kinds of nature photography. When I was travelling with my family in Costa Rica, I spent a lot of time trying to photograph different birds near the lodges where we stayed. This photograph was taken using a telephoto lens from quite close range. These birds are not at all shy, so I was able to sit quietly in the open waiting for the bird to return to this patch of flowers.

Nikon D200, 80-400mm lens. 1/100sec at f/5.6 Post-capture: no digital alterations.

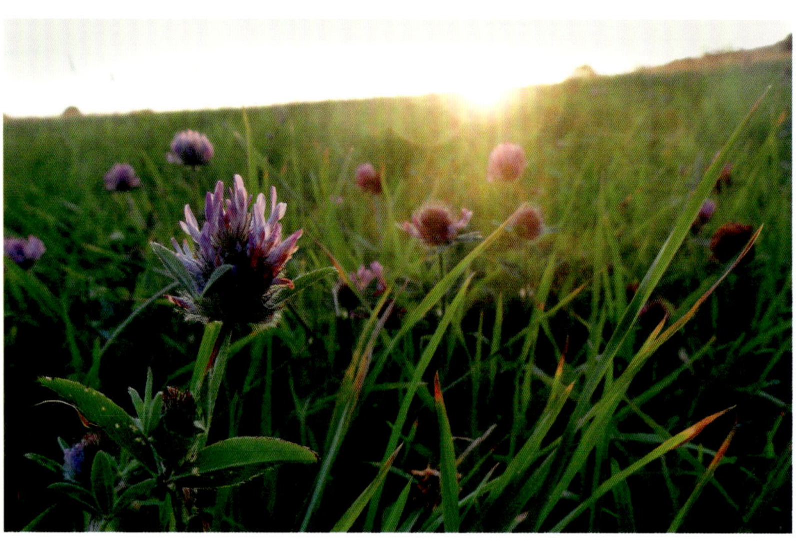

MARGUERITE CHALKLEY – AGE 13 2ND PLACE, FRAGILE LANDSCAPES

Downland Flowers
Isle of Wight, UK

The chalk downland of the Isle of Wight is home to loads of lovely wildflowers, many of which you do not see every day now. It was an amazing evening sky and the sun was lighting up the flowers in the field so beautifully. I particularly liked the way the colour of the red clover flowers glowed in the evening sun. I wanted to take a backlit shot which can be difficult. But I think it worked quite well as the sun was low by the time I took the photograph. I took it lying down in the grass and got very close to the flowers.

Sony Cyber-shot DSC-H55, 25mm wide angle lens. 1/40sec at f/4.0. Post-capture: slight cropping.

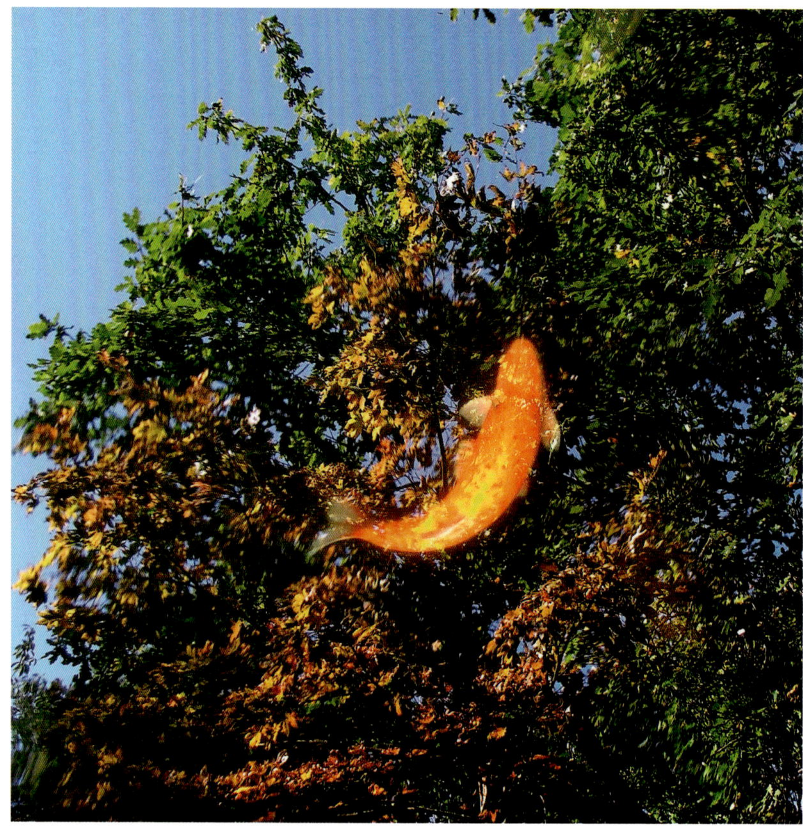

JASMINE CLEGG – AGE 10 3RD PLACE, BEAUTIFUL GARDENS

Spirit Fish
Japanese Gardens, Newquay, Cornwall, UK

A golden fish swimming through the reflection of the overhanging trees in the pond at the Japanese Gardens in Newquay, Cornwall. I liked the way it looked like the fish was swimming through the trees. I leant over the edge of the bridge that went over the pond and tried to get a photo just as a fish passed through the reflection.

Fuji Finepix S5000. 1/42sec at f/2.8. Post-capture: I cropped the photo into a square and turned it upside down, to make it look more like a garden view, with the sky at the top.

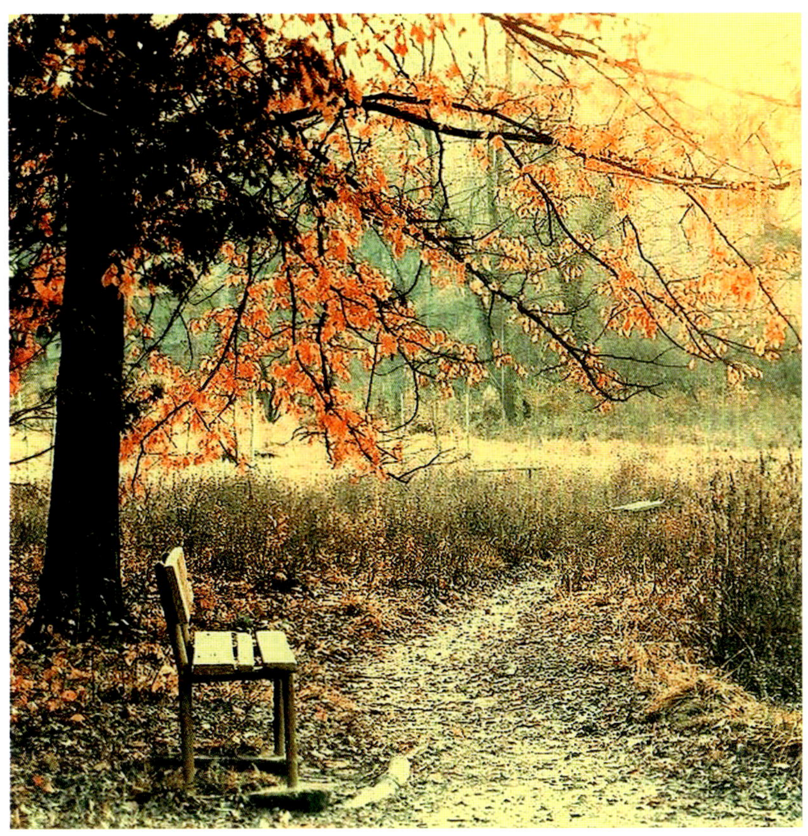

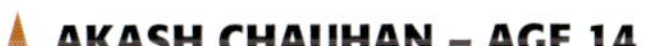

AKASH CHAUHAN – AGE 14 — HIGHLY COMMENDED, THE BEAUTY OF PLANTS

Colourful Leaves on a Half-dried Tree
Sevoke, near Siliguri, India

When I was passing by the forest near Sevoke, my eyes just went to the half-dried tree. It was the only tree there with colourful leaves and it looked beautiful near the dry forest. I had my camera with me and I asked my uncle to stop so I could take this shot.

Nikon S3100. Post-capture: no digital alterations.

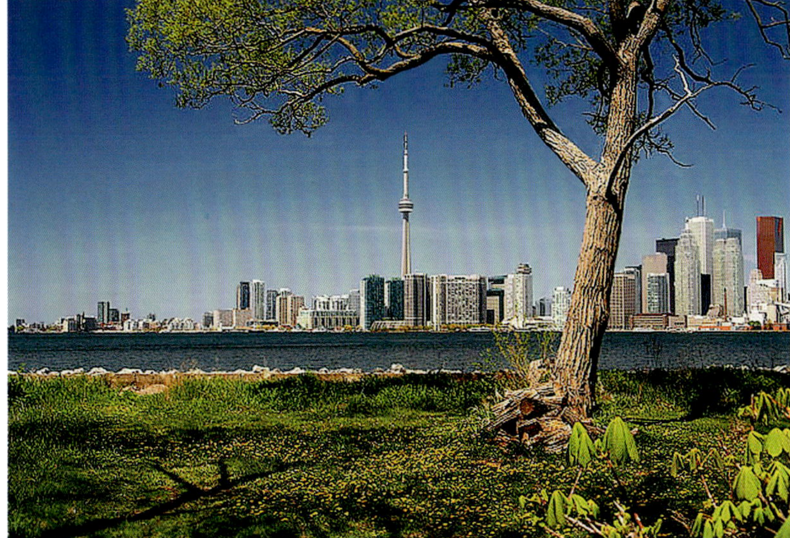

AKASH CHAUHAN – AGE 14 — FINALIST, GREENING THE CITY

Green View out of a Busy City
Kolkata, India

This was the view from a small garden outside of the city. Taking the shot through the tree meant the tree was slightly tilted. There was less greenery within the metropolitan city.

Nikon S3100. Post-capture: no digital alterations.

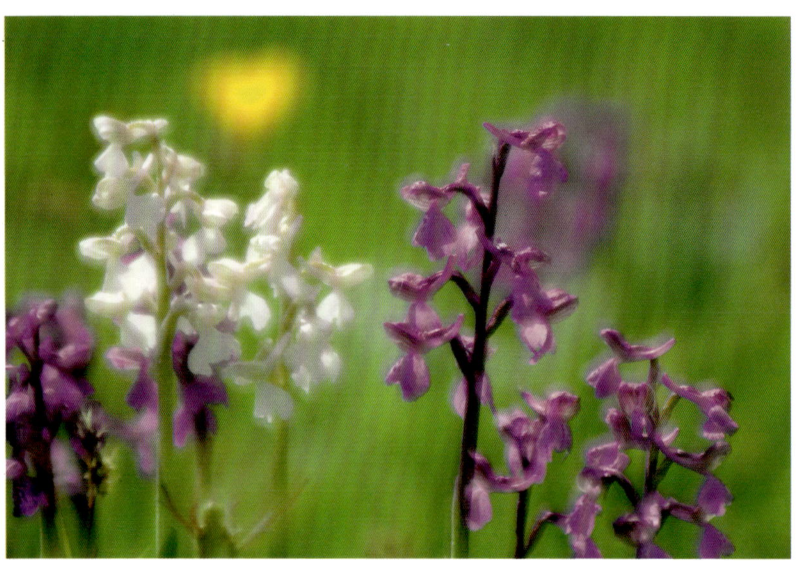

PATRICK CORNING – AGE 15 HIGHLY COMMENDED, FRAGILE LANDSCAPES

Green-winged Orchids
Marden Meadow, Kent, UK

These are Green-winged Orchids growing at Marden Meadow, a Kent Wildlife Trust reserve where thousands of this wild orchid species bloom in early May. The purple flowers are the standard form, and the white flowers growing alongside are the less common 'alba' variety. The soft-focus effect in this photograph is created by making a double-exposure in the camera, one shot sharp and the other slightly unfocused.

My Dad and I visited this reserve in early May specifically to photograph this species. I often try different techniques to make my photographs more abstract, in this case using an in-camera multiple exposure. I took this photograph lying down on the path through the reserve, using my telephoto lens to isolate the flowers.

Nikon D200, 80-400mm lens. 1/1500 sec at f/5.6 Post-capture: no digital alterations.

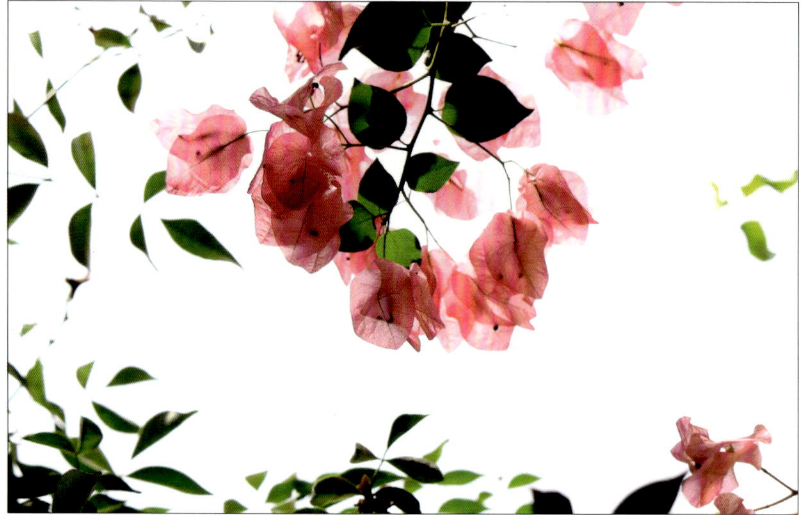

MATTHEW SECOMBE – AGE 15 FINALIST, THE BEAUTY OF PLANTS

Majorcan Colour
Majorca, Spain

In the garden of a restaurant in Majorca I looked up and saw these bougainvillea flowers against the contrast of a white sky. I had been taking photos of other plants in the garden when I happened to look up and spotted this striking flower. The white sky helped me show the vibrant colours. The fairly slow shutter speed I used on such a light day gives the sky a completely smooth texture, and to throw some of the higher up flowers out of focus, I used a medium depth of field, giving the photo contrast and depth.

Canon EOS 1000D, Canon 55-250mm lens. 1/250sec at f/7.1. Post-capture: no digital alterations

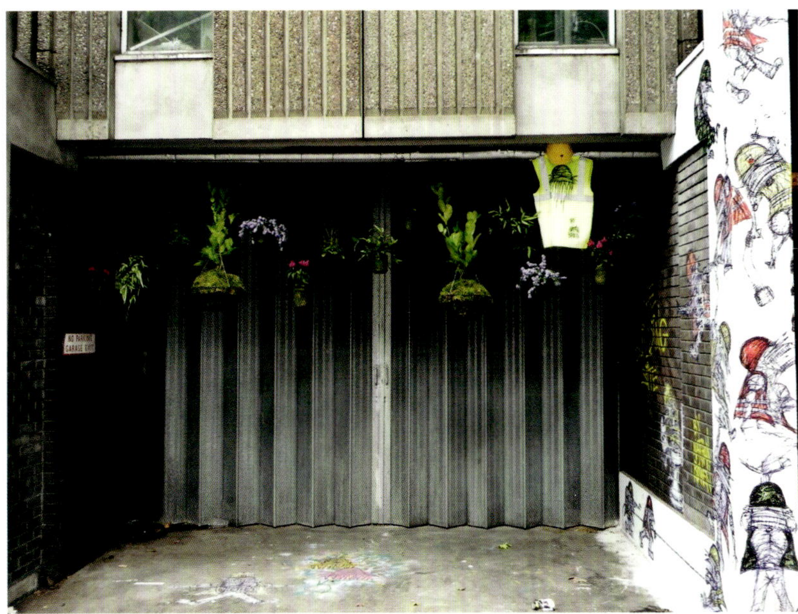

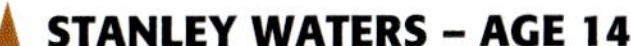

STANLEY WATERS – AGE 14 FINALIST, GREENING THE CITY

Hanging Plants in Bristol
Old Market, Bristol, UK

This photograph is like a piece of guerrilla gardening in inner city Bristol. Baskets hang within an urban garage enclosure and the plants do not look like they are meant to be there, which is one of the reasons why I entered it into Greening the City category. I photographed the whole of the garage doorway so that it would act as a frame and show the urban setting.

Nikon Coolpix P100. f/3.2. Post-capture: no digital alterations.

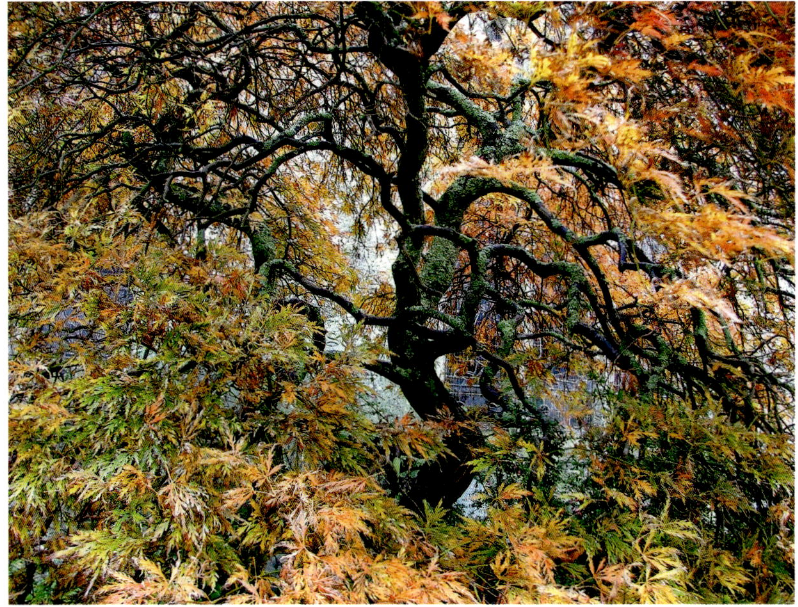

JASMINE CLEGG – AGE 10 HIGHLY COMMENDED, TREES, WOODS & FORESTS

Tree of Souls
Cornwall, UK

A majestic Acer tree in autumn colours in Gulval churchyard, Cornwall. It reminded me of the 'Tree of Souls' in the film *Avatar*.

Fuji Finepix S5000. 1/70sec at f/2.8. Post-capture: no digital alterations.

COMMENDED IMAGES

WILDLIFE HAVENS

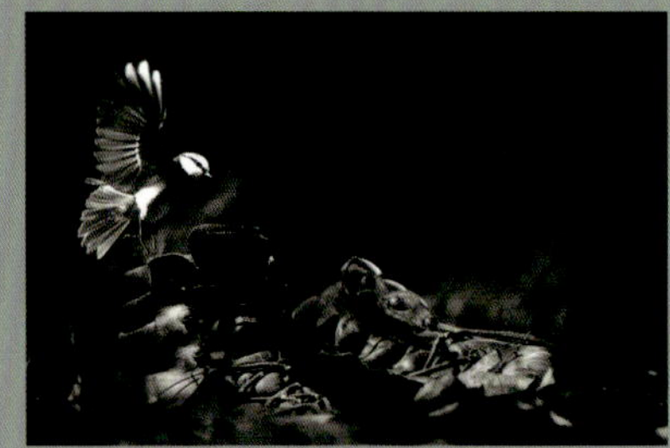

SOME DAYS NEVER END

JAMIE UNWIN

WILDLIFE HAVENS

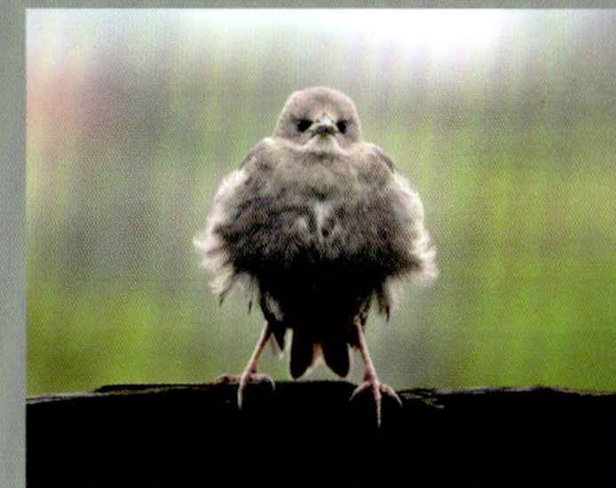

WHO'S THE BOSS?

SUSAN BRADNAM

BREATHING SPACES

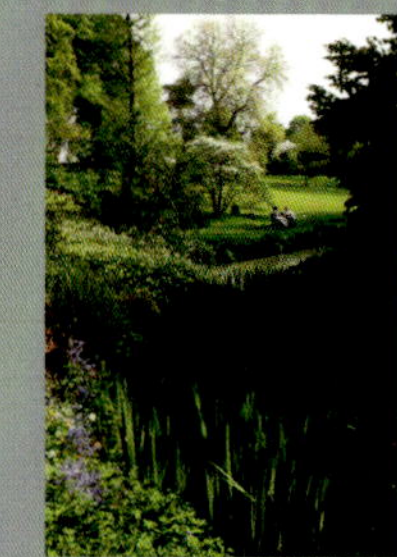

UNWINDING IN WIGHTWICK MANOR GARDENS

HESTER BLEWITT

TREES WOODS AND FORESTS

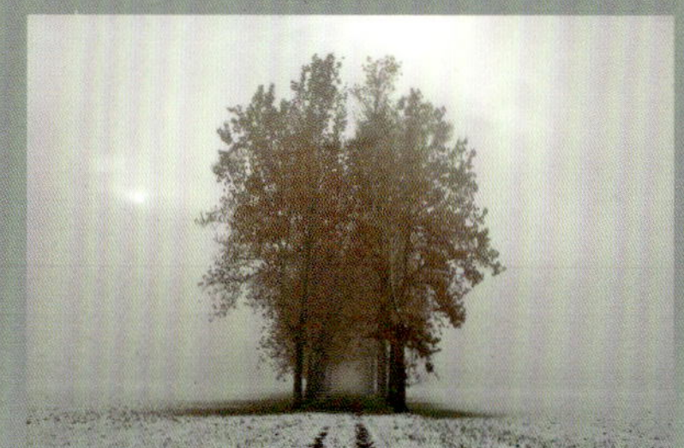

AVENUE IN WINTER

CARLO SILVA

WILDLIFE HAVENS

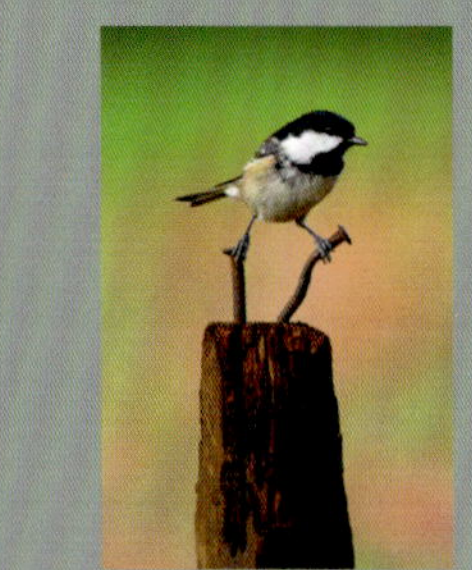

AUTUMN COAL TIT

SIMON ROY

BREATHING SPACES

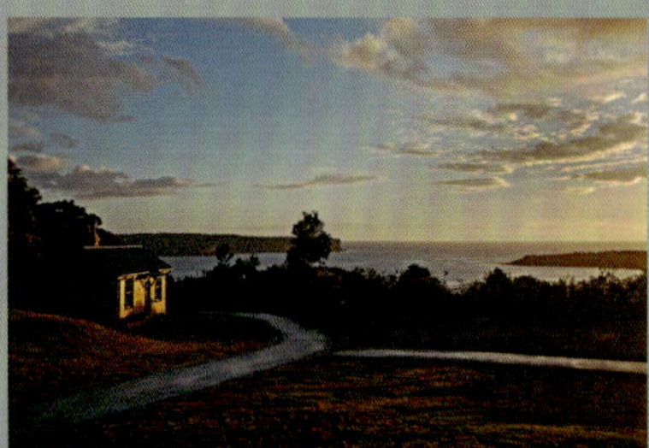

THE GUNNER'S HUT

GARY STEER

BREATHING SPACES

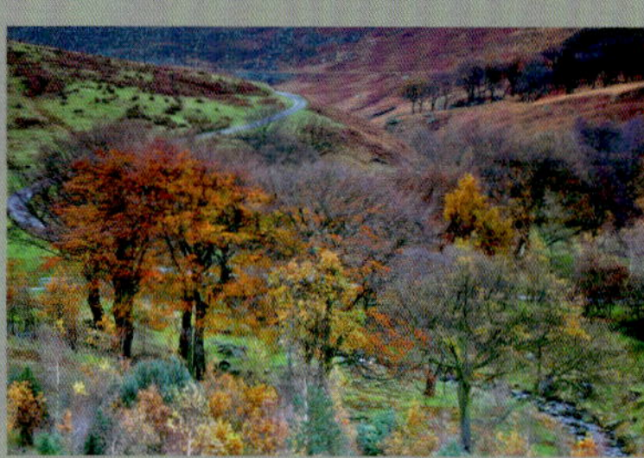

PATH TO PEACE

RACHEL HINDLEY

TREES WOODS AND FORESTS

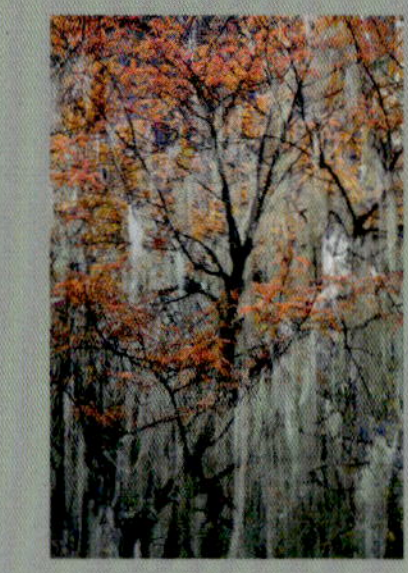

BHUTAN TREE

LAURO DINI

WILDLIFE HAVENS

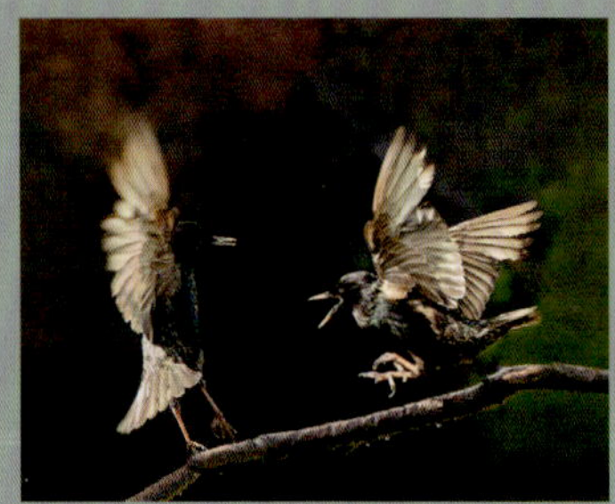

STARLINGS - HOPPING MAD

HAZEL BYATT

BREATHING SPACES

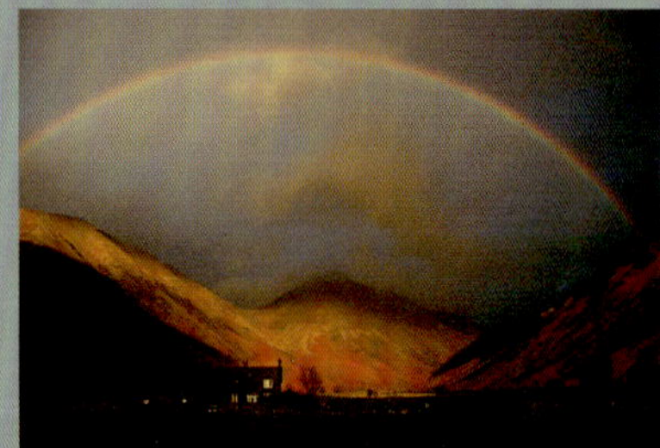

WASTWATER, NOVEMBER 2009

MAURICE ROETYNCK

TREES WOODS AND FORESTS

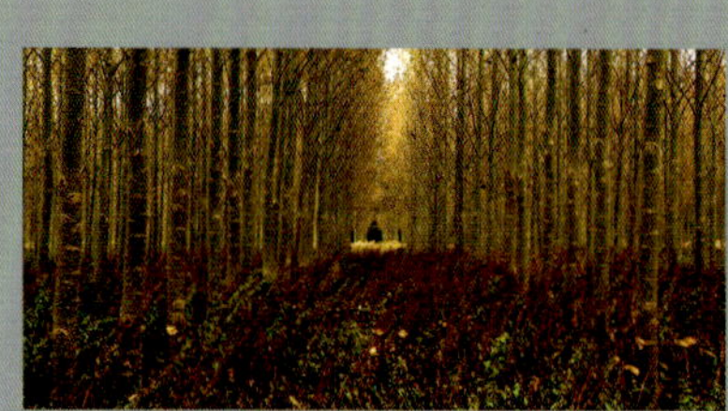

POPLARS

JAMES KERR

TREES WOODS AND FORESTS

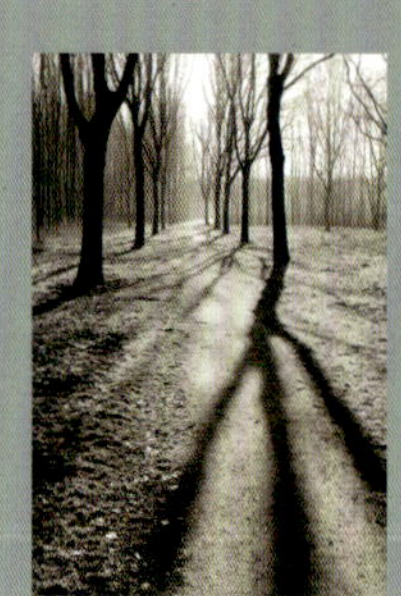

LONG SHADOWS

MICHAEL TURNER

TREES WOODS AND FORESTS

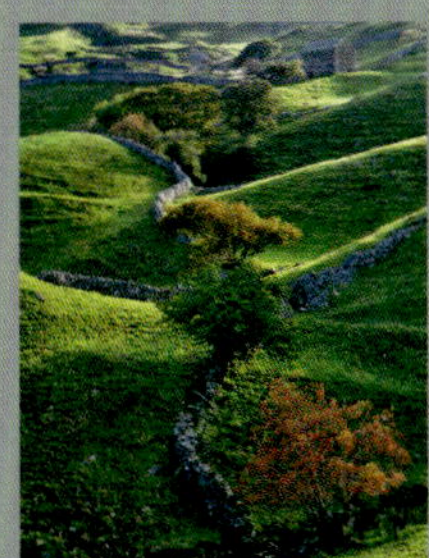

OXNOP, YORKSHIRE DALES

ROSS BROWN

THE BOUNTIFUL EARTH

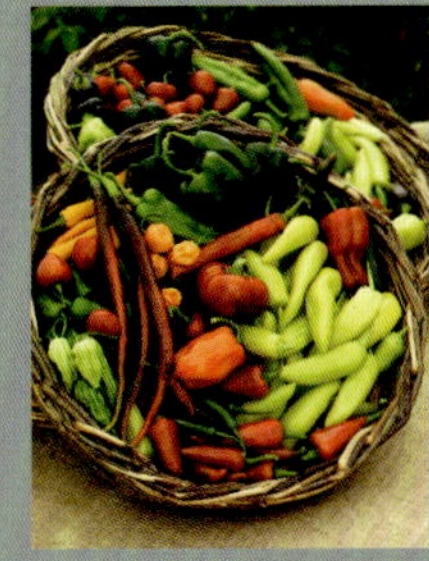

TOO HOT TO HANDLE

NICOLA STOCKEN TOMKINS

GREENING THE CITY

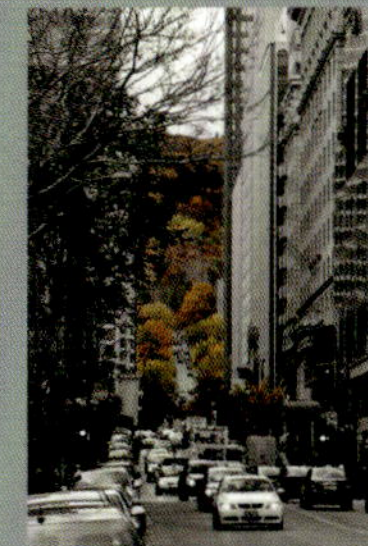

LAST GLIMPSE OF AUTUMN

SYLVIE PINSONNEAULT

YOUNG GARDEN PHOTOGRAPHER OF THE YEAR

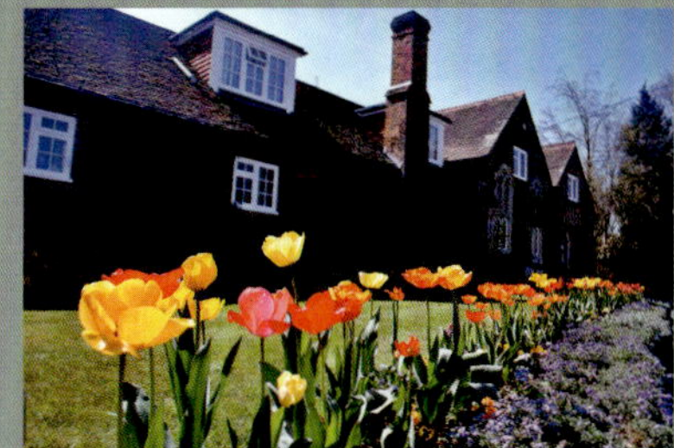

TULIP GARDEN

ALICE BROMFIELD

FRAGILE LANDSCAPES

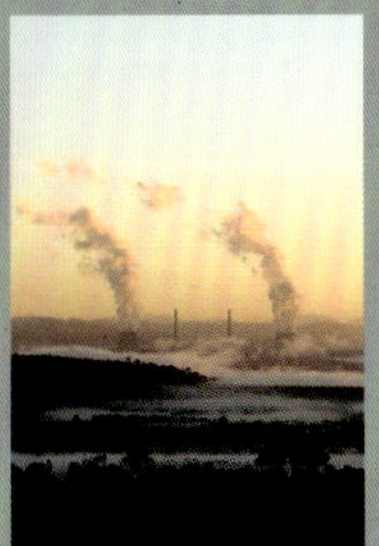

EARLY MORNING POLLUTION

LUCY ROBERTS

BEAUTY OF PLANTS

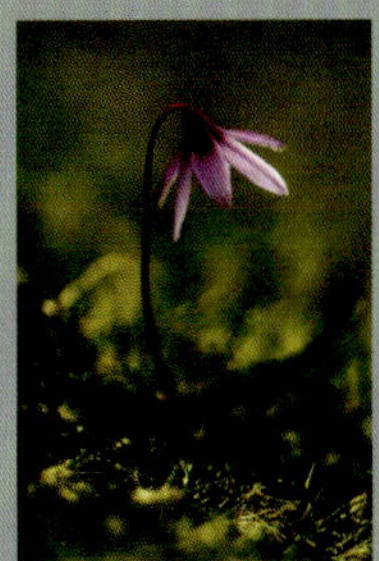

SADNESS

ANA SAIZ ROJAS

GREENING THE CITY

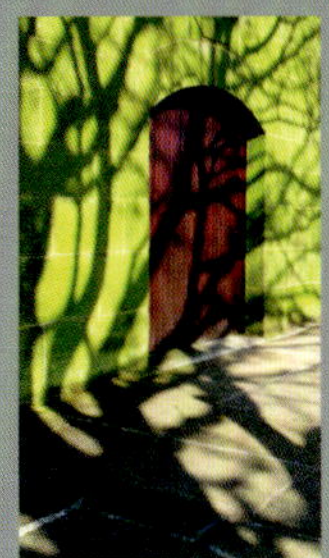

TREE SHADOWS ON A CHURCH WALL

MICHAEL TURNER

YOUNG GARDEN PHOTOGRAPHER OF THE YEAR

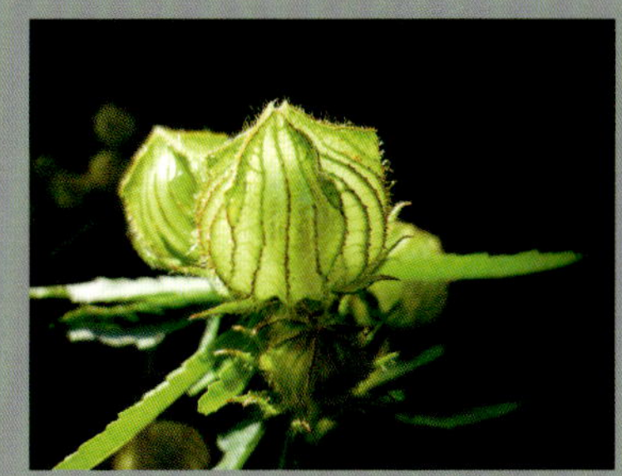

EVEN GREEN CAN BE BEAUTIFUL

MATTHEW UNWIN

THE BOUNTIFUL EARTH

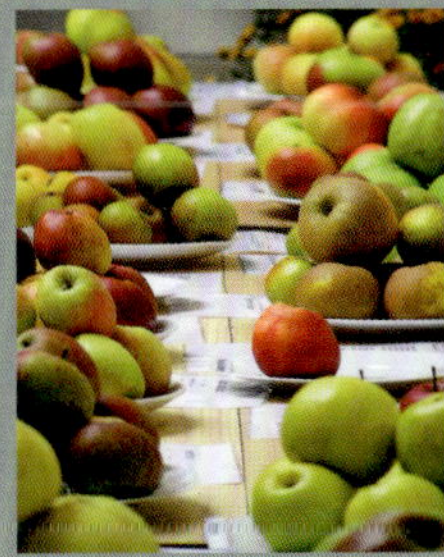

ALL SHAPES AND SIZES

DANIEL ROLLITT

GREENING THE CITY

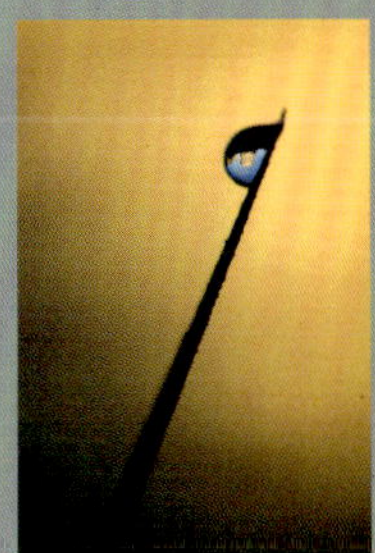

CITY REED AND TOWERBLOCK

RAOUL SLATER

GREENING THE CITY

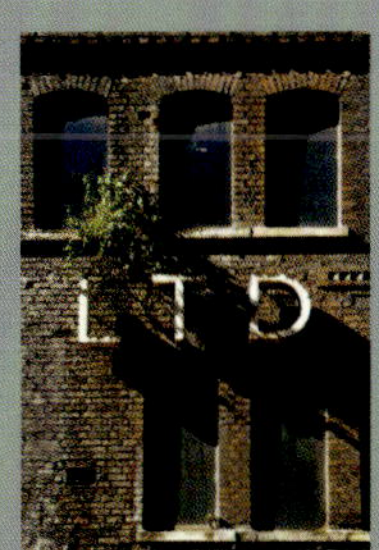

'LIMITED' GROWTH

LIZ EVERY

YOUNG GARDEN PHOTOGRAPHER OF THE YEAR

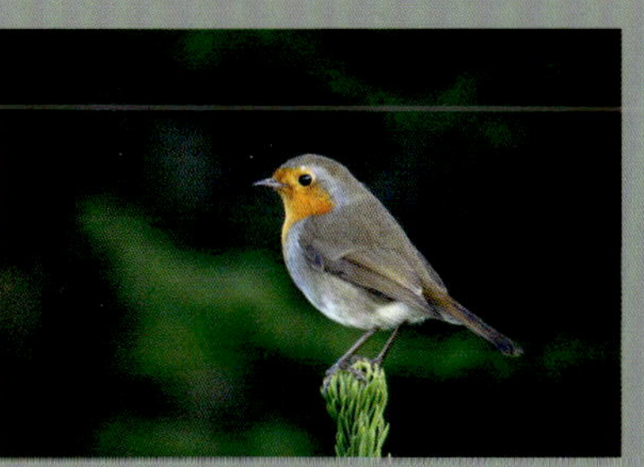

BRIEF MOMENT

MATTHEW SECOMBE

JOANNA STOGA 1ST PLACE, THE BEAUTY OF PLANTS

Qi

Wroclaw, Poland.

ROYAL PHOTOGRAPHIC SOCIETY GOLD MEDAL

This portfolio expresses my fascination with plants and is dedicated to my favourite photographer Karl Blosfeld. The title of the portfolio refers to Qi energy, which in traditional Chinese culture is an active principle present in every living thing, or 'life energy'. The x-ray technique not only reveals the remarkable forms and structures of plants, but also gives us the opportunity to feel this energy. This kind of photography requires a focus on the shape of the plants and image composition. When I started this project, I was assisted by my good friends and radiology technicians Jaroslaw Mszanski and Rafal Susser. Over the three years of this project I used x-ray equipment at three clinics, and also worked closely with Wroclaw Botanical Garden and Professor Tomasz Nowak.

Kodak MIN-R S Film Quantum Q-Rad ODYSSEY and Quest, GE Diamond. No lens. Post-capture: scanned using a high-resolution scanner. In some of the photographs brightness and contrast is adjusted.

1–Hosta 2–Aesculus 3–Pteridophyta 4–Unknown Plant 5–Hemerocallis 6–Nelumbo

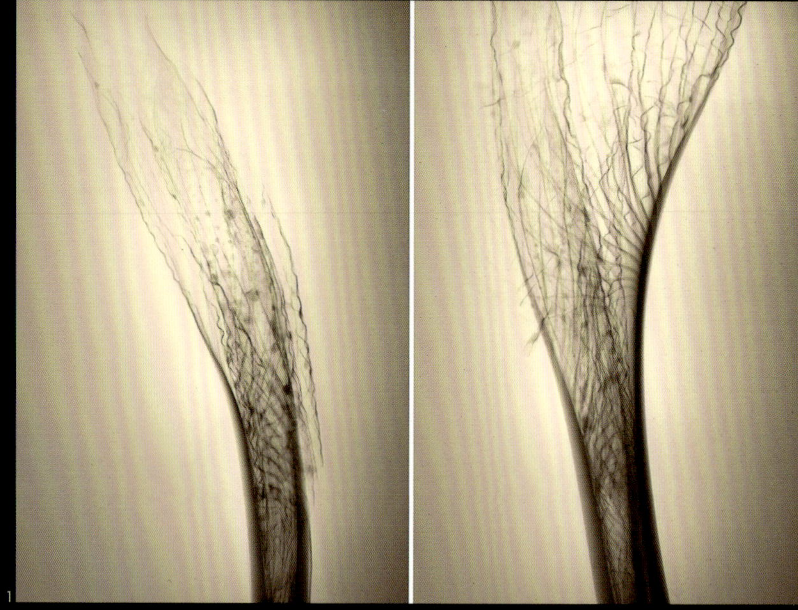

1

2

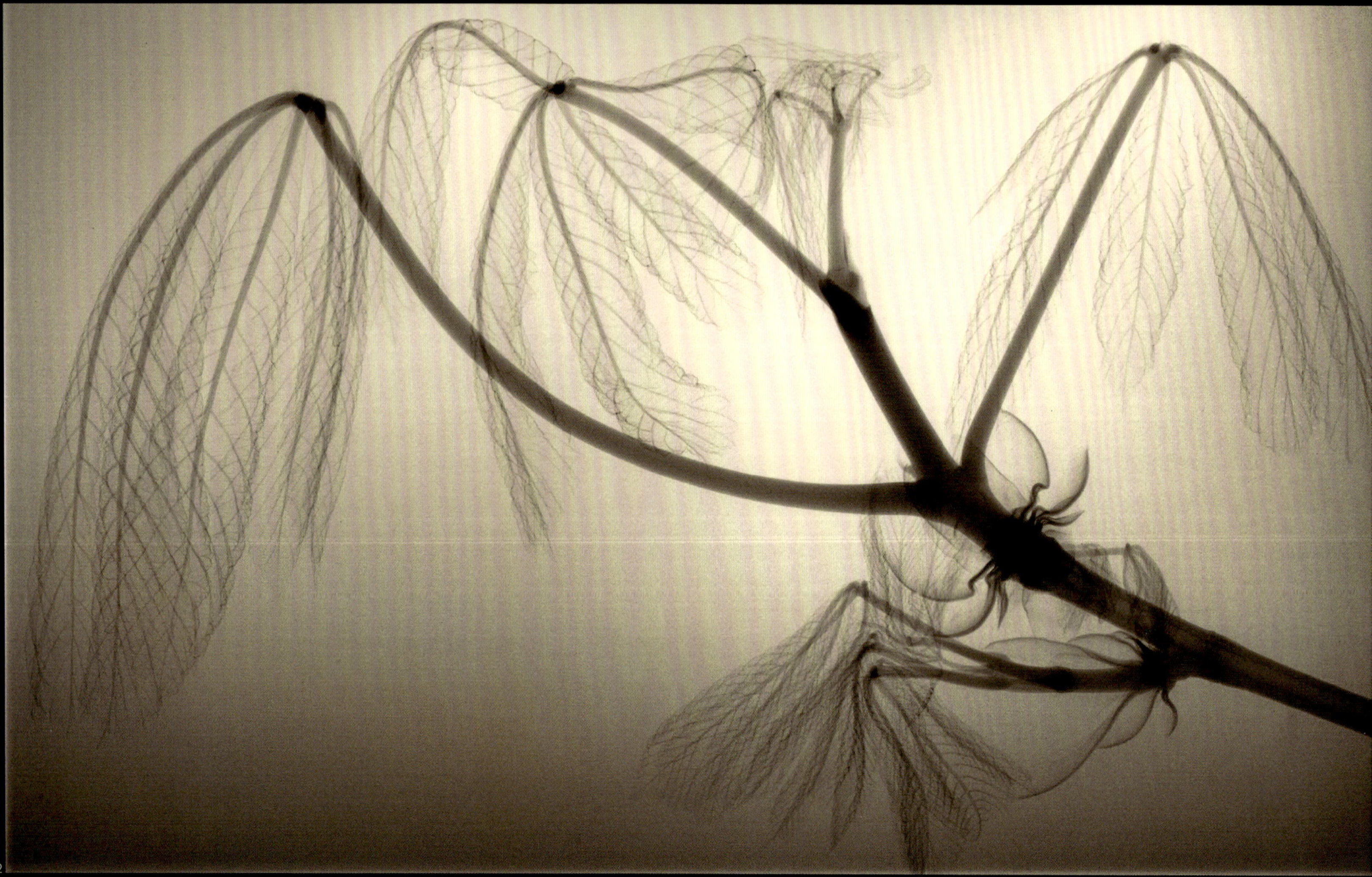

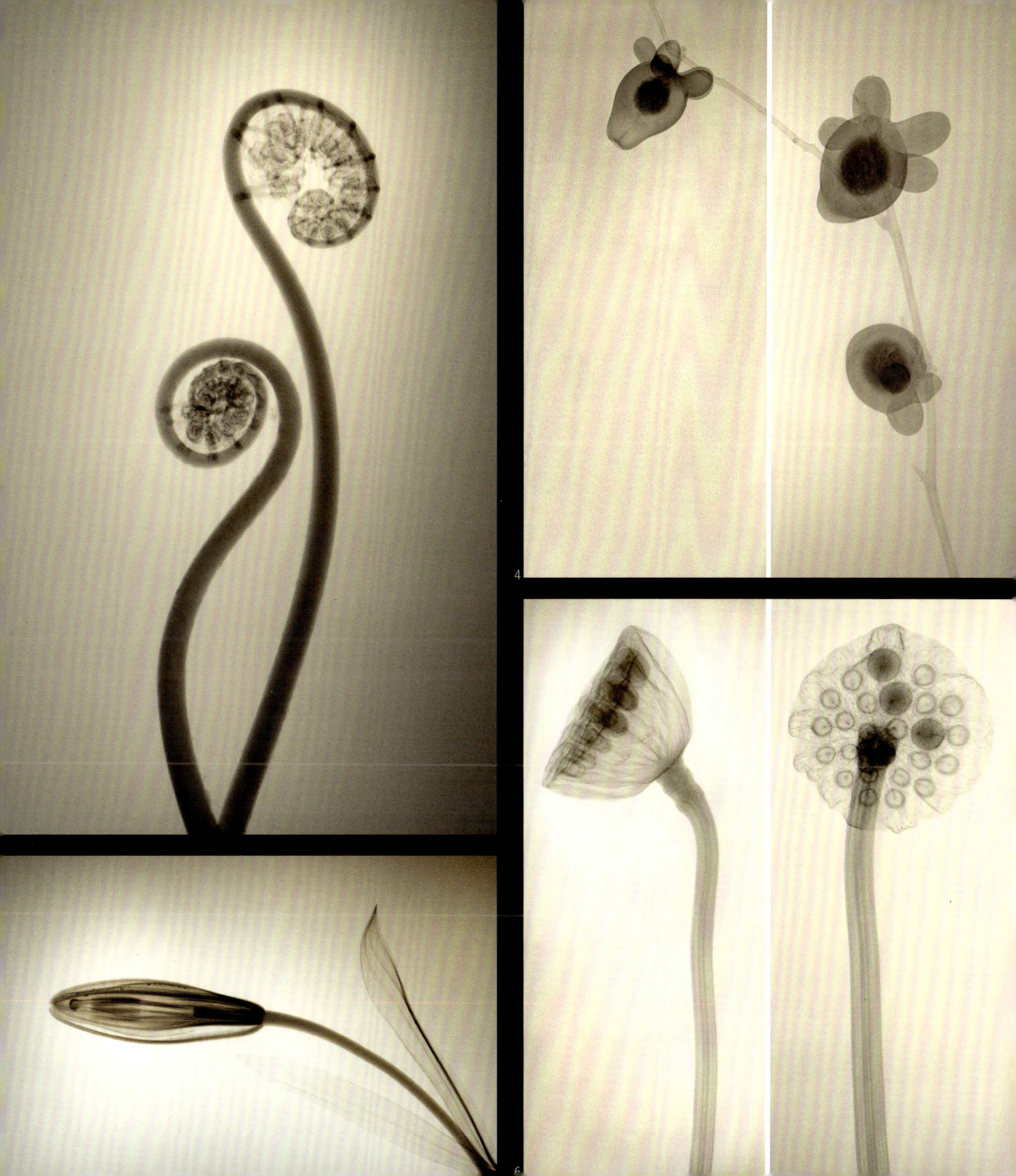
4
6

JOHN GRANT | 2ND PLACE, THE BEAUTY OF PLANTS

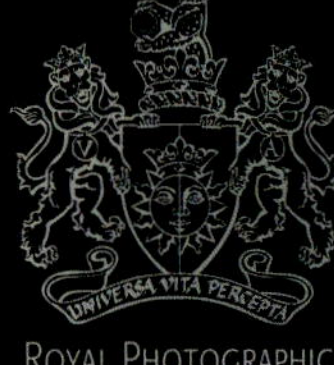

ROYAL PHOTOGRAPHIC SOCIETY SILVER MEDAL

Solace: Adrift with Flowers

My studio, with use of natural light, Virginia, USA

Sometimes when I make an arrangement of flowers in a clear glass vase, I am struck by the beauty of what is below the waterline. Displayed and magnified by the water and glass, the flowers and detritus come alive when lit by the right natural light. Often I allowed the blossoms to float for several weeks, making them diaphanous and very delicate. The fact that they are essentially 'weightless' gives them maximum grace. The results of the work could never be predicted directly and required patience, steady observation and a lot of perseverance. All of the specimens were grown in my own garden.

Canon EOS 5D Mark II, 100mm lens. Post-capture: in a few cases, the images were realigned to fit the frame better.

1–Romeo
2–Kimono
3–Adrift
4–Pastel
5–Visitation
6–Regeneration

1

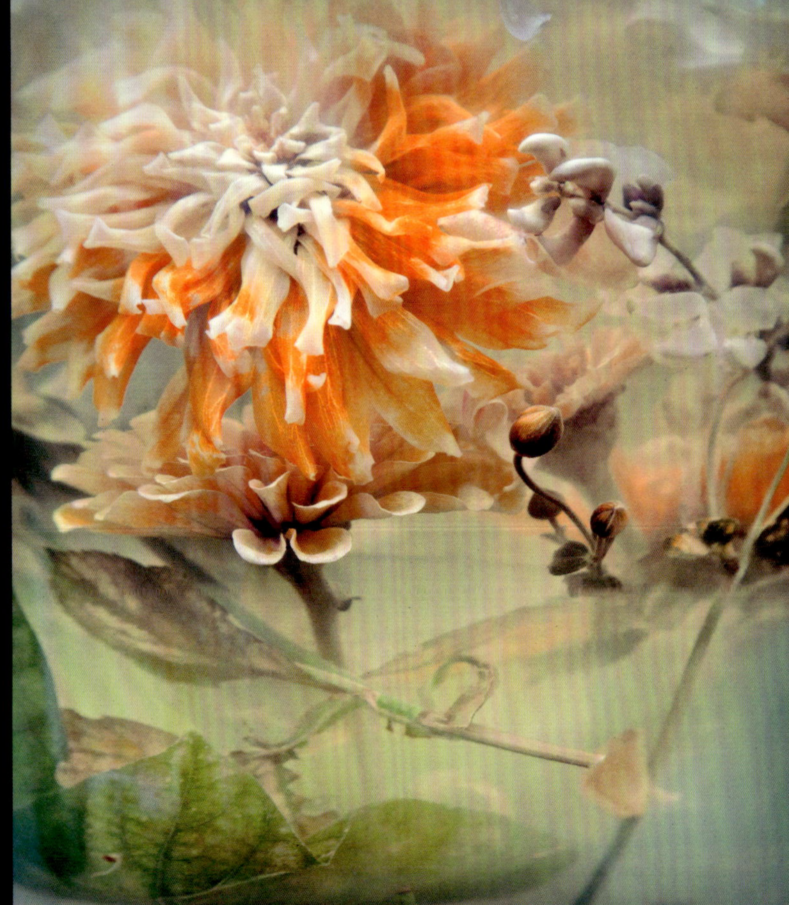

2

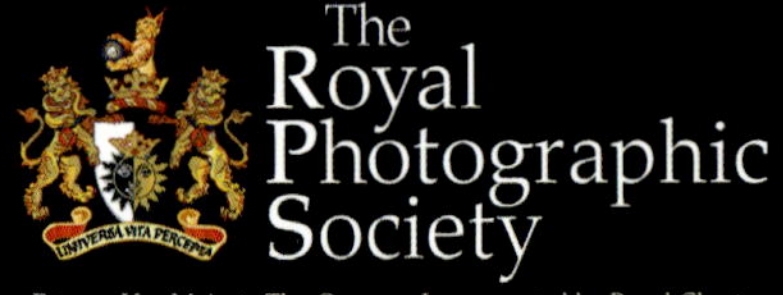

Patron: Her Majesty The Queen. Incorporated by Royal Charter

Gold, silver and bronze medals awarded by the Royal Photographic Society

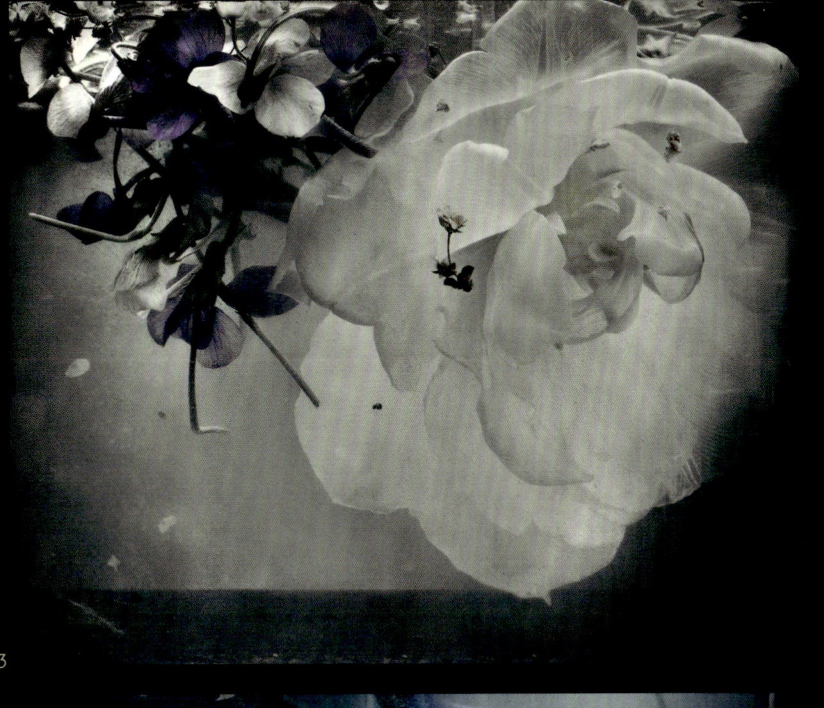
3

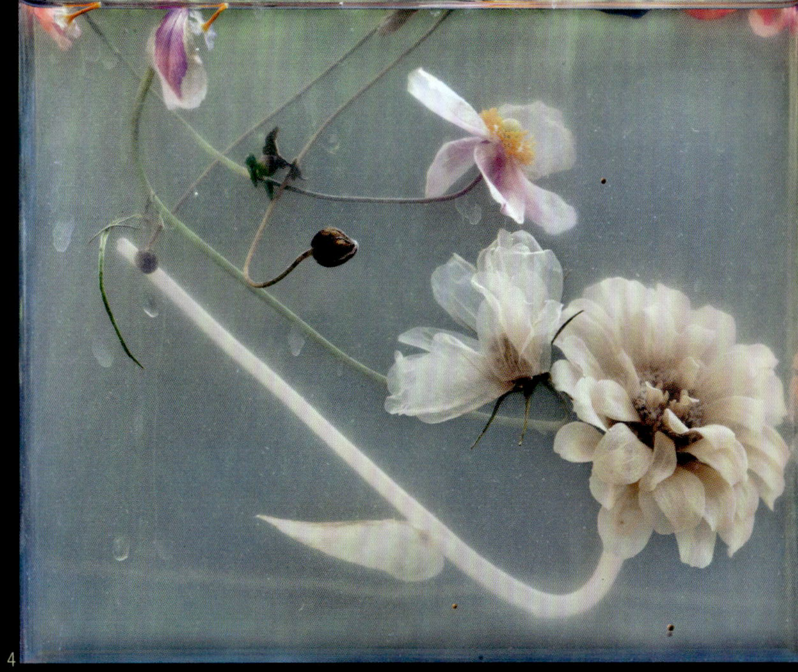
4

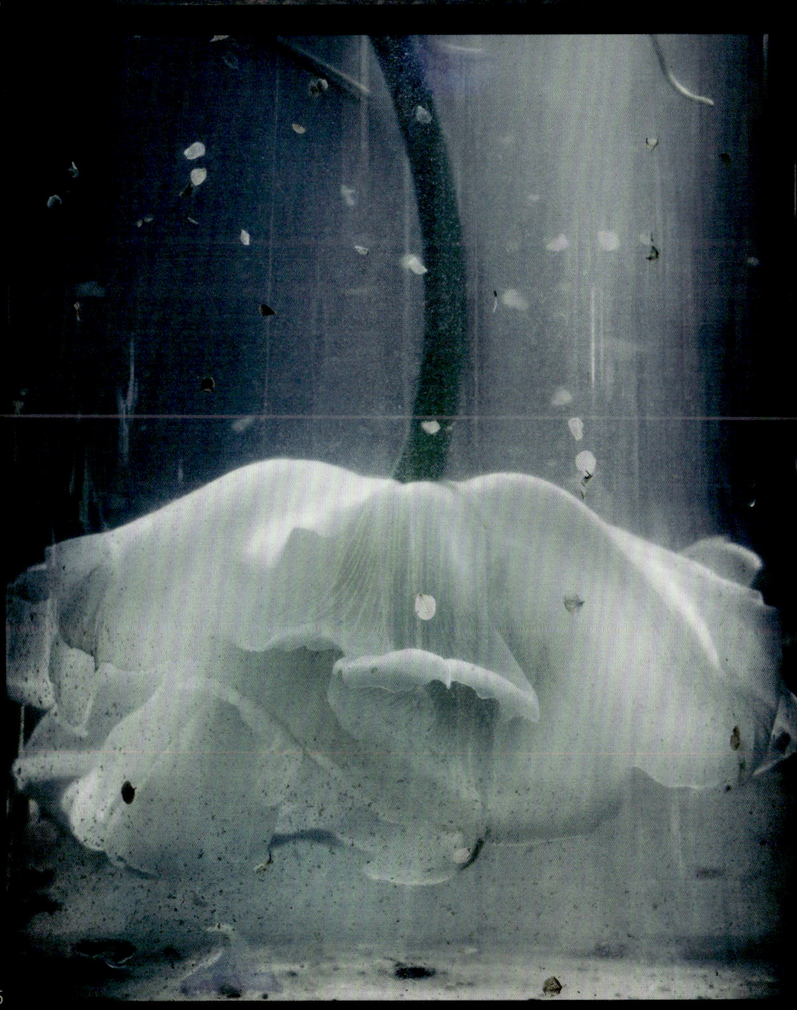
5

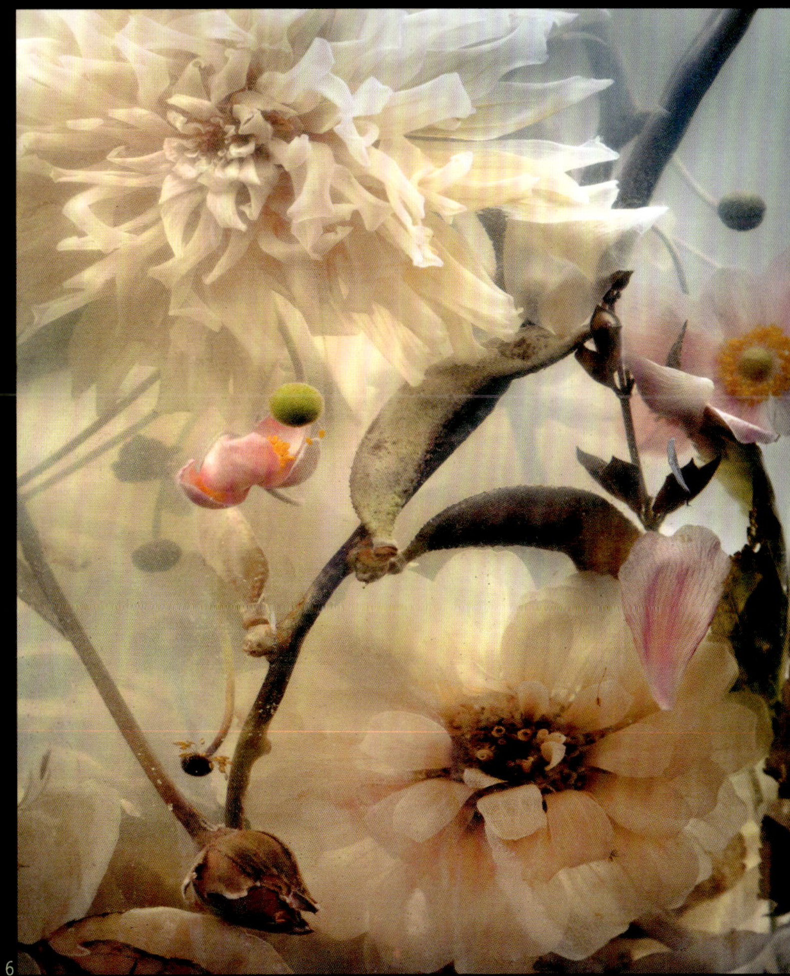
6

NIKKI DE GRUCHY 3RD PLACE, BEAUTIFUL GARDENS

A garden of walls in a border town

El Paso, Texas, USA

Landscape architect: Martha Schwartz Inc.

With kind permission of Sam and Anne Davis

ROYAL PHOTOGRAPHIC SOCIETY BRONZE MEDAL

A Mexican wall garden designed by Martha Schwartz. This garden sits as a kind of 'folly' amidst an English-style garden in the city of El Paso, Texas. Typically in a garden the plants would be the stars of the show, but here that accolade rests with the walls, with the sparseness of the planting a reminder of the arid aloofness of the surrounding desert.

Canon EOS 5D Mark I. Post-capture: None.

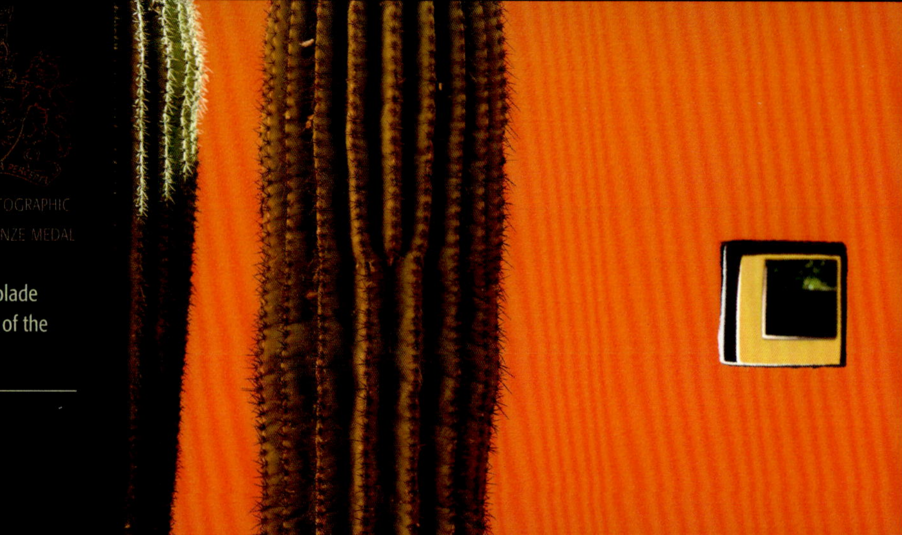

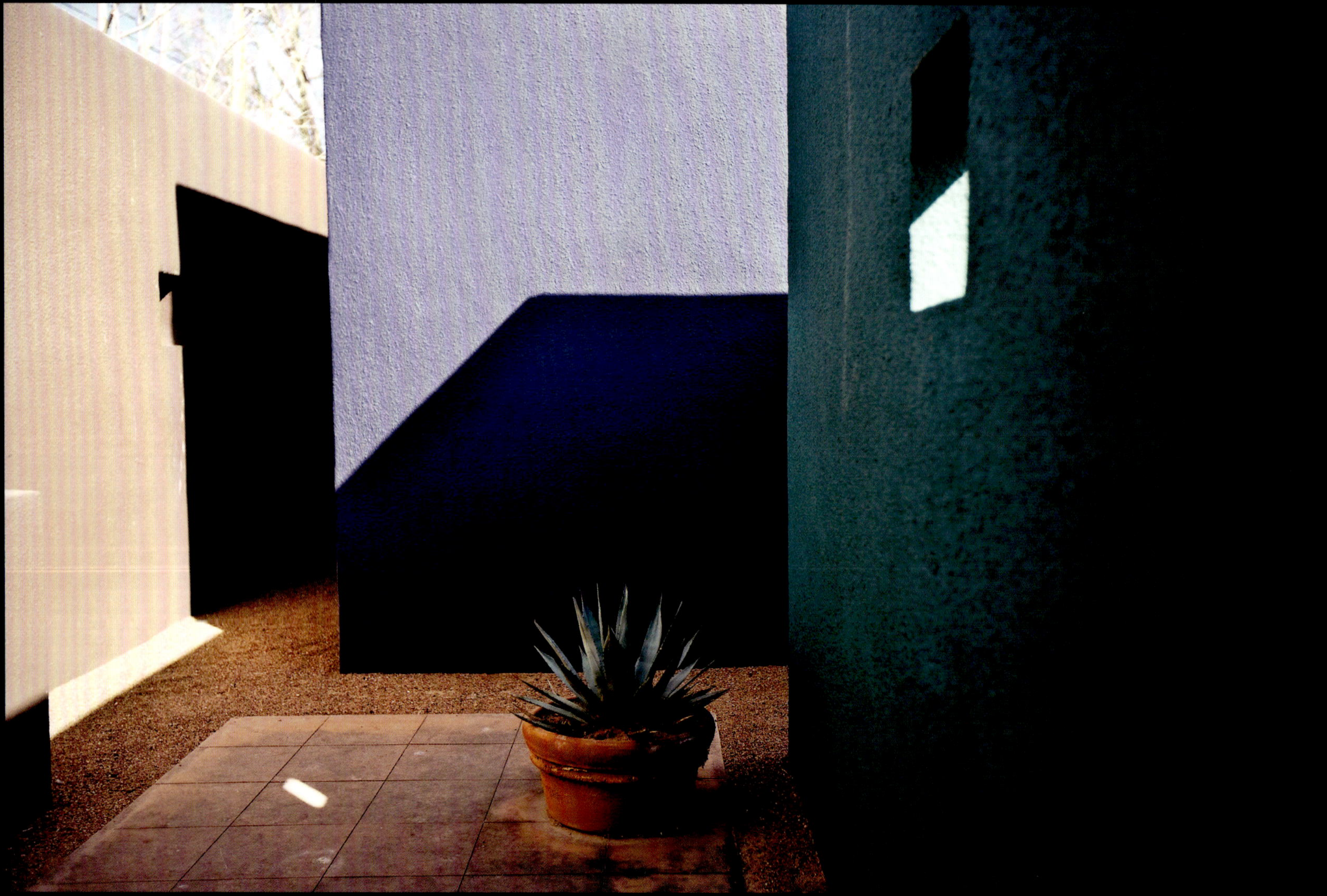

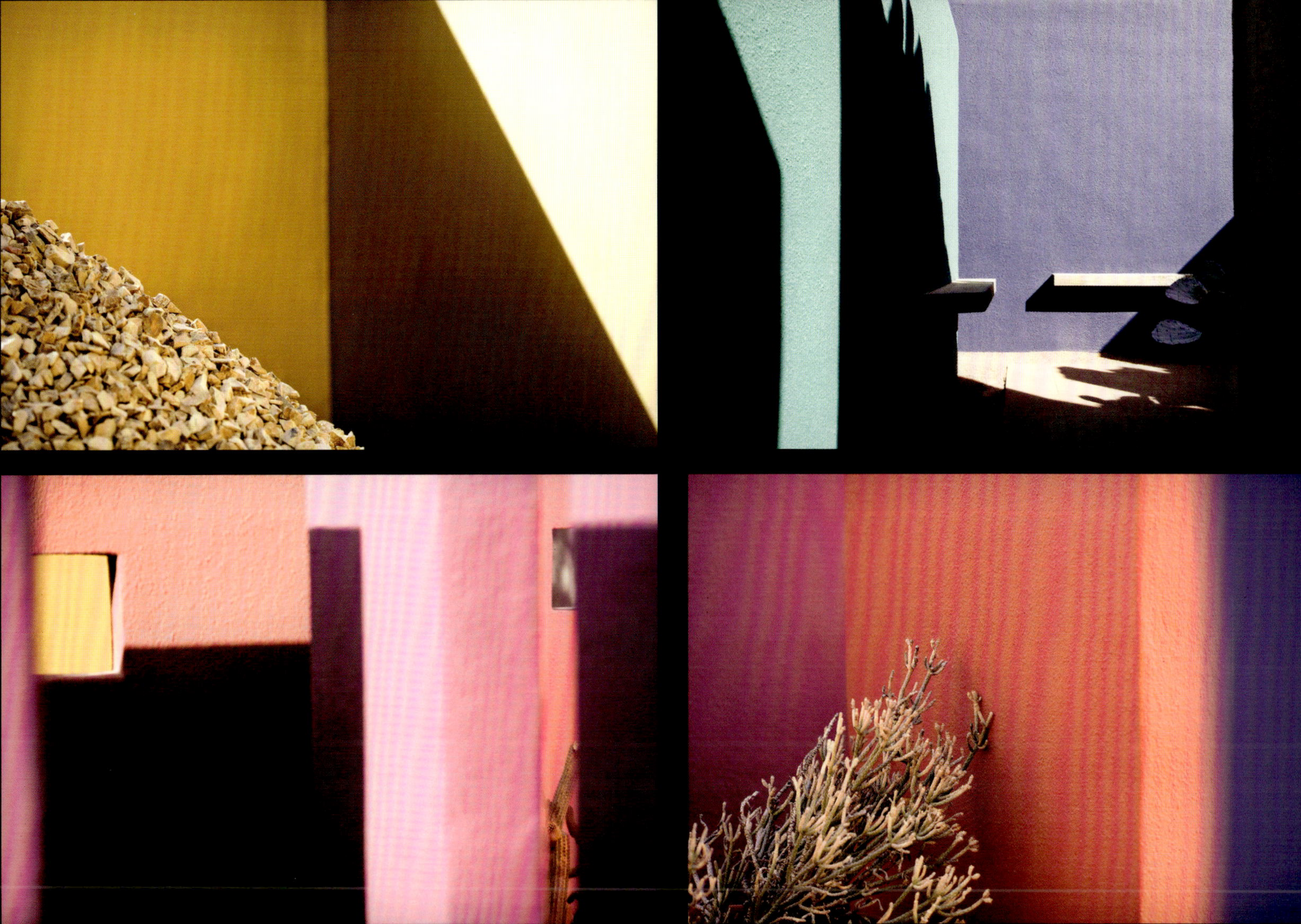

Land Girls
Various locations in the Midlands and Southern England

A series of portraits of contemporary garden journalists, presenters, authors, bloggers and campaigners who all grow their own food. Usually well known faces in the industry, the aim is to give a personal insight into the often unseen gardens or plots referred to in their public work. This is an ongoing project, currently with 30 portraits. The original inspiration for this project was a Land Girls poster from World War Two. The stylized theme and vivid colour of the poster was adopted to create a series of portraits of ladies working in the gardening industry or campaigning about green issues. The approach was to take each portrait with the same lens to keep a similar perspective, with each person a similar height within the frame for consistency.

Canon EOS 5D, 40mm lens approximately 1/60 to 1/125sec at approximately f/5.6.
Post-capture: the sky was often darkened to create a more dramatic effect, with some dodging and burning, much as I would have done when working in a darkroom.

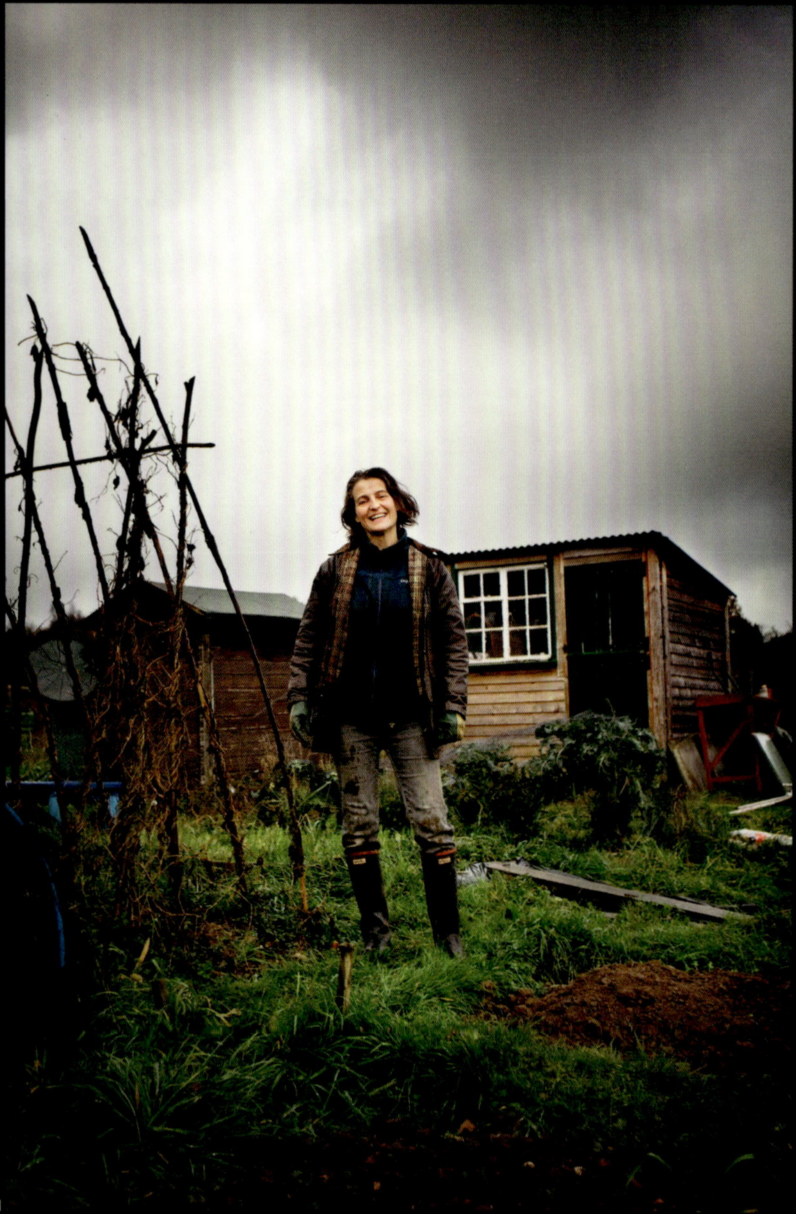

1

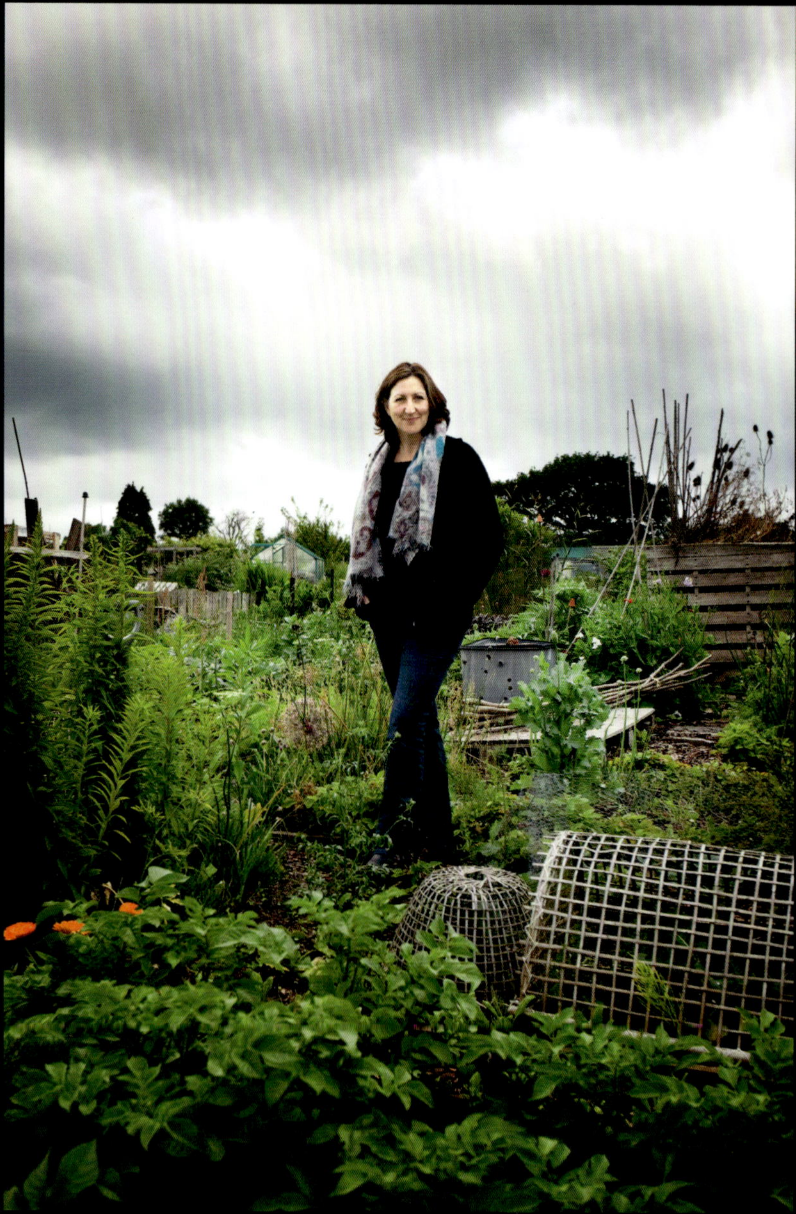

2

1–Portrait of Sally Nex on her allotment
2–Portrait of Juliet Roberts on her allotment
3–Portrait of Lia Leendertz on her allotment
4–Portrait of Beth Chatto in her vegetable garden
5–Portrait of Helen Yemm on her allotment
6–Portrait of Alys Fowler on her allotment

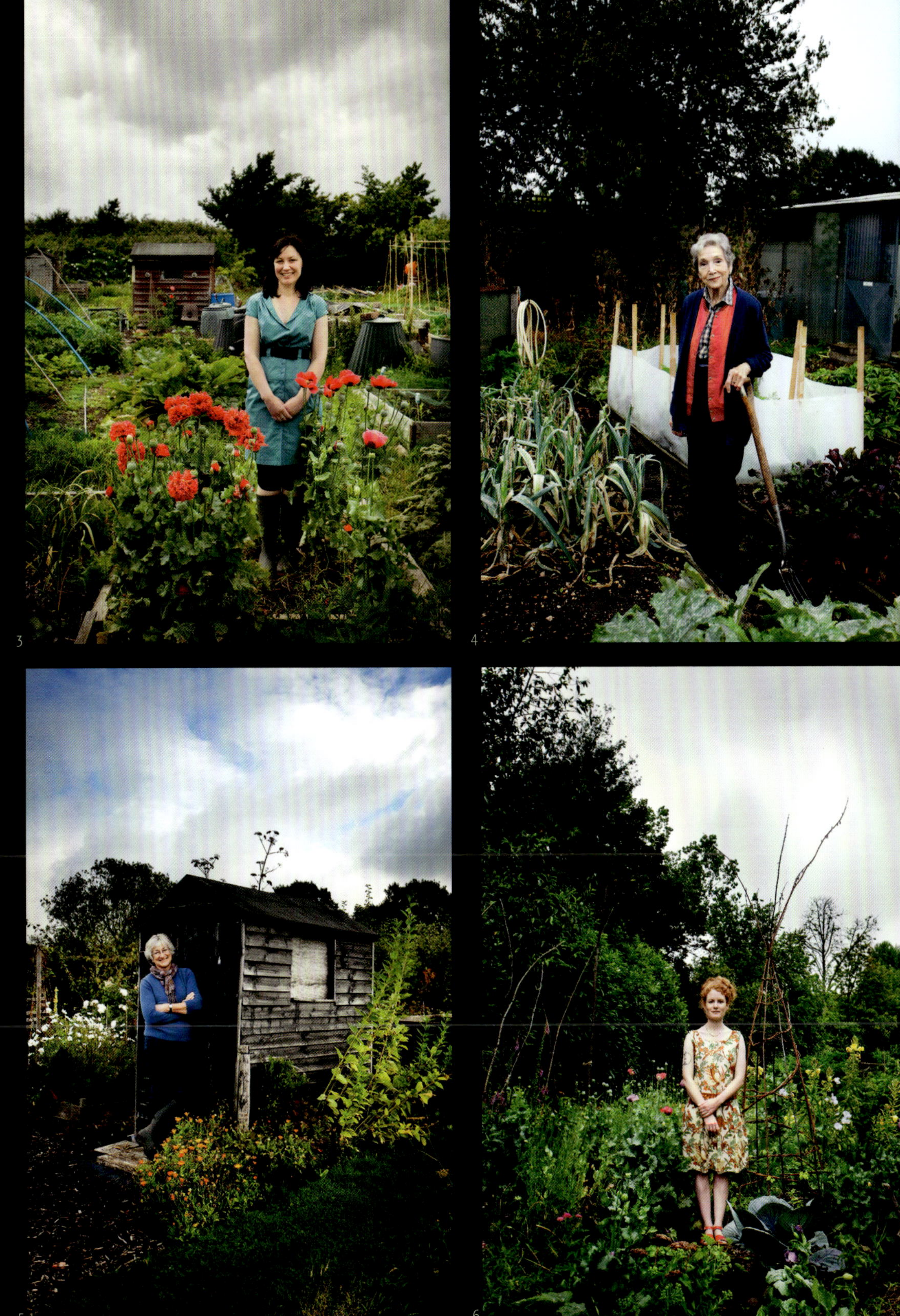
3
4
5
6

Window Dressing
Cambridgeshire, UK

My aim was to create a series of floral studies with a warm and nostalgic feel. Fresh-cut flowers taken from the borders of my garden during the summer months are arranged in glass containers ranging from jam jars to fine crystal vases, with the inclusion of a fine net draped behind or over the flowers to create an informal scene. I chose the Cosmos, Hydrangea, Dicentra, Petunia, Poppy and Michaelmas daisy as my subjects as I wanted each to be different in colour and flower shape but also working together. My inspiration is drawn from the beautiful natural colours, textures and diverse forms of flowers that give such wonderful scope for photography. Three bracketed shots were taken for each image to capture a high dynamic range of the tonal values. Using three exposures at a stop apart allowed me see a greater dynamic range between the lightest and darkest areas than if I had used just a single photograph.

Canon EOS 7D and Canon EOS 450D, Canon 50mm lens, Tamron 60mm and Tamron 90mm lenses. Post-capture: I combined the three shots I had taken together. I also photographed a variety of fine net fabrics and merged them into the floral image to add more interest and create a feeling of movement.

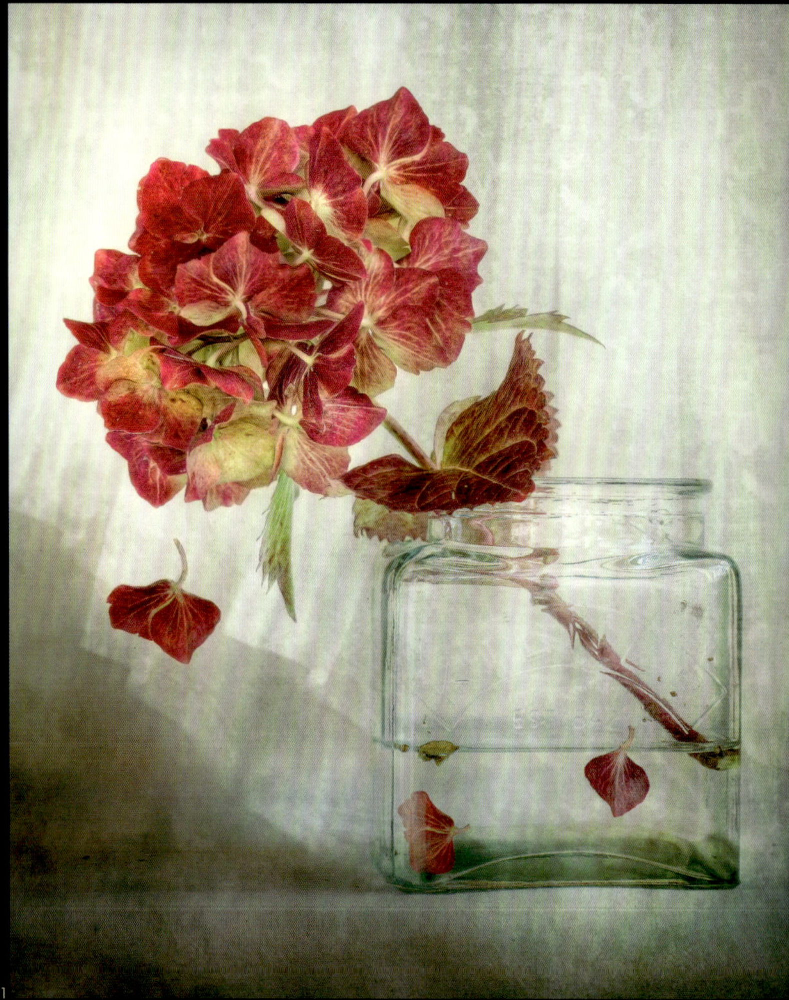

1

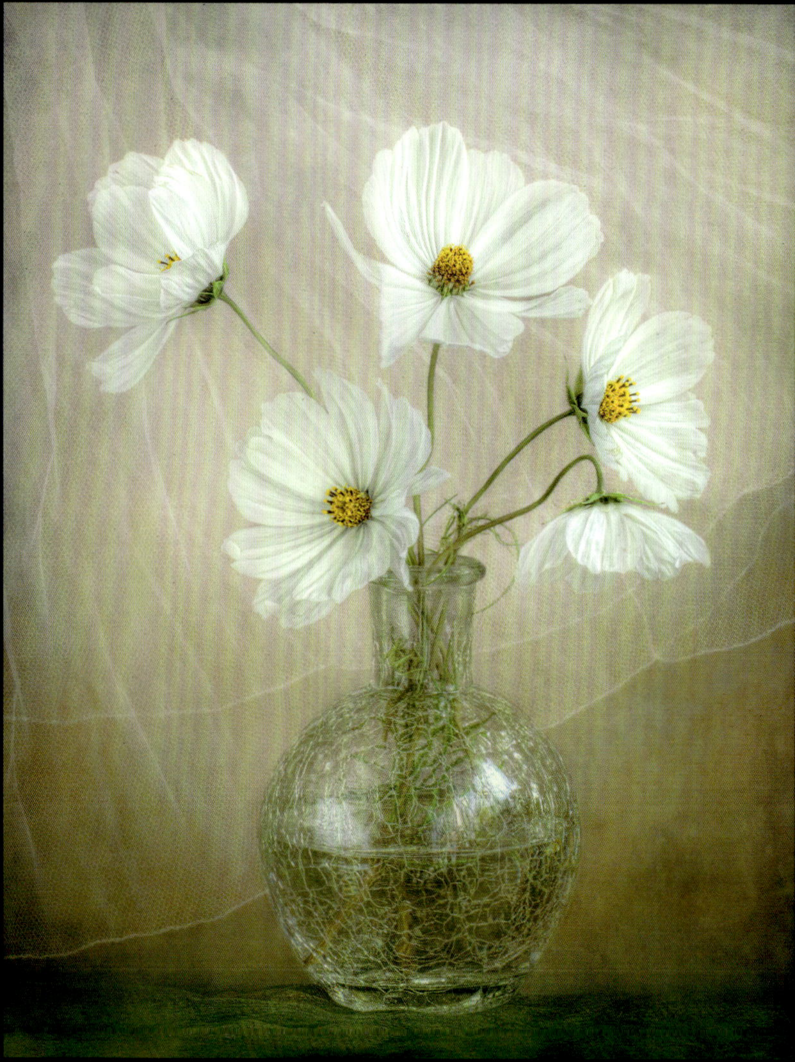

2

1–Cherish
2–Pure
3–Romance
4–Joy
5–Celebration
6–Cheer

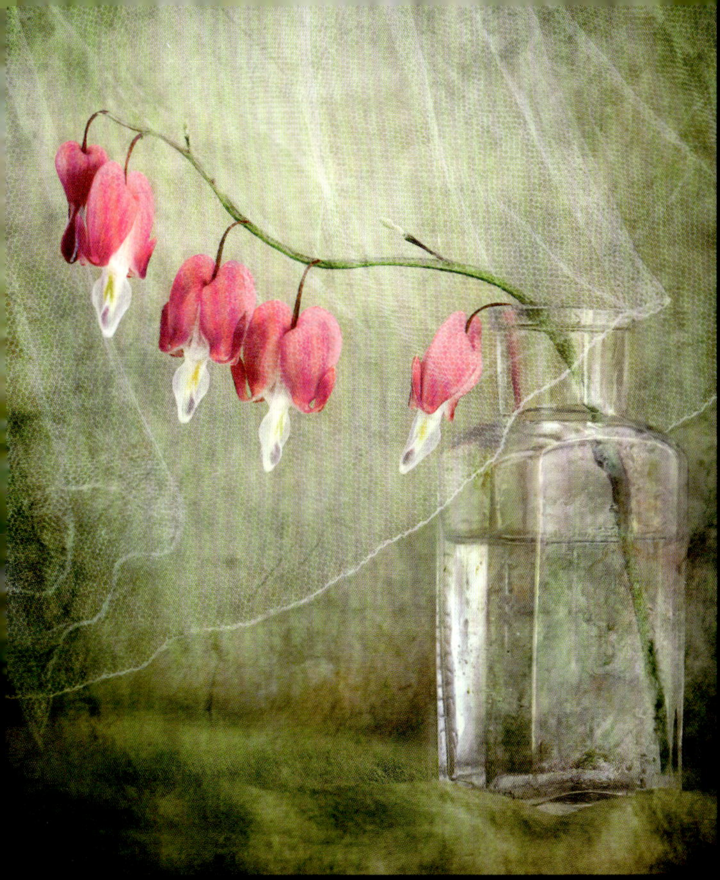

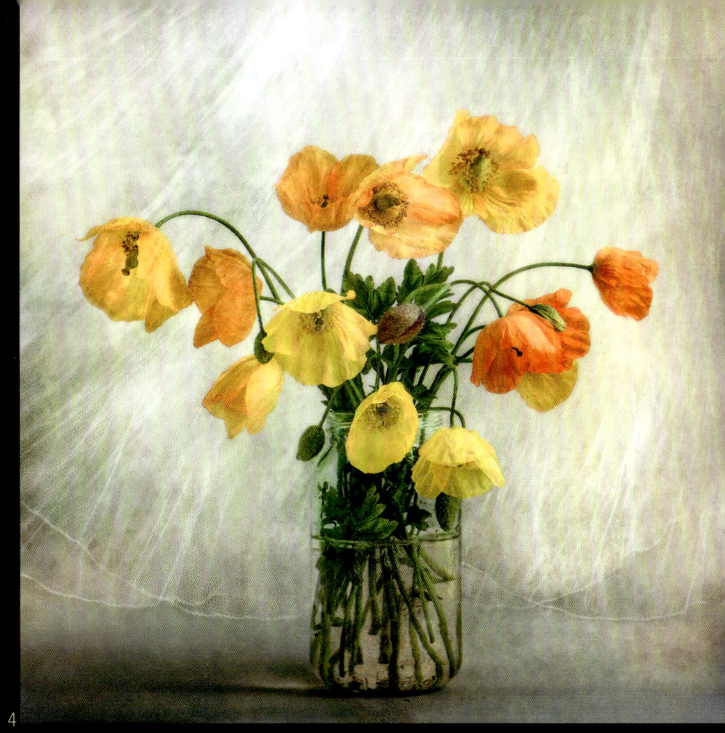

4

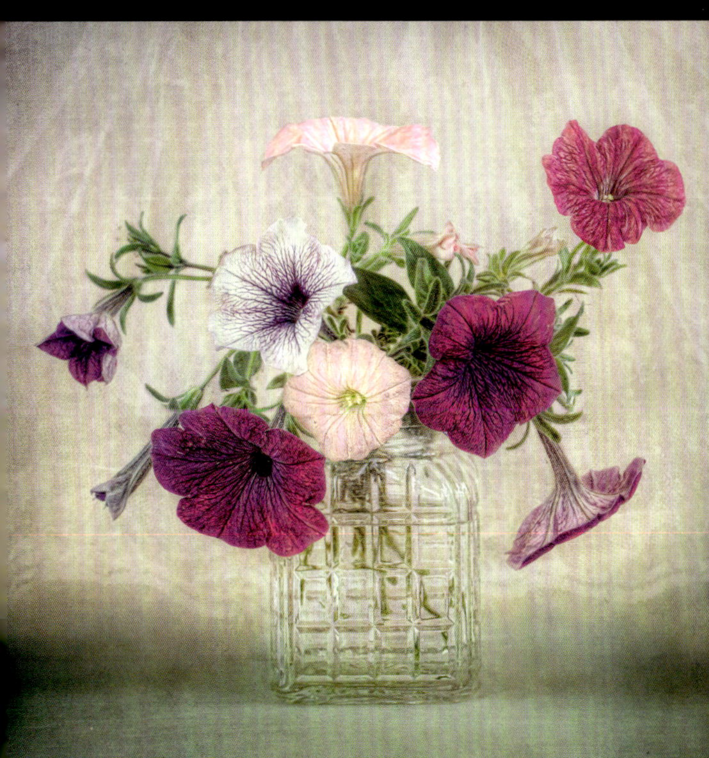

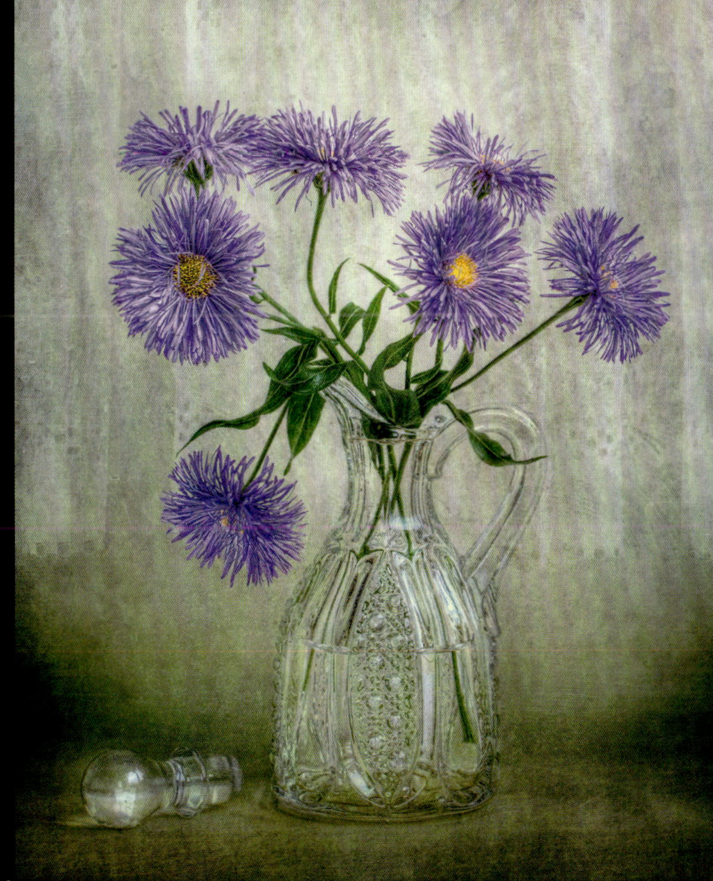

6

MARY KOCOL | HIGHLY COMMENDED, THE BEAUTY OF PLANTS

The Poetics of Nature

Somerville, Massachusetts, USA

Drawing upon themes of the garden, landscape, and the seasons, I create ice tablets of botanical specimens. Blooms are collected from various gardens and are frozen into a block of ice, becoming ethereal constructions. Since ice is temporary, the photograph becomes the record that this ephemeral garden once briefly existed. I am inspired by three pioneers of photography: Julia Margaret Cameron, Henry Fox Talbot, and Anna Atkins, whose early photographic experiments incorporated their gardens directly into their work. With the exception of the cherry blossom branch from a friend's garden in Bethesda, Maryland, I grow all these plants myself in an urban garden.

Canon Digi Rebel T2i, Canon Zoom 17-40mm lens. Post-capture: no digital alterations.

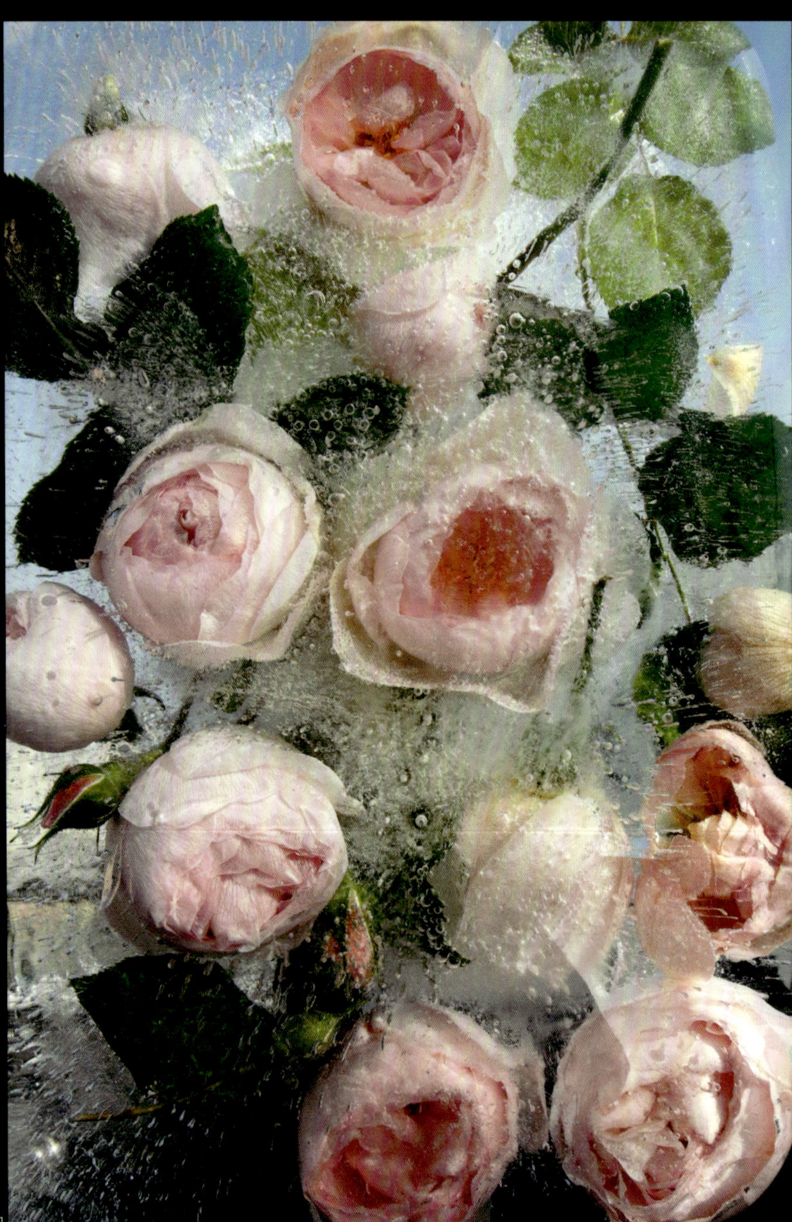

1

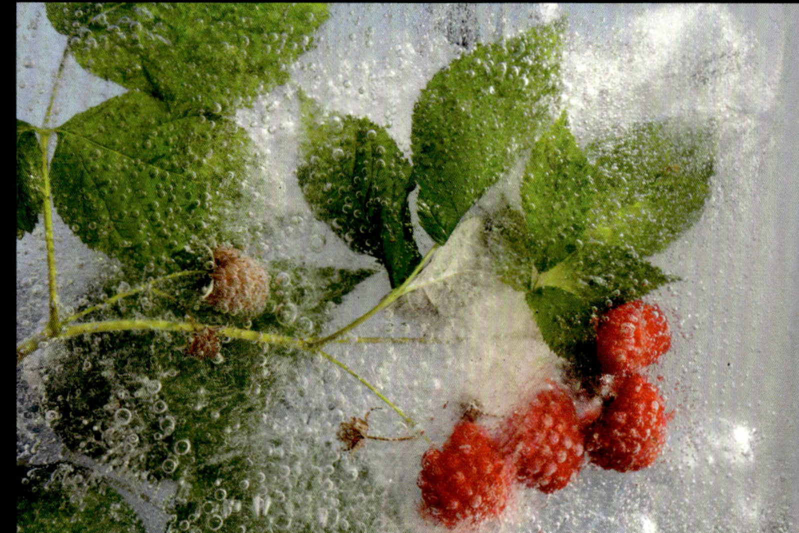

2

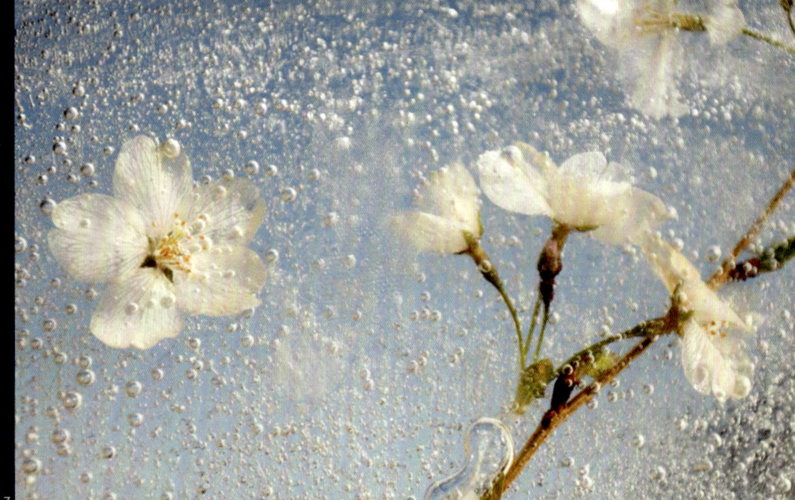

3

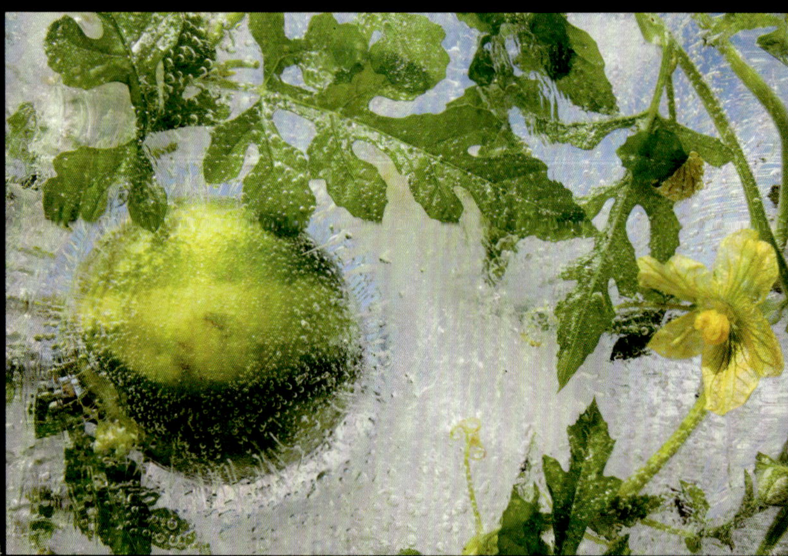

4

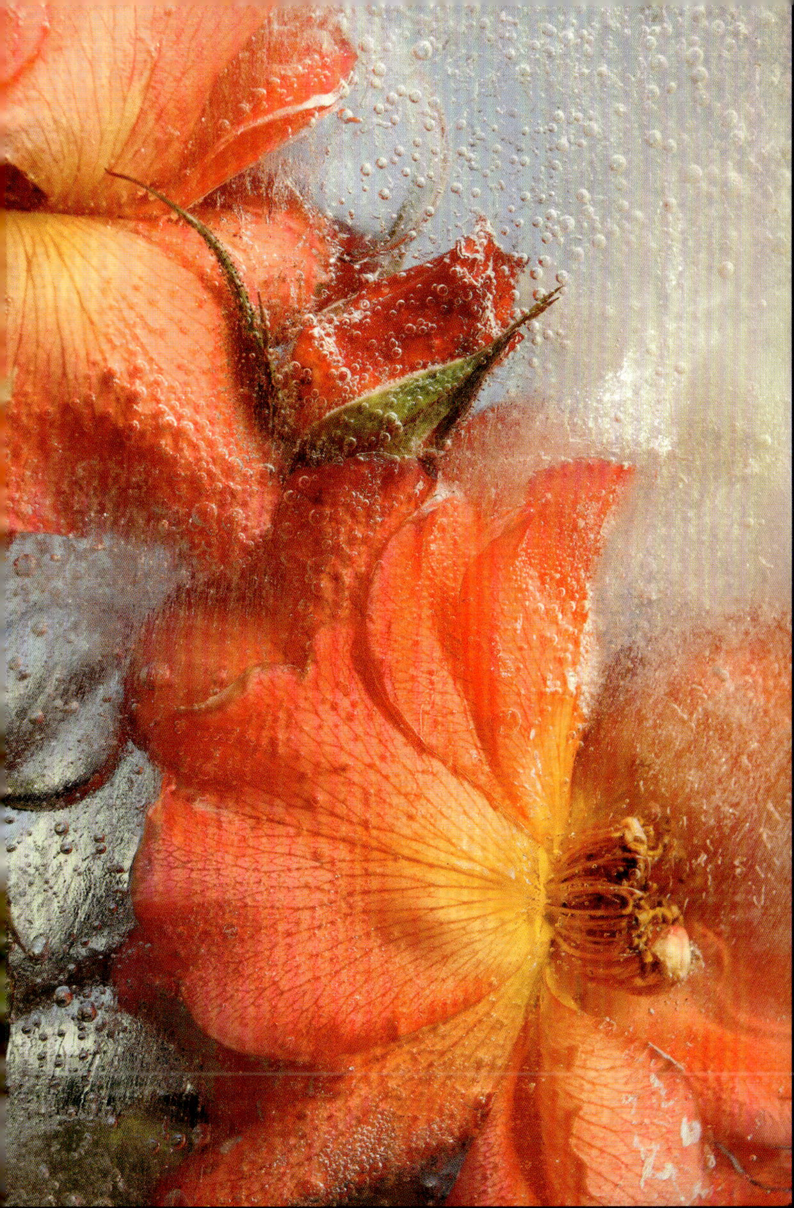

6

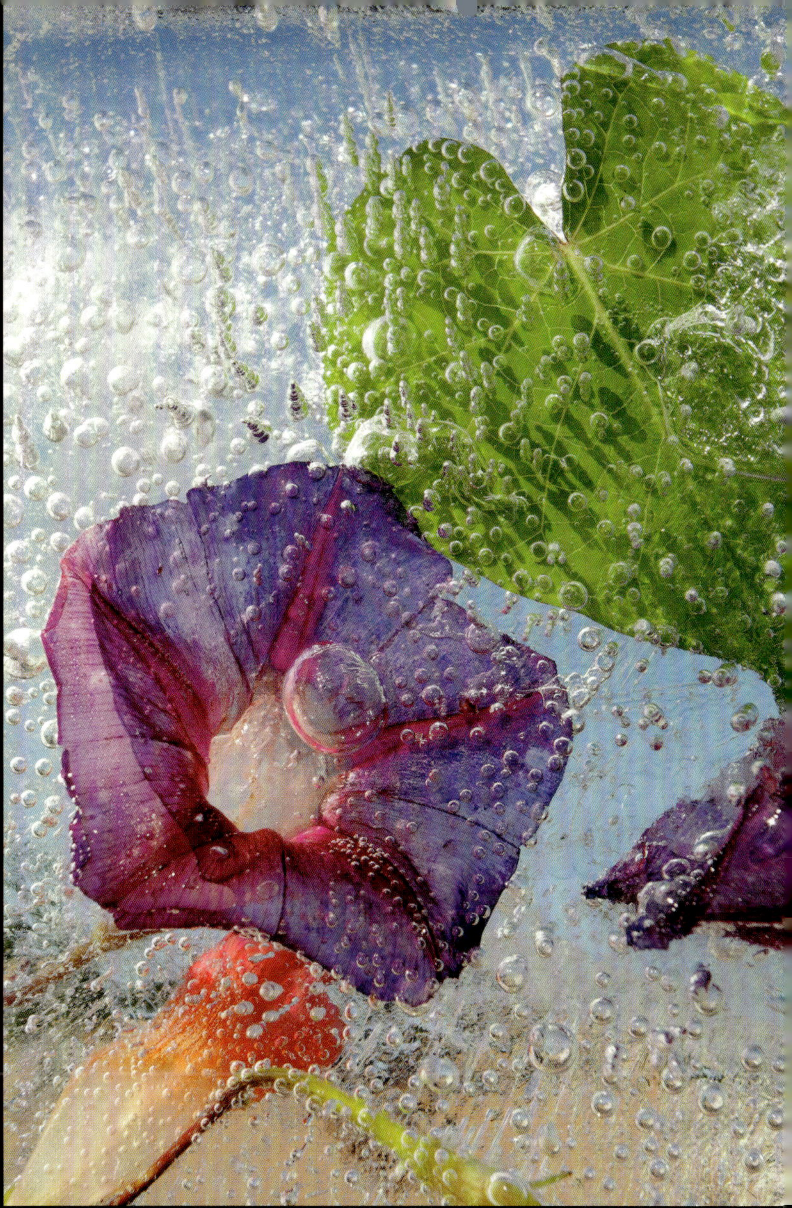

–Pink English Roses, Iced. These David Austin 'Heritage' pink roses are a favourite in my garden. They have inspired many creative photographs.
2–Raspberries, Iced. This year was the best yet for my raspberries: it was difficult to part with this cluster and not eat it. Some plants lose their colour when frozen into a block of ice, but the raspberries held up very well.
3–Cherry Blossoms from Bethesda, Iced. This fragile blossoming branch made it all the way from Bethesda to Boston on an airplane. After a particularly harsh winter, I made a special trip to Washington D.C. to capture the first breath of spring.

4–Baby Watermelon and Blossom, Iced. This year I grew watermelons in pots on my roof deck garden. I was attracted to the bright yellow flower, strong vine, and chartreuse striped melon.
5–Oranges Roses, Iced. These orange roses are incredibly fragrant: one can even smell them as the ice melts. When making this ice plate, I was inspired by the background detail of Botticelli's Birth of Venus where flowers fall against blue sky and green sea.
6–Morning Glory, Iced. Morning glories are difficult to embed in ice as they are very fragile and resistant to being in water. I was happy to see this one with the bubble detail, and its color held up well. When I work with this plant, I'm inspired by Japanese morning glory print designs.

A Vision becomes a Garden
Hilden, Germany

I came to know Peter, a young garden designer and plantsman, when he started to plan his garden in Hilden, Germany about four years ago and I was fascinated by his passion and professional work. Since then I met him regularly at his garden through the seasons. I have tried to show the magic and variety of the various aspects of the garden: the woodland garden, the gravel garden, the border garden, the exotic garden and the water garden. I visited and photographed Peter's garden many, many times and it was amazing to see how the garden has developed with surprising new aspects and plant combinations.

This garden project became an adventure for Peter and me, so we decided to make a book out of it which will be published in Germany in spring this year.

Nikon D3 and D3X, Nikkor 55mm lens. Post-capture: basic colour management.

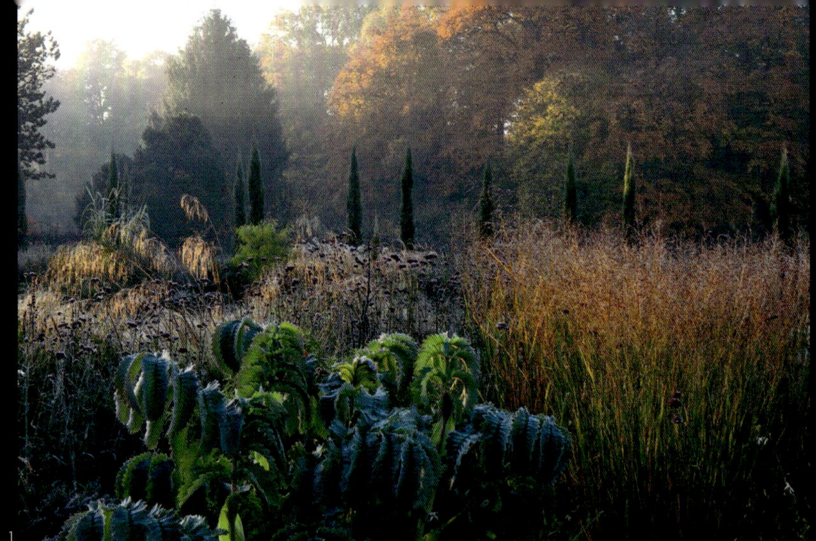
1

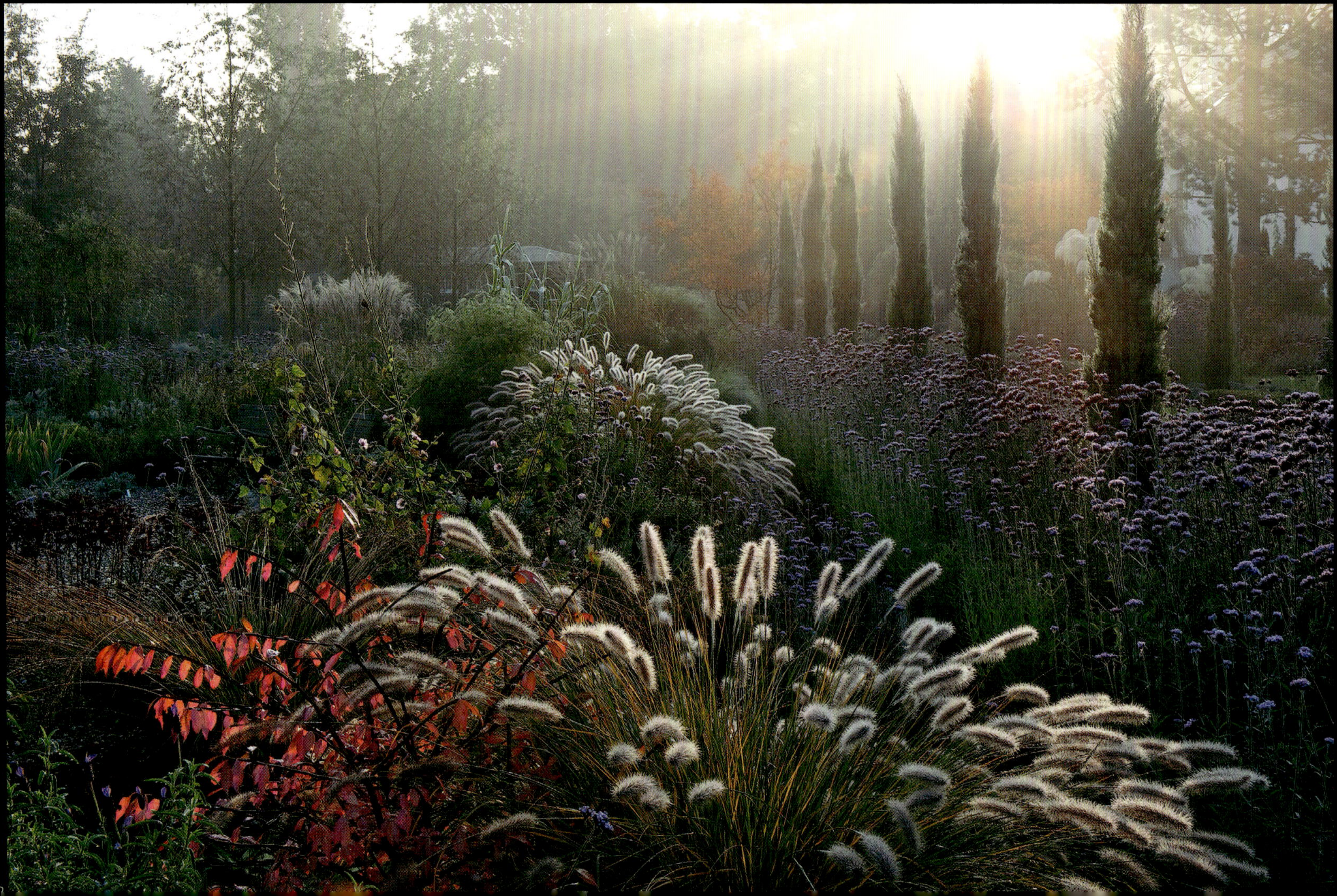

2

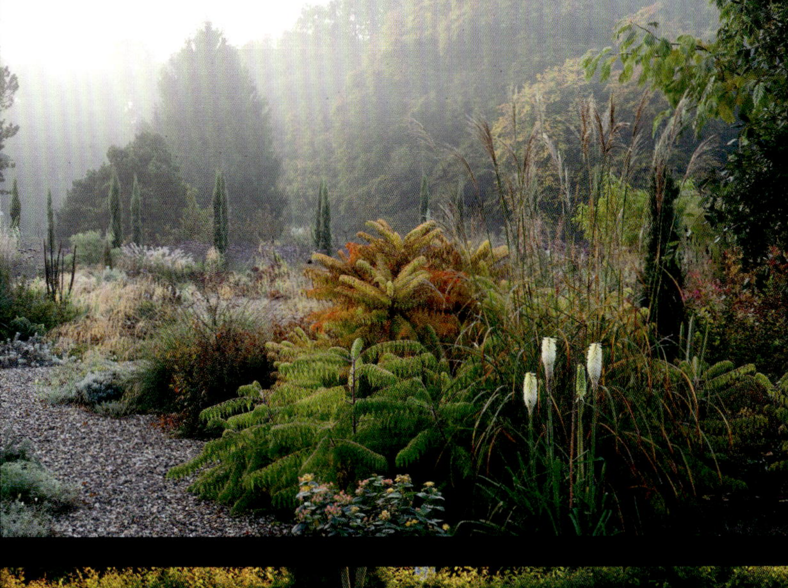

4

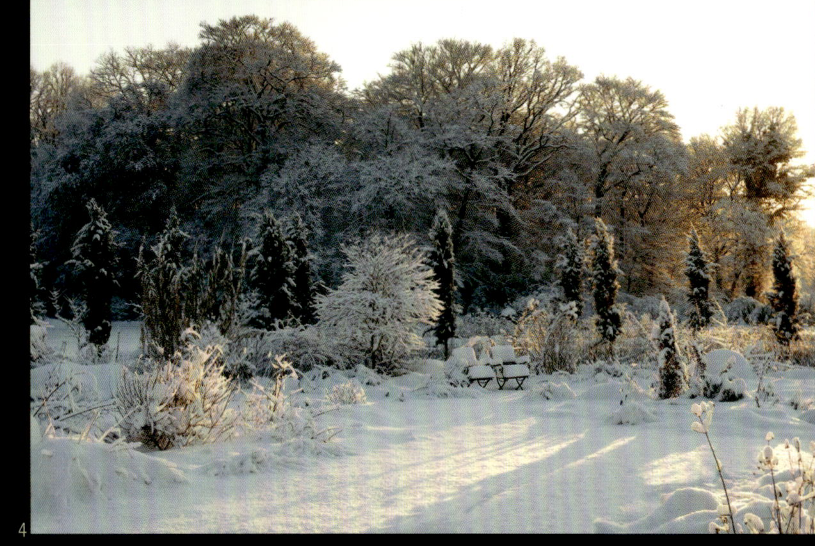

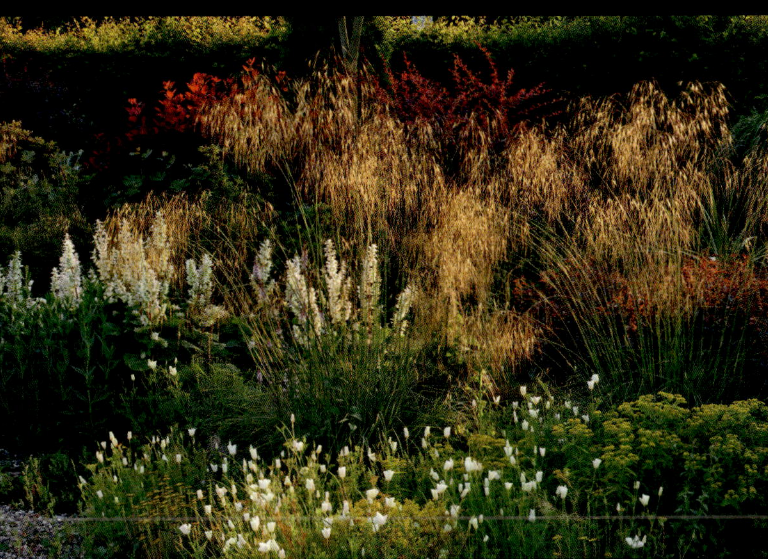

6

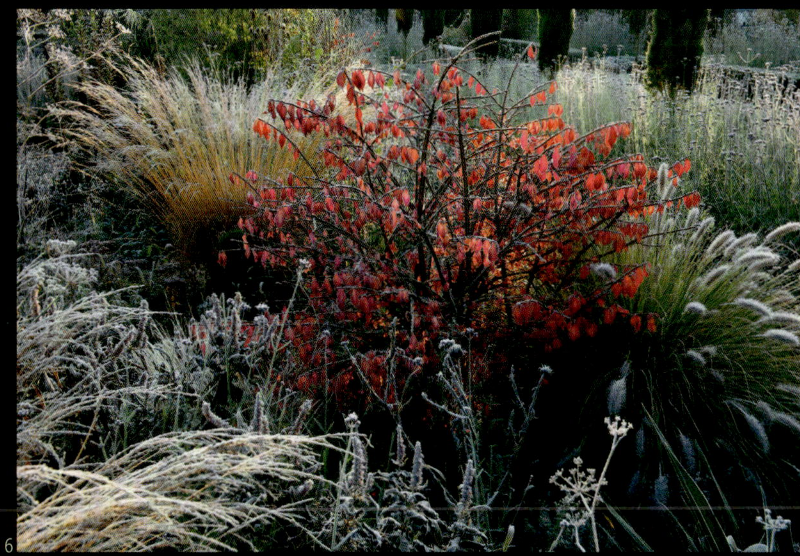

1–Early frost in the grass border
2–Pennisetum, verbena, euonymus in early morning light
3–Miscanthus, stipa, kniphofia in autumn
4–Snow in Peter's garden
5–Grass border in high summer
6–Early frost on the leaves of euonymus

Japanese Gardens of North America

United States

I spent much of 2011 photographing Japanese gardens throughout the United States and Canada. I love doing this, and I also had an assignment to photograph them for an upcoming book. The six portfolio images were some of my favorites from the year, and the image from Portland, Oregon was from an earlier shoot in 2009.

For me this garden landscape portfolio captures the magical early morning light and the moody images you can get on foggy days. Since Japanese gardens are also about seasons, I wanted to represent a few of them here.

Canon EOS 5D, Canon 24-70mm lens, except on Fort Worth image - Canon 70-200mm lens. Post-capture: five of the six images were channel blended; in the image from Phoenix, Arizona I erased one electrical plug.

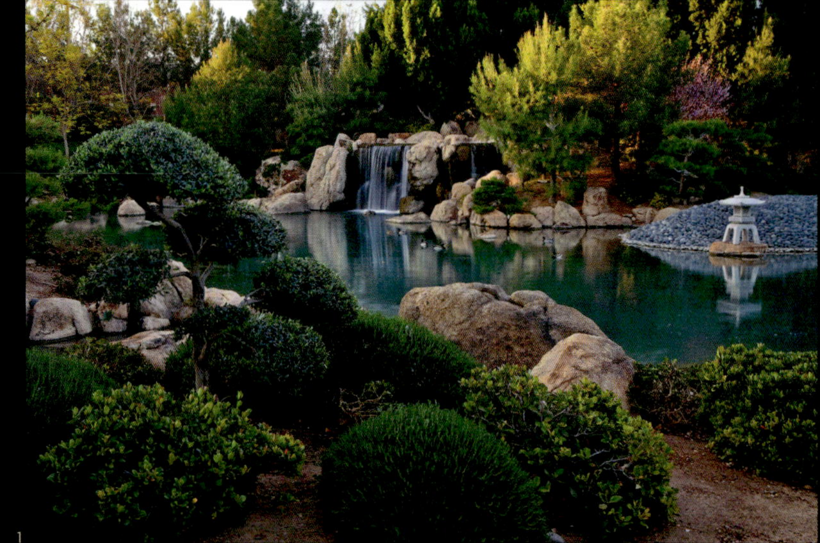

1

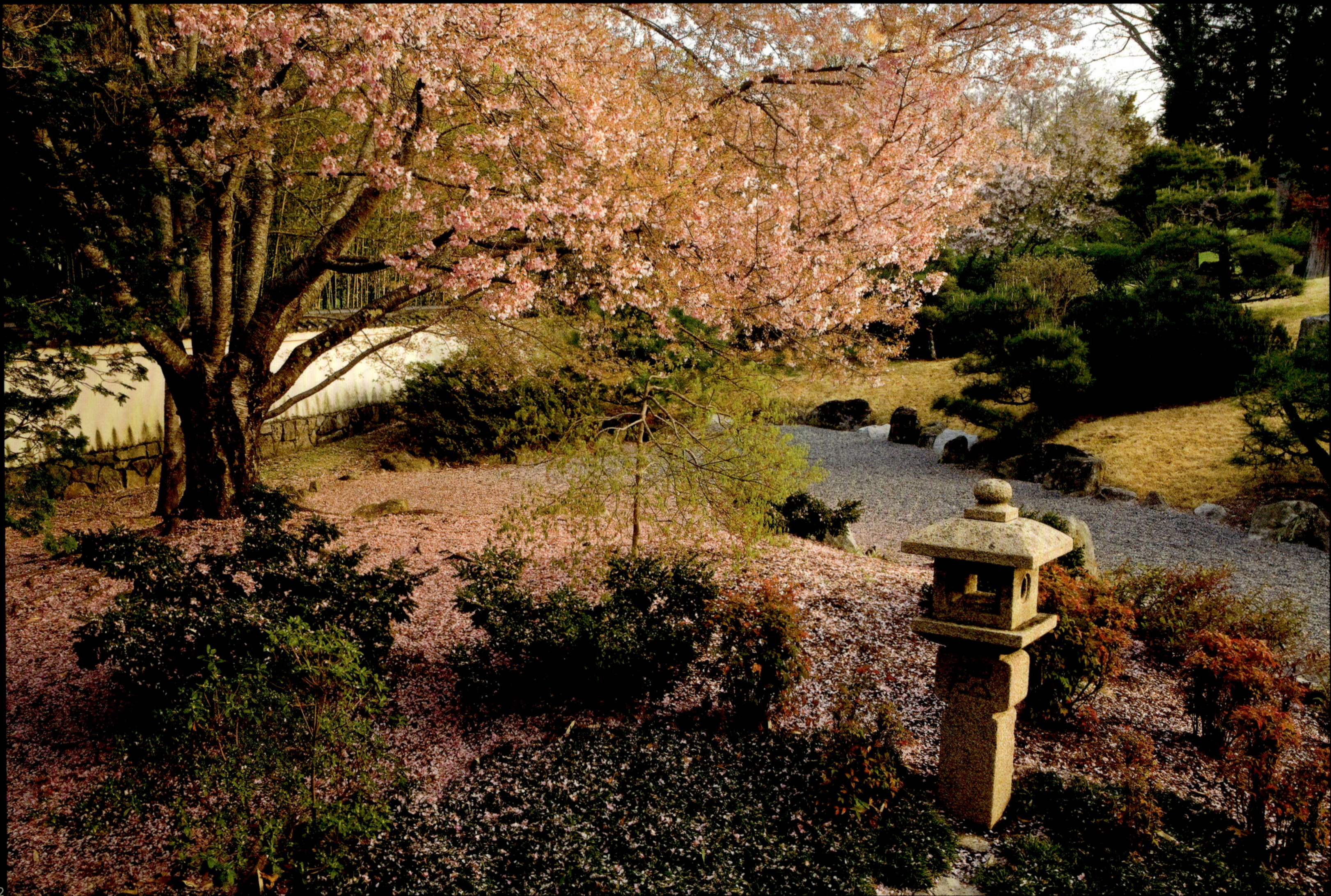

2

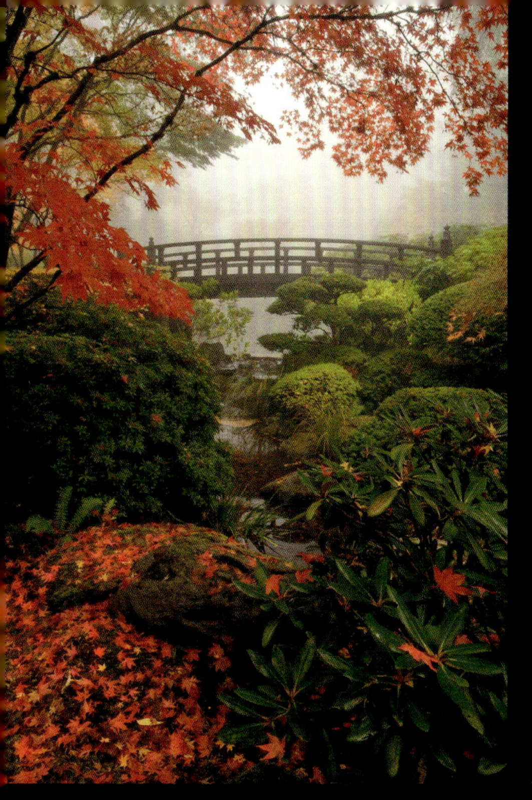

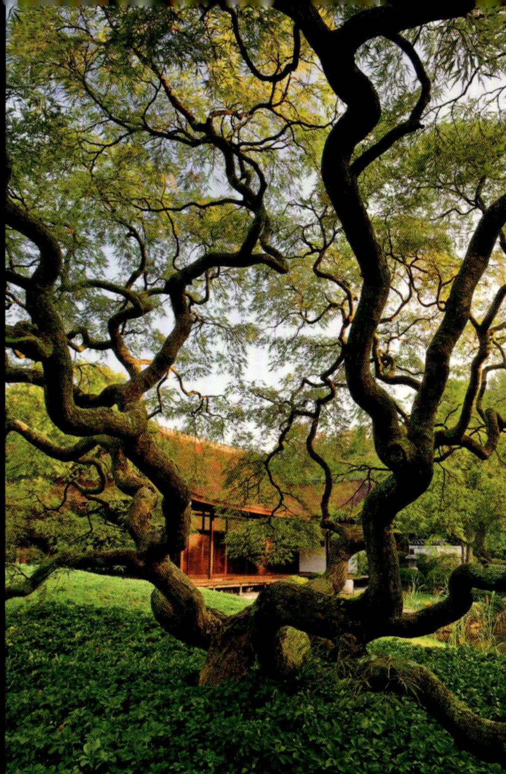

4

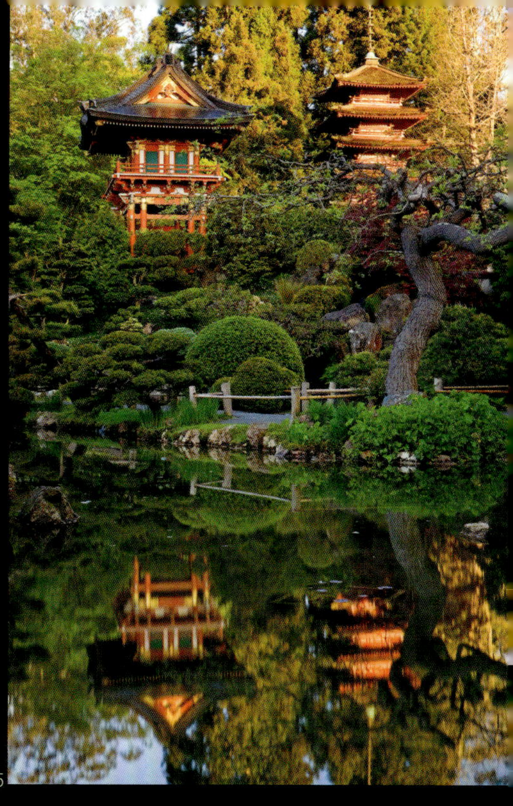

5

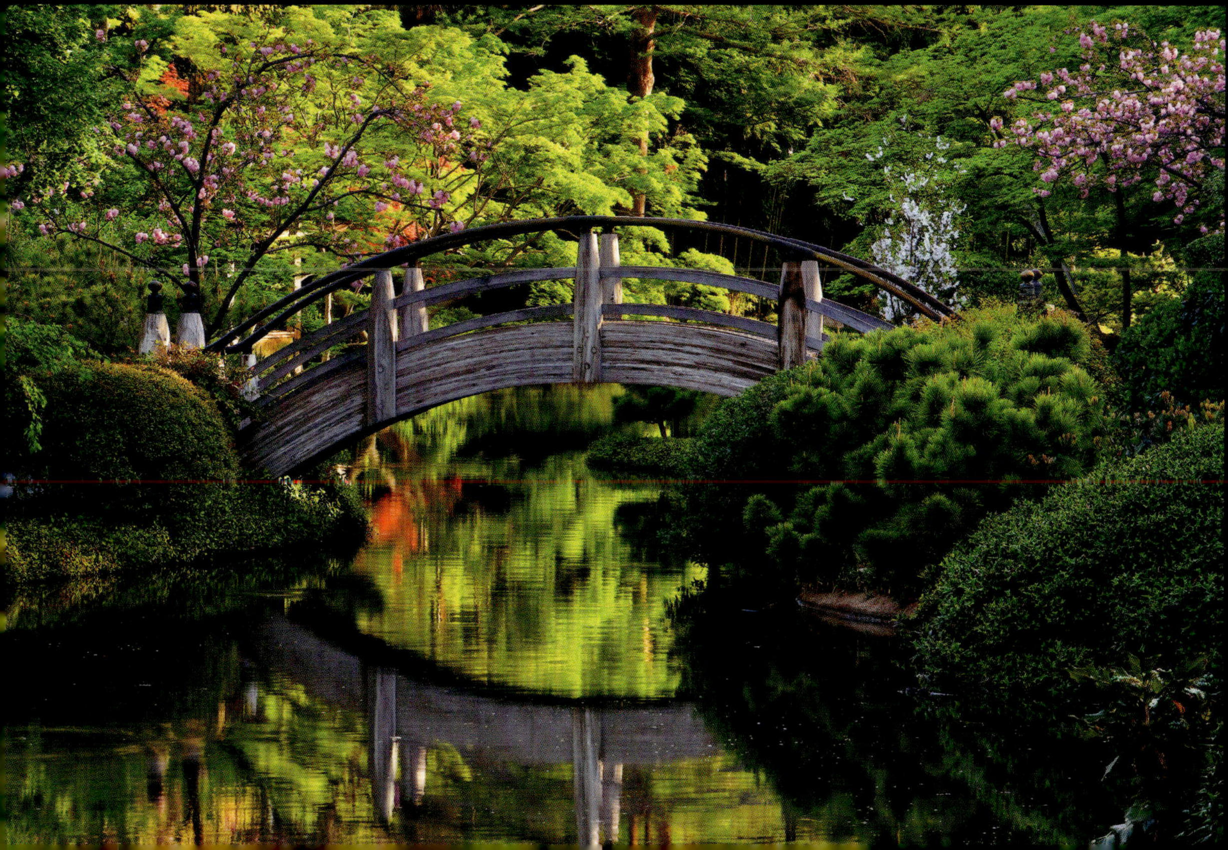

1–A Japanese garden desert setting at the Friendship Garden, Phoenix, Arizona.
2–Morning cherry blossoms at the Shomu'en, Cheekwood.
3–Fog arrives in the Portland Japanese Garden, Oregon.
4–A Japanese maple frames the tea house at the Shofuso in Philadelphia.
5–Pagoda Reflections. First light on the Pagodas at the Japanese Tea Garden in San Francisco, California.
6–First light on the Moon Bridge at Fort Worth Botanical Garden, Texas.

LIZ EVERY HIGHLY COMMENDED, THE BEAUTY OF PLANTS

The August Garden
My garden in Cheshire, UK

I found all of these flowers and seed heads in my garden during August. They are the quiet, intricate, smaller treasures that need close inspection to reveal their beauty. All the subjects are single specimens of buds, flower heads or, in one case, a seed head photographed against a white background.

Canon EOS 5D Mark II, 100mm lens. From 1/1sec at f/20 to 1/125sec at f/9.
Post-capture: contrast adjusted.

1–Clematis Seedhead. There seems to be movement in the shape of this seedhead, as if it is spinning like a Catherine wheel.
2–Dahlia Bud. The tightness of the bud and the promise of what is to come attracted me to this subject.
3–Feather Clover Flower. I noticed this small flower with its many flowers when the thousands of tiny hairs caught the light.
4–Globe Thistle. The tiny flowers seem to burst out of the ends of the spikes of the thistle.
5–Knapweed Flower. The individual red flowers are quite insignificant, but the pattern of the flower head is where the interest lies.
6–Teasel Flower. The outer, upward pointing 'leaves' seem to be protecting the tiny inner flowers.

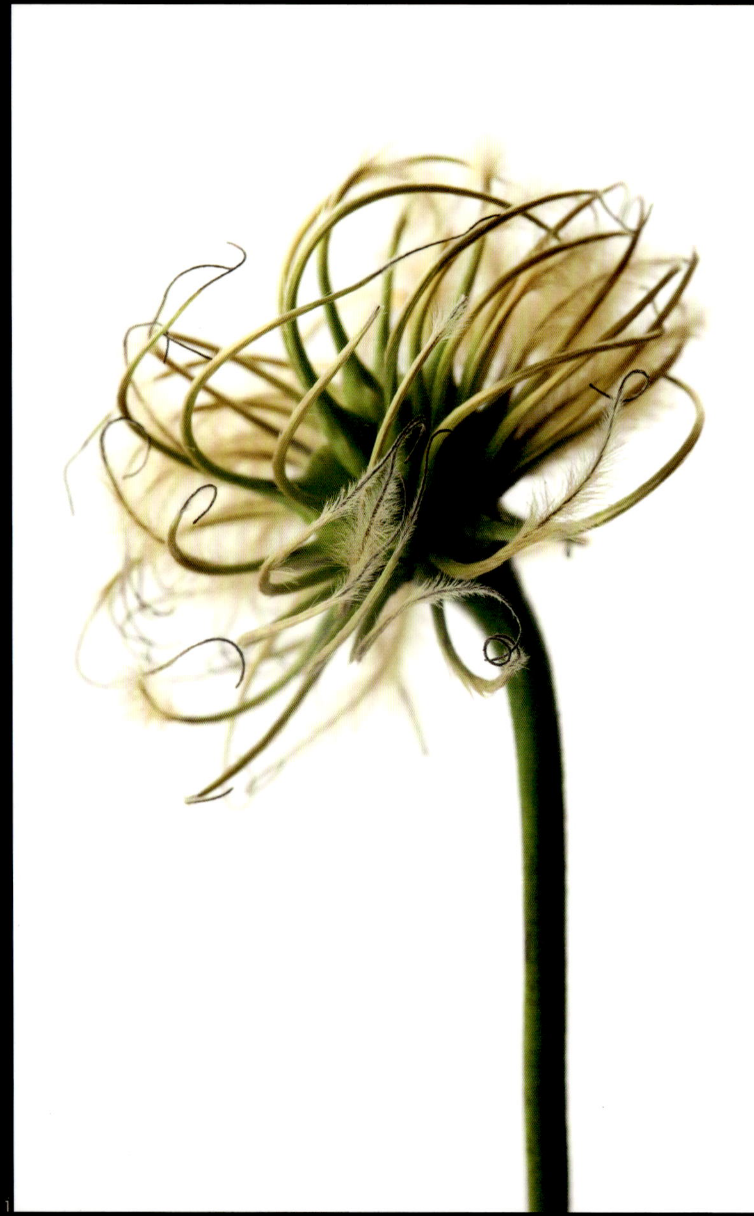
1

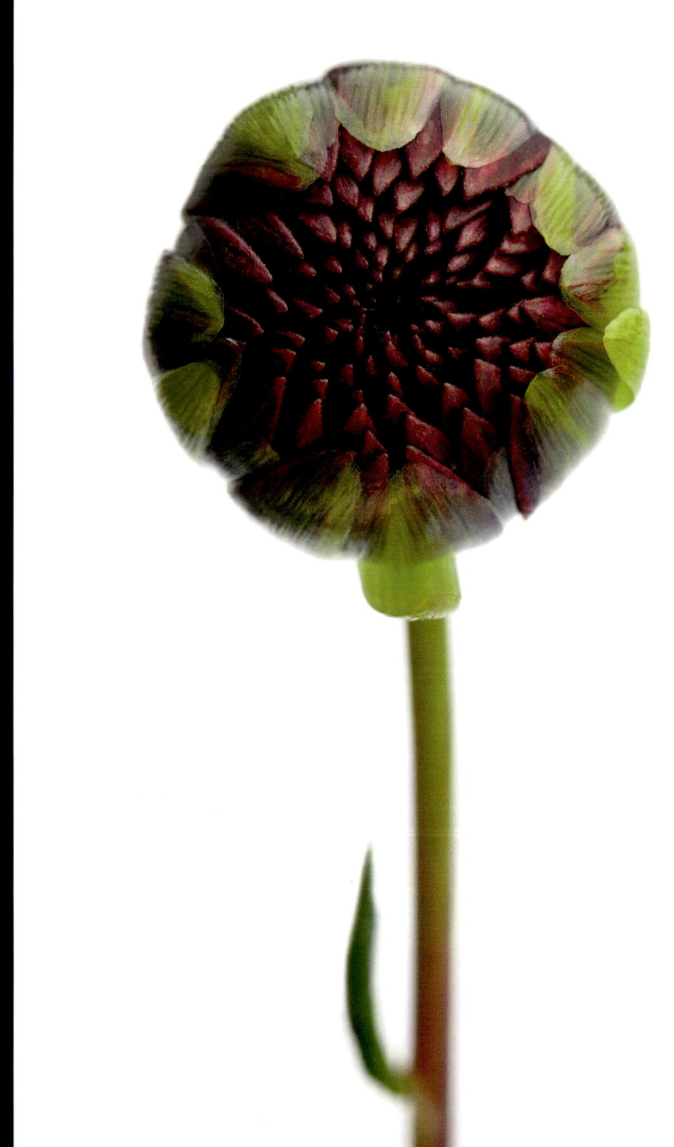
2

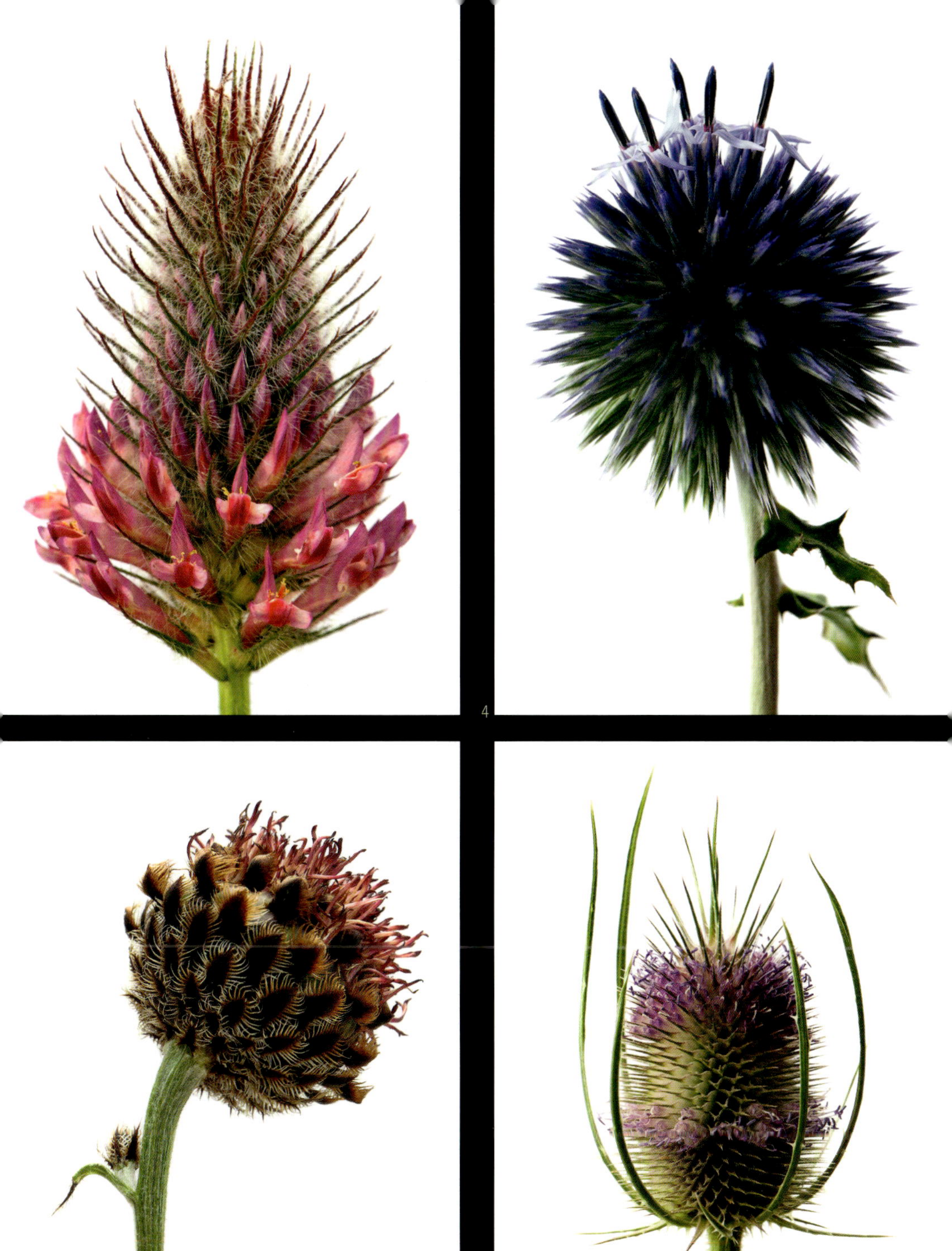
4
6

ANNEMARIE FARLEY HIGHLY COMMENDED, THE BEAUTY OF PLANTS

Impressions of a Cyclamen
Daylight home studio, UK

Just as the cyclamen (*Cyclamen persicum*) started to emerge in autumn this year I started to photograph different aspects of its personality. A lot of the time it was cold and wet outside making photography very difficult, so I ended up taking the flowers inside. I was inspired to take this portfolio in homage to French photographer Joseph Nicéphore Niépce. He produced the world's first photograph called 'View from the Window at Le Gras' (1826). In the absence of a lens, the resulting image was more 'impressionistic' than a clear recording of the scene. I did not want a sharp, posed image; I wanted more of an impression of an autumn flower fading away into winter and a sense of its character as seen in early photography. I did this by adding texture, fading the colour of the final image, and softening the original images.

Nikon D300, Sigma 105mm lens. The original image of the cyclamen was taken with soft focus to give a pinhole camera effect. Post-capture: I converted the images into black and white, then added a warmer (sepia) distressed texture over the top to create a duotone effect. I then toned the merged image with a 'blue/green' colour (a little like an aged 70s Polaroid) and reduced the vibrancy to make it look old and faded.

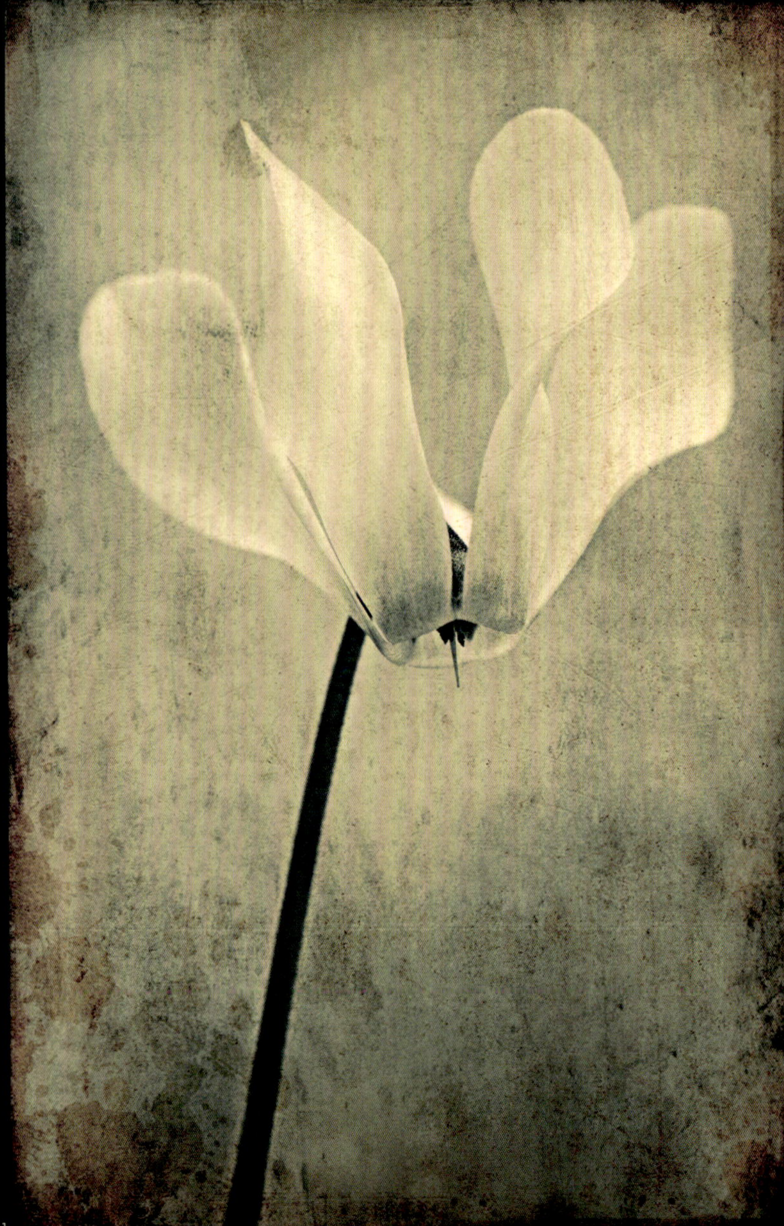

1

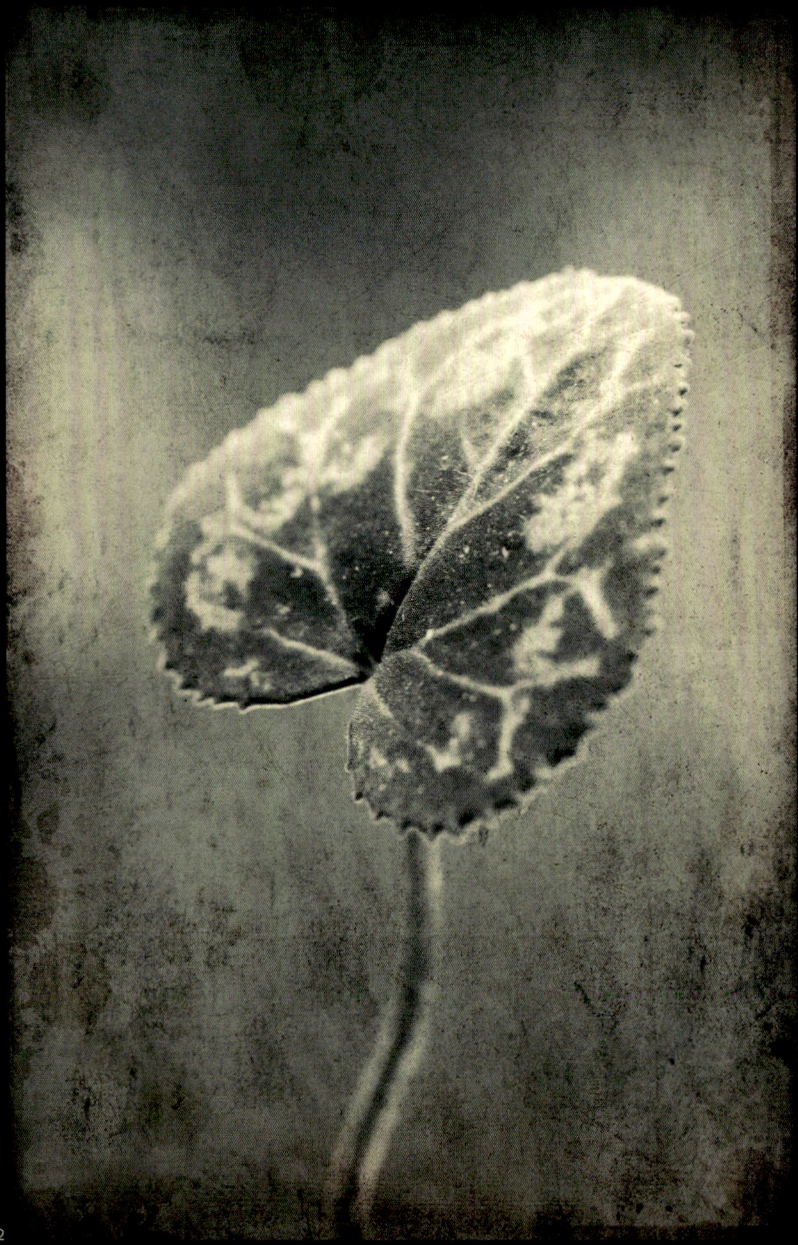

2

1–Flower head
2–Flower leaf
3–Flower bud
4–The back of the flower head
5–The front of the flower head
6–Budding flower

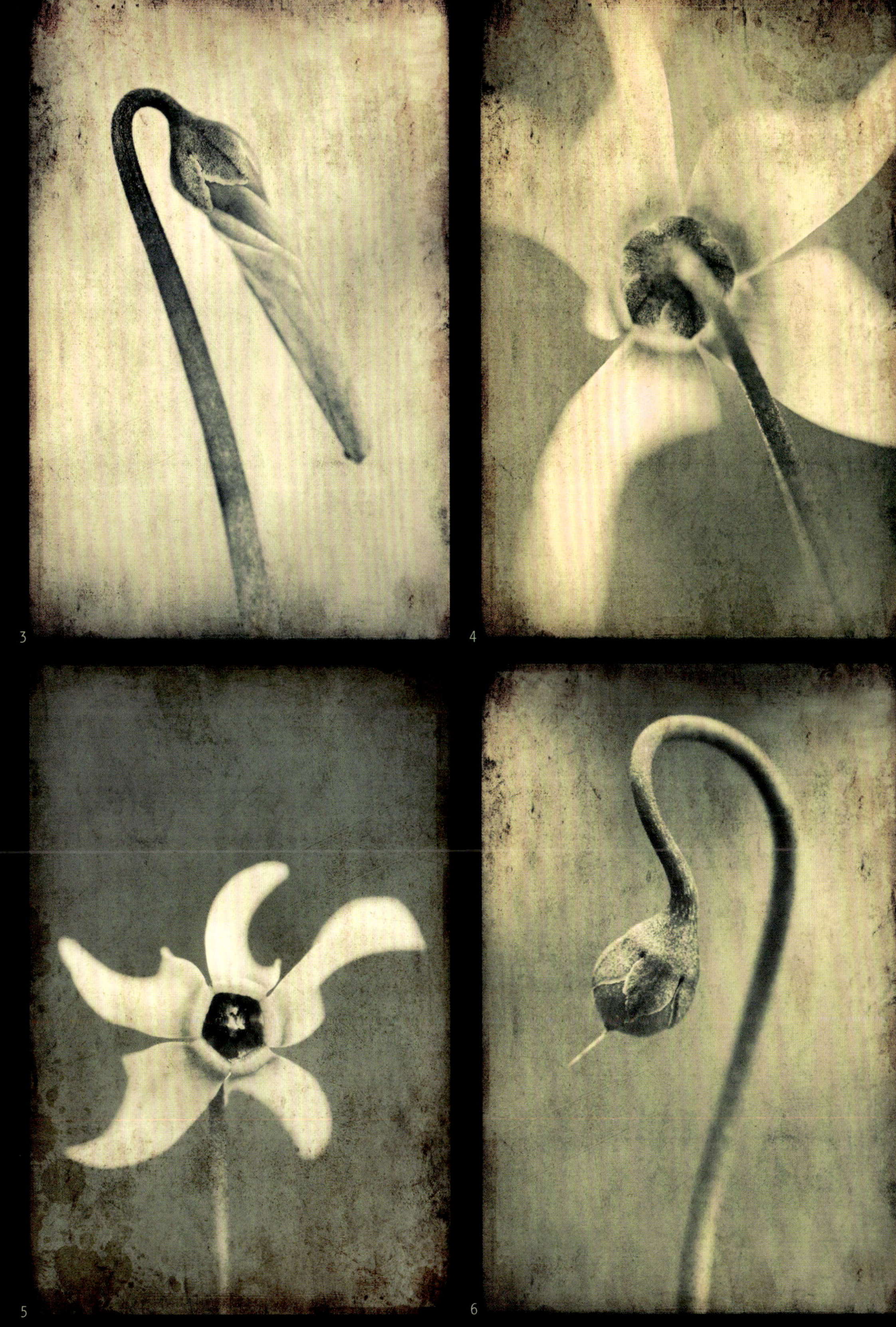

3 4 5 6

Dead Gorgeous
My garden, Devon, UK

This is part of a larger collection of images created for an exhibition inspired by the beauty discovered within the decay found around my garden and close to my home: a beauty often overlooked and too quickly consigned to the compost heap or rubbish tip. It is a reaction against the sterilisation of the world around us, and a celebration of the undesirable, the neglected and wrinkled!

Having returned to Devon in early 2011 after escaping seven years of hard labour on the construction sites of London, I decided I had to return to photography. Short of funds and unable to travel far, I challenged myself to see what I could find within walking distance of my home. Most were taken in the last days of September in a state of total panic having found myself two weeks before an exhibition with only four suitable images to hang. I applied my new philosophy to photography: try to forget any rules, don't wait for the light and just do it!

Nikon D700, 90mm and 300mm lenses. Post capture: varying degrees of both general and local tonal adjustments. Some textured overlays added.

1–I just can't go on anymore
2–Bad hair day
3–Balancing act
4–Swan lake
5–Silent song
6–Diving kingfisher

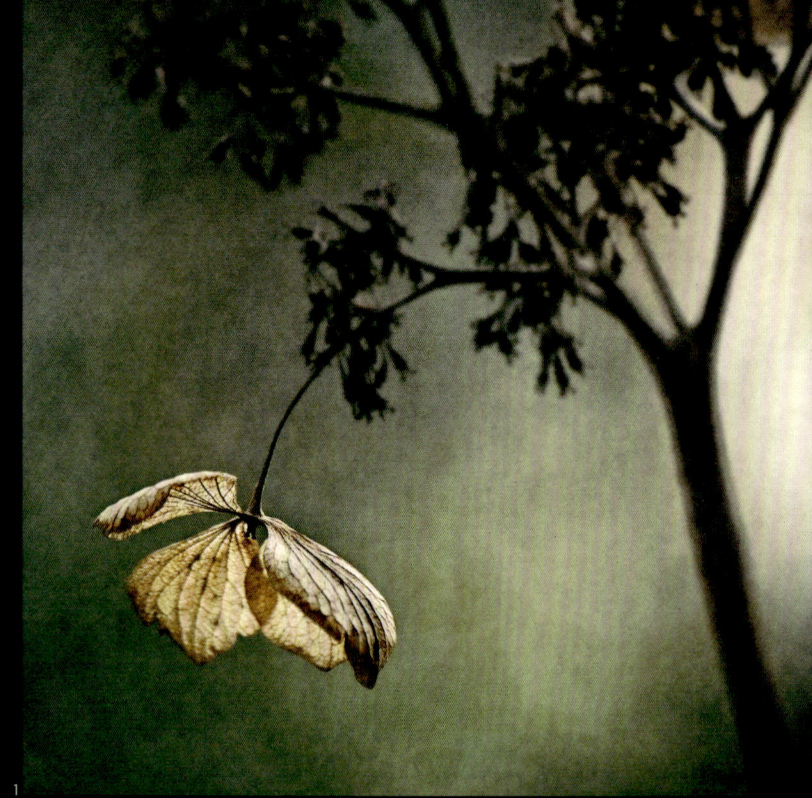
1

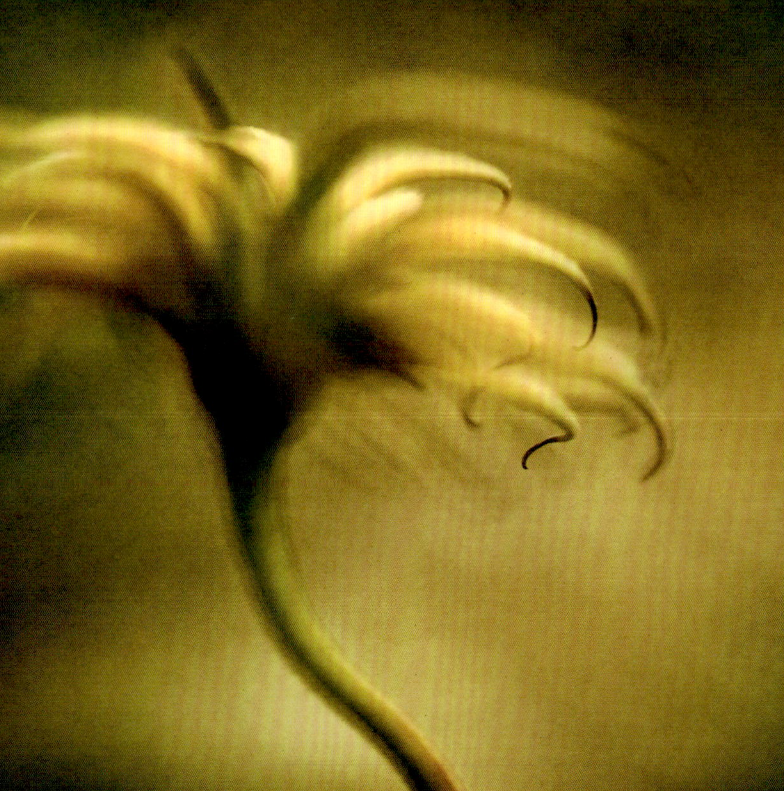
2

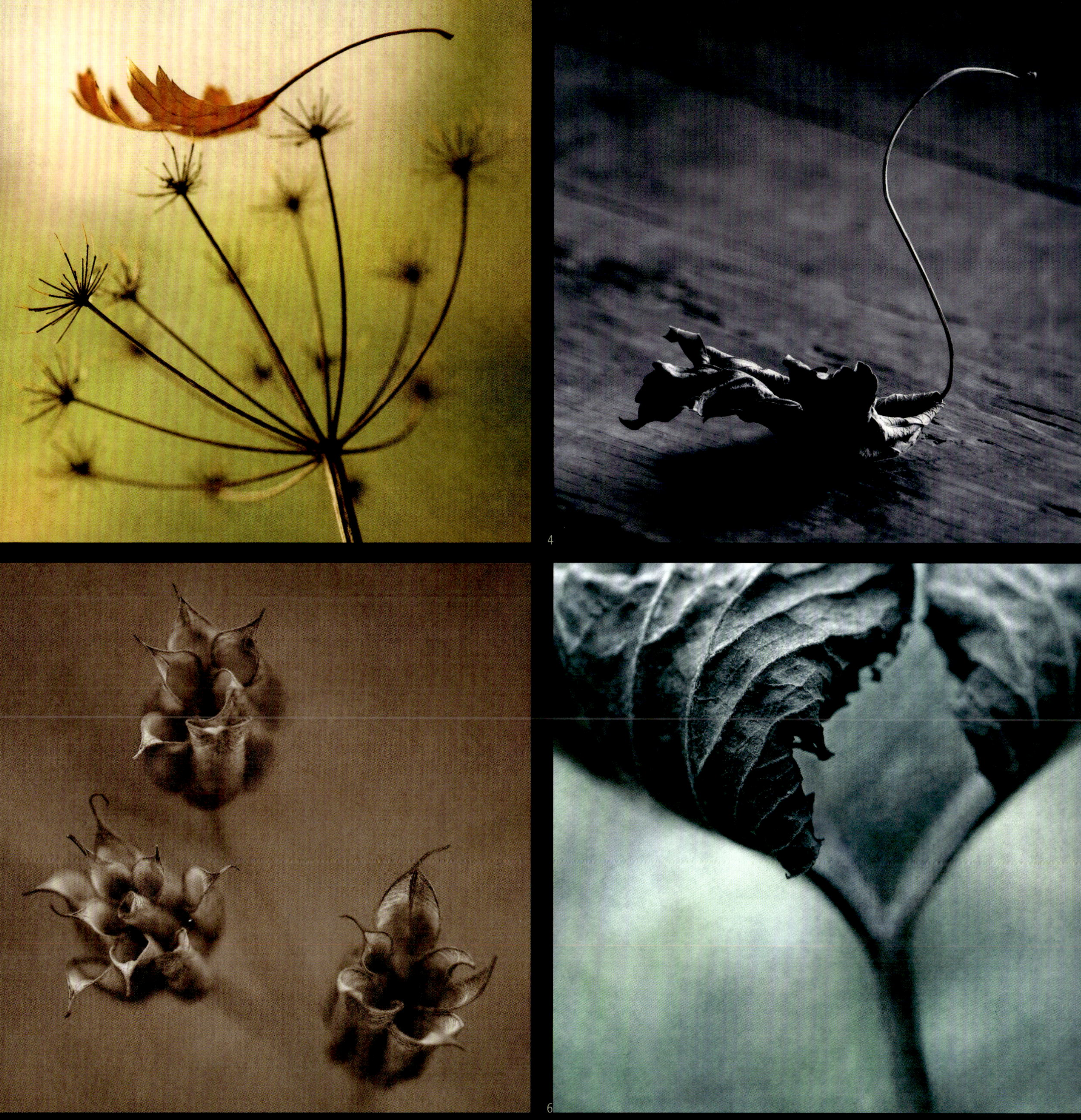

4

6

NEW GARDENS IN LANGUEDOC

JEAN DU BOISBERRANGER

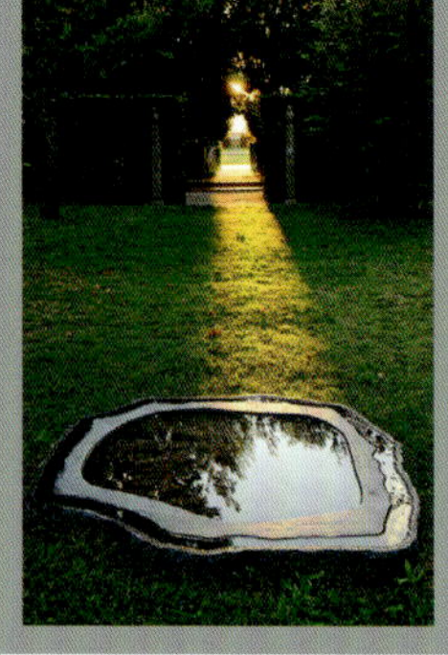
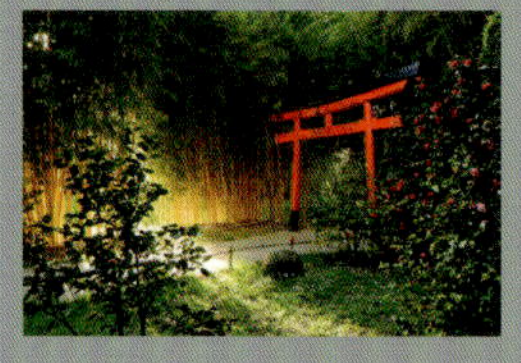
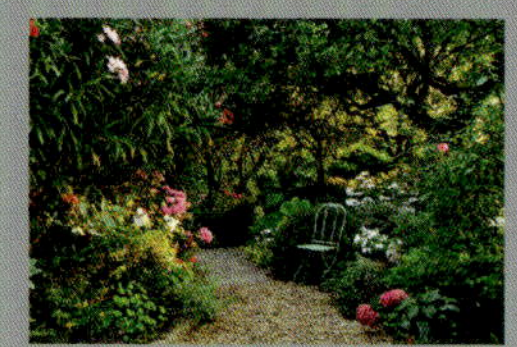
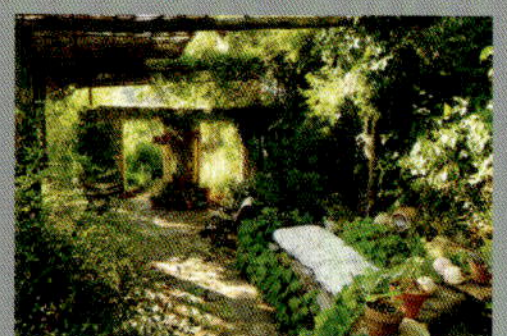
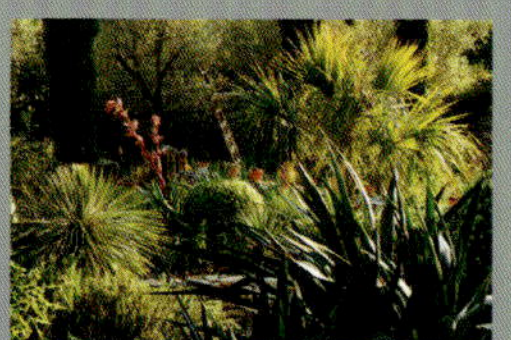
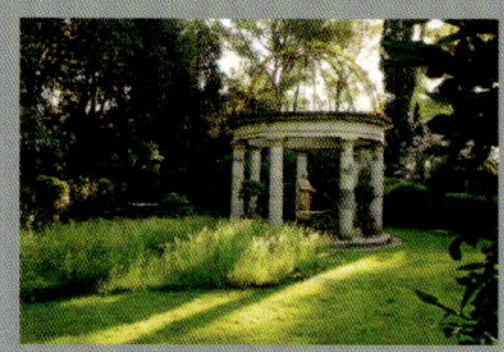

PRESSED FLOWERS

JOHN HUMPHREY

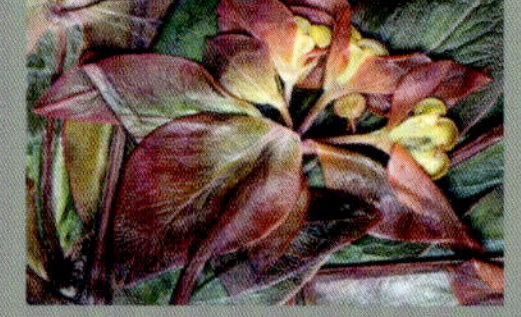
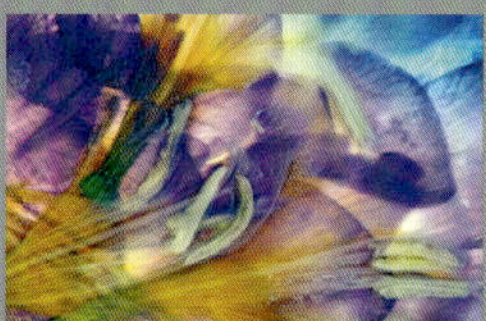
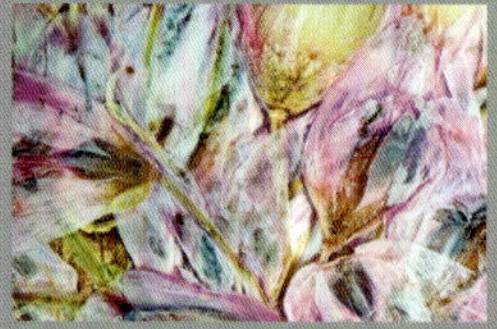
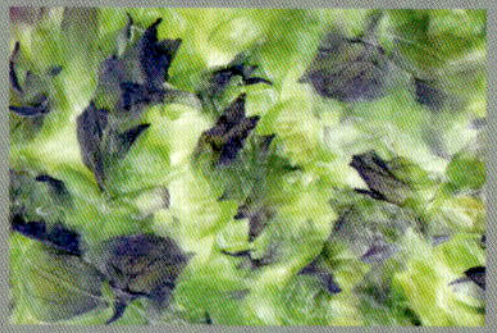
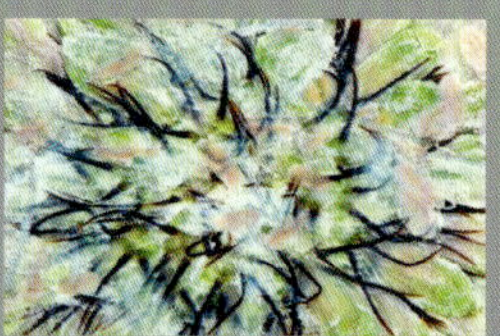
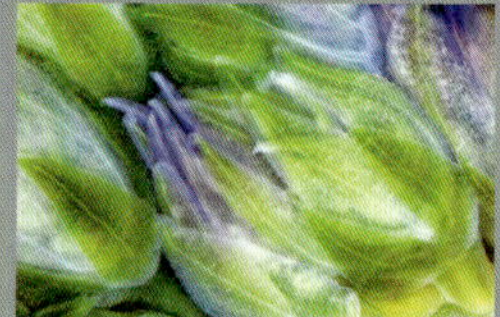

SEEKING THE LIGHT OF ENCHANTMENT

PETER DOBSON

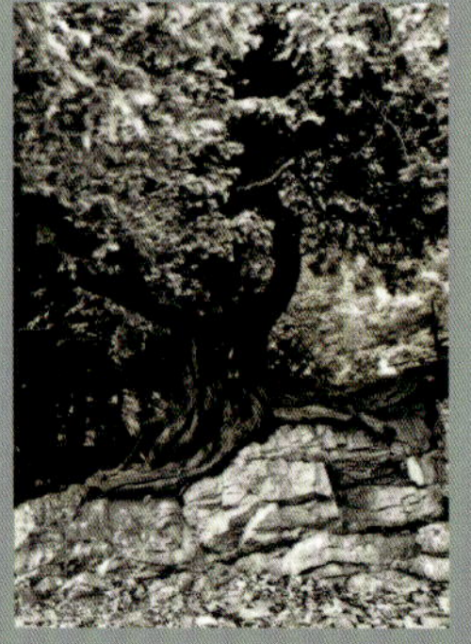
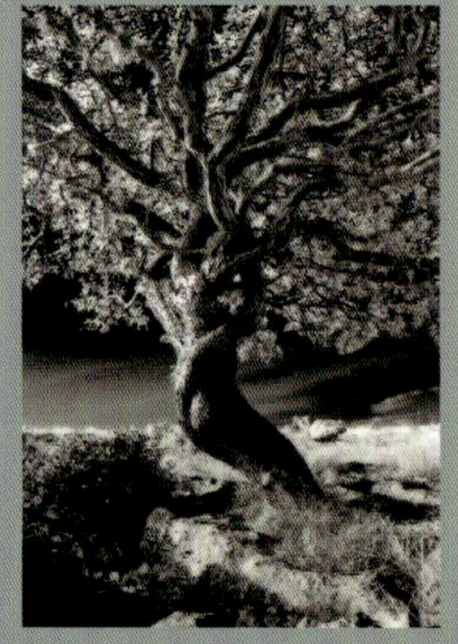
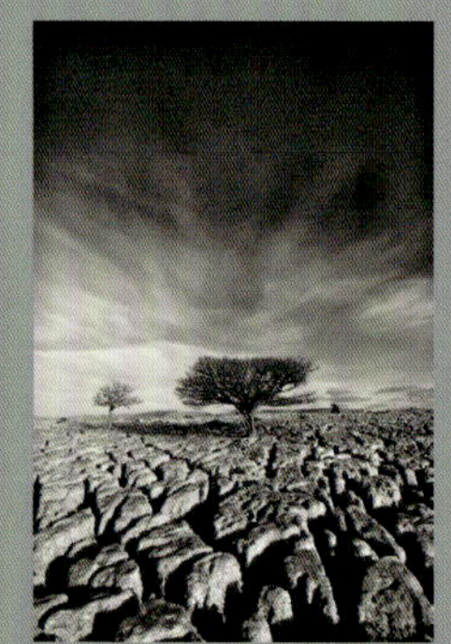
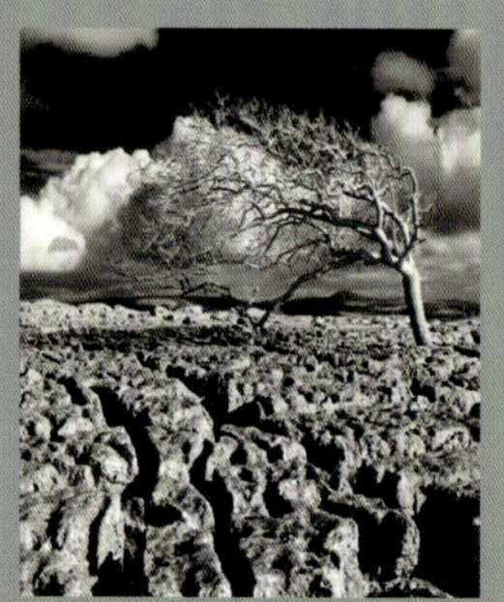
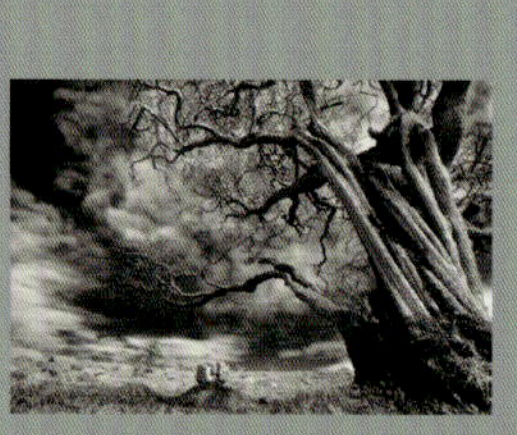
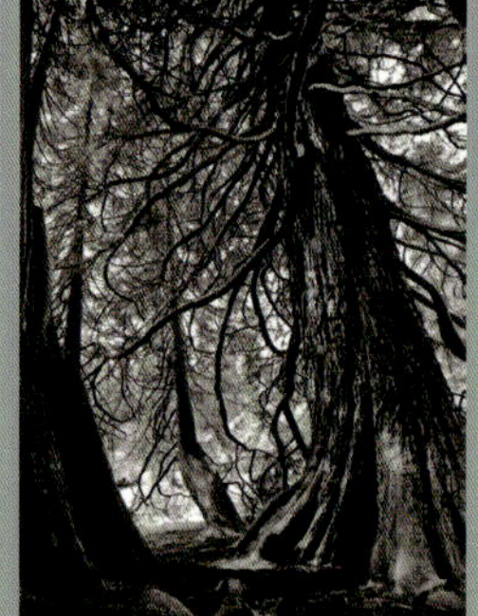

BIRD'S-EYE VIEW

NEIL OVERY

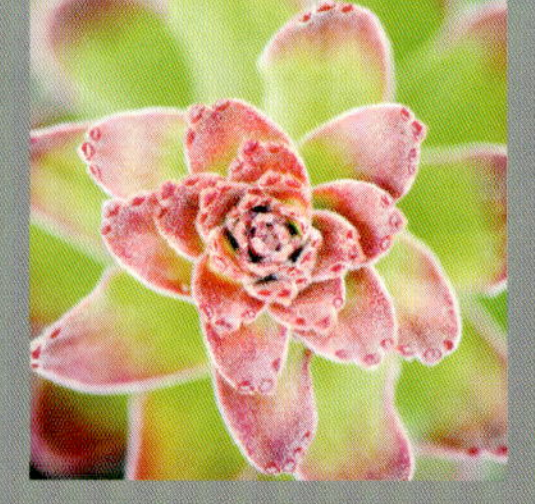
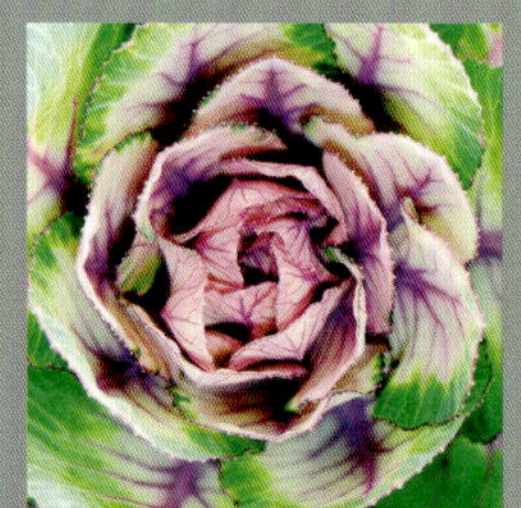
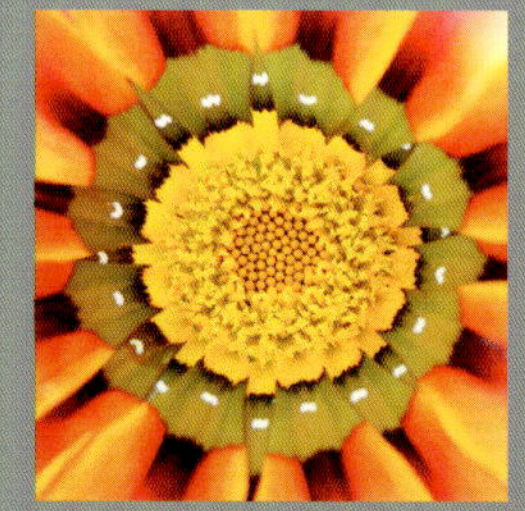
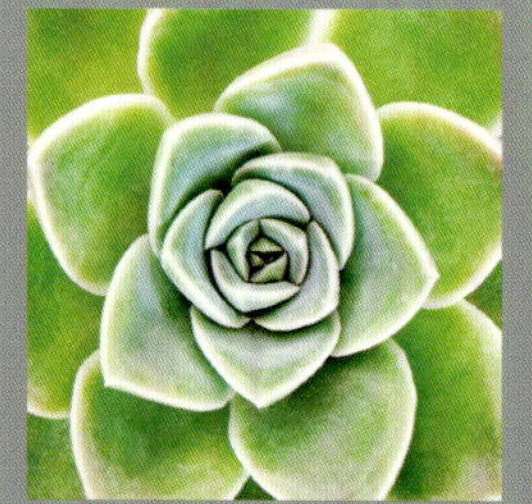
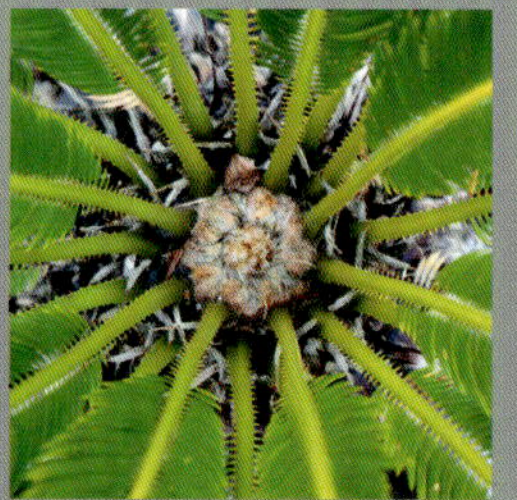
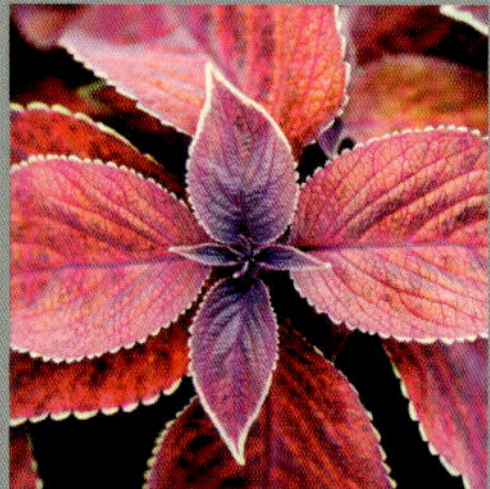

SNOW BIRDS **GRAHAM LOVE**

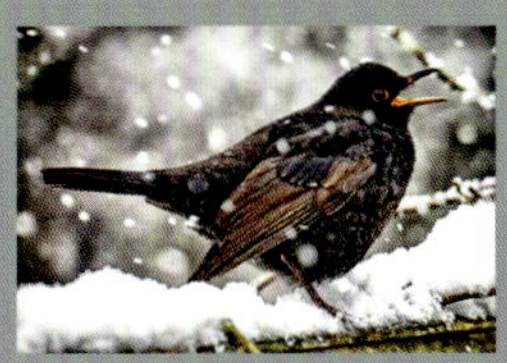
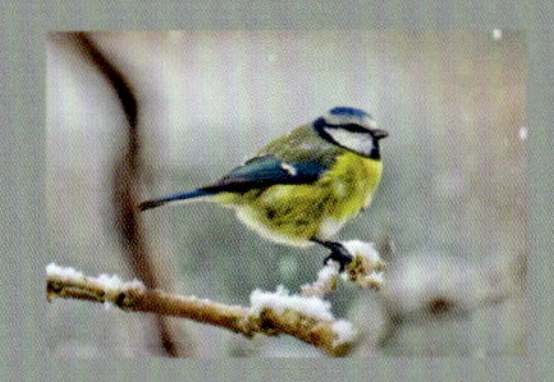
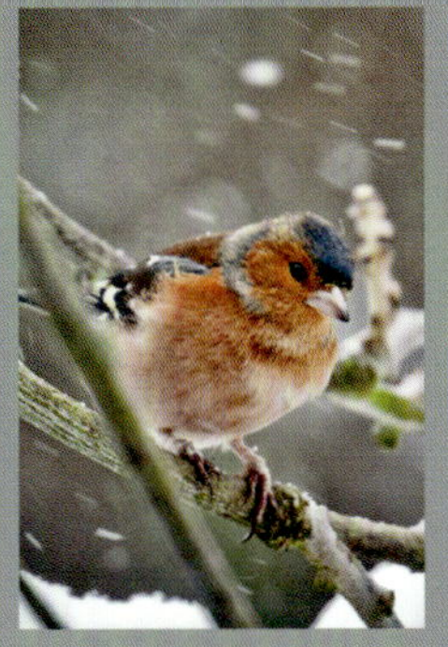
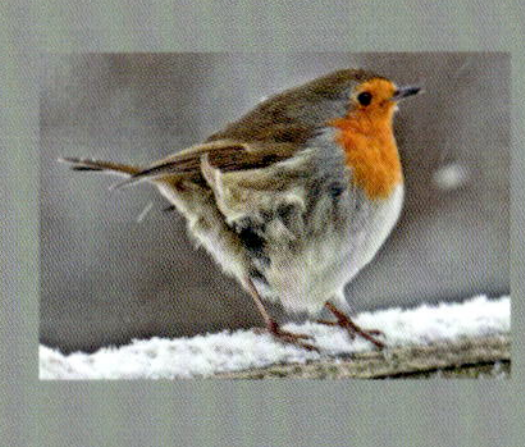
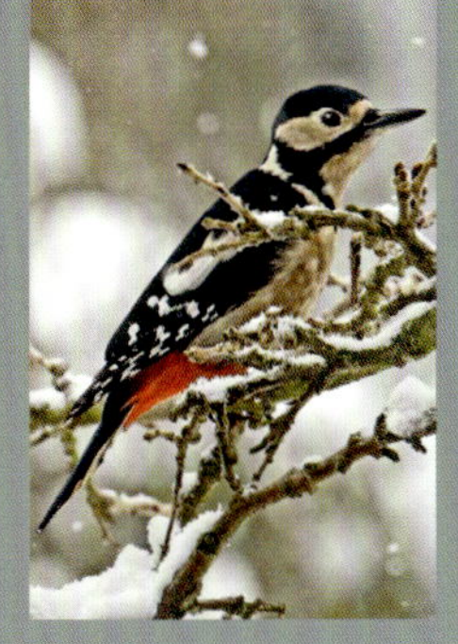
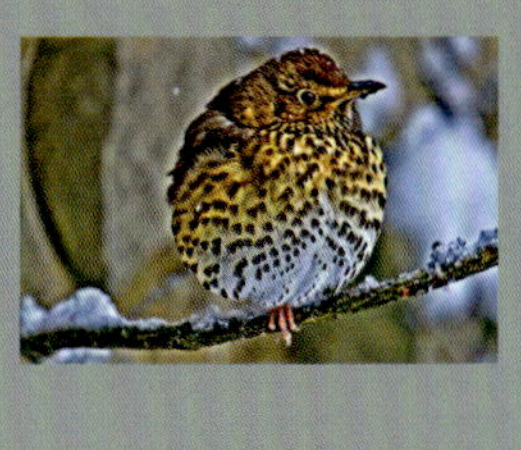

LAS POZAS SURREAL **MALCOLM RAGGETT**

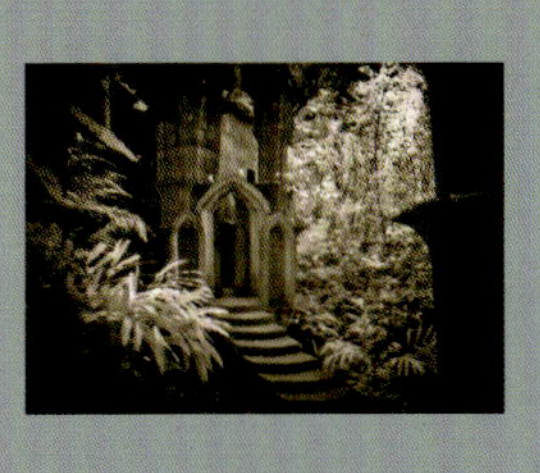
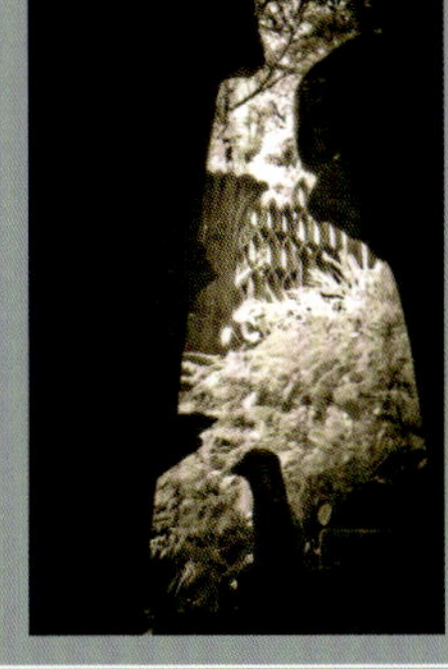
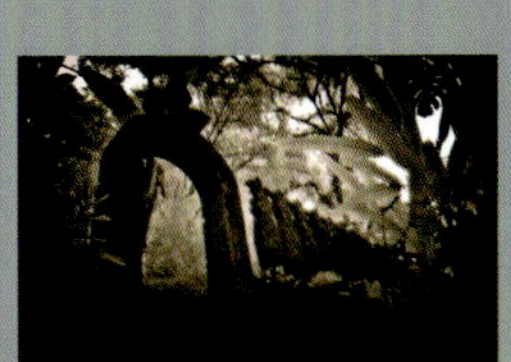
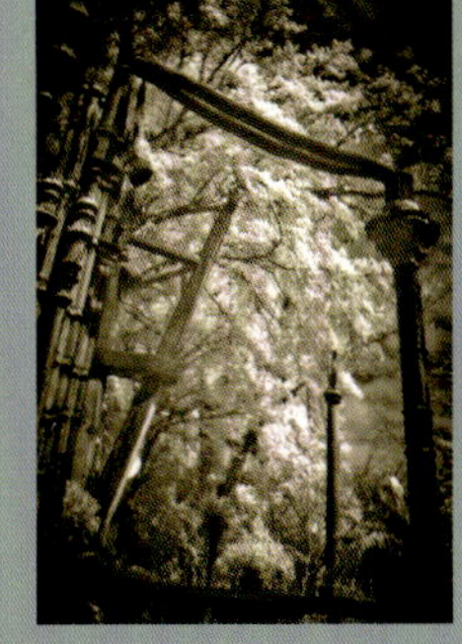
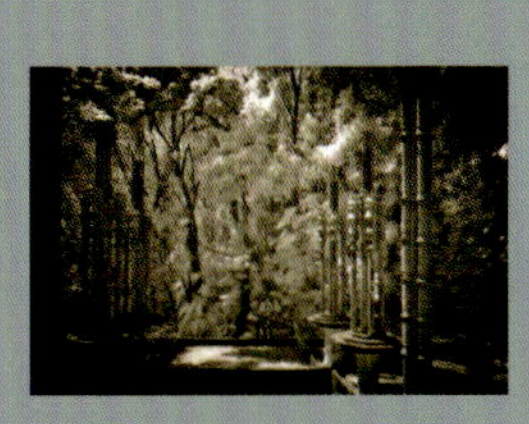
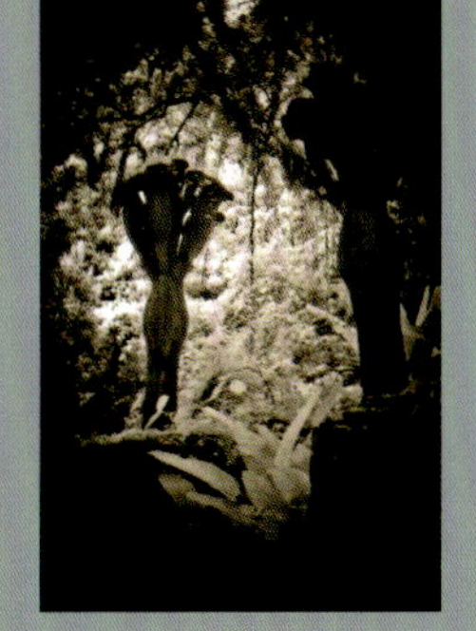

NATURE'S BARCODES (*CORDYLINE INDIVISA*) **ROSY MARSHALL**

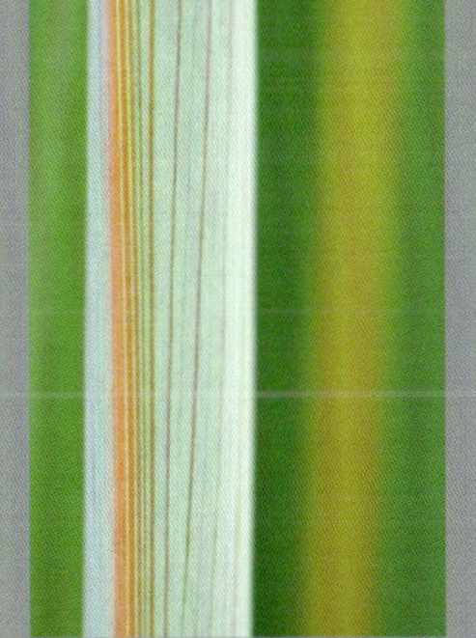
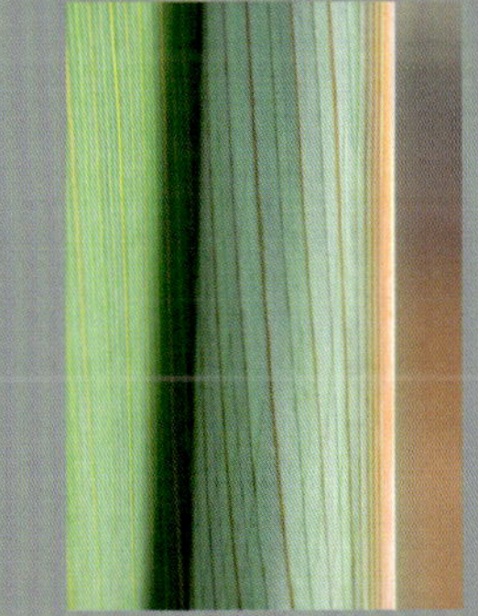
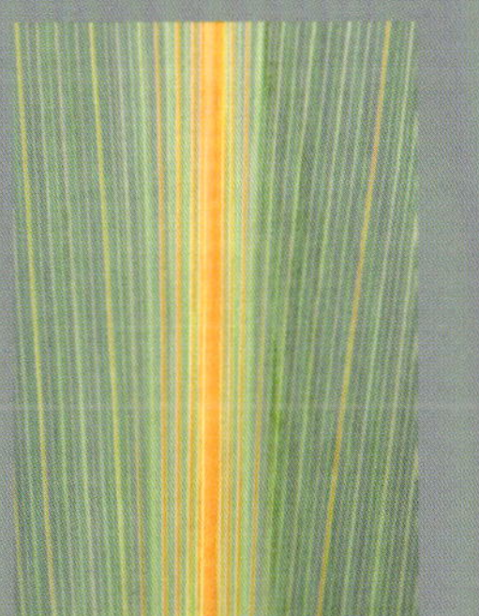
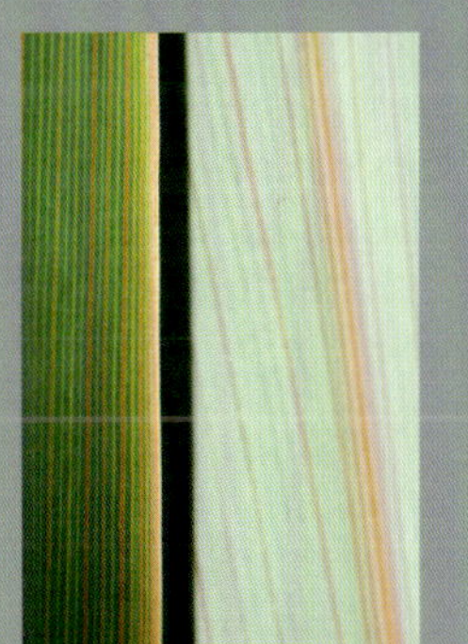
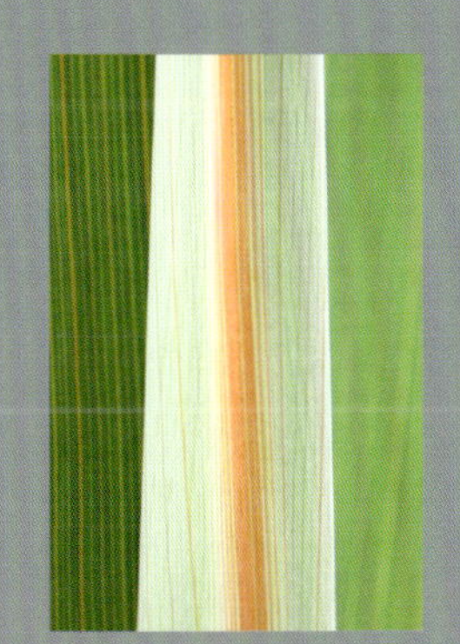
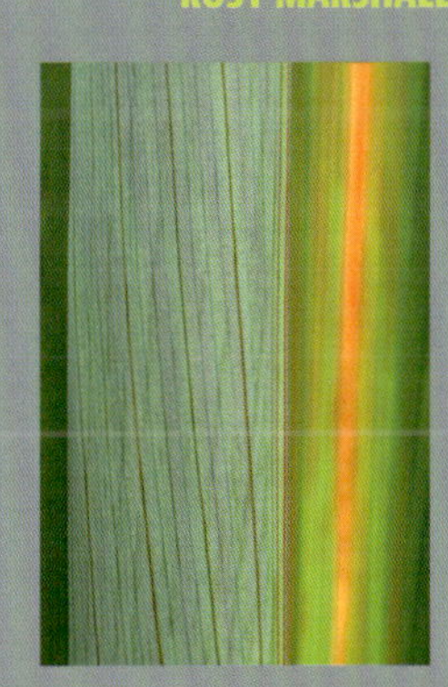
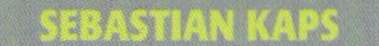

VEGETABLES **SEBASTIAN KAPS**

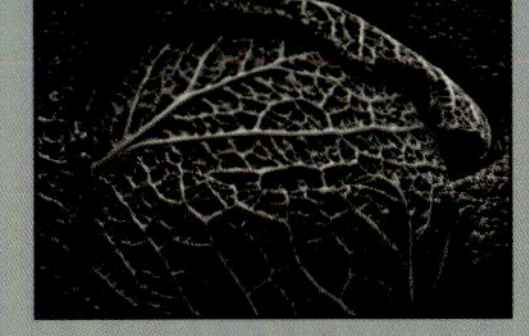
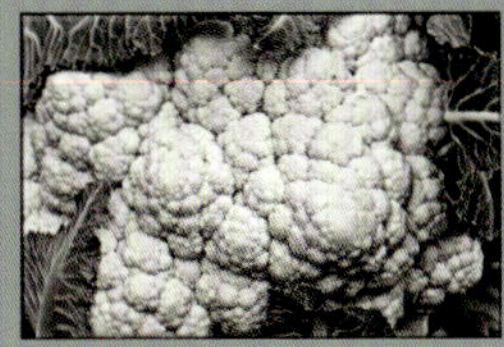
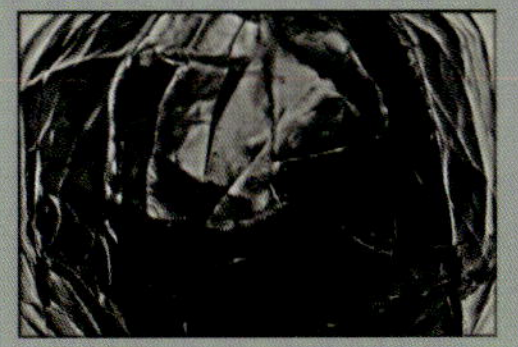
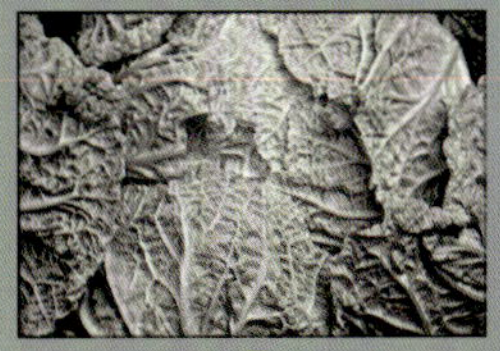
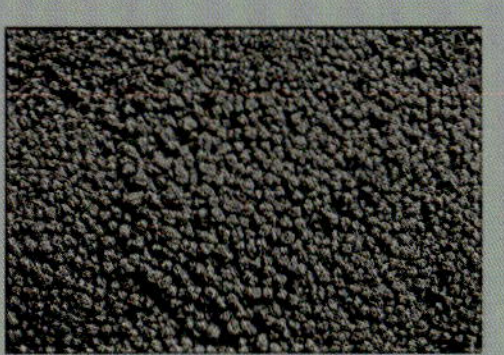
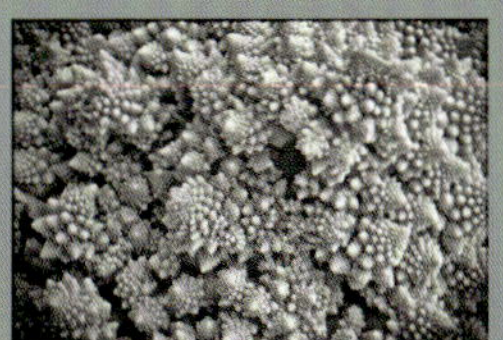

JEFF EDEN ► 1ST PLACE, MONOCHROME

Pointed Topiary in Winter

Ham House, Richmond-upon-Thames, Surrey, UK

By kind permission of the National Trust.

I was shooting a series of photographs at Ham House on a very foggy day and the repeating shapes of topiary fading into the fog caught my eye. It was so foggy that the image looked virtually black and white even before I altered it.

Nikon D300, 70-300mm lens. 1/100sec at f/11.0.
Post-capture: image was changed from colour to monochrome in software.

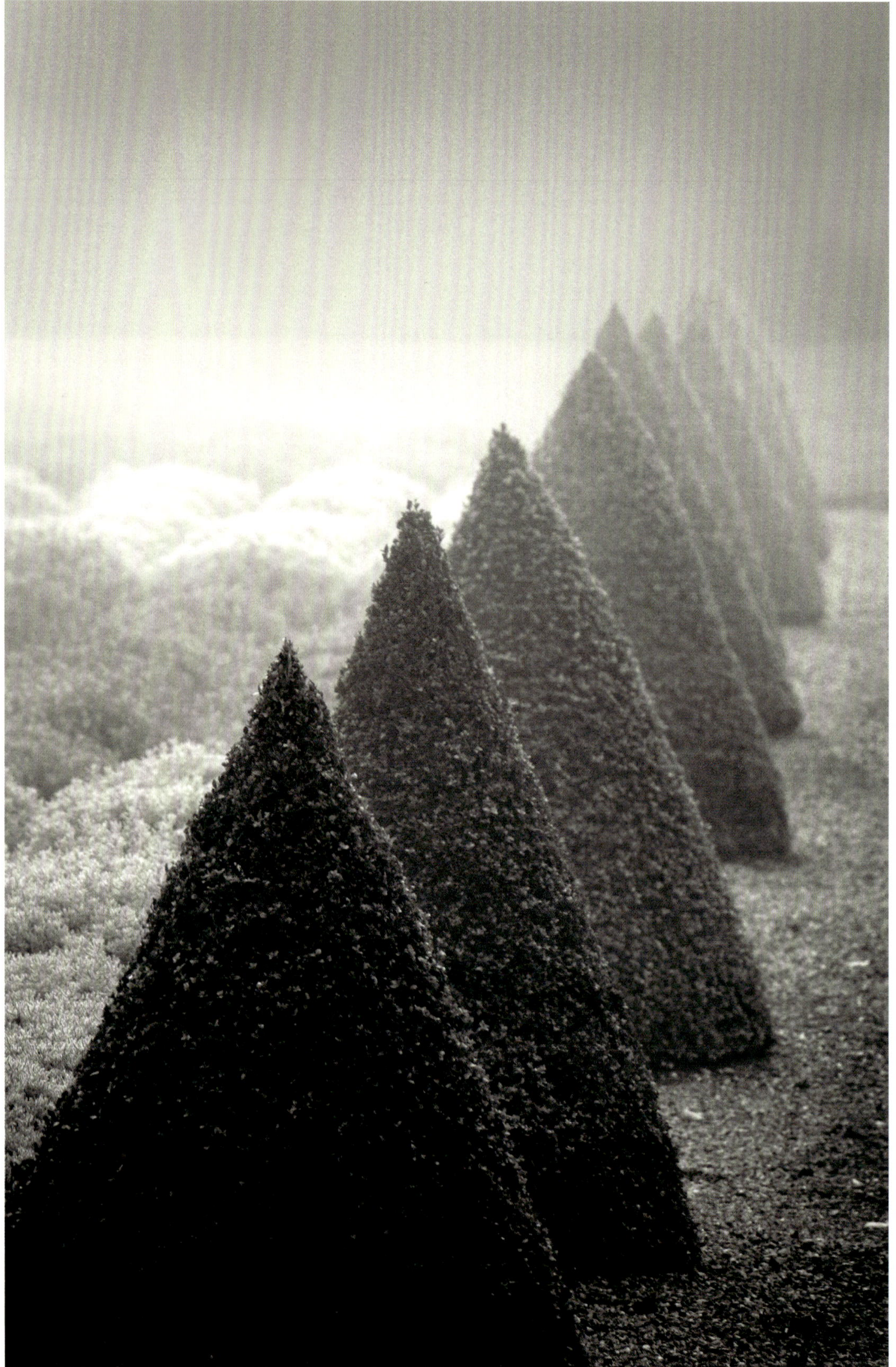

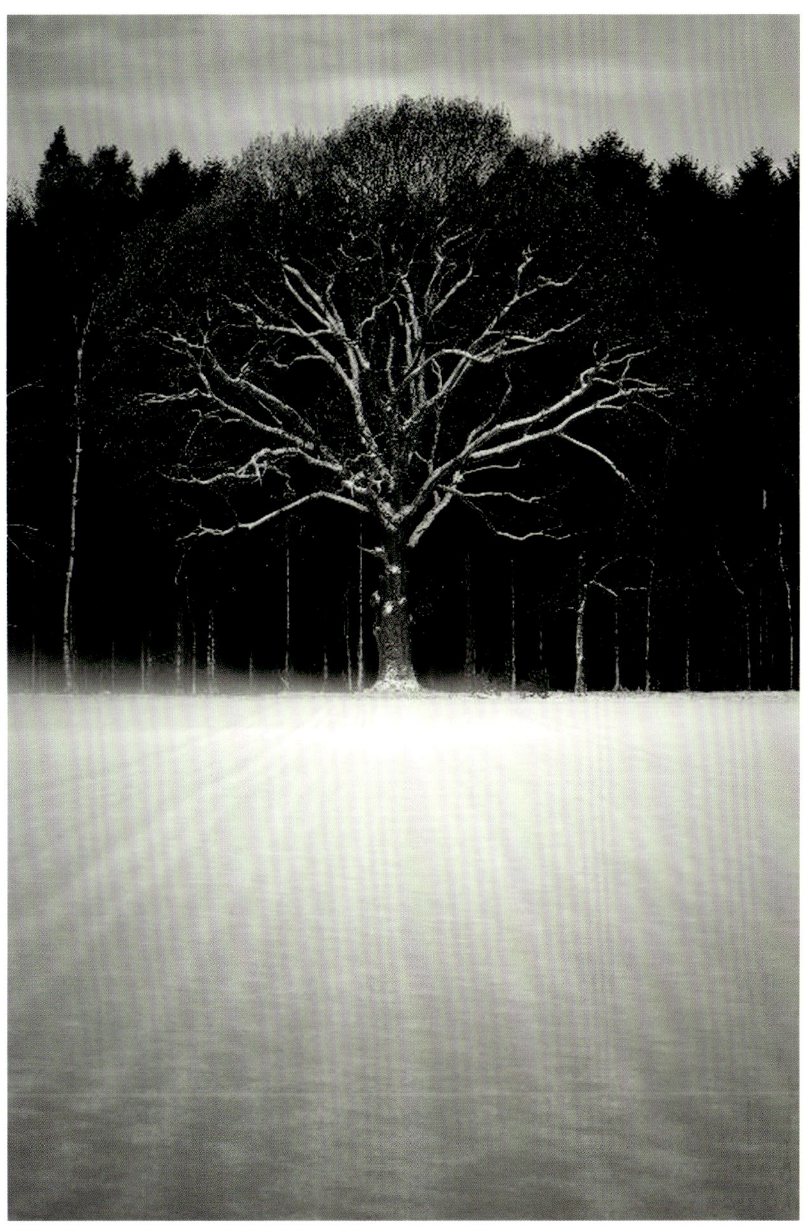

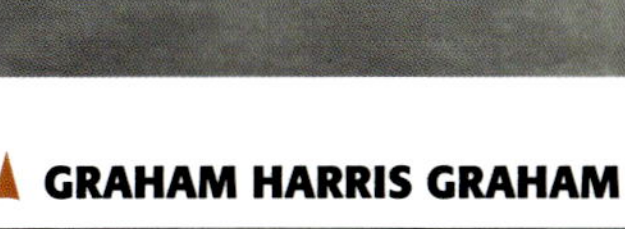

GRAHAM HARRIS GRAHAM 2nd Place, Monochrome

The Beech Tree
Near Airth, Falkirk, Scotland

Symbolising the veins of life before our very eyes, this tree appears to absorb energy from the ground it stands on.

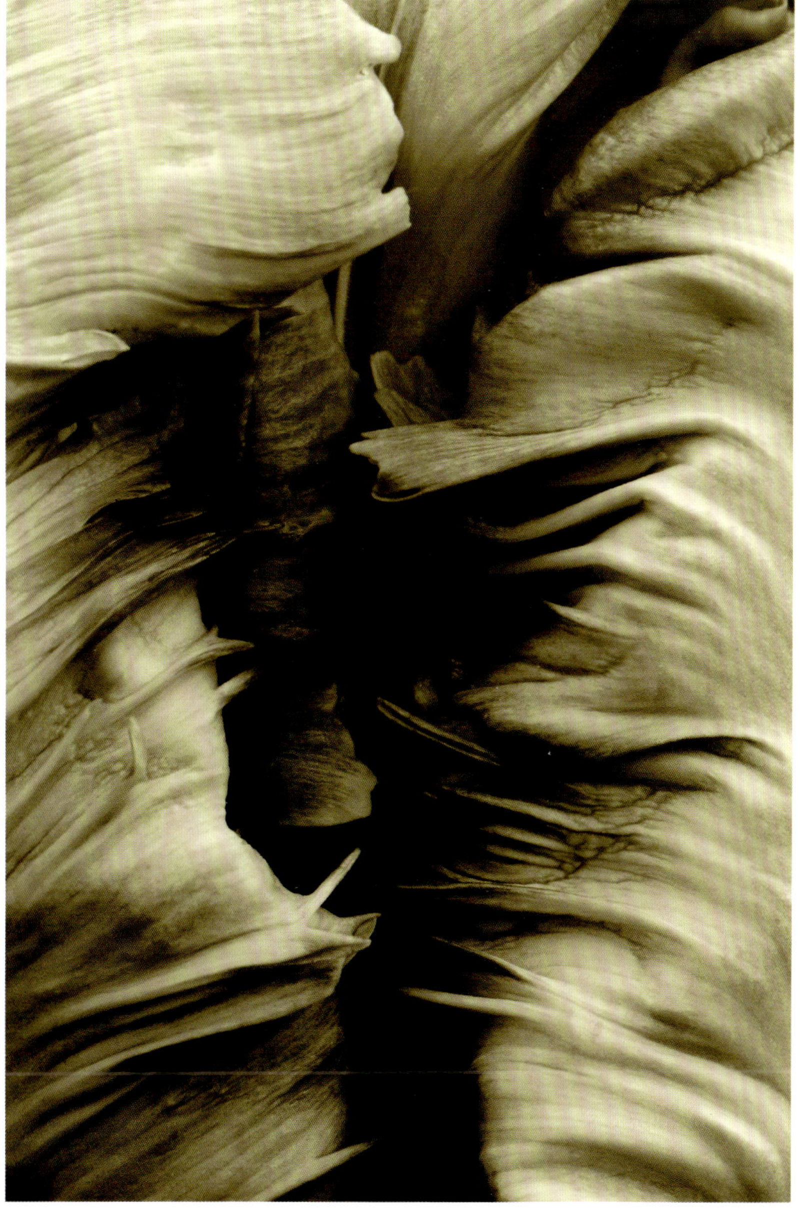

STEPHEN STUDD 3rd Place, Monochrome

Homage to Edward Weston
Malvern, UK

I remember looking at Edward Weston's amazing black and white abstracted images of nature years ago. I was drawn to the abstract viewpoint for this photograph, which could as easily be of a shell as a tulip.

Canon EOS 1Ds Mark II, 100mm lens. f/22. Post-capture: tone effects applied in software.

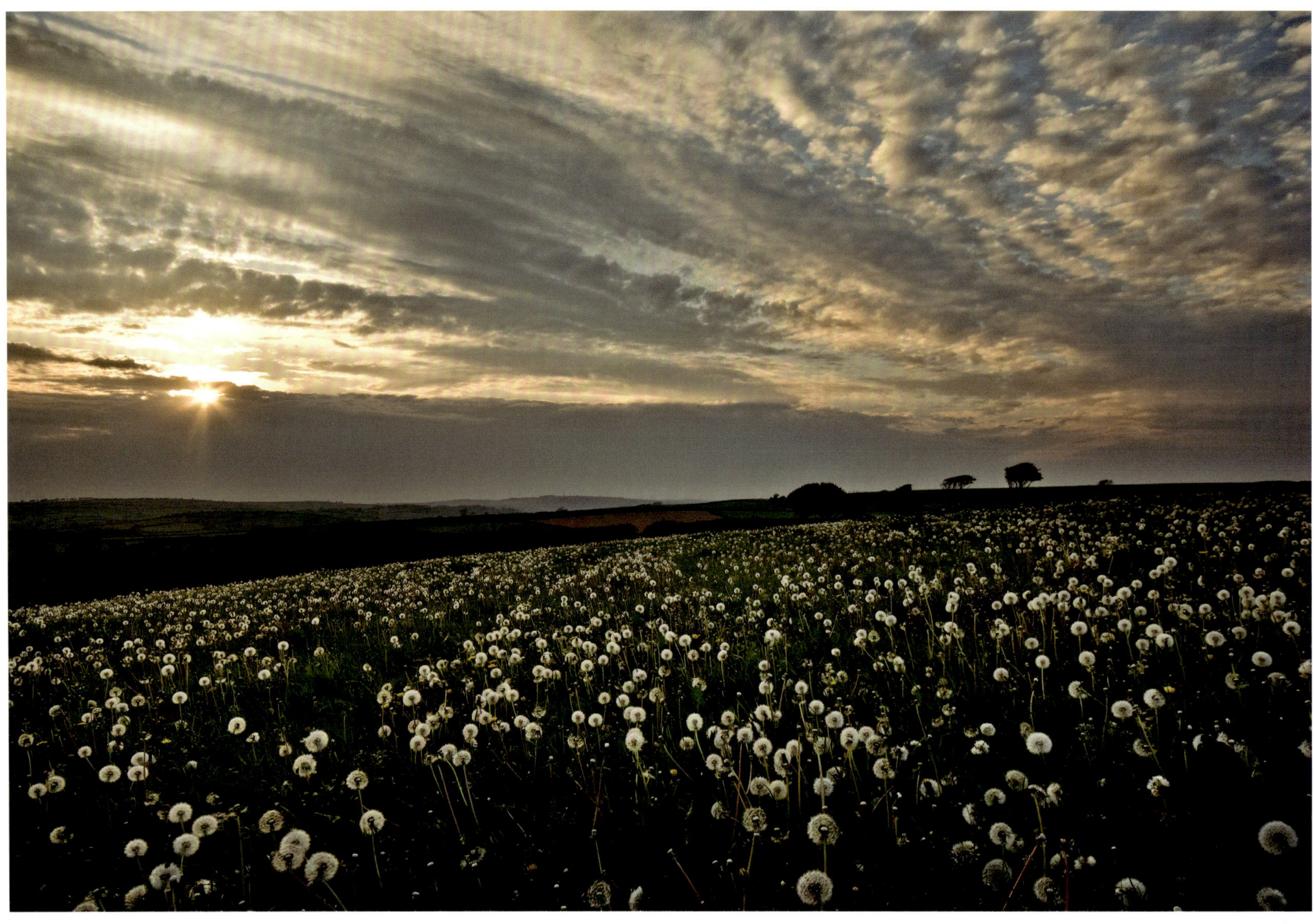

NICK SHEPHERD 1ST PLACE, NEW MORNINGS

Spring Seed
Dartmouth, Devon, UK

Backlit field of dandelion heads photographed with a low breaking sun. I waited patiently each morning for an interesting sky and carefully monitored the dandelion field to ensure the heads were at their best.

Nikon D80, Nikkor 10-20mm lens. 1/50sec at f/13. Post-capture: no digital alterations.

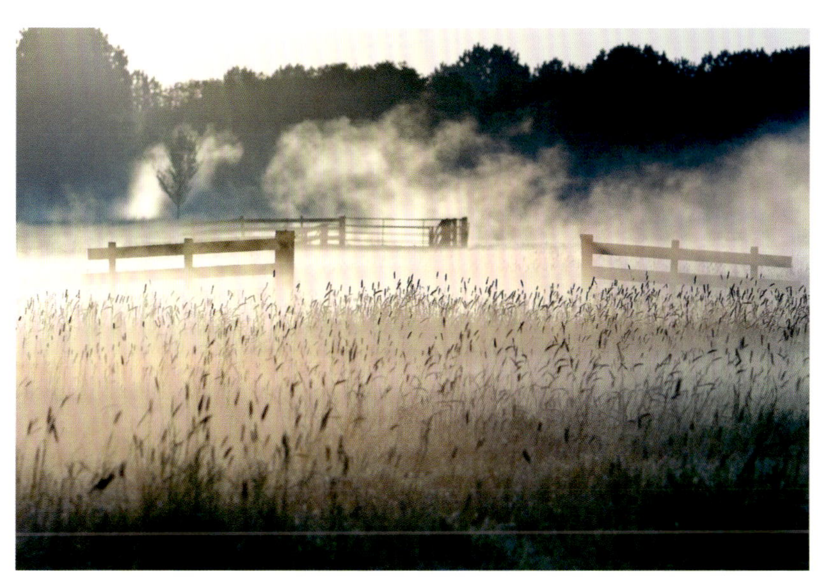

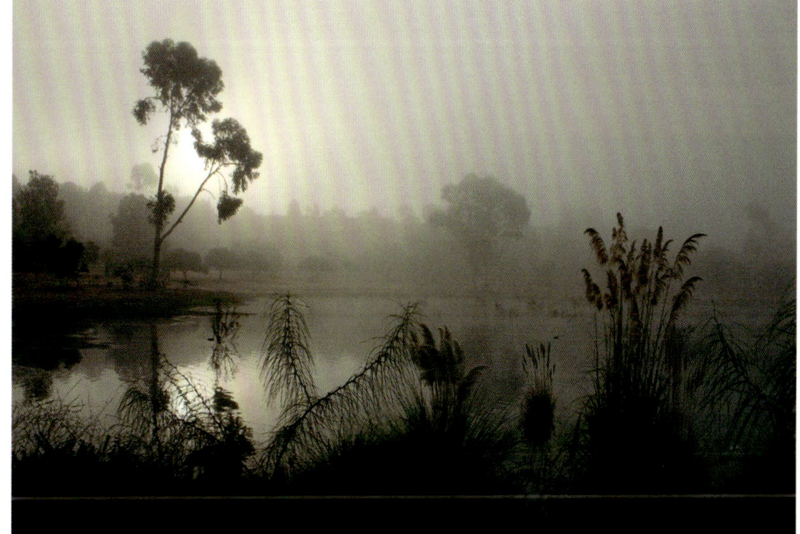

GERARD LEEUW — 2nd Place, New Mornings

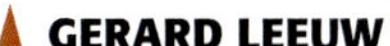

New Mornings
Cronesteyn Park, Leiden, Netherlands

The grass is high during this season so a variety of birds have a sheltered environment for building a nest. It is always exciting to be in this area during foggy weather. Lots of birds are found here and when the mist burns away the eye is able to see more every minute. Silhouettes of all kinds of geese become visible.

Nikon D300s, Nikon 200mm lens. 1/800sec at f/7.1. Post-capture: no digital alterations.

JENNIFER SPENCER — 3rd Place, New Mornings

Dawning at Lake Murray
Mission Trails Regional Park , San Diego County, California, USA

Lake Murray is a fresh water reservoir surrounded by native and non-native species of plant life, such as pampas grass in the foreground. Eucalyptus trees line parts of the lake. Since seeing fog on the lake is such a rare situation, I was intrigued by the possibility of photographing it one early autumn morning. I had never tried to photograph in fog before. Due to a mix of light from the emerging sun and the water, I tried various combinations of exposure. My objective was to re-create the feeling of a cool, moist atmosphere, and hold important detail in the foreground as well as the background.

Canon EOS Rebel, 55mm lens. 1/250sec at f/9. Post-capture: some tonal adjustments.

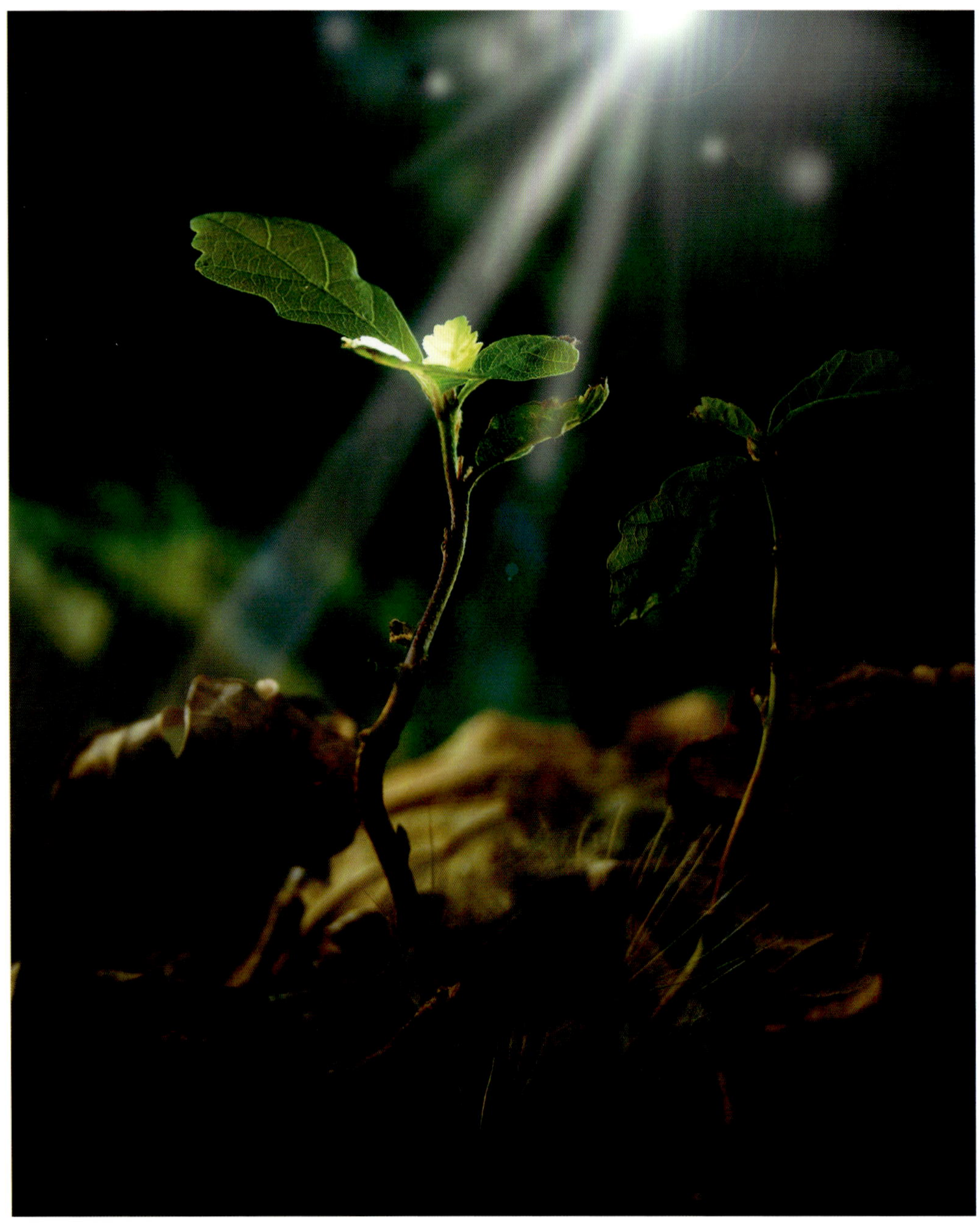

ALAN PRICE 1ST PLACE, WEATHER EYE

Oak Seedlings
Nantlle, Caernarfon, Gwynedd, Wales

The oak has always been a symbol of strength and longevity in our woodland. I wanted to capture the start of that journey and use the sun's rays to pinpoint that new beginning. I have been taking photos in my local wood for many years and know it very well, down to the lighting conditions and wildlife.

Nikon D90, Nikon 18-55mm lens. 1/60sec at f5.6. Post-capture: I darkened the background and highlighted the rays of sunlight to give more punch. The oak leaves were sharpened and given more contrast. To finish, I darkened the base of the foreground to really add more impact to the sunlit area.

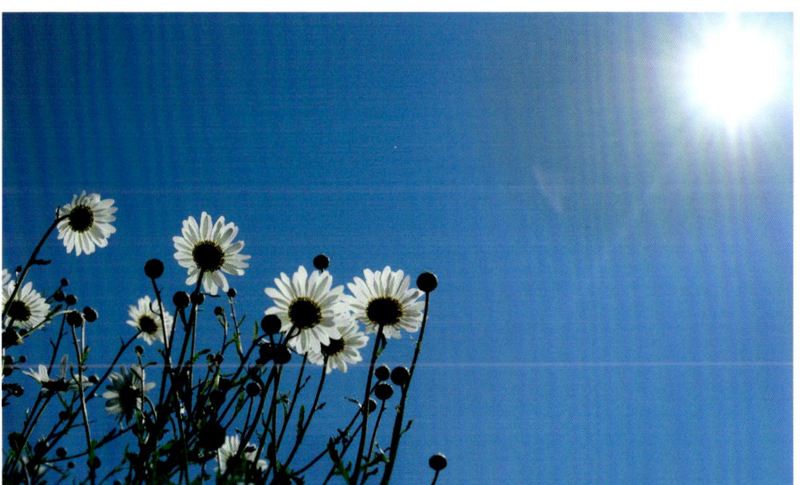

ALAN PRICE 2ND PLACE, WEATHER EYE

Ox-eye Daisies
Nantlle, Caernarfon, Gwynedd, Wales

The ox-eye daisies form a centrepiece to my garden and are accessible from all directions. Having spent many hours sitting out in the garden, I was amazed at the way in which the heads of certain flowers tracked the sun's position. I wanted to try to capture that image.

Nikon D90, Nikon 18-55 lens. 1/4000 sec at f7.2. Post-capture: basic colour management.

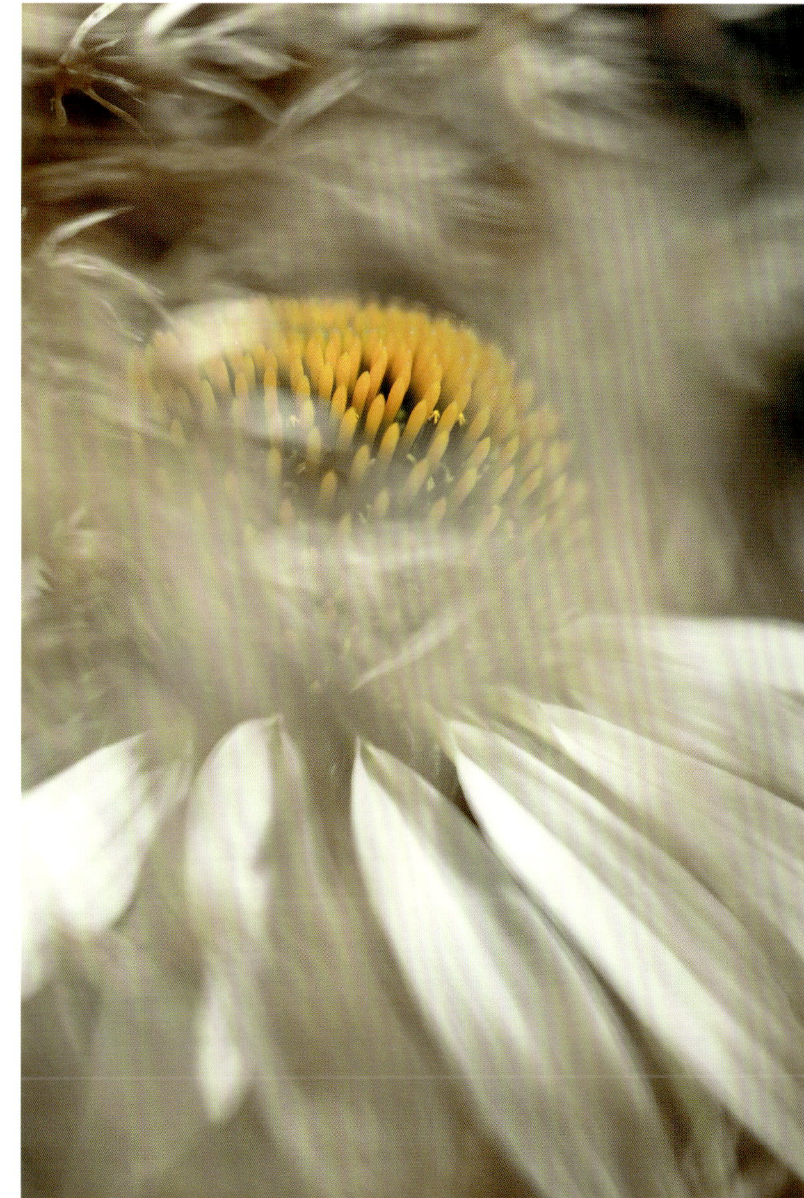

GERTIE B GRANVIK 3RD PLACE, WEATHER EYE

Summer Breeze
The Royal Garden (Kungsträdgården), Stockholm, Sweden

Wind through faded alliums softens the beautiful yellow and white rudbeckia. It was a wonderful, stormy day in Stockholm's Royal Garden.

Canon EOS 5D Mark II, Sigma 180mm lens. 1/1000sec at f/3.5. Post-capture: basic colour management.

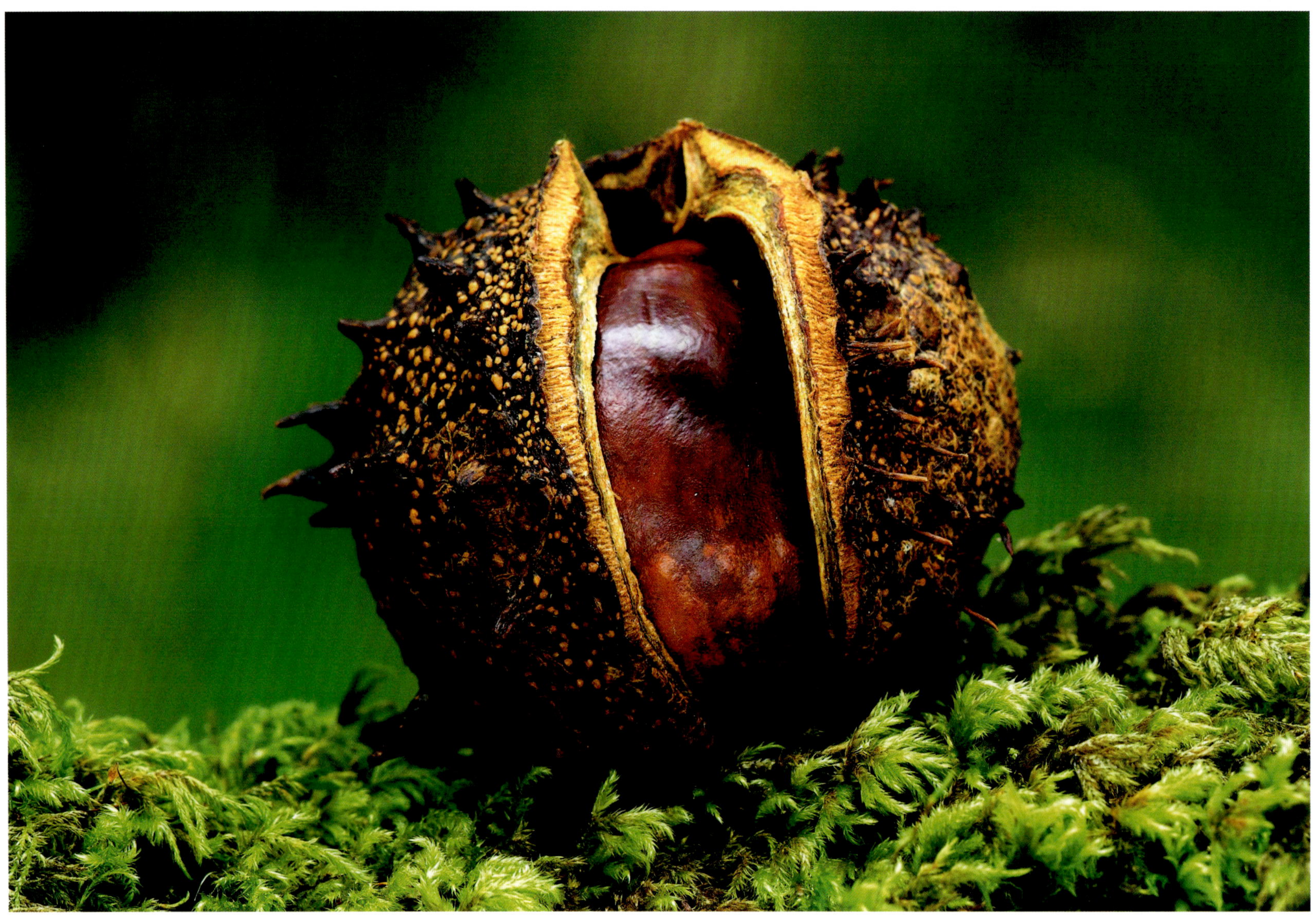

COLIN VARNDELL 1ST PLACE, TEXTURES

Horse Chestnut
Woodland garden in Netherbury, Dorset, UK

Autumn horse chestnut (*Aesculus hippocastanum*). I noticed the conker had fallen onto a mossy stump and chose to shoot from a low angle so it would be isolated from the background.

Nikon D200, Sigma 150mm lens. 1/3sec at f/16. A piece of kitchen foil was used to fill in the shadows with reflected light from the overcast sky. Post-capture: no digital alterations.

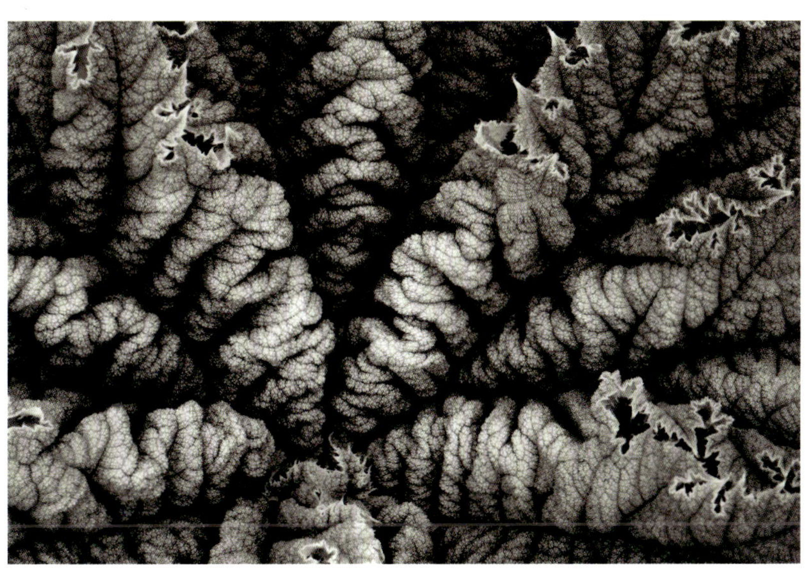

JOANNA CLEGG 2ND PLACE, TEXTURES

Gunnera Leaf
Cornwall, UK

Not native to Cornwall, the gunnera, also known as giant rhubarb, has very prickly stems and undersides to the leaves. As the name suggests, the leaves can be enormous. Using a macro lens and a tripod, my aim was to capture as much detail in the leaf texture as possible, whilst also portraying the larger radiating pattern of the leaf ribs.

Canon 5D Mark II, Tamron 90mm lens. 1/100sec at f/20. Post-capture: I converted the image to black and white to emphasise the textural quality of the leaf.

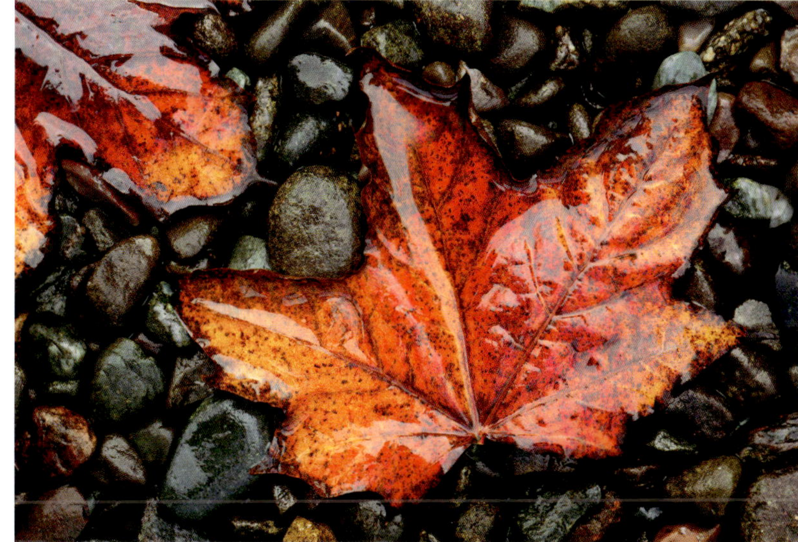

GRAHAM HARRIS GRAHAM 3RD PLACE, TEXTURES

Leaf and Pebbles
South Alloa near Falkirk, Scotland

I was initially struck by the deeply saturated, blood red colour of the leaf but upon framing the shot I realised that the homogenous backdrop of river pebbles made the image more complete. A tripod holding the camera to look directly down avoided reflections from the overcast sky and enhanced the colour saturation.

Canon 5D Mark II, 135mm lens. 0.8 secs at f/22. Post-capture: no digital alterations.

4 SEASONS FINALISTS

MONOCHROME

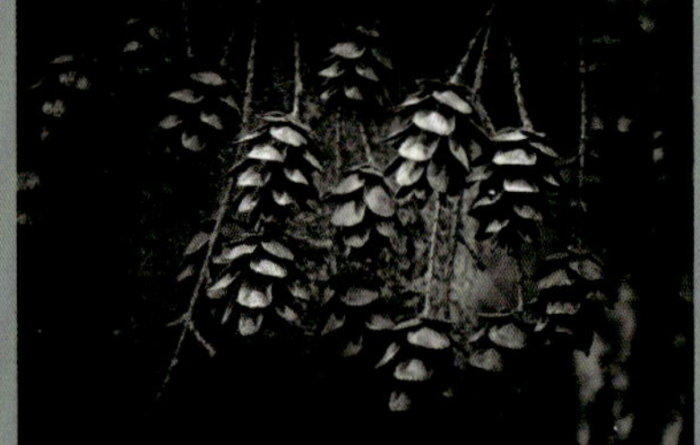

IN LONBUIE WOODS

COLIN CAMPBELL

MONOCHROME

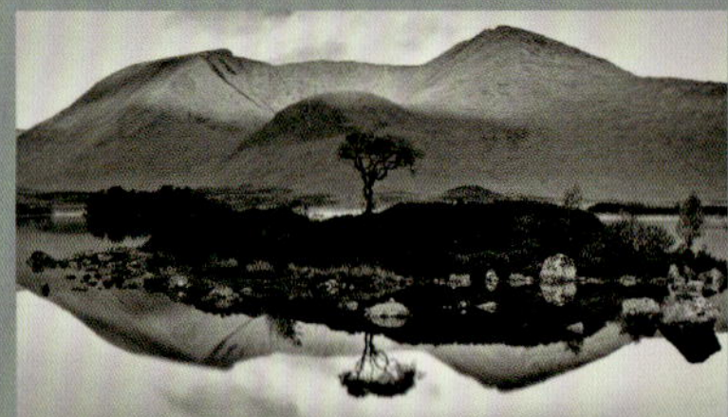

MÓINTEACH REANNACH

GRAHAM HARRIS GRAHAM

MONOCHROME

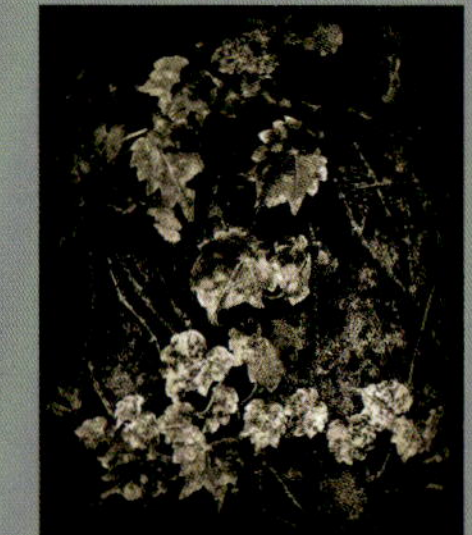

STEEL LEAVES

MICHAEL JARDEEN

MONOCHROME

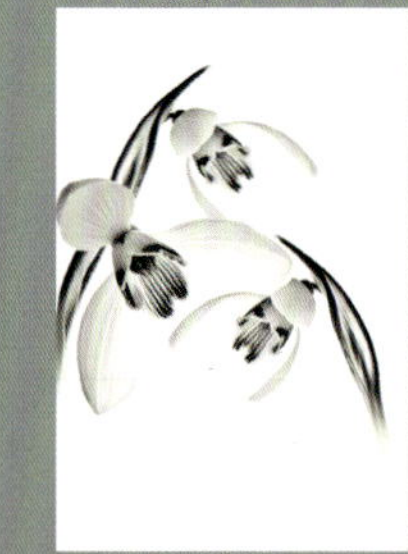

GALANTHUS RIZEHENSIS

BARRY BOLON

MONOCHROME

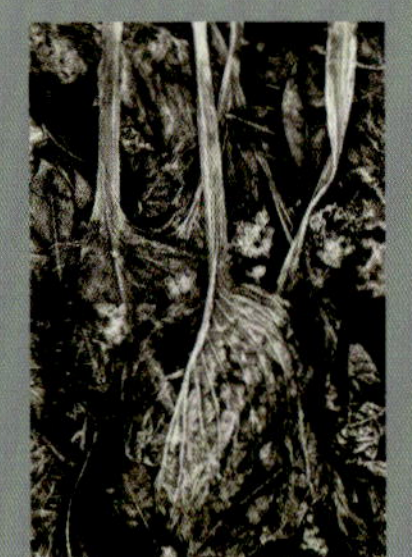

HOSTA IN DECAY 2

LOTTE PEDERSEN

MONOCHROME

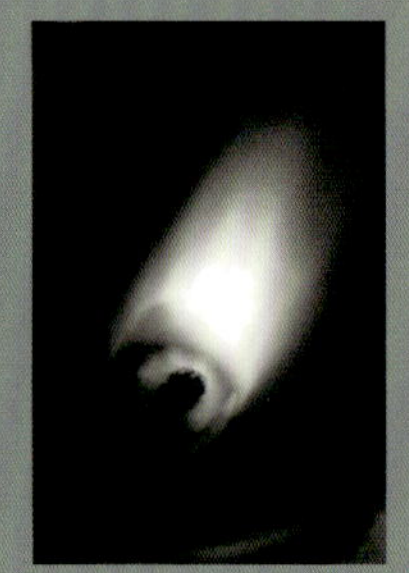

ARUM LILY

GERTIE B GRANVIK

MONOCHROME

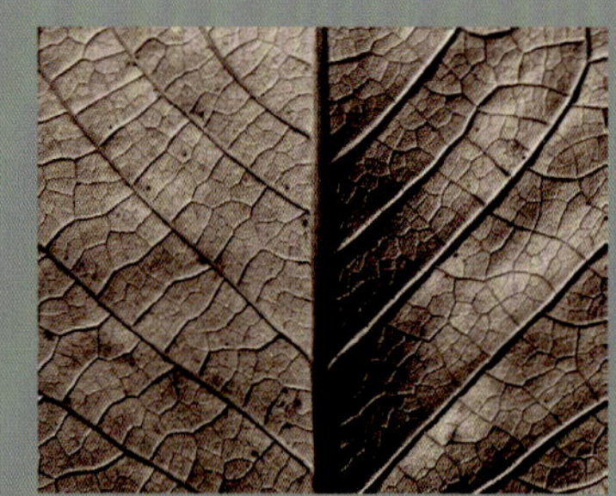

LEAF VEINS

BRAD MAILER

MONOCHROME

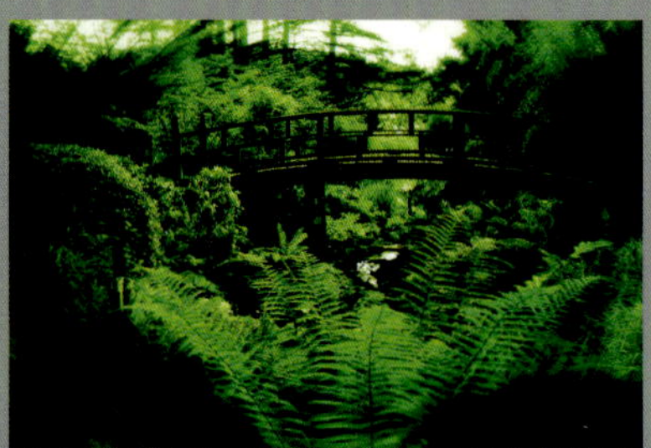

JAPANESE BRIDGE

DEREK GALON

NEW MORNINGS

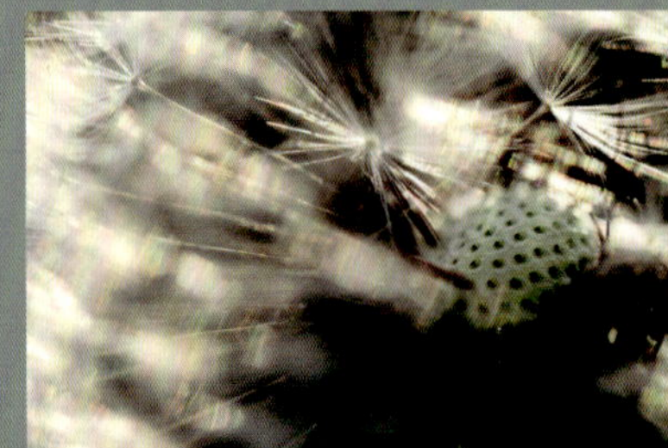

EARLY MORNING DANDELION

DEBBIE HARTLEY

NEW MORNINGS

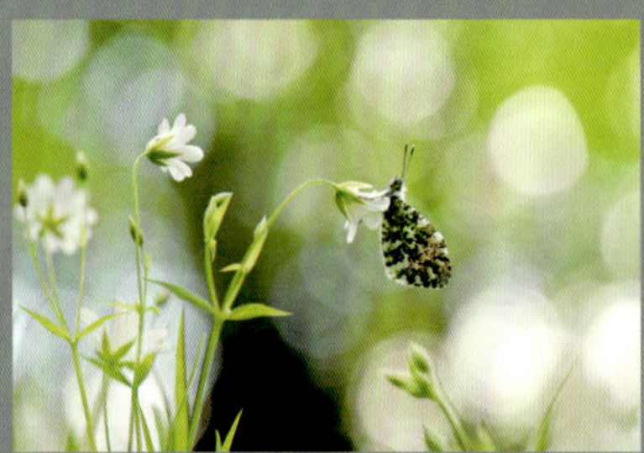

SPRING ARRIVALS

SARAH-FIONA HELME

NEW MORNINGS

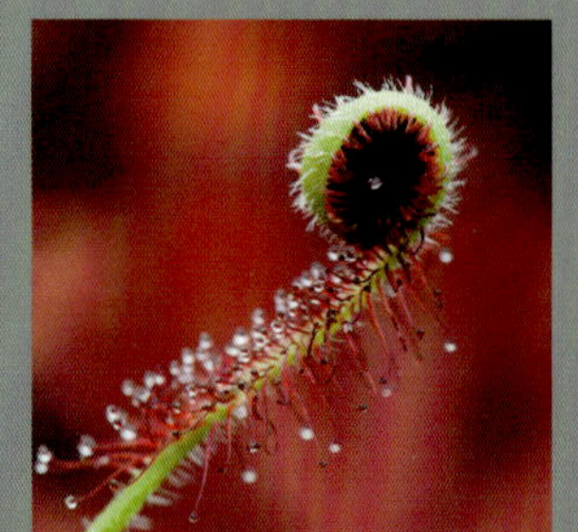

DROSERA CAPENSIS UNFURLING

STEPHEN STUDD

NEW MORNINGS

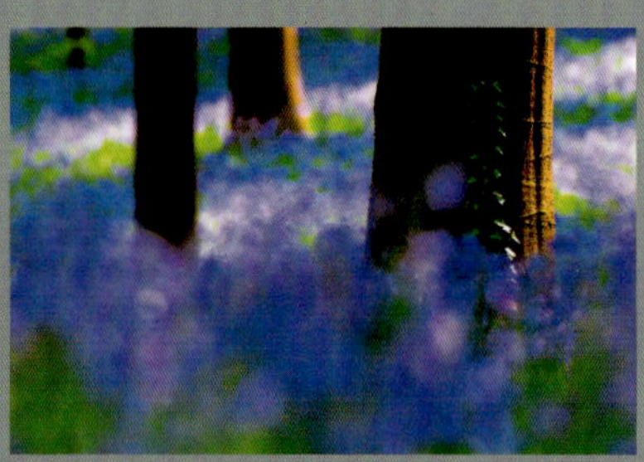

CLIMBING UP THE TREE

GERARD LEEUW

NEW MORNINGS

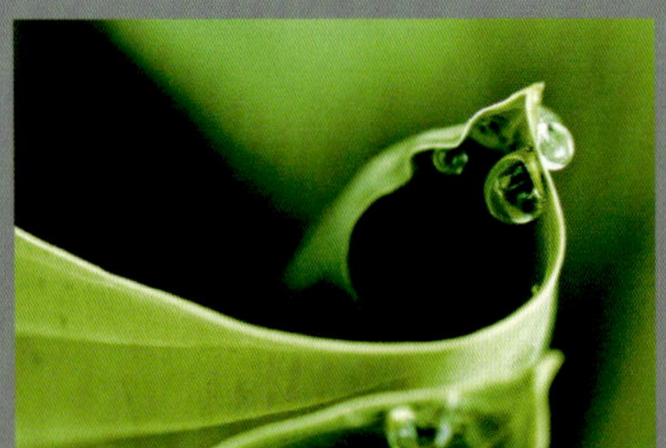

GREEN

ARIANN ISAKSSON

NEW MORNINGS

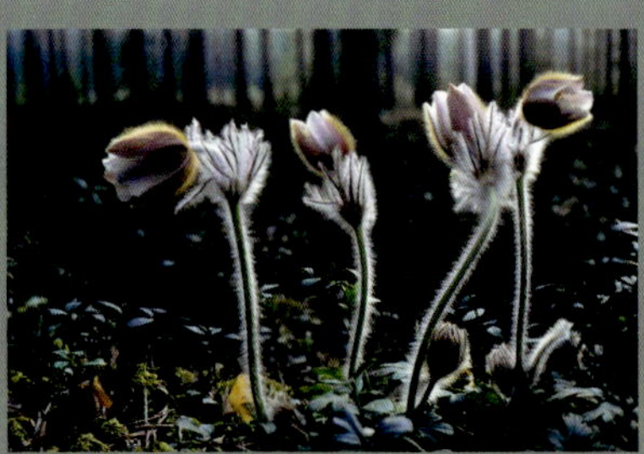

PULSATILLA VERNALIS

NILS-OLOF HOLGERSSON

NEW MORNINGS

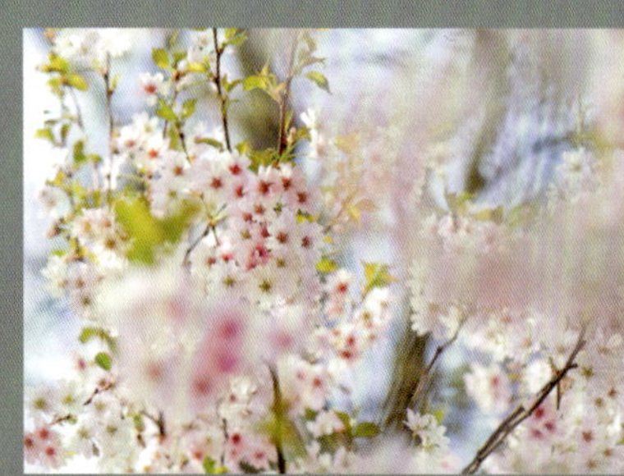

GLORY OF SPRING

SARAH-FIONA HELME

NEW MORNINGS

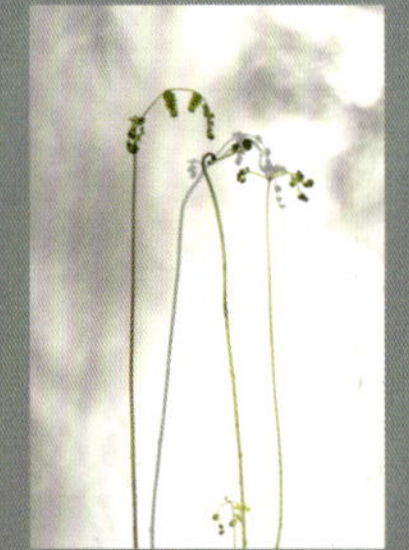

AWAKENING

LASSI KALLEINEN

WEATHER EYE

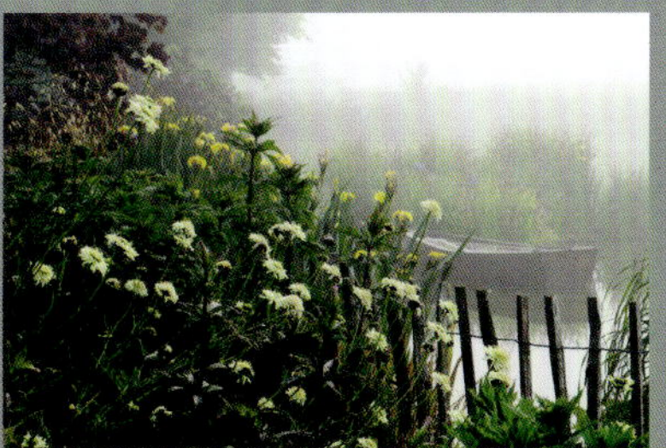

MISTY MORNING

HEATHER EDWARDS

WEATHER EYE

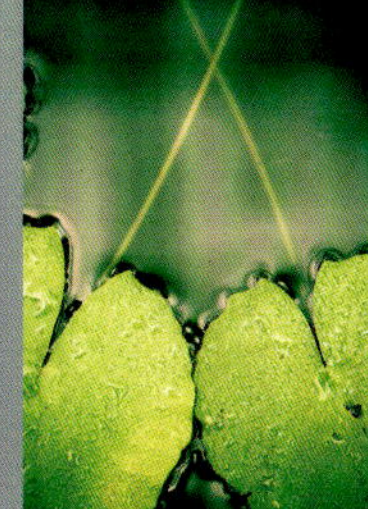

LOVE PLANET

LENA PESULA

WEATHER EYE

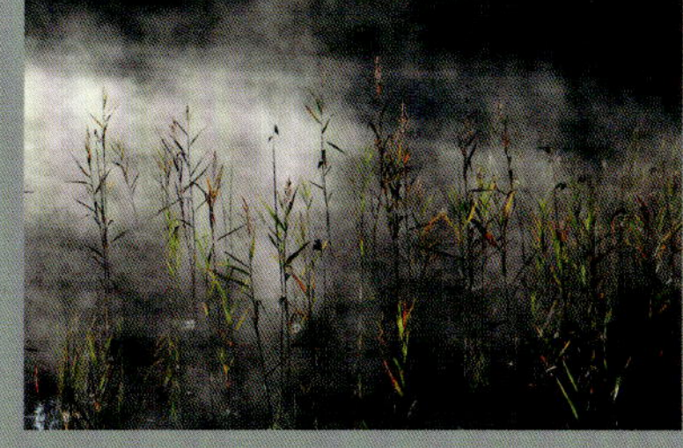

REEDS IN MIST

NILS-OLOF HOLGERSSON

WEATHER EYE

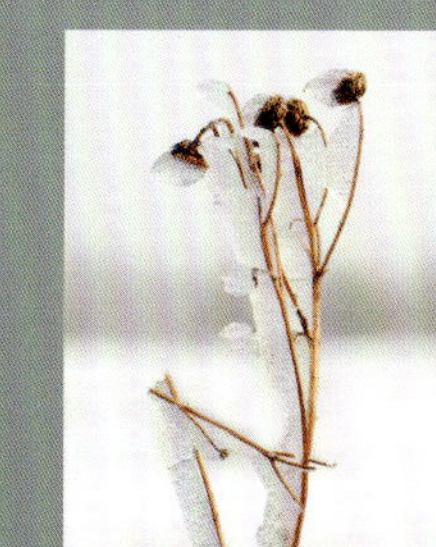

ICE COLD MORNING MIST

LEENA HOLMSTRÖM

WEATHER EYE

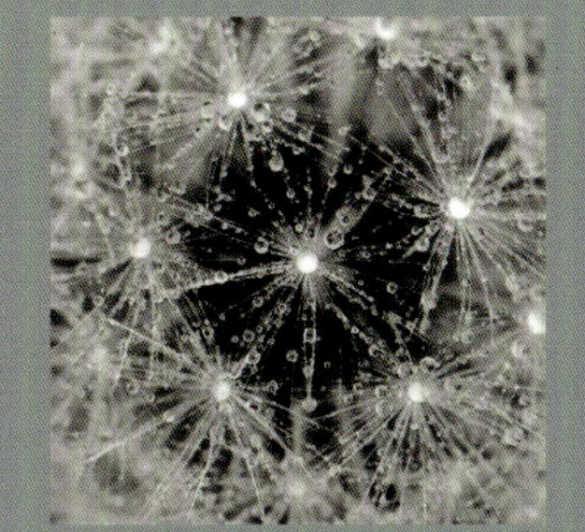

JEWELS

JOANNA CLEGG

WEATHER EYE

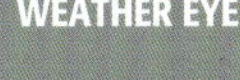

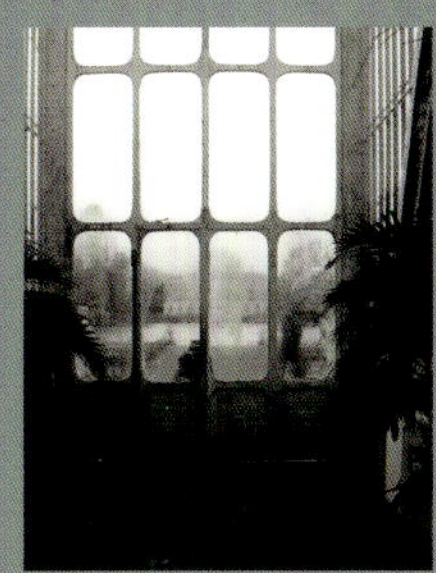

PALM HOUSE AT KEW

VOLKER LAMPE

WEATHER EYE

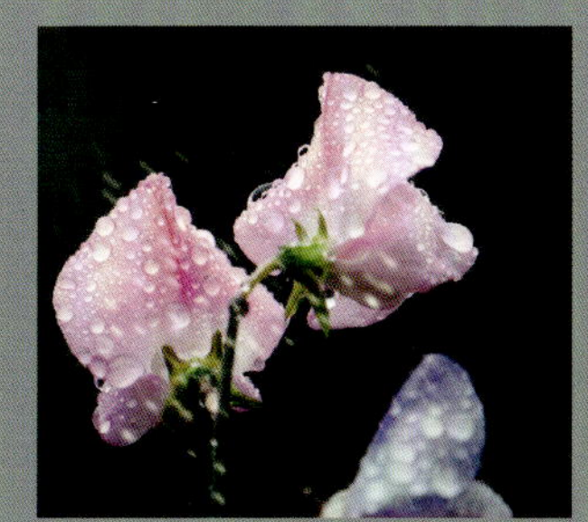

SWEET PEAS

ALAN PRICE

WEATHER EYE

GARLIC CHIVE SEEDHEADS

STEPHEN STUDD

TEXTURES

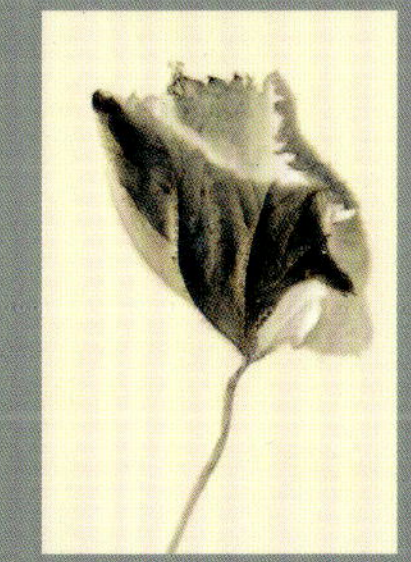

ALCHEMILLA

VOLKER LAMPE

TEXTURES

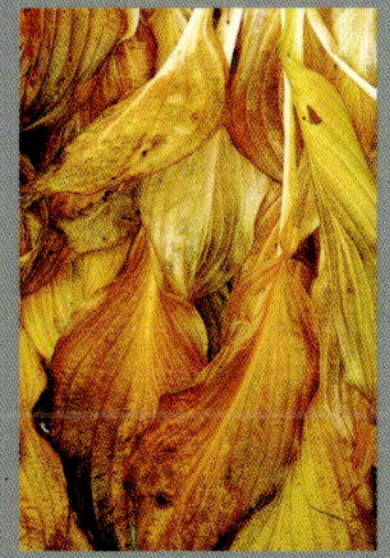

HOSTA IN DECAY

LOTTE CHRISTINA ANDERSEN PEDERSEN

TEXTURES

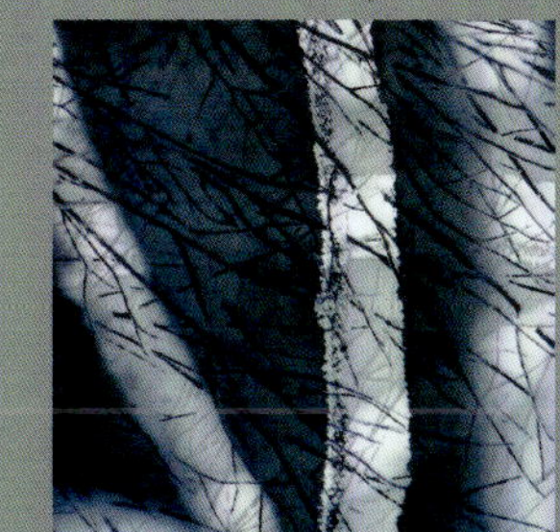

BIRCH ABSTRACT

LASSI KALLEINEN

TEXTURES

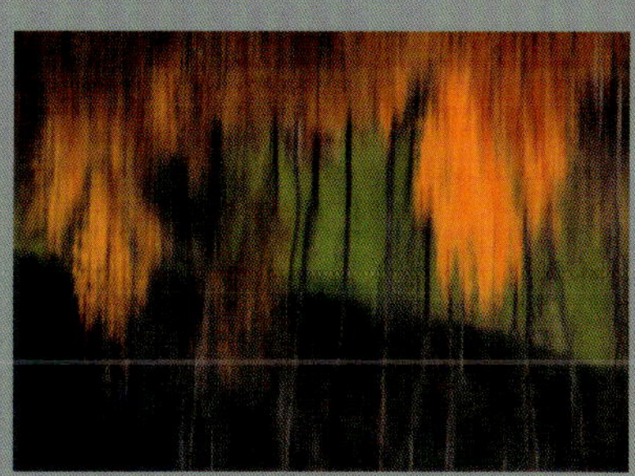

AUTUMN IMPRESSIONS

MONICA SIRI

TEXTURES

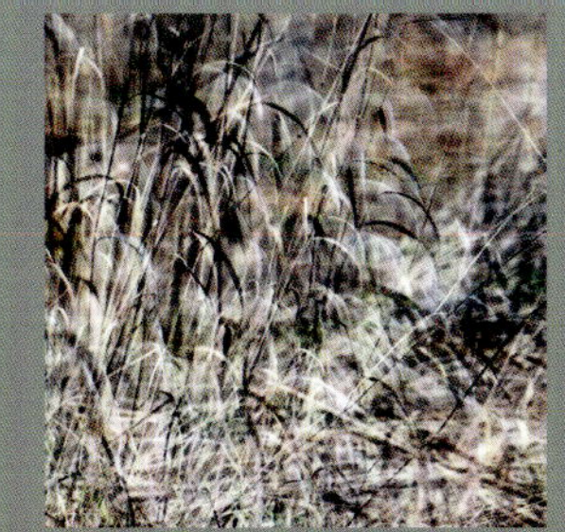

SMALL REEDS

LEENA HOLMSTRÖM

TEXTURES

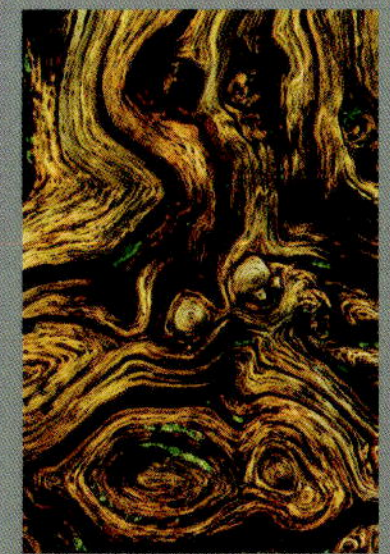

OAK WOOD

COLIN VARNDELL

TEXTURES

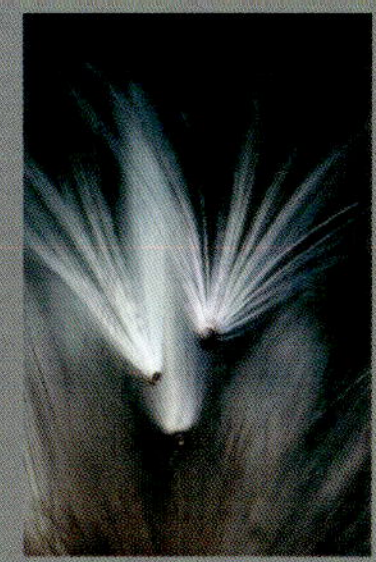

THISTLE

LOTTE CHRISTINA ANDERSEN PEDERSEN

TEXTURES

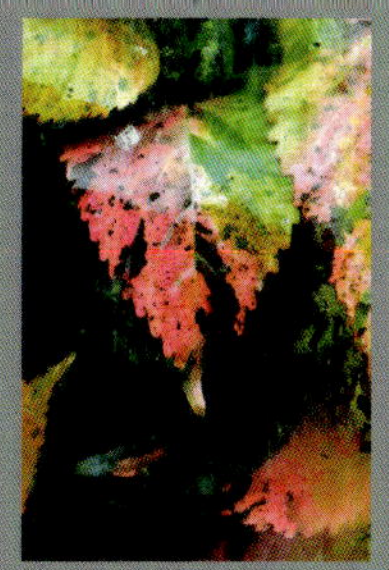

FALL THROUGH THE GLASSHOUSE WINDOW

ALLYSON BROWN

MONOCHROME

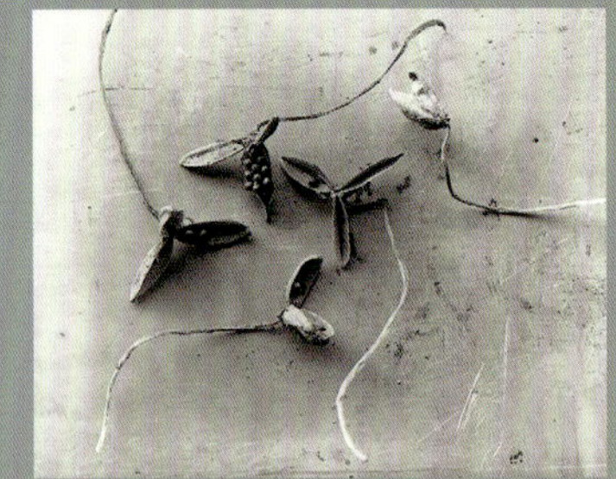

SEEDS

DAVID BALLANTYNE

MONOCHROME

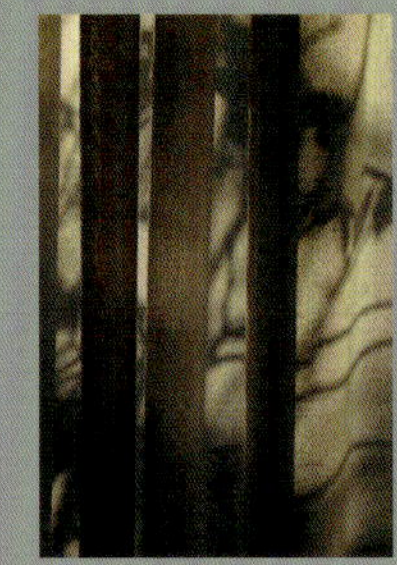

SHADOW GARDEN 2

CHRISTINE LLOYD-FITT

MONOCHROME

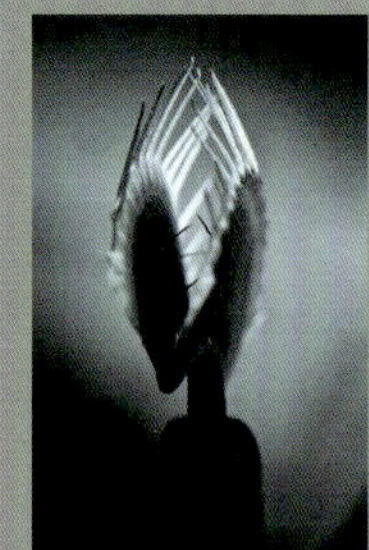

PUNK

STEPHEN STUDD

MONOCHROME

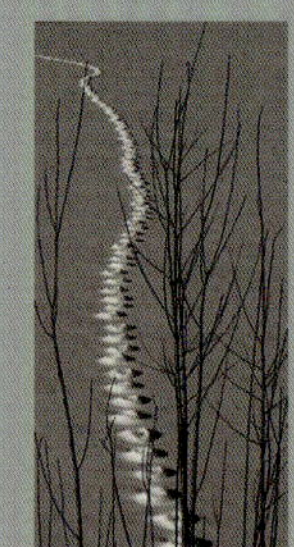

WINTER DEER TRACKS

JAMES SCHOSTER

MONOCHROME

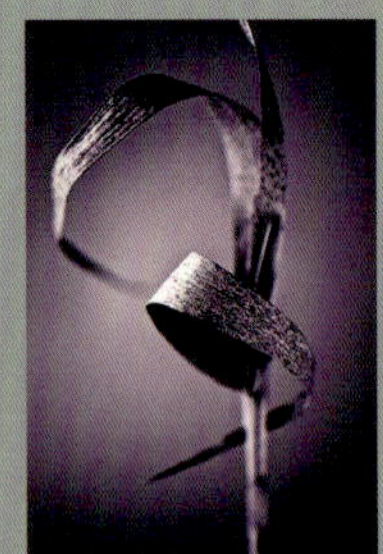

REED GRASS

DEE FISH

MONOCHROME

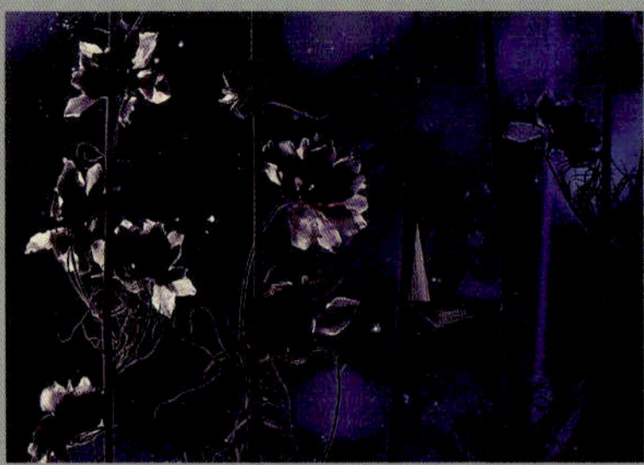

DRIED FLOWERS AT NIGHT

LASSI KALLEINEN

MONOCHROME

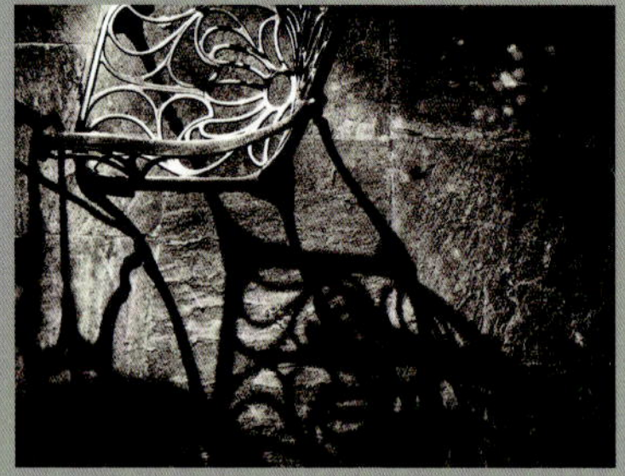

SHADOWS

GRAHAM LOVE

MONOCHROME

MATINAL

CORINE OOSTERLEE

MONOCHROME

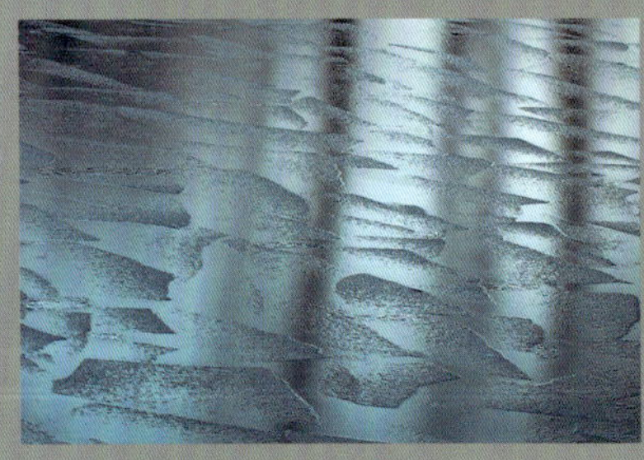

TREES IN ICY BLUE

GERARD LEEUW

MONOCHROME

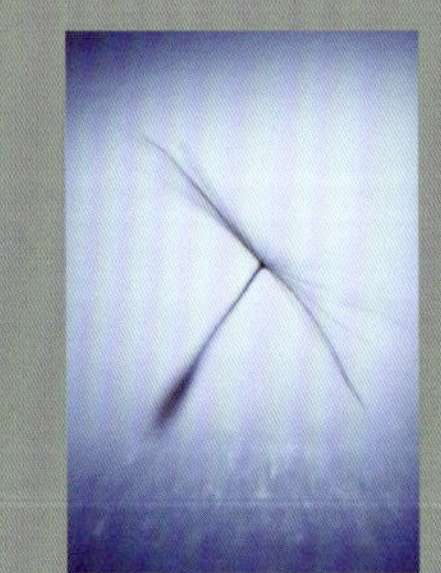

CLOCK

DAVID MAITLAND

MONOCHROME

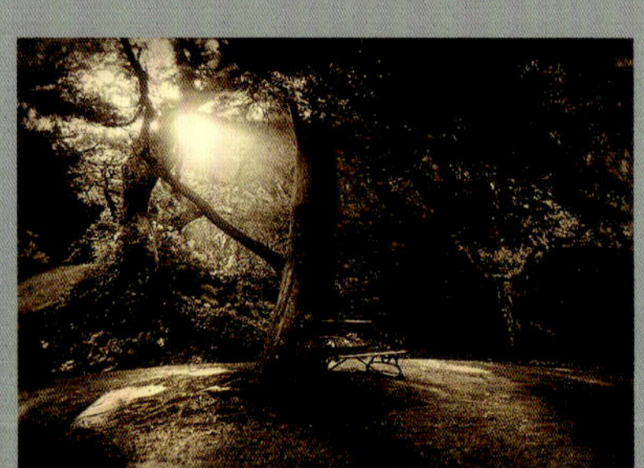

I WISH YOU WERE HERE

PETER KURDULIJA

MONOCHROME

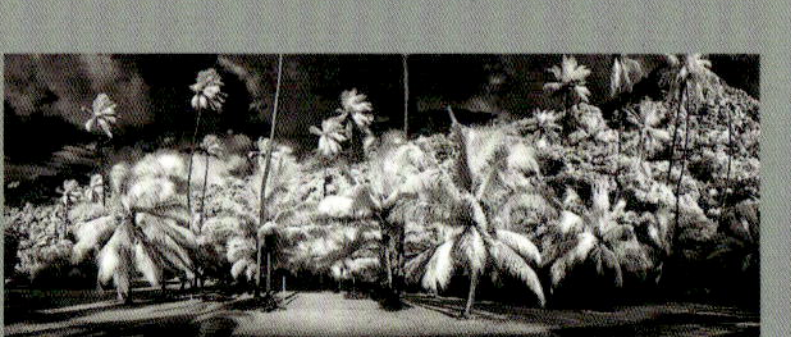

JALOUSIE GARDEN

LESZEK NOWAK

NEW MORNINGS

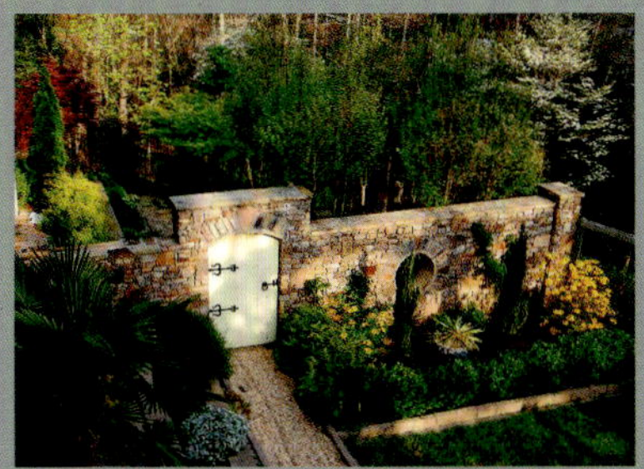

NEW MORNING IN OUR GARDEN

JOHN ROGER PALMOUR

NEW MORNINGS

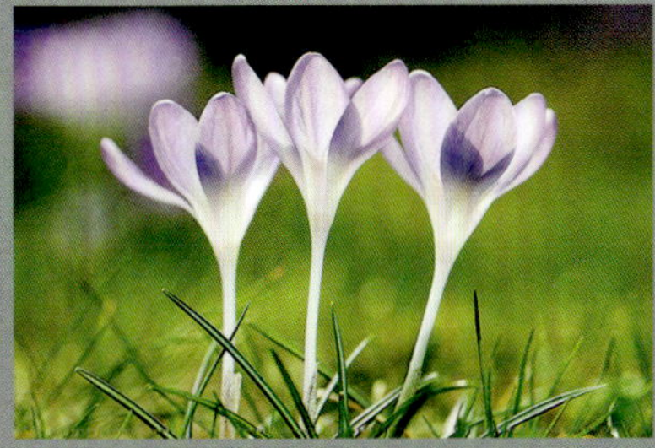

6181 CROCUSES

KEVIN HOWCHIN

NEW MORNINGS

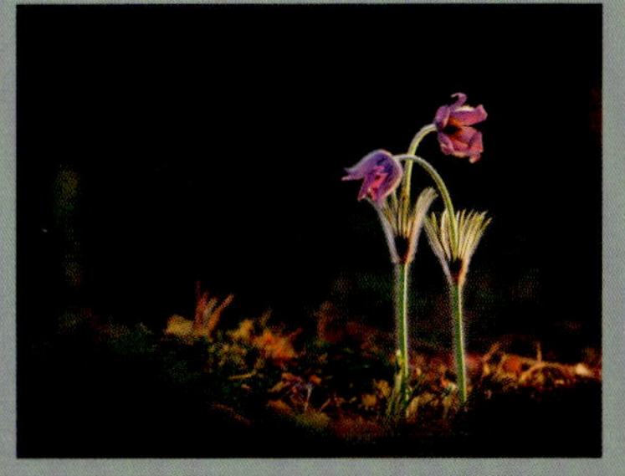

PULSATILLA PATENS

OLEGAS KURASOVAS

NEW MORNINGS

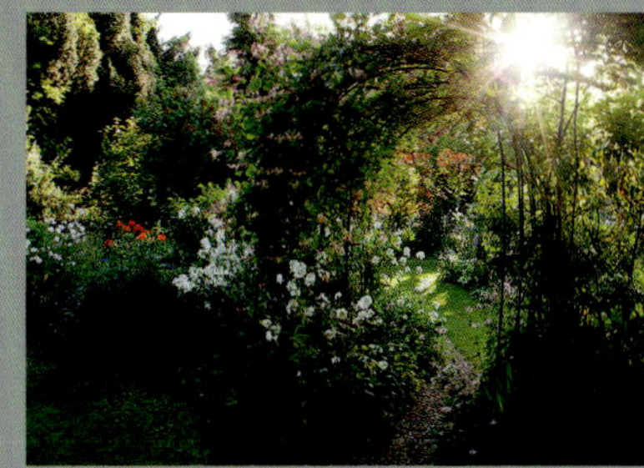

A BRAND NEW DAY

CLARE FORBES

NEW MORNINGS

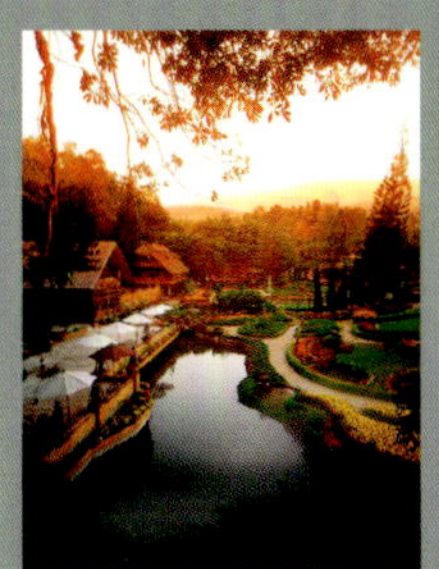

FIRST LIGHT

HANSA TANGMANPOOWADOL

NEW MORNINGS

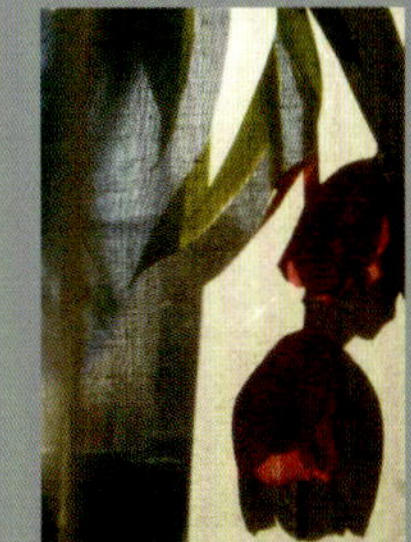

WINDOW TULIPS 2

CHRISTINE LLOYD-FITT

NEW MORNINGS

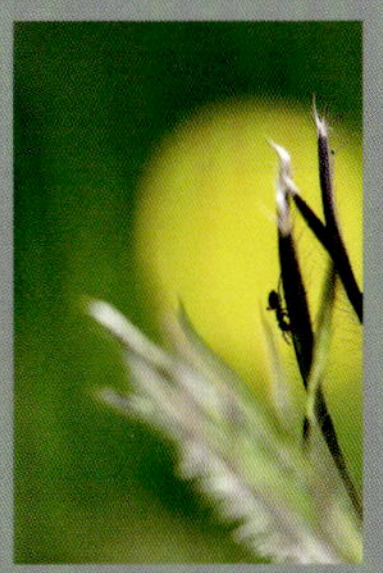

DANDELION

GERTIE GRANVIK

NEW MORNINGS

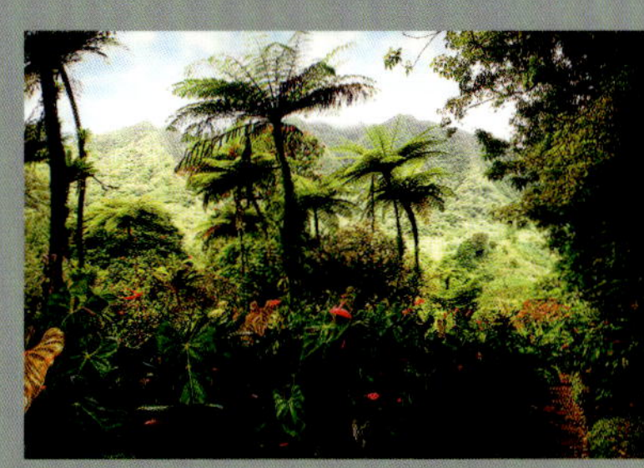

CARIBBEAN MORNING

DEREK GALON

NEW MORNINGS

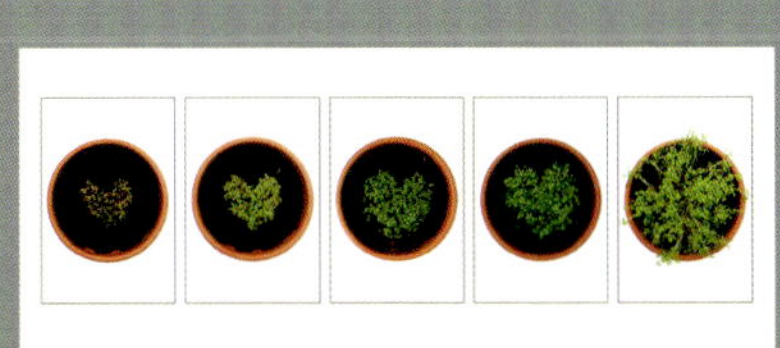

FIVE DAYS

ANNE GILBERT

NEW MORNINGS

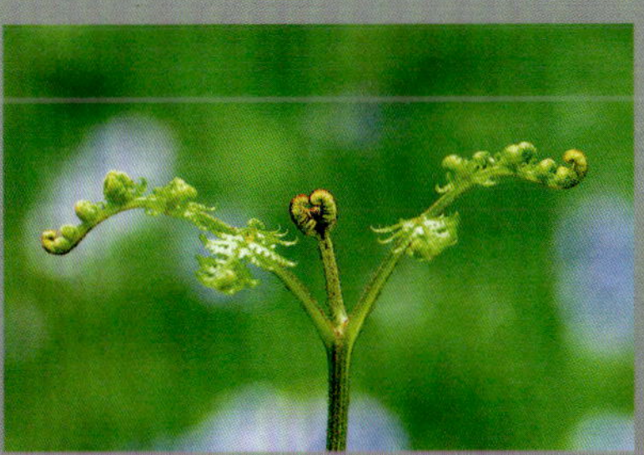

BURSTING

GERARD LEEUW

NEW MORNINGS

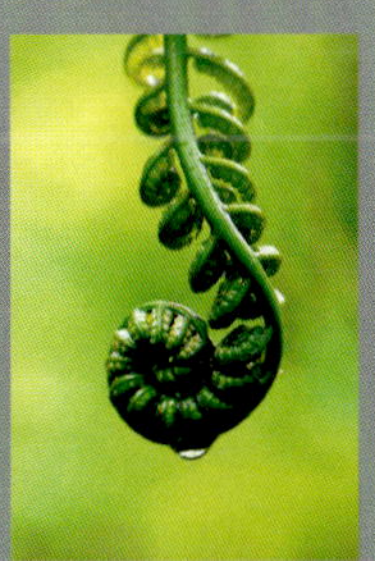

UNFURLING FERN FROND

ALLYSON BROWN

NEW MORNINGS

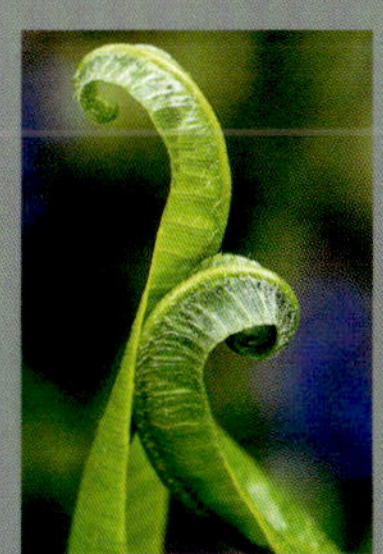

FERNS UNFOLDING

GLORIA KING

WEATHER EYE

FIRST RIME

ANDREW GEORGE

WEATHER EYE

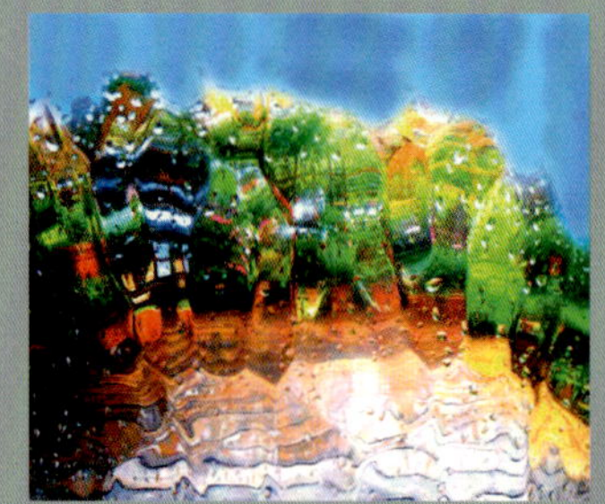

RAIN ON MY WINDOW

SUSAN EDWARDS

WEATHER EYE

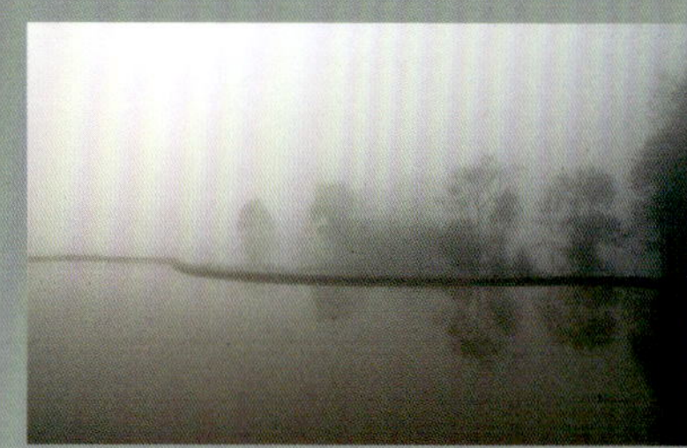

MORNING MIST ON THE RICE FIELDS AT YUANYANG

JOSEPH HENDLEY

WEATHER EYE

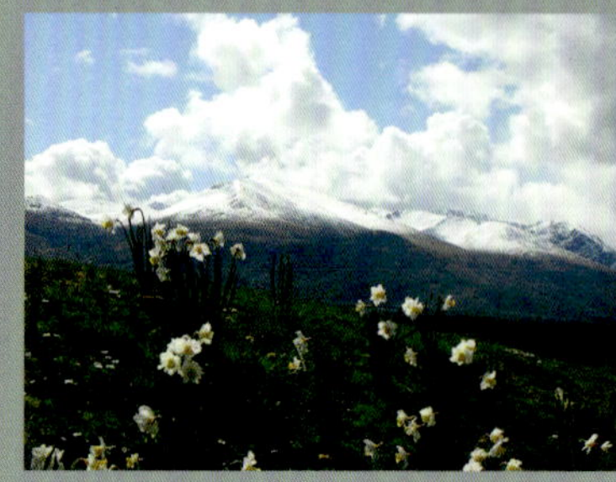

SUN AND SNOW

ROCHELLE DON

WEATHER EYE

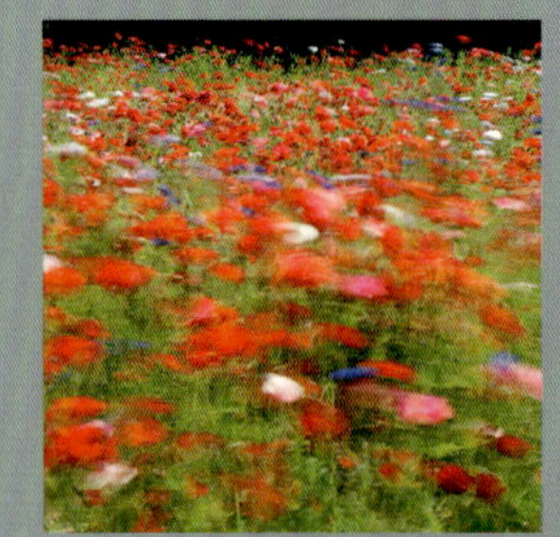

GOING WITH THE FLOW

CLARE FORBES

WEATHER EYE

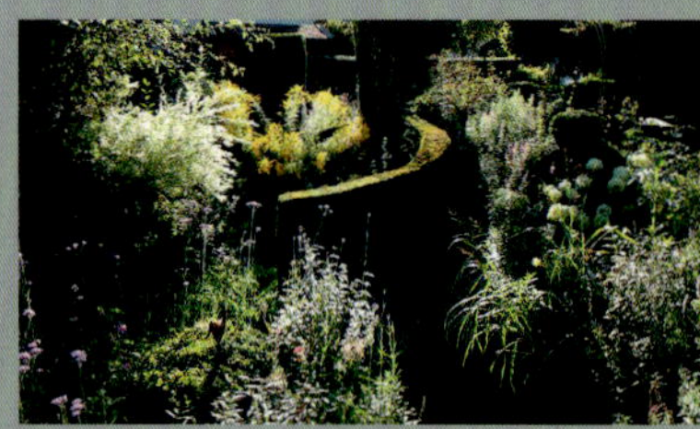

THE END OF A SUNNY DAY

THOMAS VOLLMERT

WEATHER EYE

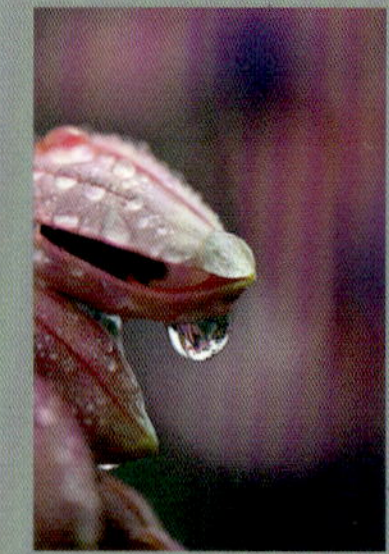

SUNLIT FUCHSIA

GERTIE B GRANVIK

WEATHER EYE

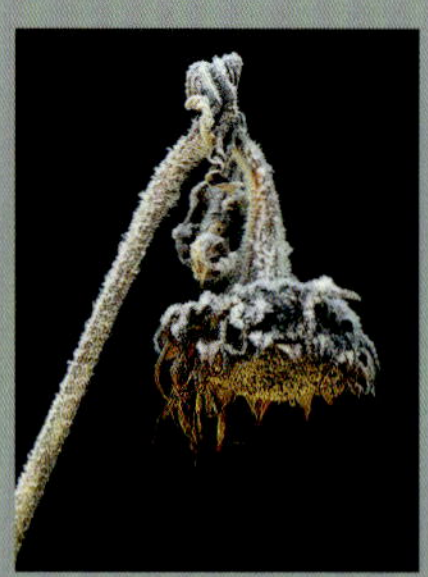

FROSTY SUNFLOWER HEAD

CHRISTOPHER BESTALL

WEATHER EYE

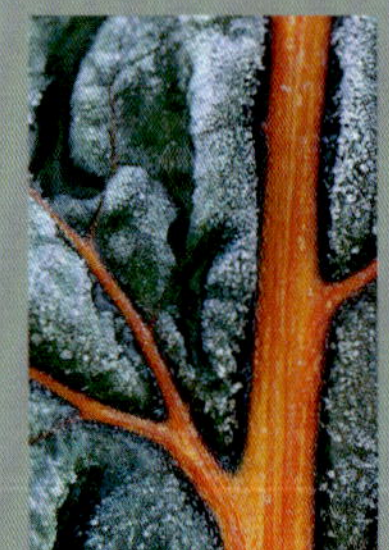

FROSTY CHARD

SYLVIE PINSONNEAULT

WEATHER EYE

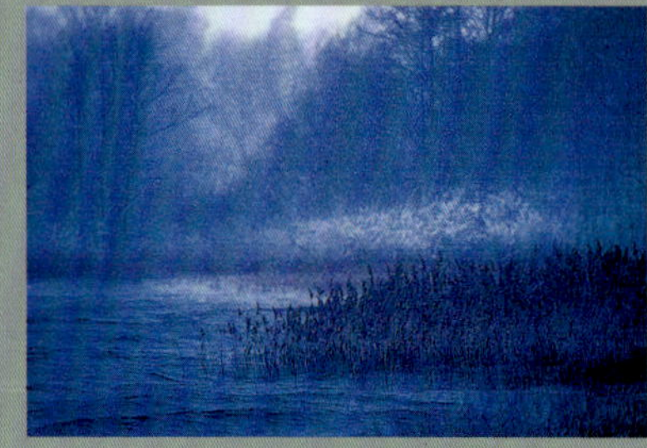

BLIZZARD

ARIANN ISAKSSON

WEATHER EYE

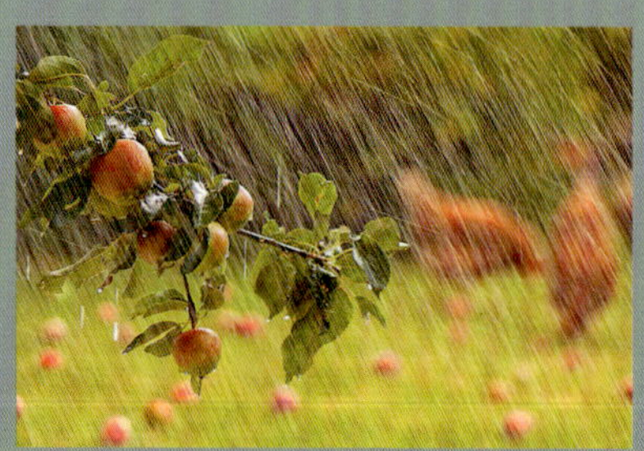

BRITISH SUMMER TIME

JENIFER BUNNETT

WEATHER EYE

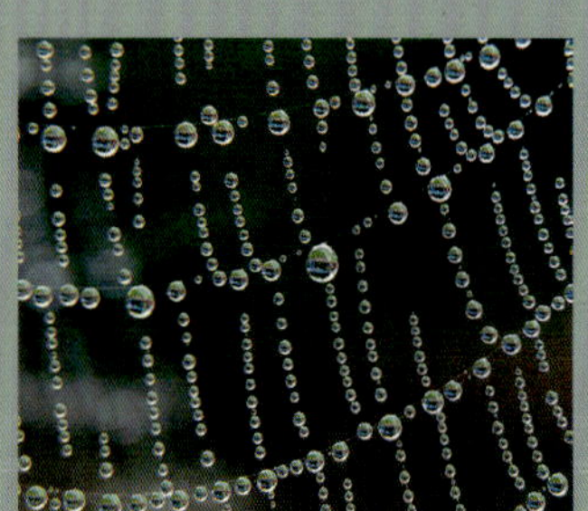

RAINDROPS ON WEB

COLIN MOLYNEUX

TEXTURES

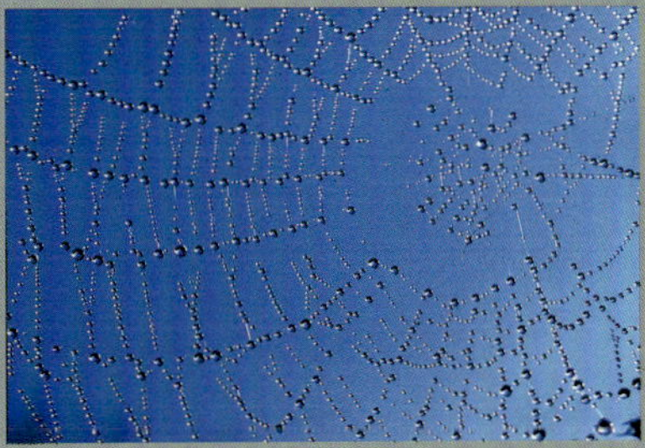

DEW LADEN COBWEB

COLIN VARNDELL

TEXTURES

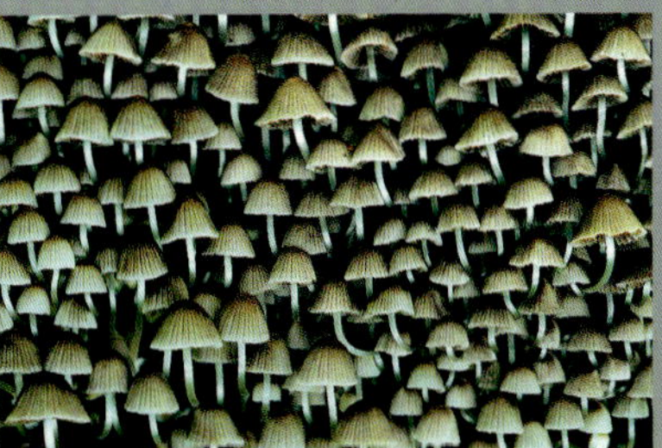

TROOPING CRUMBLECAP

COLIN VARNDELL

TEXTURES

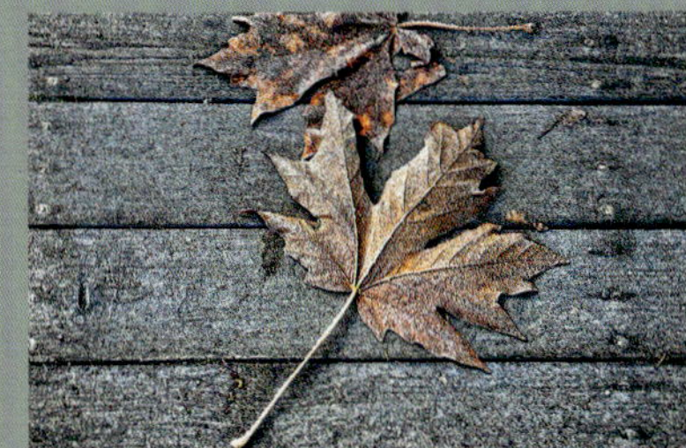

FIRST FROST

DEREK GALON

TEXTURES

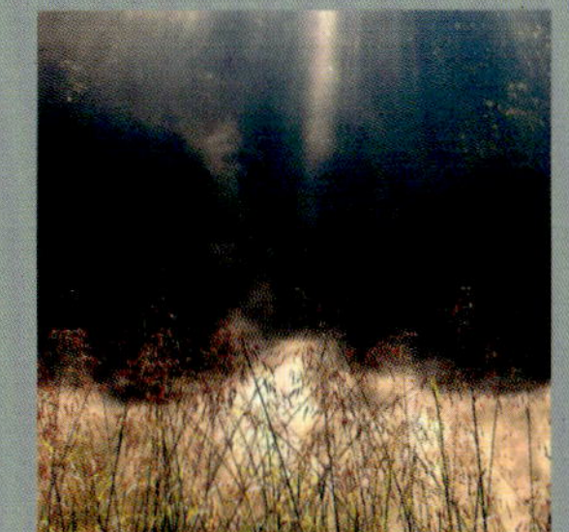

"LET THERE BE SOFTNESS!"

JOHN ROGER PALMOUR

TEXTURES

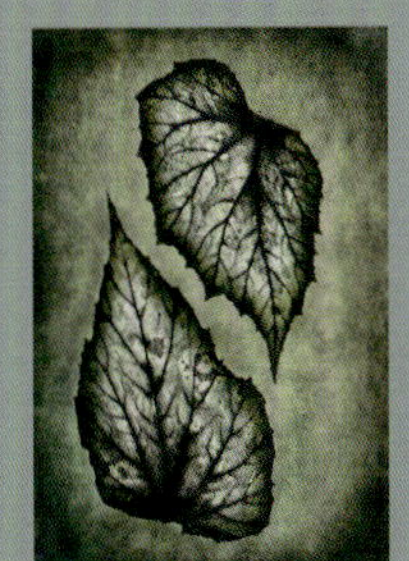

AUTUMN LEAVES

LOTTE CHRISTINA ANDERSEN PEDERSEN

TEXTURES

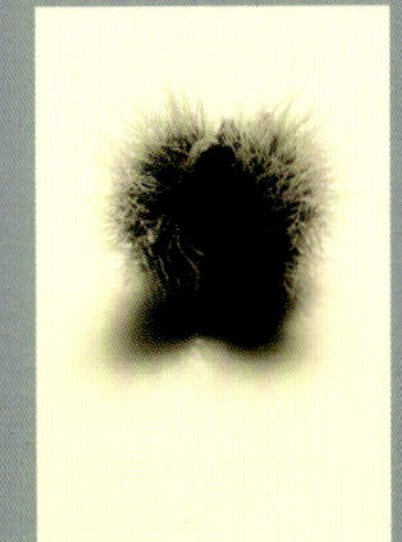

INVITATION TO A PRIVATE VIEW

COLIN PEARCE

TEXTURES

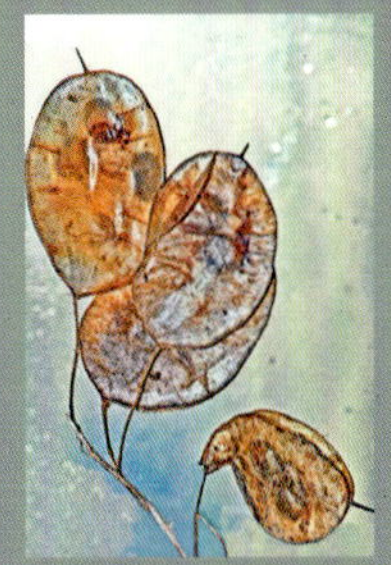

RIPE FOR COLLECTION

SUSAN EDWARDS

TEXTURES

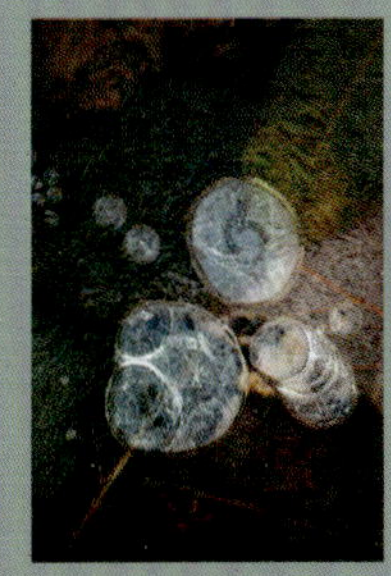

ICECOVERED

GERTIE B GRANVIK

TEXTURES

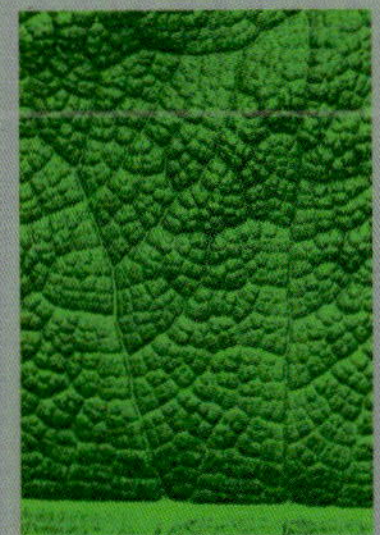

GUNNERA HIDE

NIGEL SYMINGTON

TEXTURES

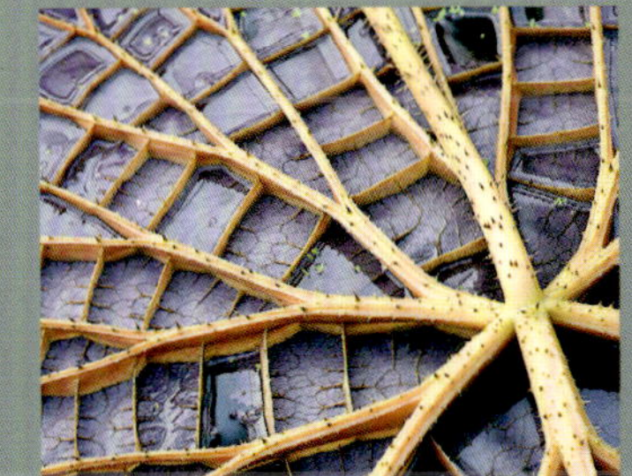

WHAT LIES BENEATH

RACHEL CHAPPELL

TEXTURES

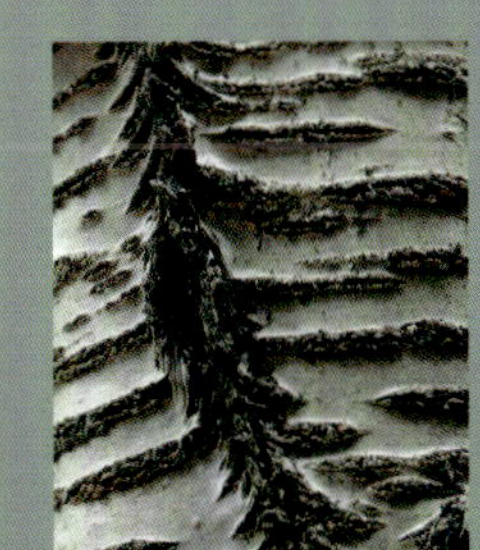

PRUNUS SP.

HANA MARTINKOVÁ

TEXTURES

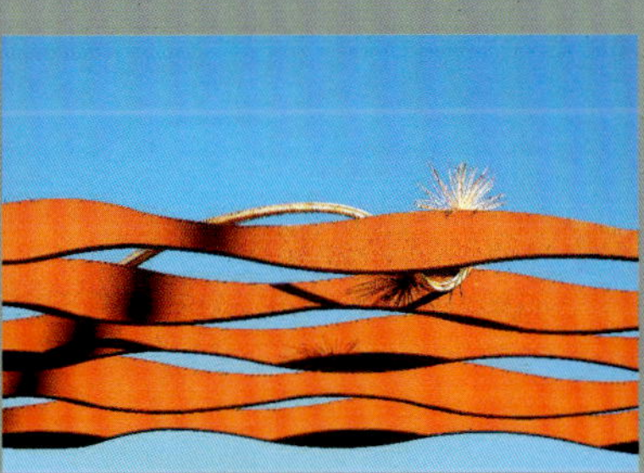

AUTUMN WAVES 1

FIORELLA GAGGERO

THE SKY IS ALWAYS MINE

THE HELEN BAMBER FOUNDATION

This year, International Garden Photographer of the Year has offered support to the Helen Bamber Foundation.

The Helen Bamber Foundation is a UK-based human rights organisation, formed in April 2005 to help rebuild lives and inspire a new self-esteem in survivors of gross human rights violations. At the Helen Bamber Foundation we believe that survivors are by nature courageous and resilient. We seek to draw upon their inner resources providing them with the support they need to recover from past trauma, deal with current hardships and lay the foundations for a better future.

The Photography group consists of a mixed group of around ten students from countries as diverse as the Congo, Bangladesh and Iran, led voluntarily by current photography professionals. In a group of human beings coming from destructive experiences we aim to find ways of moving forward positively, generating self esteem through respect, understanding and creativity.

Our workshops consist of a mixture of practical photography sessions, exhibition visits (for example to Kew Gardens), and photographic lectures. We often use photography competitions and festivals as an outlet for our work, which also leads us to interact with the wider photographic community, not only furthering our learning potential, but also developing and redefining ourselves as 'photographers' rather than 'asylum seekers' or 'refugees'.

We have used the common group experience to produce work where relevant, but the workshops are really a space to try to forget about problems past and present, to develop friendships and hobbies, make high quality work and simply to have fun. We are keen to make work stemming from our individual interests and are grateful to the International Garden Photographer of the Year competition 2011 for providing the opportunity to promote our activities. We are a close knit, yet welcoming group whose members encourage each other both creatively and personally, and there is always a lot of laughter during the sessions!

Images by Nicole & Kam, Abe Hussein, Adel Khelifa and Esha.

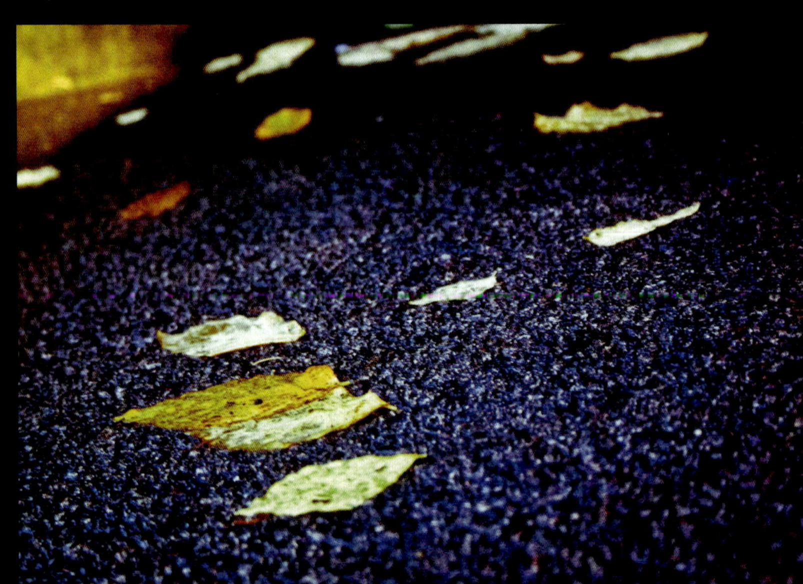

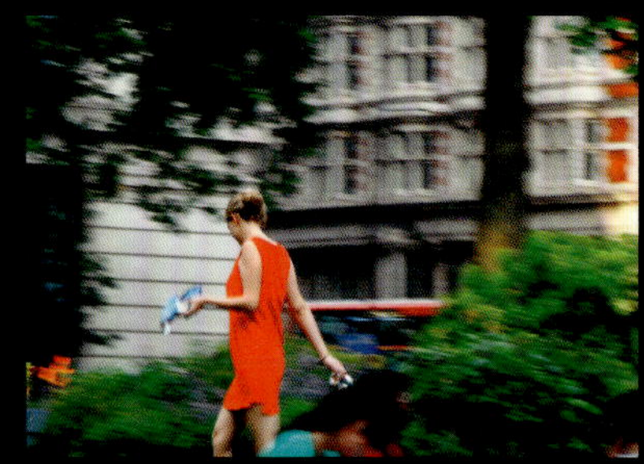

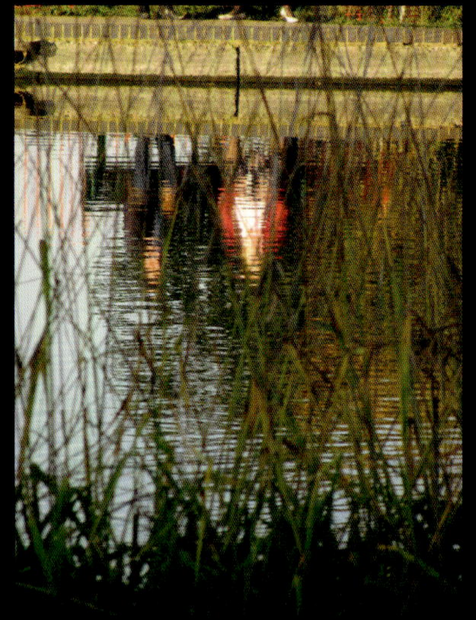

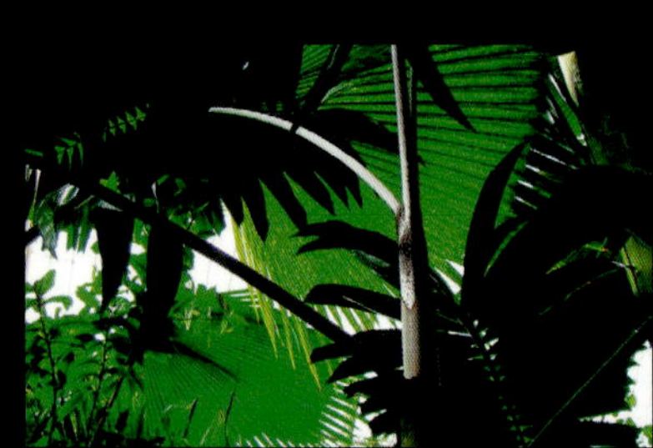

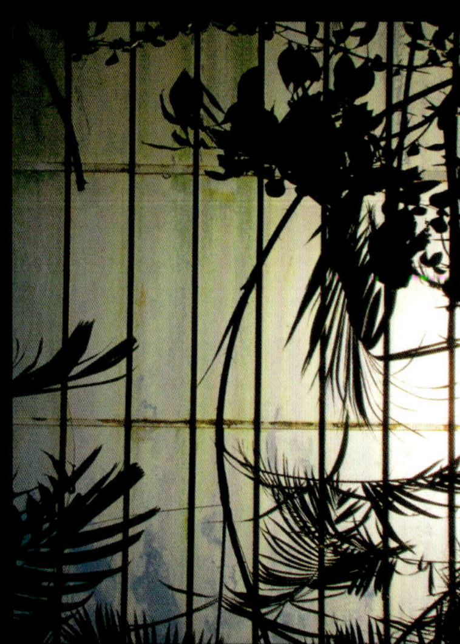

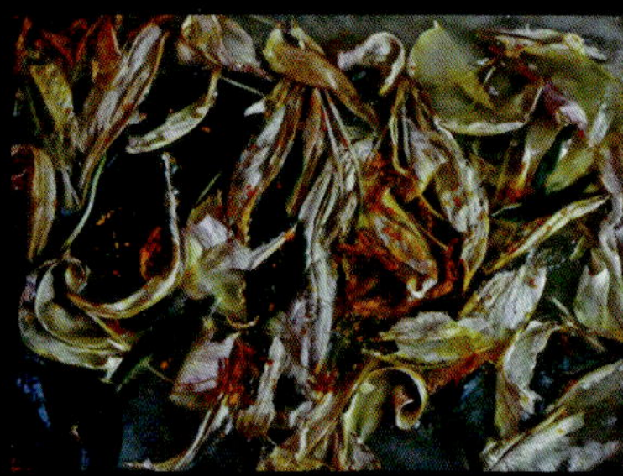

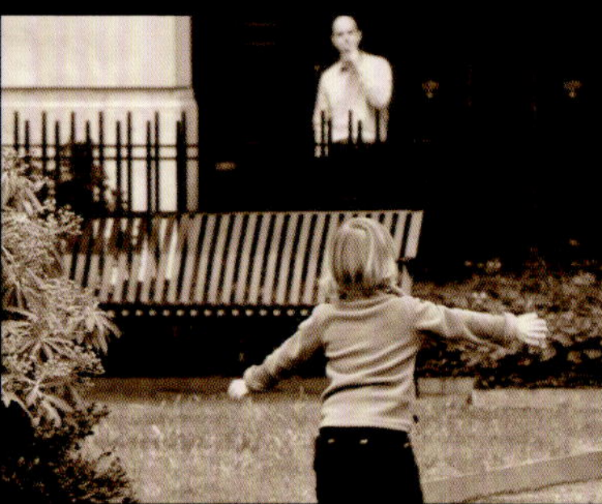

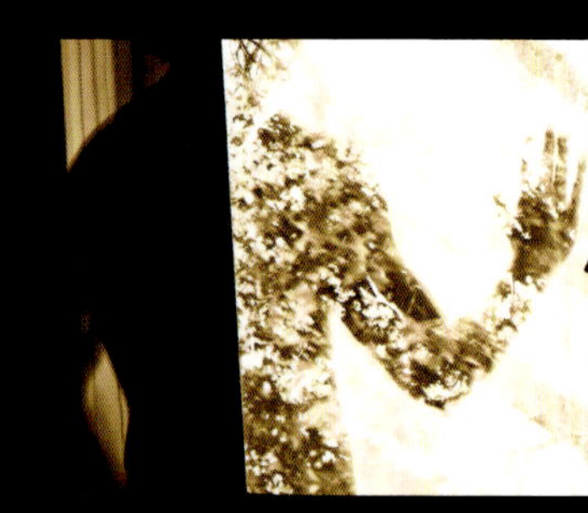

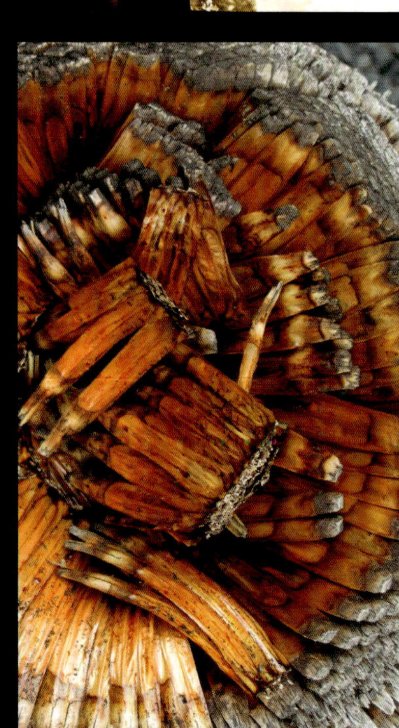

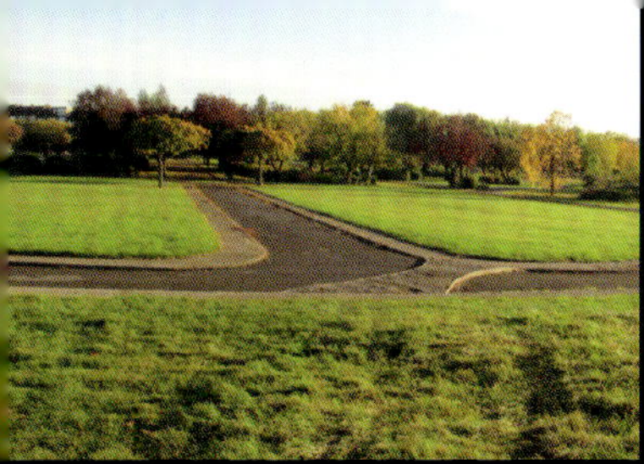

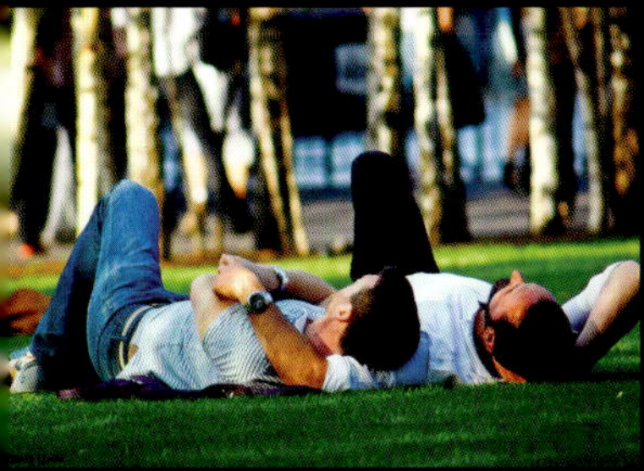

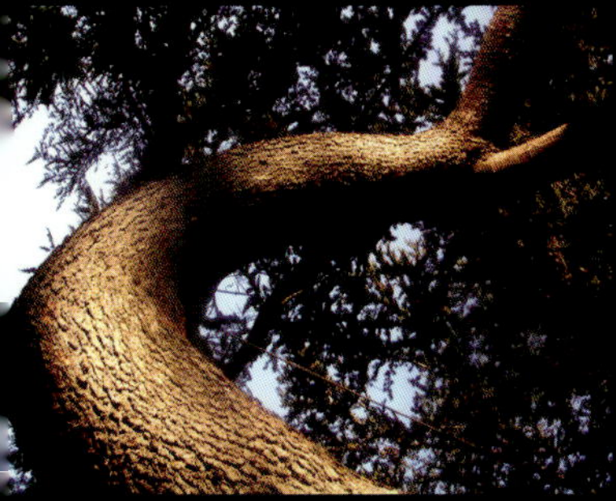

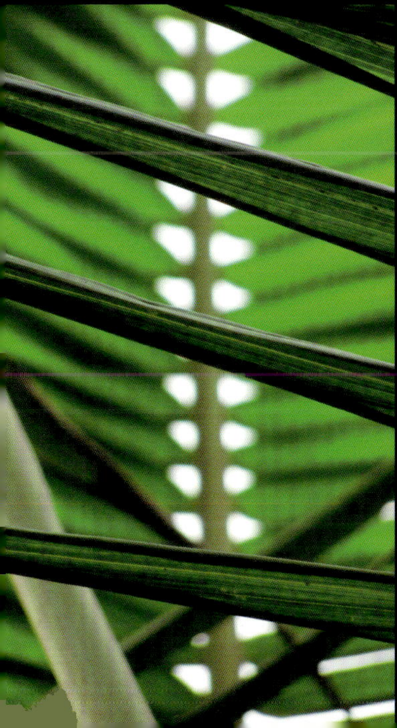

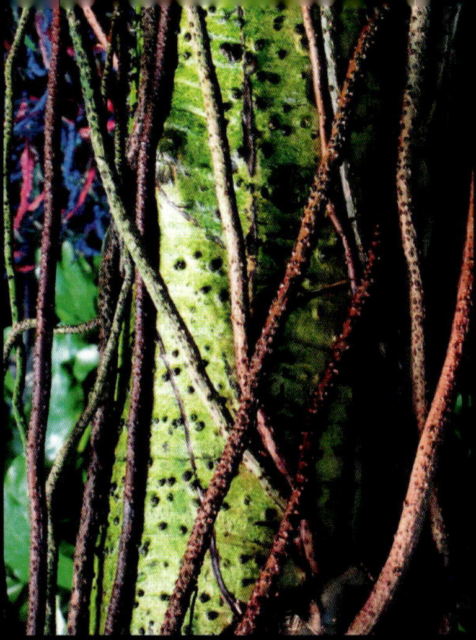

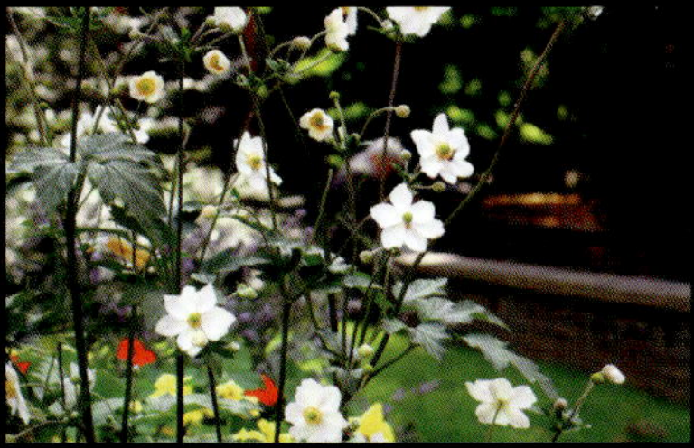

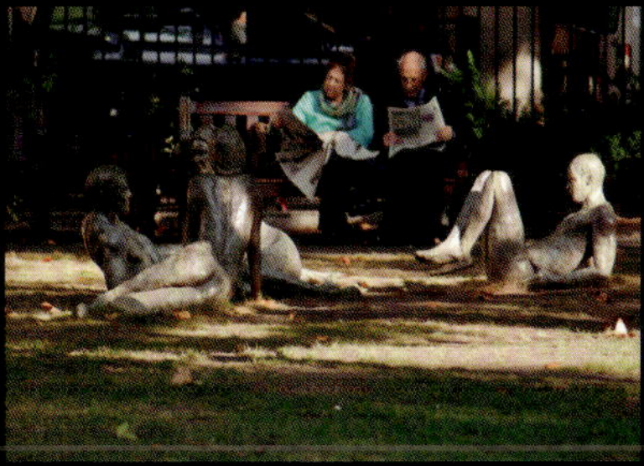

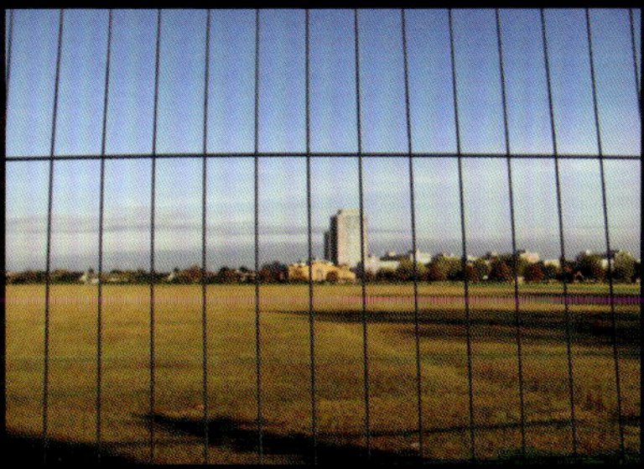

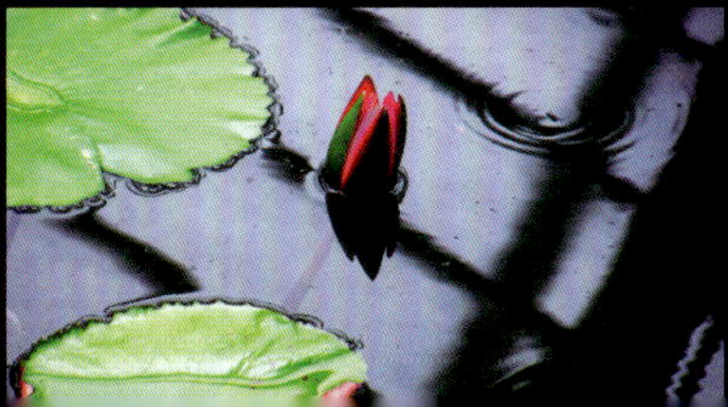

To let our students speak:

"When I joined the class with so much apprehension, I had no idea of what to expect. After 15 minutes, I realised that I was relaxed and so much into the photos that were shown on the projector. At that very moment, I understood this is the place where I wanted to be."

"The photography class gave me a sense of worthiness which I lost a long time back. The tutors are so welcoming that they allow us to push our creative boundary further without slightest burden on our shoulder. I forget about my stress when I see my photos are evaluated by the tutors or edit my photos. I can never thank enough to them for their time. They not only teach us, they listen to us and feel our problems."

"In the Helen Bamber Foundation they say 'wherever I go, the sky is always mine'. The photography class made me believe that the sky is always mine."

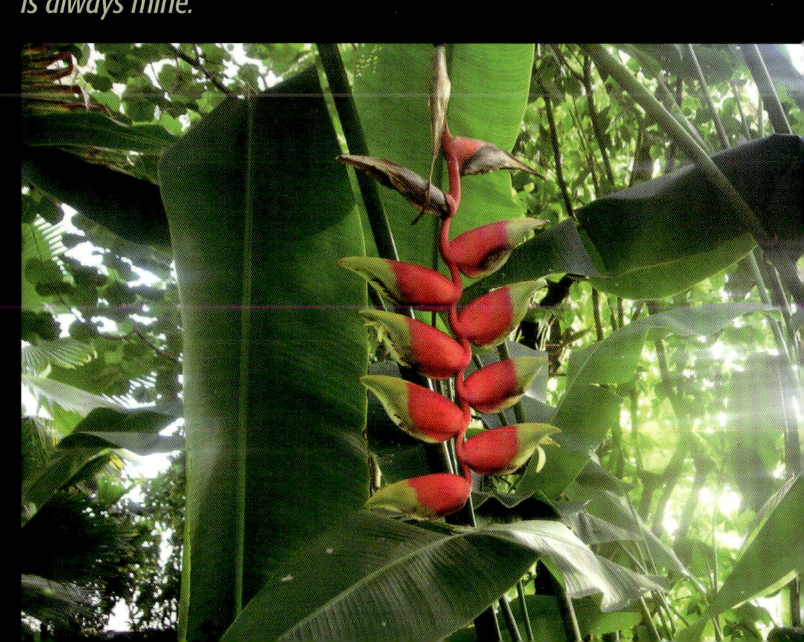

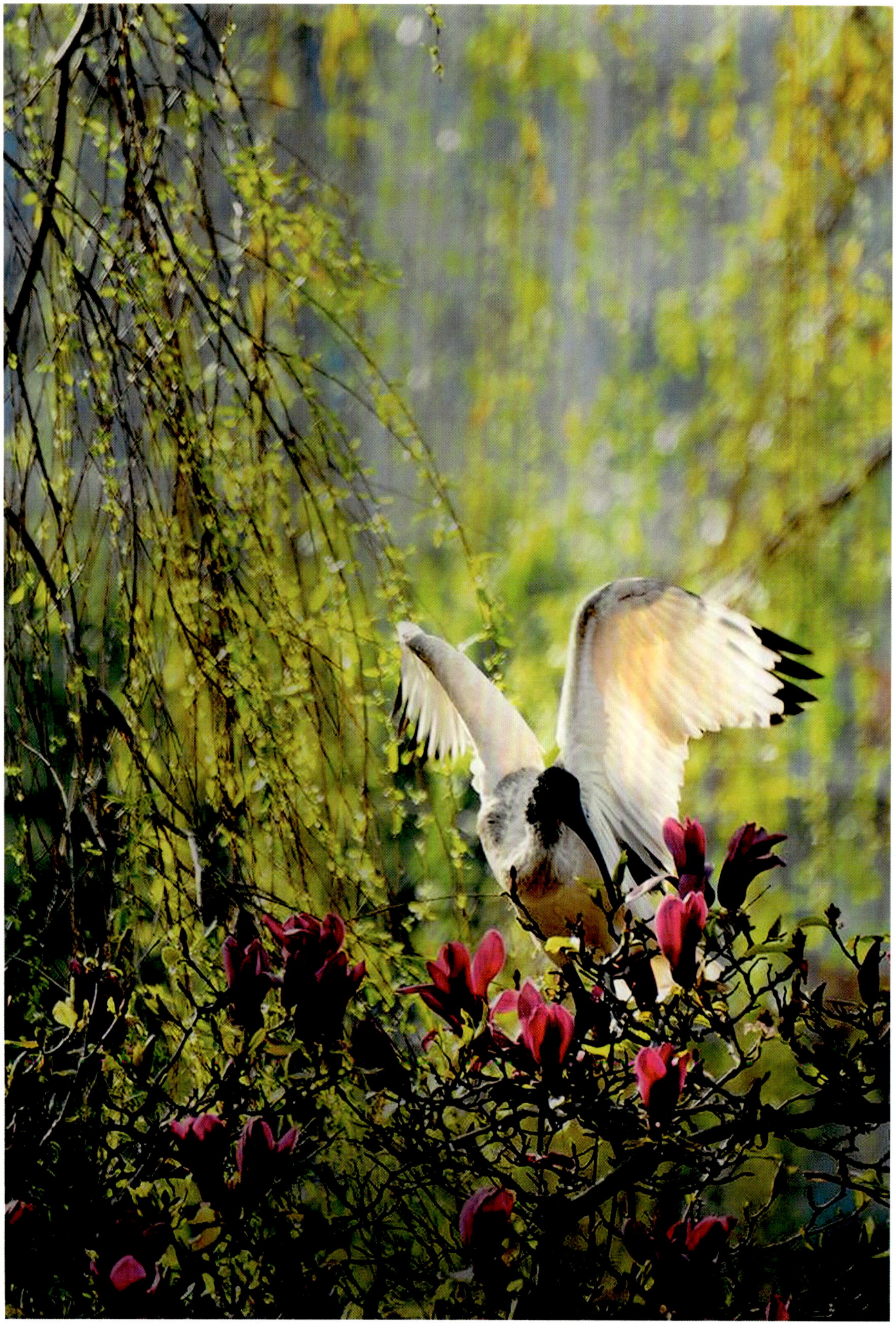

GARDENS IN FOCUS

'Gardens in Focus' Competition 2010.Organised by Friends of the Botanic Gardens, Sydney, Australia.

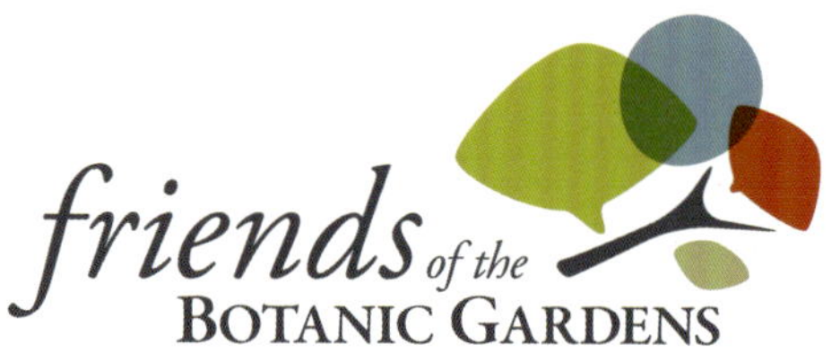

◄ **SUGIANTO YAHYA** 1ST PLACE

Ibis on Magnolia
Royal Botanic Garden, Sydney

This photo was taken in the morning while the sun shone with a golden colour from behind the tree, though it was drizzling. I found an ibis at rest on a branch of the magnolia tree in full bloom. I grabbed my 70-300mm lens and Nikon D700 and waited patiently until the ibis began to stir, hence the superb view of its wings.